Questioning Architectural Judgment

There is a growing insecurity among practitioners and academics concerning how we should judge architecture—through the aesthetic lenses of the canon, as we have for centuries, or through various quantitative measurements of performance that have emerged in the shadow of climate change over the last decade.

This book is not the first to observe that these two criteria for excellence appear to be in conflict. It is, however, the first book to observe that the advocates of either side generally fail to recognize that both sets of criteria are *socially constructed*. The purpose of this book is, then, to theorize (on the basis of historical and empirical data) a synthetic mode of judgment—one that will neither compromise opposing standards nor simply state new standards to replace existing ones. Rather, this book provides practical and theoretical tools to empower a civil society discourse for remaking standards directed at the built environment in the 21st century.

The book shines light on the problem of judgment, particularly in the realm of architectural "technics" and the codes that regulate it. The struggle to define "sustainability," and thus judge architecture through such lenses, is but one dimension of the contemporary problem of judgment. By providing the reader with an inherently interdisciplinary study of a particular discipline—architecture—it brings to the topic lenses that challenge the too frequently unexamined assumptions of the discipline. By situating architecture within a broader cultural field and using case studies to dissect the issues discussed, the book emphasizes that it is not simply a matter of designing better, more efficient, or more stringent codes to guide place-making, but a matter of *reconstructing the boundaries of the systems to be coded.*

Steven A. Moore is Bartlett Cocke Professor of Architecture and Planning and Director of the Graduate Program in Sustainable Design at the University of Texas at Austin, USA.

Barbara B. Wilson is an Assistant Professor of Planning and Sustainable Design and the Director for the Center of Sustainable Development at the University of Texas at Austin, USA.

Questioning Architectural Judgment

The Problem of Codes in the United States

Steven A. Moore and
Barbara B. Wilson

Routledge
Taylor & Francis Group
LONDON AND NEW YORK

First edition 2014
by Routledge
4 Park Square, Milton Park, Abingdon, Oxon OX14 4RN
605 Third Avenue, New York, NY 10017

Routledge is an imprint of the Taylor & Francis Group, an informa business

British Library Cataloguing in Publication Data
A catalogue record for this book is available from the British Library

Library of Congress Cataloging in Publication Data
Moore, Steven A., 1945– author.
Questioning architectural judgment: the problem of codes in the United States/Steven A. Moore and Barbara B. Wilson.—First edition.
pages cm
Includes bibliographical references and index.
1. Architecture—Evaluation. 2. Building laws—United States. I. Wilson, Barbara B. (Barbara Brown), author. II. Title.
NA2540.M66 2013
720.1—dc23 2013003823

ISBN: 978-0-415-84080-4 (hbk)
ISBN: 978-0-415-84081-1 (pbk)
ISBN: 978-0-203-79665-8 (ebk)

Typeset in Univers
by Florence Production Ltd, Stoodleigh, Devon, UK

Steven A. Moore dedicates this book to a good man,
Michael Cornelius Moore (1942–2011).

Barbara B. Wilson dedicates this book to
Bailey Ellen Wilson, my inspiration.

Citation Program
AUSTIN
CODE
COMPLIANCE
TX
Code Compliance

About the frontispiece

During the intensely hot Texas summer of 2011, I was engaged in two activities: writing chapters for this book and supervising the construction of a small retaining wall that separated my rear garden from the adjoining property. The retaining wall was made necessary by the sale of that property and a minor dispute with the seller concerning responsibility for drainage and soil stabilization. The wall was the technology that resolved our disagreement.

As I was typing away one afternoon—convinced of the seriousness of my work—there was a knock on the door, followed by appropriate barking by my dog, upset at being disturbed from her equally serious nap. Seeing an oddly uniformed officer through the glass, I was puzzled but opened the door with a pleasant greeting—"Can I help you?" After a few perfunctory questions—"Are you the owner of the house?" "Yes." "Are you building a swimming pool in the back yard?" "No"—the officer gravely informed me that I was in violation of the International Building Code. Before another word could be uttered, I burst into animated laughter. After I composed myself, the officer, completely perplexed, asked why I was laughing—"Most people," he offered, "get angry or defensive when I come to the door."

A few thousand dollars later, the same door was embellished with ten separate permits, and construction resumed. Having been "busted" for code violation, I felt new authority to question architectural judgment.

Steven A. Moore

Contents

Figure Credits

1.1 Courtesy of James Ewing Photography from The Museum of Modern Art exhibit, *Forecloses: Rehousing the American Dream*.
1.2 Courtesy of the authors.
1.3 Courtesy of the authors.
1.4 Courtesy of the authors.
1.5 Courtesy of the authors.
1.6 Courtesy of the authors.
1.7 Courtesy of the authors.
1.8 Courtesy of the authors.
2.1 Courtesy of the School of Architecture, The University of Texas at Austin.
2.2 Courtesy of the School of Architecture, The University of Texas at Austin.
4.1 Courtesy of Electa, Barcelona. *Cerda: The Five Bases of the General Theory of Urbanization*. ed. Arturo Soria y Puig.
5.1 Courtesy of publisher Niggli; in: Schnaidt, Claude. 1965. *Hannes Meyer* (p. 21). Teufen.
5.2 Courtesy of the School of Architecture, The University of Texas at Austin.
5.3 Courtesy of Scott Gilchrist and Amy Fry.
5.4 Courtesy of the University of Tennessee Press. In, Glassie, Henry. 1975. *Folk Housing in Middle Virginia* (p. 110).
5.5 Courtesy of Fernando Luiz Lara.
5.6 Courtesy of Instituto Lina Bo e P.M. Bardi, São Paulo, Brazil.
5.7 Courtesy of Instituto Lina Bo e P.M. Bardi, São Paulo, Brazil. Photographer Romulo Fialdini.
6.1 Courtesy of Harry Ransom Center of the University of Texas.
6.2 Courtesy of Harry Ransom Center of the University of Texas.
6.3 Courtesy of Hughes and Larkin, *Tudor Royal Proclamations*.
6.4 Courtesy of Edition Axel Menges.
6.5 Courtesy of Edition Axel Menges.
6.6 Courtesy of the University of Texas Library.
6.7 Courtesy of the University of Texas Library.
6.8 Courtesy of Harry Ransom Center of the University of Texas.
6.9 Courtesy of the University of Texas Library.
6.10 Courtesy of Harry Ransom Center of the University of Texas.
6.11 Courtesy of the University of Texas Library.
6.12 Courtesy of Harry Ransom Center of the University of Texas.
6.13 Courtesy of the University of Texas Library.
6.14 Courtesy of Harry Ransom Center of the University of Texas.

6.15 Courtesy of Catie Carter.
6.16 Courtesy of Frank Miller, photographer for Erdman Development Group, Inc. 2012.
6.17 Courtesy of Marjorie Moore.
7.1 Courtesy of Adrian Tinniswood. 2003. *By Permission of Heaven: The Story of the Great Fire of London* (pp. 76–77). London: Jonathan Cape.
7.2 Courtesy of Iwan Baan, photographer for Herzog and de Meuron Architects.
7.3 Courtesy of the Library of Congress.
7.4 Courtesy of Cote, Ron, ed. 1997. *Life Safety Code Handbook*. 7th ed. (p. 58). National Fire Protection Association.
7.5 Courtesy of Dr. Andrew Karvonen.
7.6 Left image: Courtesy of the University of Texas at San Antonio Library special collections. Right image: Courtesy of Marjorie Moore.
7.7 Courtesy of Behnisch Architekten. Photo by Anton Grassl.
8.1 Courtesy of the Library of Congress.
8.2 Drawing: Courtesy of Belinda Banks. Photograph: Courtesy of the authors.
9.1 Courtesy of Rachel Tepper.
9.2 Courtesy of Joan Leon and Zona Roberts.
9.3 Courtesy of HolLynn D'Lil.
9.4 Courtesy of Bush Presidential Library.
9.5 Courtesy of Roger Borgenicht, Assist Inc., A Community Design Center.
9.6 Courtesy of Roger Borgenicht, Assist Inc., A Community Design Center.
10.1 Courtesy of Texas State Library and Archives Commission.
10.2 Courtesy of Austin History Center.
10.3 Courtesy of the authors.
10.4 Courtesy of Kate Vickery.
10.5 Courtesy of Kate Vickery.
10.6 Courtesy of Cayce Bean.
10.7 Courtesy of Cayce Bean.
10.8 Courtesy of Rachel Tepper.
10.9 Courtesy of Elizabeth Walsh.
10.10 Courtesy of graduate students enrolled in *Topics in Sustainable Development*, 2009.
10.11 Courtesy of Jody Horton Photography.
10.12 Courtesy of Sarah Gamble.
10.13 Courtesy of Rachel Tepper.

Acknowledgments

Books are conversations that, in our case, usually begin with students and continue with readers. In between, however, are those pivotal conversations with colleagues in the hallway, over coffee, via email, or at conferences that shape the observations and arguments developed over years. At the University of Texas, we are particularly grateful to Richard Cleary, Michael Oden, and Fernando Lara, who read early drafts of chapters and provided detailed comments concerning issues outside our own realms of expertise. Likewise, we are grateful to colleagues at the Manchester Architecture Research Centre (UK), Simon Guy, Ralf Brand, and Andy Karvonen, who each provided critical reading of troublesome chapters. Colleagues elsewhere—David Hess at Vanderbilt University, Rob Imrie at King's College London, and Vincent Canizaro at the University of Texas at San Antonio—provided critiques of several chapters that proved indispensable in clarifying our thesis. To them, we are indebted. At Arizona State University (ASU), Sherry Ahrentzen, David Guston, Clark Miller, Daren Petrucci, and Emily Talen provided exceptionally helpful comments at an early presentation of the project at ASU. Equally helpful comments came from Matthew Carmona and Michael Guggenheim at an early presentation of the work at Manchester.

Action research of this kind could not happen without the collaboration of local partners. We are extremely thankful to Michael Gatto, Director of the Austin Community Design and Development Center (ACDDC), Mark Rogers, Director of the Guadalupe Neighborhood Development Corporation (GNDC), and their respective staffs for the investment of precious time in academic pursuits. The future of the Alley Regeneration Project has, in turn, been made possible by Lucia Athens, Chief Sustainability Officer of the City of Austin, along with Kalpana Sutaria and Melissa Martinez. Our hope is that the work will, in return, contribute to their communities.

In addition to these individuals, we are indebted to the institutions that supported the work over several years. The National Science Foundation provided a substantial Individual Scholar Award, in the form of grant number SES-0849147, that allowed time away from other responsibilities. With the indispensable support of Dean Frederick Steiner, the University of Texas generously provided a Faculty Research Award at a key time in the research. Certainly not least, Manchester University (UK) supported the work in the form of a Simon Visiting Professorship for the fall of 2010, where much of the analysis was completed.

The publication process itself brings welcomed insight and valuable criticism through the peer review process. We are indebted to the anonymous referees who helped us recognize just how unique this research is to the United States, but also relevant everywhere for its aspirations.

Finally, we owe the greatest debt to those anonymous individuals from the disability rights movement and from the City of Austin, who offered their time and insights to help us learn about their struggles in constructing sociotechnical codes for their respective communities.

General Introduction

Questioning Knowledge and Judgment in Architecture

> In the last century or two of social disruption, we were tempted by an excess of faith in the machine to do everything by means of it. We were like children left alone with a paint brush who applied it impartially to unpainted wood, to varnished furniture, to the tablecloth, to his toys, and to his own face. When with increased *knowledge and judgment*, we discover that some of those uses are inappropriate, that others are redundant, and that others are inefficient substitutes for a more vital adjustment, we will contract the machine to those areas in which it serves directly as an instrument of human purpose.
>
> We have now to work out the details of a new political and social order, radically different by reason of knowledge that is already at our command from any that now exists. And to the extent that this order is the product of scientific thought and humanistic imagination, it will leave a place for irrational and instinctive and traditional elements in society which were flouted, to their own ultimate peril, by the narrow forms of rationalism that prevailed during the past century.[1]
>
> (Lewis Mumford, 1963[1934]; our emphasis)

In these passages from 1934, Mumford makes the hopeful forecast that future generations, such as our own, will exercise the "knowledge and judgment" required to select and govern technologies through a process that "serves directly as an instrument of human purpose." His reasoning is that, once we figure out which new technologies are "inappropriate," "redundant," or "inefficient," we will be able to "contract the machine" in two ways: First, to *contract* or reduce the scope of technology to the areas of use where it is most helpful to us, where it is most life enhancing. But he also means, we surmise, that we might also make a *contract with* technology and thus regulate what isn't appropriate, what isn't life enhancing. In a word, he argued that we have the social capacity to *code* the machine and, indirectly, our future. Yet he also recognizes that such a "new social and political order" must avoid the "narrow forms of rationalism" and technological hubris employed by the extremes of both the Right and Left that dominated his time.[2]

Although 1934 was certainly a time already foreshadowed by the dark events to come, Mumford was then optimistic. But, as many have observed, by the end of his long life in 1990, he was far less so. It is not that the body of knowledge produced by technoscience failed to keep up with his expectations, but that society, or the sum of governmental and civil institutions, collectively failed to exercise the sound judgment required to serve "human purpose" through it.

By comparison, our own position is neither overly optimistic nor pessimistic, but we do stand in Mumford's shadow by adopting his caution. To employ knowledge without judgment will serve what Mumford called the "machines of the future" more than humanity itself. But, conversely, judging our machines without knowledge is no more likely to succeed, because there is no informed basis to do so. Following Mumford's logic, in this book we examine methods of building in the United States through what he called "technics"—studying our way of doing things rather than the distinguished things that we produce. In the chapters that follow, then, our hope is to shine some light on the problem of judgment, particularly in the realm of architectural "technics" and the codes that regulate it. The struggle to define "sustainability," and thus judge architecture through those lenses, is but one dimension of the contemporary problem of judgment.

In our investigation, we have concluded that what Davis refers to as "cultures of building," or "the coordinated system of knowledge, rules, procedures, and habits that surround the building process in any given place and time,"[3] are regional or national in nature. In other words, there is no single or universal "system of knowledge, rules, procedures, and habits" by which we should judge how we build. Although the forces of globalization have surely created nearly universal pressures of development,[4] how those pressures are interpreted, practiced, and codified remains a matter of ever-evolving local habit. This is particularly true of the US, which has, as we document in Chapter 3, a unique history with regard to regulating technologies of any kind.

This claim to unique history necessarily opens a discussion concerning "American exceptionalism"—de Toqueville's idea that the US is unlike other nations because we have voiced, through the act of revolution and ever after, a historical mission to spread democracy and freedom around the globe. That global mission of liberation, however, frequently comes into conflict with the idea of local "building cultures," because freedom in the US is too often conflated with the ideals of neoliberal capitalism and standardized production. This is a topic that is of global concern and to which we will return throughout the book.

We have, then, limited our investigation to the building culture(s) of the US, but with the clear purpose of making our findings about the social construction of codes relevant to other cultures. How we go about doing this is made clear in subsequent chapters. For the moment, it will suffice to say that the highly social process of regulating practices, things, and spaces is more shared by diverse peoples than is the regional or national character of what is coded, exactly how it is coded, and by whom. Coding the built world in this very broad sense is, then, a meta-cultural practice, if not a universal one.

Neo-traditional town planning, New Urbanism, or form-based codes (FBCs) is one evolving example of contemporary code-making that originated in the US but that has gained increasing recognition elsewhere.[5] FBC advocates, who have contributed significantly to the revived interest in code-making, have argued that the sound judgment that Mumford desired can be more efficiently embodied in the codes that guide architectural production than in the minds of young architects or municipal planners through their education.[6] Simplistically stated, this position argues that, if we can get the code right, then the city too will be right.[7] Although we sympathize with the ideals embodied within that assertion, we have found the situation to be more complex. Although codes do indeed influence the spaces and buildings we construct, the influence is not always what code-makers intend. As FBC advocates have themselves observed, the legislation of floor-to-area ratios (FARs) in cities has resulted, not in places of distinction, but in monotony.[8] In our view, it is not simply a matter of designing better, more efficient, or more stringent codes to guide place-making, but a matter of *reconstructing the boundaries of the systems to be coded.*

By *systems*, we refer to the normal scheme, arrangement, or classification of activities in contemporary society. School systems, for one example, are generally designed and managed by groups of people who have very little overlap with water systems. Likewise, power systems are generally designed and managed by groups who have very little overlap with housing. Any seasoned planner can tell you, however, that the operation of each of these systems has a profound impact on the others. We may conceive and regulate them in isolation from each other because it seems rational to do so, but that is not how they actually work in the world. The location of a new school, for example, affects the demand placed on power and water systems, not only because the school consumes more of those resources, but also because it attracts new housing that consumes even more. In turn, the consumption of power and water affects, not only air quality, but also the incidence of childhood asthma adjacent to the roads needed to serve new development. In what follows, we will challenge the autonomy of conventional systemic categories so as to consider the integration of code-making and cities themselves.

Simply put, our hypothesis is that all technological codes, whether we recognize it or not, have social and environmental consequences, as well as technological ones. If we can empirically demonstrate this dynamic relationship, it stands to reason that we should, then, construct our codes with social and environmental, as well as technological, judgment. In other words, the making of socially just and environmentally sustainable codes of technology requires participation by individuals with appropriate training or experience. But, before we can propose why and how our system boundaries might be redrawn, it will be helpful to first sketch the structure of our investigation, so that the reasoning behind the construction of new categories of code-making can unfold at a reasonable pace.

The book is structured in three parts:

In Part One, we reconsider the Cartesian categories that divide the world in binary pairs: mind/body, male/female, black/white, nature/civilization, or art/science—the last pair being a distinction that has dominated architectural judgment in the modern era.[9] By conducting an analysis of contemporary literature, we conclude not only that the modern duality of art and science is more complex and nuanced than is generally acknowledged, but also that this dualism conceals what it is that architects actually talk about. Rather than two opposing categories, in our review of the literature we found 23 distinct categories of concern that could, in turn, be grouped into five or three meta-categories. Even these three might be considered reductive, let alone the Cartesian dualism of art versus science.

For classical figures in architecture (Vitruvius, Palladio, Alberti, et al., as well as contemporary romantics), architecture is an art form, even if one more complex than painting, sculpture, or media. Although we appreciate the benefit of interpreting architecture through a lens forged in the philosophy, history, and criticism of art—what we will henceforth refer to as *art studies*—we find that the changing nature of cities and architectural practice requires additional lenses.

One such lens emerged in the mid 18th century. Considering architecture to be a technology—a way of solving problems rather than a representation of cosmological order—is a major historical shift. It is a concept and practice at the core of modernism. As a technology, architecture has always had more flexibility than, say, making a hammer or even a transistor. But, even though a loose fit, understanding buildings as technology reflects fundamental social changes associated with the era of Enlightenment. The study of our tools in themselves is, however, still insufficient to understand what Mumford called *technics*.

A third lens has been more recently added: Beginning with the philosophy of technology in the late 19th century[10] and science and technology studies[11] in the mid 20th century, architecture can be studied, not only as a technology, but one with significant social as well as environmental consequences—what we will henceforth refer to as *technology studies*. In this literature, a technology is not only a thing, but it is also a body of knowledge and a social practice.[12] In other words, we cannot hope to understand contemporary architecture as an aesthetic artifact, or a way of solving problems, unless we also understand it as an evolving and ever more professionalized system of managing flows of people, information, energy, water, and materials. Rather than suppress how contemporary firms actually operate in day-to-day practice, in comparison to, say, Brunelleschi in the 15th century, we consider in what follows how shifting power relationships in the building industry are a necessary part of understanding architecture as a thing and as a process.

In Part One (Chapters 1–3), we argue that interpreting architecture requires all three kinds of knowledge, as well as related traditions in geography, engineering, and the social sciences. In short, we argue for a kaleidoscopic view, not only a singular aesthetic, technological, or dualistic one.[13] Part One provides the background required to investigate the power relations embodied in the structure of different kinds of code considered in Part Two.

Part Two (Chapters 4–7) is a taxonomy of codes—here we categorize the types of code that have emerged to regulate city-making. Although there is popular interest shown by contemporary architects in the *decoding* of the human genome as a metaphor for architectural production,[14] our own interest is focused on the highly practical, political, and concrete process of *encoding* the built environment. To do so, we adopt "frame analysis" as a methodological tool. If we are proposing to examine architectural production through a kaleidoscope of competing assumptions, we need a tool that will help us appreciate the multiple modes of interpretation, or *frames*, that are used, not only by architects, but also by others to make sense of the built environment.

In the balance of Part Two, with the help of frame analysis, we characterize four general types of code: *tacit, sumptuary, economic*, and *sociotechnical*. Each of these is an ideal type that employs a specific kind of logic to influence human behavior in combination with specific classes of artifact—shingles, pipes, freeways, watersheds, parking spaces, or 2x4s. In practice, ideal code types are typically combined in hybrid forms that are catalyzed by local conditions, and yet their internal logic can still be assessed and made concrete through the examination of historic examples. Looking at concrete examples through the logics contained in ideal code types allows us to better understand how they work to influence social and environmental conditions, as well as technological ones.

In Part Three (Chapters 8–11), we empirically investigate two in-depth cases of sociotechnical codes, because we find in them Mumford's early optimism for the future of the built world. We begin the section by first theorizing "sociotechnical codes," by which we mean those that self-consciously seek to make simultaneous and symbiotic changes in the realms of technology, the environment, and society. Sociotechnical codes, in other words, erode the system boundaries between social, environmental, and technical systems, because code-makers recognize that *all* technological change, either positively or negatively, has impact not only on the environment, but also on particular social groups. Code-makers consciously, then, intend to benefit specified groups through sociotechnological regulation. That definition establishes the groundwork to examine the disability rights movement (DRM) in the US and the case of S.M.A.R.T. Housing in Austin, Texas, as examples of sociotechnical code-making. In sum, these case studies provide an empirical and historical perspective on the relationship between three primary variables: the *relevant social groups, technological frames*, and *focal issues* that move history in one direction or another. The definition of these specialized terms will unfold in the context of these stories.

Finally, we conclude by observing that sociotechnical codes are not (usually) constructed by the state, by industry itself, or by second-party certifications made by industrial associations such as the Underwriters Laboratory (UL). Given the unique history of regulation in the US, and the globalization of production, sociotechnical codes are now being developed by third-party civil society groups engaged in what some refer to as the "certification revolution."[15] At issue is the role that traditionally aloof design professionals will play in the sociotechnical code-making that is already redefining architectural production. Chapter 11, and the book as a whole, conclude with a series of ten propositions that point in the direction of sociotechnical code-making through the knowledge and judgment sought by Mumford.

This broad outline of the book should suggest to the reader that it is an inherently interdisciplinary study of a particular discipline—architecture. By this, we mean that we bring to the study of regulating architecture not only art, technology, and professional studies, but also related tools we have borrowed from several related disciplines. Our purpose in doing so is to bring to the topic lenses that challenge the too frequently unexamined assumptions of the discipline. As have others, we find that those who promote the "autonomy of architectural discourse" are those who benefit most from its isolation among like-minded persons.[16] By situating architecture within a broader cultural field, we hope that our study will be of value, not only to architects, but also to the other disciplines noted above, as well as policymakers, social scientists in general, not to mention thoughtful citizens who are engaged in city-making. This observation suggests, in turn, that there may be several ways to read the book.

Architects who are practitioners, for example, may want to skim Part Two, A Taxonomy of Codes, and invest their time in Parts One and Three, which focus directly on the concerns of practice. In contrast, social scientists may be primarily interested in Part Two, but will also take interest in the application of sociotechnical codes proposed in Part Three. Historians and geographers, however, might be most interested in the Taxonomy of Codes section, because that section is mostly focused on the social construction of codes across time and space.

The singular problem presented by reading the book nonsequentially is that we do develop specialized terms that are defined, generally, only at their first use. Reading the chapters out of order may, then, lead to missing the definition of key terms. For this reason, we have included a glossary of specialized terms after the concluding chapter. Readers who wish to skip some sections can, then, turn to the glossary to find the theory constructed throughout the book. We hope, however, that all readers will find our interdisciplinary approach throughout the book to be of interest precisely because it challenges disciplinary assumptions about "knowledge and judgment" that so concerned Mumford in the 20th century, and that now challenge the citizen code-makers of the 21st century.

Part One

Art, Technology, and Professionalism

Introduction

Part One reconstructs the competing lenses through which we interpret architectural production. We begin by challenging the historical assumption that architecture is a fine art, and because that characterization alone proves valuable, but insufficient, we turn to empirical analysis to find out what it is that contemporary architects actually think and talk about. Through a content analysis of a recognized North American journal of architecture over several decades, we found 22 specific topics of concern that we subsequently grouped into five, and finally three, meta-categories—*art, technology,* and *professionalism.* Our claim is that these meta-categories serve as an index, albeit a reductive one, of contemporary architectural thinking.

The journal analysis in Chapter 1 required, in turn, that we consider one alternative view in Chapter 2—that architecture should be interpreted not only as a fine art, but also as a *professional culture* and a *technology,* understood in the broadest meaning of those terms. This proposal requires that we employ, not architectural history, but the history of technology, philosophy of technology, as well as science and technology studies (STS) to study architectural production. Our reasoning is that lenses forged in a single discipline are in themselves insufficient to understand the complexity of the built environment. Architecture is not only artistic and technical, but it is also managerial and highly social. Simply put, the traditional categories that frame our understanding of architecture tend to be reductive and solipsistic—meaning that they are self-referential and thus conceal as much as they reveal about artifacts and the societies that produce them.

If, as we argue in Chapter 2, neither art, technology, nor professional studies are sufficient in themselves to interpret architecture, our investigation must begin with the understanding that architecture in the world is inevitably interpreted by multiple and competing kinds of knowledge, not just architectural knowledge. Each of the different kinds of knowledge—public health, business, real estate, politics, biology or street smarts—has its own assumptions and codes of judgment. This observation compels at least two related questions: First, how are the codes of art (taste), technology (laws), and professional conduct (business ethics) constructed and by whom? And second, in whose interest is it to prefer one set of codes over the others? These are inherently political questions and lead us to adopt the concept of *sociotechnical* codes in response. Through this kaleidoscopic approach, we find that there are significant ontological and political consequences at stake in the making of technical codes—they are not purely, or merely, technological.

Taken together, these perspectives set up Chapter 3, in which we first provide a historical background for code-making in the US. How did the people of this nation assemble the codes that now govern our built world? Most readers will be surprised to know that the very idea of standardizing technology through code-making is embodied in the U.S. Constitution itself.

This background provides, in turn, a foundation for considering the contemporary critique of technological codes, understood in the broadest sense to include laws, ordinances, policies, and programs that attempt to influence social behavior related to the built world. Although each of these terms does have different meanings and derives from different sources, we will use them interchangeably to avoid a lengthy etymology—that is a good project for another time. In sum, Part One provides the background to investigate the power relations embodied in the structure of different kinds of code examined in Part Two.

Chapter 1

Maintaining Frames

Architecture-as-art

> In all matters, but particularly in architecture, there are these two points: the thing signified, and that which gives it its significance. That which is signified is the subject of which we may be speaking; and that which gives significance is a demonstration on scientific principles. It appears, then, that one who professes himself an architect should be well versed in both directions. He ought, therefore, to be both naturally gifted and amenable to instruction. Neither natural ability without instruction, nor instruction without natural ability can make the perfect artist. Let him be educated, skilful with the pencil, instructed in geometry, know much history, have followed the philosophers with attention, understand music, have some knowledge of medicine, know the opinions of the jurists, and be acquainted with astronomy and the theory of the heavens.[1]
>
> (Vitruvius, 1960[15 BCE])

From within the canon of architecture, the discipline is regarded as an art form, a high-culture practice in which the essence of the age is expressed and given form by individual designers with "natural ability." In the quote above from Vitruvius' *Ten Books of Architecture*, which is thought to have been published about 15 BCE and which remains a foundational text in architectural studies, he challenges the architect to be the "perfect artist"—not just skillful in drawing and geometry, but also knowledgeable in history, philosophy, music, medicine, law, astronomy, and theology. Yet, for a list so long, it is conspicuous, at least from a contemporary architect's perspective, that technology, administration, climate change, and politics are all absent from this litany of knowledge deemed relevant to the discipline.

Unlike contemporary architects, however, philosophers and historians would not find the absence of these different kinds of knowledge in Vitruvius' litany at all odd. To the contrary, they would have found the inclusion of such concepts to be historically impossible. Technology, in particular, is a thoroughly modern concept that could not be known to Vitruvius. In its place, he might have considered the Greek term *techne*, or "poetic making," to be a related idea, but one dramatically different in meaning and practice from the technological practices of our time.[2] Nor would Vitruvius have understood what we mean by "administration," the day-to-day management of contracts, bidding, specification writing, and shop drawing approvals. In its place, he might have considered the Greek term *metis*, or the social application of abstract knowledge, to be a related idea, but again, it is one dramatically different in meaning and practice.[3] This is not to say that the architects of Vitruvius' time had no such worldly responsibilities, but that they were incorporated into a "culture of building" (as we defined this term in the General Introduction) that operated with entirely different assumptions and practices than those of our time.[4]

Our point in making this brief comparison between the kinds of knowledge deemed relevant by Vitruvius and those required by contemporary practice is to emphasize, not only how much the world has changed in nearly 22 centuries, but also how little the criteria for canonizing architectural works have changed. To be clear, we use the term "canon" to mean the collection of exemplary works used by experts in the field as the "basis for judgment" in determining the significance of any particular architectural work.[5] Although that term is commonly used only in reference to the code of classical architecture, we use it here in the common sense that every architectural period develops its own canon as an extension of, or in response to, the period it succeeds. This is to say that, although the exemplars of good judgment change significantly over time, the process through which the canon is constructed has changed relatively little. Constructing and forever reconstructing the canon is a highly social process through which experts in the field compete to define what Bourdieu calls "cultural competence," a topic that we investigate more thoroughly in Chapter 6.[6]

One significant change in the process of canonizing architectural works did occur in the Renaissance, some 16 centuries after Vitruvius set out his criteria. In studying the works and career of Andrea Palladio (1508–1580), Habraken documents a shift in judgment regarding the cultural competence of individual architects. Where Vitruvius' *Ten Books of Architecture* served to document the collective works of Greek and Roman building cultures as a whole, Habraken argues that Palladio's *Four Books of Architecture*, published in 1570, demonstrated an entirely new and proto-modern format. Rather than documenting the collective works of a people, as Vitruvius had done, Palladio's books were "a record of a personal *œuvre* and, as such, a new way of defining architecture."[7] In short, Palladio became the model for individual artistic authorship that students and practitioners of today still emulate. What made Palladio's books so revolutionary was that, for the first time in history, they associated the genius of a single individual, rather than a people, with a building style or manner of building.[8]

A second consequence derives from the first: In making books that could be transported from place to place, unlike buildings linked to a particular place, or craftsmanship linked to a particular problem, artist–architects could seek international recognition and autonomy from particular cultural and ecological conditions. They did so, not by participating in a local building culture, but by appealing to a neoclassical "elite transcending political boundaries, united by education in the arts, history, Latin and Greek."[9] This is to say that the basis for judgment for admission to the canon of architecture was becoming, not only individualized, rather than being based on the collective works of a people, but also abstracted from local context and transportable as a universal system of form, proportion, and order.[10] Habraken's two-part argument is, first, that, from Palladio onward, the tradition of architectural judgment changed to focus on individual artist–architects, rather than on building cultures. But second, the process of judgment itself changed hardly at all—as it was for Vitruvius, judgment is still dominated by the elites of our time, who are able to demonstrate cultural competence to each other.

From his distant perspective in the 1980s, Donald Schön observed that architecture is a profession steeped in this tradition. Architecture, he holds, "crystallized as a profession before the doctrine of technical rationality had established itself, and therefore carries the seeds of an earlier view of professional competence and knowledge."[11] In this reflection, Schön clearly recognized that it is not at all surprising that architecture has been historically interpreted through lenses forged by art studies. There are at least two reasons why: First, although Vitruvius and Palladio could both distinguish between architecture and the other arts, the boundaries between them were relatively porous in comparison with our own time of restrictive professionalism and specialization. And second, the purpose of architecture in the time of Vitruvius and Palladio, like that of painting and sculpture, was not so much to serve an institutional or economic purpose, as we understand the concept of *program* today, as it was to represent to the public the power and authority of those elites who sponsored architectural production.

Emerging from this ancient and neoclassical cultural context, it seemed perfectly logical for early moderns, like those before them, to classify buildings through the categories developed in art history—*form*, *style* and *type*.[12] Likewise, it seemed perfectly logical to interpret the significance of particular buildings through the categories developed in art studies—*intention* and *meaning*.[13] However, from our contemporary perspective, it now seems necessary, even overdue, to ask if—given the radically changed nature of the world and practice—it is still perfectly logical for us to interpret the built world *only* through the five lenses of form, style, type, intention, and meaning?

Within the world of contemporary art studies, many artists and critics have, of course, moved well beyond the limits of interpreting works through these five traditional lenses.[14] The problem is that, unlike in the European Union (EU) and elsewhere, many schools of architecture in the US cling to traditional categories of interpretation instilled in "studio culture."[15] Put in slightly different terms, Habraken (who taught at MIT for many years) argues that there is a contemporary "disconnect," or dissonance, between how we architects see ourselves—as the "children of Palladio"—and what it is that we actually do every day in the office. Other critical observers of architectural practice in the US have similarly argued that this dissonance has rendered the profession isolated from the communities that its members serve, because they imagine their works will be judged only by the canon of architecture, and its keepers, rather than by those who inhabit, experience, maintain, and pay for the buildings they design.[16] In a word, the dominant model of the discipline in the US teaches architects to seek *autonomy* from normal life.[17]

Architect Peter Eisenman serves as a good contemporary exemplar of the quest for modern autonomy from everyday life. Eisenman argues, "Originality and newness have traditionally comprised the two dominant modes of legitimation in architecture. Radical or resistant behavior was always linked to the avant-garde, with the pursuit of the ever new and thus the original." In this passage, Eisenman argues that architecture is "legitimated," or judged by the canon, primarily on the basis of its originality—the degree to which it distinguishes itself from traditional vocabularies (as well as the works of contemporary competitors).

A sympathetic reading of Eisenman's quest for autonomy is generally grounded in a critique of neoliberal capitalism as the dominant cultural context of our time. If capitalism is inherently consumptive and thereby unsustainable, such reasoning goes, then, responsible architects should distance themselves from the day-to-day operation of markets and the consumption of clichés in the form of shopping centers, housing, car washes, corporate headquarters, or fast-food restaurants.[18,19] Although younger architects within the Critical Theory tradition have thoughtfully updated this line of reasoning, the tradition still suffers from the use of simplistic dualisms—capitalist/noncapitalist, conventional/avant-garde, art/technology, etc.[20] To move beyond such duality and disengagement from people in need, other architects of the same generation abandoned orthodox Critical Theory and either affiliated themselves with the pragmatist tradition or have simply abandoned theory in favor of action.[21]

In his own writing, Eisenman painfully recognizes that the modern avant-garde has been essentially "reactive" to the status quo, to normal life, and thus not fully free from its social context. It is not enough, in his view, to say "black" just because traditionalists say "white," or vice versa. In other words, it is not enough to choose "abstraction" over references to "cliché" or the comforting forms of everyday life—a double-hung window, a shaded porch, or a belvedere. To become fully context-free, or autonomous from the demands of society, Eisenman argues that architecture must get beyond "a judgment of taste or value," which is to say that, "architecture's autonomy presents no need for judgment." To be clear, Eisenman holds in these passages that, to achieve the goal of artistic autonomy that begins with Palladio, architects should exercise *no judgment at all* in matters of cultural context. Rather, he reasons, architects should look to artificial techniques, such as computation or chance, to arrange patterns of space and material that are "wrested from any present preference for the normative."[22] Eisenman's reasoning, as we understand it, serves to *anesthetize* architects from the responsibilities of individuals in society, and to *aestheticize* the sometimes-harrowing problems of ordinary people.

Perhaps the most egregious recent example of such work is the exhibition hosted by the Museum of Modern Art (MoMA) in 2011, *Foreclosed: Rehousing the American Dream*. The exhibition featured works by five teams of architects "that would open new routes through the mortgage-foreclosure crisis that continues to afflict the United States."[23] But, in lieu of seriously trying to assist vulnerable families to find "new routes" toward a more sustainable life, these artist–architects produced visually seductive images that served only their abstract, formal interests. In effect, they ridiculed the victims of the banking crisis to aggrandize their own sophistication and distance from it. In the contemporary US, where a majority of humans now live in suburbs, what could be a more appropriate topic for serious design investigation?[24] But, to reduce

Figure 1.1 A Sardonic Solution for Vulnerable People. Michael Meredith and Hilary Sample, MOS. 2011. The Oranges, New Jersey: Thoughts on a Walking City. In *Forecloses: Rehousing the American Dream*. New York: Museum of Modern Art.

that investigation to self-indulgent formalism is profoundly asocial and warrants even more criticism than it received.[25]

We should be clear that, in arguing that nothing could be less autonomous than architecture, we are not arguing against art for art's sake.[26] Rather, what we are arguing is that *architecture is never just Art—it is architecture*. If architecture did coevolve with the social production of art, it has long ago evolved as a social practice quite distinct from the categories of excellence articulated by Vitruvius in 25 BC.[27] This position will be further developed in Chapter 2. Before we do so, however, it is necessary to provide empirical evidence that demonstrates how contemporary practice and research in the US is radically different from the Palladian model to which so many architects still cling.

MEASURING THE CHANGING NATURE OF PRACTICE

In Chapter 6, we make the observation that social groups tend to make the most extreme claims when they are most threatened from the outside, or when a particular social order has already experienced significant decline. That observation may explain why elite North American architects such as Eisenman and Frank Gehry, who feel closest to the tradition of Vitruvius and Palladio, are vehement in arguing for the autonomy of architectural practice.[28] Yet it would be overstated or ideological to claim that all well-known architects and academics in the US, let alone elsewhere, see the situation similarly. How, then, might the field be measured?

Like Habraken's theoretical observations, Imrie and Street's highly empirical analysis of contemporary architectural practice documents that most architects, well known or not, are very aware of the changing nature of practice. In a survey they conducted with several hundred architects currently practicing in an office, 80 percent of the respondents "either agreed or strongly agreed that they spent more of their time on red tape and bureaucratic procedure than 5 years ago," and 93 percent "feel that regulation is becoming more complex."[29] In referring to the "crisis of regulation," architects from the EU, the British Commonwealth, and the US all reported the increasing tension and conflict between the artful demands propagated by the canon and the more technological and administrative demands imposed by contemporary architectural production. Not only are buildings becoming more and more technologically complex, but the regulation and management of those technologies require time that might otherwise be invested in becoming the "perfect artist" demanded by Vitruvius. It is "like playing two games on the same field with two sets of goalposts. To play it effectively requires a feel for both games (art and technology) and to score both goals simultaneously."[30]

In this colorful sports metaphor, Owen and Dovey make good use of Bourdieu's observation that there are competing "fields of cultural production" in society that depend on different kinds of knowledge.[31] Where technological knowledge has become increasingly analytic and quantitative, the aesthetic knowledge valued and held by the keepers of the canon remains tacit and qualitative, by which we mean that it is hard to articulate because it is embedded in our cultural assumptions about beauty and taste—a topic that we take up in Chapter 5. When conflict occurs in any contemporary architect's office, as it does on a daily basis, the advocates of art bring out one kind of knowledge in support of their claims, and, correspondingly, the advocates of technology bring out another kind of knowledge in support of theirs. The problem, or perhaps opportunity, for architects is that they must have command of both kinds of knowledge in order to play simultaneously on one field regulated, or judged, by the canon and another judged by modern notions of technological efficiency, health, safety, and welfare.

In order to better understand this problem, these spheres of knowledge must be mapped as contested fields of cultural production. To put this in simpler terms would be to ask—what is it that contemporary architects think and talk about when they have the opportunity to be reflective? What are their categories of conversation? With this intent in mind, we evaluated contemporary architectural discourses by reviewing the major themes discussed within the *Journal of Architectural Education* (*JAE*) throughout its publication over a period of 18 years, from 1982 through 2010. We selected the *JAE* because it is the principal peer-reviewed journal of architecture in North America and has a broad international readership. Given that status, the *JAE* provides, we hold, a reliable index of the concerns held by architects who are also academics.[32] Of course, the interests and concerns of academics do not necessarily represent those individuals who are involved daily in the construction industry—practitioners, engineers, contractors, subcontractors, as well as those who commission, finance, regulate, and use buildings. And that is the point. By analyzing the discourses of academics, who are influential gatekeepers of the canon, there is an opportunity to determine what kind of knowledge is being pursued by them and how it fits into the categories of art and/or technology studies.

In our content analysis, we reviewed and categorized by theme 1,381 texts from the *JAE*. Entries evaluated included peer-reviewed articles, book reviews, op-ed pieces, and editorial introductions to special issues. Each entry in our manual "sort" comprised the article abstract, or, if no abstract was provided, the first and last paragraph of the text. Each entry was then pre-printed on a quarter sheet of paper and placed in a pile initially named, or categorized, by one of four researchers.[33] Each category was defined by all four of us as it was being constructed. Individuals made frequent queries about particular entries, so that a common understanding of each category emerged as the day went on. We all agreed that sorting conducted by four people, in which categories are debated and negotiated, is a more reliable method than coding by a single person, even when repeated more than once.

A rule emerged during our sort that nine "cites" were required to maintain a category. Those that did not survive this test included: *language, consumption, space, naming, branding, public communication*, and *landscape*. Each of these themes was then subsumed in other categories. The categorizing process also worked the other way: one large category—"interpretation"—was eventually divided into "history" and "theory/criticism" when it got disproportionately large. "Interpretation" was, however, later reinstated as a meta-category under which new categories were identified.

After the sort was completed, we had 22 categories of contemporary architectural discourse. We concluded that it would be helpful to re-order these 22 categories under a smaller number of related meta-categories, which the researchers created by association. We ended up with the following five meta-categories: (1.) architectural heritage, (2.) interpretation, (3.) cultural politics, (4.) technology, and (5.) professional culture. Each represents an identifiable sector of discourse within the discipline of contemporary architecture and is illustrated by Figure 1.2. In the remainder of this chapter, we summarize each

Figure 1.2 Five Meta-categories and 22 Categories of Contemporary Architectural Discourse.

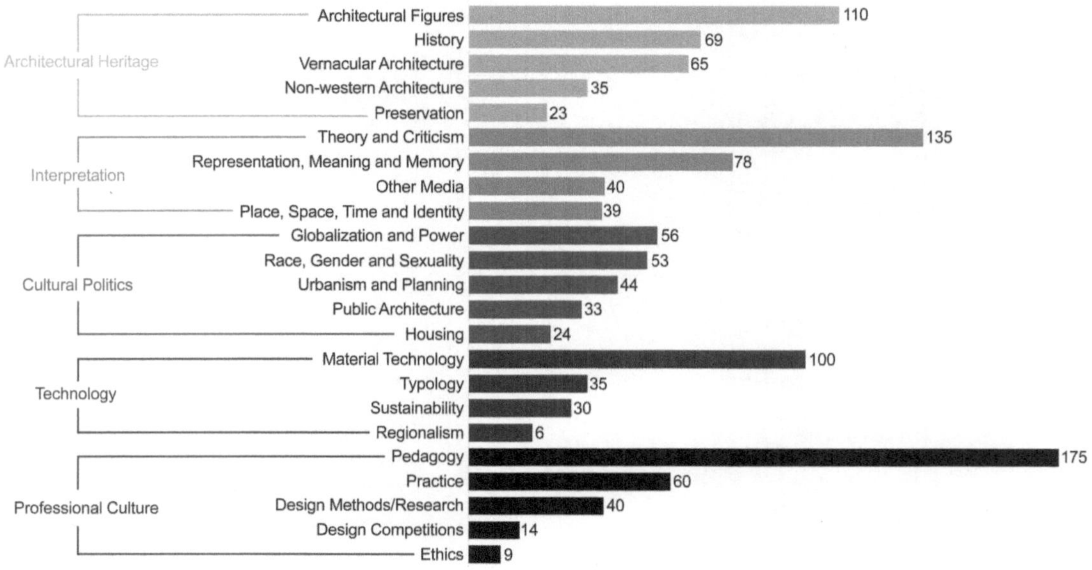

meta-category in order to further flesh out the results of our review, and to identify patterns within the literature.

ARCHITECTURAL HERITAGE

Architectural heritage, or the documentation and analysis of historical artifacts and cultural landscapes, was the most popular of the meta-categories we identified within the *JAE* (with 302, or 21.9 percent, of the total articles). Within this meta-category, the team included five categories: *architectural figures,*[34] *history,*[35] *vernacular architecture,*[36] *non-Western architecture,*[37] and *preservation*[38] (Figure 1.3).

What we found was that the discourse on architectural heritage has been focused, as in art studies, primarily on the formal characteristics of Western, elite building culture. This discourse has a keen interest in the practices of a few leading figures championed by the field and the analysis of the sociopolitical climates that influence differentiated periods of architectural form. Though still significant, the political tensions inherent in the preservation of this elite architectural heritage and the social influences of vernacular and non-Western building cultures are lesser-valued topics within the discourse. We do surmise, however, that a longitudinal investigation of this literature, although not within the scope of this project, would illustrate that this allergy to buildings outside of the Western, elitist confines of the traditional architectural canon is slowly dissipating as the literature begins to expand beyond its formal boundaries. And, although *architectural heritage* might be more resistant to changes in tradition by its very nature, this same logic would infer that the equally popular meta-category of *interpretation* should be very sensitive to the intricacies of cognitive evolution.

INTERPRETATION

Interpretation, or the endeavor to make sense of the built world, emerged as another popular meta-category during our review of the *JAE* (with 292, or 21.1 percent, of the total articles). This analytical and introspective lens within the

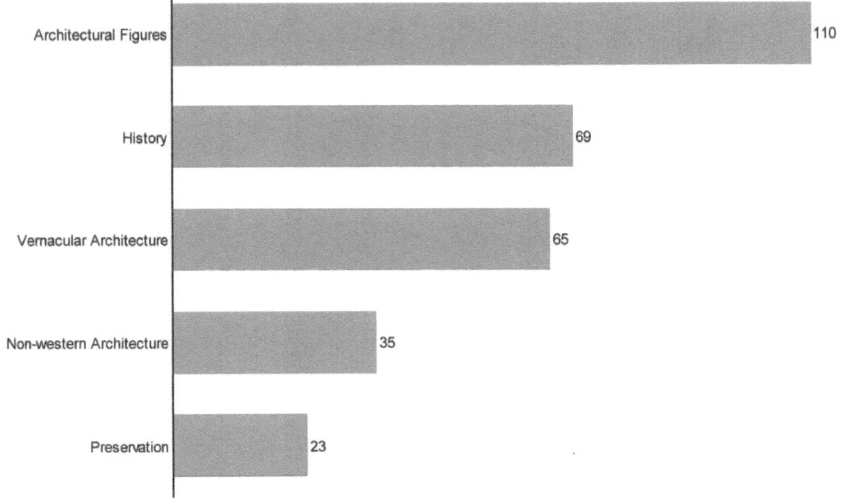

Figure 1.3 Categories of Architectural Heritage.

discipline of architecture encapsulates four categories: *theory and criticism*,[39] *representation, meaning, memory*,[40] *other media*,[41] and *place, space, time and identity*.[42]

Although the meta-category of *interpretation* captures the various modes and means of representing space through artistic endeavor, like the *architectural heritage* meta-category, the themes within this category do not seriously consider the social and political pressures influencing the production of our built environment. Even in the most political arenas—the civic memorial—these spaces are often analyzed primarily, if not entirely, in terms of their symbolic and formal characteristics, as in art studies.

CULTURAL POLITICS

Cultural politics, or how the built world influences, and is influenced by, power relations, is dealt with in an entirely different manner than the historical and interpretive articles published in the *JAE*. Categories within this meta-category include *globalization and power*,[43] *race, gender, and sexuality*,[44] *urbanism and planning*,[45] *public architecture*,[46] and *housing*.[47] It constituted a total of 210 articles (15.2 percent) in our review.

The meta-code of *cultural politics* captures those articles that turn the traditional elitist, paternalistic notion of architectural practice and critique on its head. Focusing on the messiness of participatory processes, the contentious political battles that contribute to any civic building project, and the contributions made from the situated perspectives of minority and nonexpert actors, authors contributing to this body of literature tend to be consciously avoiding discussions of architectural form and representation in exchange for deeper investigations of the socially charged and practically applied challenges of the built world. This discourse, then, overlaps only slightly with art studies. Although many artists also deal with cultural politics, just like architects they draw from the literature developed in other disciplines, including technology studies, to do so.

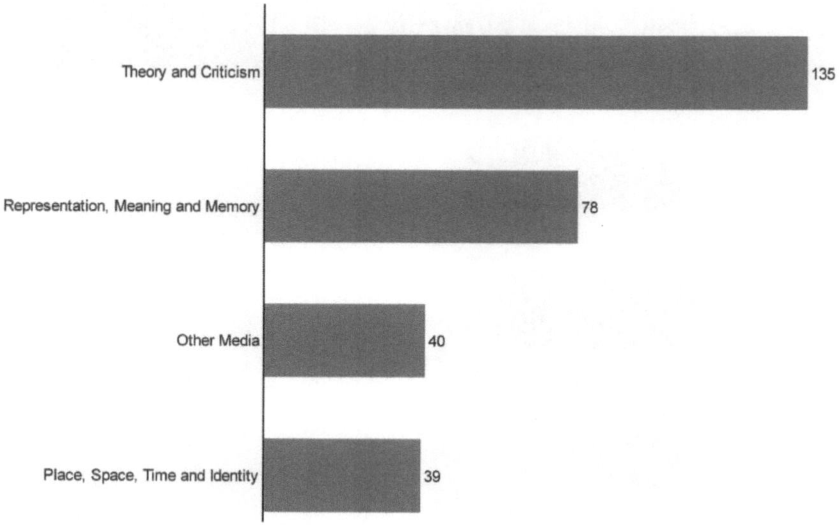

Figure 1.4 Categories of Interpretation.

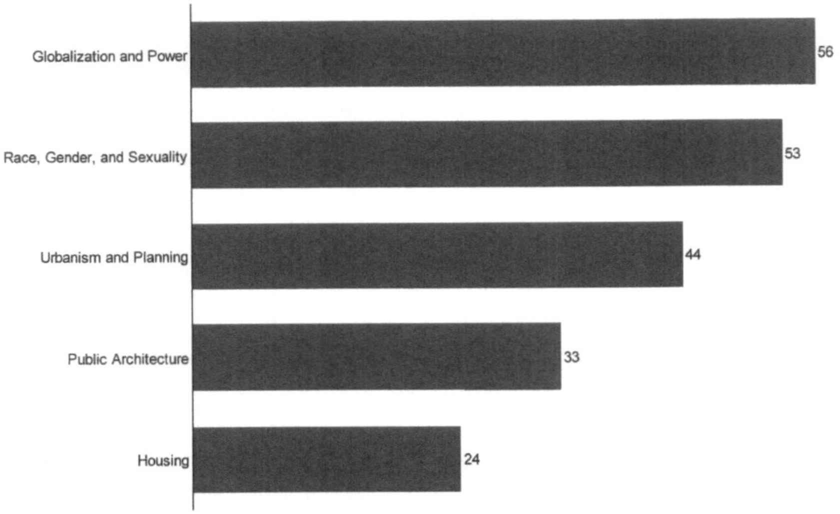

Figure 1.5 Categories of Cultural Politics.

TECHNOLOGY

In our review, we defined "technology" to be the combination of "knowledge, artifacts, and practices"[48] by which societies modify their environment. In doing so, we consciously reframed the concept from the popular understanding of "things," to emphasize the material consequences of building practices. This meta-category encapsulates four main categories in our search: *material technology*,[49] *typology*,[50] *sustainability*,[51] and *regionalism*[52]—for a total of 181 articles (13.1 percent) in our search of the *JAE*. Although this meta-category has the capacity to grapple with the sociotechnical side of architectural production, most of the articles found still focus on the formal properties of the buildings produced by and through various technological means. We will expand on this limitation in Chapter 2.

Figure 1.6 Categories of Technology Studies.

In the technologically oriented meta-category, these articles tend to grapple most directly with the realities of architectural practice in application. The authors tend to recognize, more than the authors represented in previous meta-categories, that materiality and environmental responsiveness are intrinsically related to one another. Although the social consequences of architectural production are not as richly engaged in this category, the two categories do seem to embrace the political dynamics of publicness in similar ways. Part of the project herein is to suggest viable avenues to pair tools from the literature rich in cultural and technological analyses in order to buttress the dominant, art studies-orientation of architecture with a dynamic, critically applied, and socially relevant tradition of technology studies. This should not suggest, however, that art-based literature does not also contribute to our understanding of technology. But, before we head down that kaleidoscopic path in Chapter 2, let us first finish our review of the literature by quickly summarizing the most transparent set of themes within the discourse—those discussing professional culture.

PROFESSIONAL CULTURE

The professional culture of architecture, as it is considered by *JAE* authors, includes five major categories: *pedagogy,*[53] *practice,*[54] *design methods/research, design competitions*, and *ethics.*[55] Relatively straightforward in nature, these themes are the most predictable of all the topics that emerged for a total of 298 articles (21.6 percent).

In sum, we can argue that the discourses of contemporary architecture are indeed complex, but there are also identifiable patterns illustrated by Figure 1.2. A second-level analysis of our review of the literature also suggests that it is reasonable to further compact the meta-categories from five to three. We have already noted that the meta-categories of *architectural heritage* and *interpretation* are strongly related. These two might be reframed as the search by *JAE* authors for intention and meaning—or, more simply, art studies—within

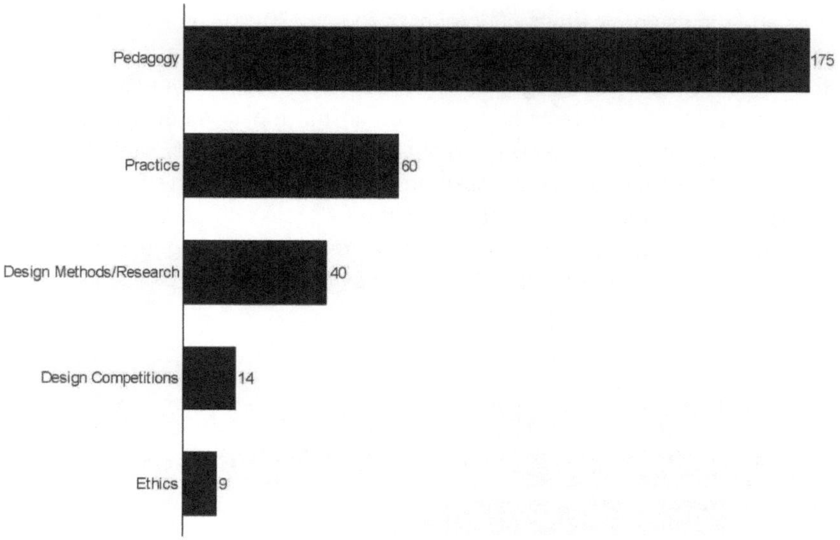

Figure 1.7 Categories of Professional Culture.

the built world. Likewise, we have also noted above that the meta-categories of *cultural politics* and *technology* are strongly related through the concerns of *JAE* authors for the social and environmental consequences of architectural production—or technology studies. That pairing leaves the meta-category of *professional culture* standing between art studies and technology studies, as illustrated in Figure 1.8.

Some readers will, no doubt, smile in recognition that this is hardly a new finding—many architects were advised to enter the field by their high-school guidance counselors because they were good at both math and art. These cultural constructs are long in the making. However, what the figure illustrates is not a simple binary opposition between the *immutable* values of art and those of technology, as if these categories of cultural production somehow existed before Vitruvius appeared on the scene. In the opening of this chapter we argued that Vitruvius would not have recognized "project administration," or the meta-category of professional culture that now drives more that 20 percent of contemporary architectural discourse.

Our review of contemporary architectural discourse suggests, then, that the conflict between art and technology studies is not an inevitable or binary one, but one that has coevolved with the need to understand the emerging nature of contemporary professional culture—the third meta-category in our analysis in Figure 1.8. No matter how thickly we attempt to bundle the categories of contemporary architectural discourse, we cannot get below three, and even these should be understood as reductive by being overly broad. The five meta-categories illustrated in Figure 1.2, and the 22 categories that comprise them, are a more accurate representation of the messy conversation that now engages architectural academics.

The result of this exercise is to document that architectural discourse is, like any other, *political*. It is political because the conflict between categories of interpretation, or judgment, embodies the changing values of social groups who would construct the canon of architecture differently than we now do. Above, we defined the "canon" of architecture as the collection of exemplary works used by experts in the field as a "basis for judgment." Our finding, then, is that art studies dominate the judgment of roughly 30–50 percent of the *JAE* authors reviewed—those who seek to understand architecture as a practice of artistic intention and meaning, yet remain autonomous of everyday life. In contrast, we found that technology studies, in the most limited use of that term, currently dominate the research of about 13 percent of *JAE* authors. The balance employs a combination of assumptions and methods. This finding does not suggest that we should advocate for the balancing of judgment through art and/or technology studies as binary opposites. Rather, it suggests that we should advocate for more hybridity and complexity as it already exists. In other

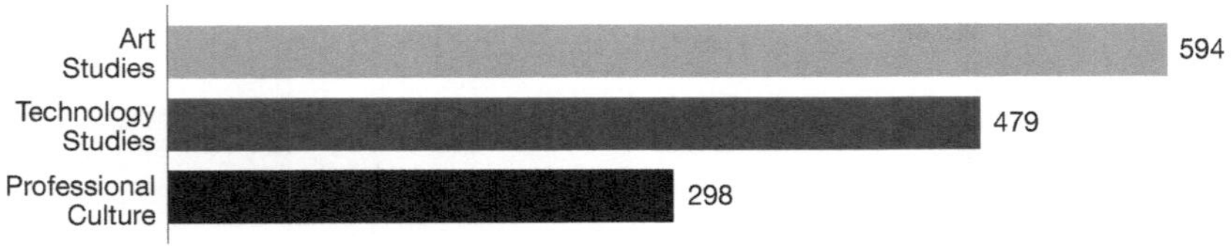

Figure 1.8 Three Meta-categories of Architectural Discourse. Compacting the categories this densely is reductive, because they become too broad. Figure 1.2 is a more accurate representation of contemporary discourse.

words, the art/technology dichotomy is a false one. Our analysis demonstrates that a surprising number of *JAE* authors are already employing mixed methods of interpretation—a condition that we find hopeful, because it opens up new kinds of knowledge and possibilities for judgment unrecognized by Vitruvius, Palladio, or Eisenman. And, because we find the methods developed in STS to be particularly helpful in the study of such complexity, we turn to that field in Chapter 2.

Chapter 2

Expanding Frames

Architecture-as-technology

For most of us, it is surprising to learn that the word *technology* did not come into general use in North America until the 1920s. How, we might ask ourselves, could a word so central to modern life be so new? Historian Leo Marx has developed an account of the word so as to dramatize its short life. The hybrid pairing of the Greek *techne* with the Latin *logy* "first entered the English language in the seventeenth century," but, he holds, "did not catch on in America until around 1900," when the term was used by such influential writers as Thorstein Veblen and Charles Beard. It did not, however, come into common use until two decades later. Marx's argument is that the appearance of this new word signals a fundamental shift in culture. Although the original meaning of the term was, as its roots indicate, the study of *techne*—what we then understood as the *mechanical arts*—its contemporary meaning refers not to the study of mechanical artifacts, but to the artifacts themselves. In contemporary society, the term has taken on an even more limited context and can refer only to digital devices, such as computers, cell phones, and iPads.

In his account, Marx documents an 1847 speech, given at Lebanon, New Hampshire, in which the orator Senator Daniel Webster employed the then novel word "technology" to mark the opening of a new railroad line. Marx uses Webster's speech to illustrate the conceptual turn toward modern technology, this desire that a new generation of Americans

> manifestly sought . . . was to identify—to name—a novel form of human power with far greater efficacy and scope than that previously ascribed to the mechanical or useful arts. The power attributable to those age-old arts was limited because, for one thing, they had for so long been identified with the handicrafts—the skilled handiwork of individual artisans. Besides, the very notion of arts devised for mere utility carried a stigma of coarseness or vulgarity. Ever since antiquity, the *useful arts* in their various guises had been considered intellectually and socially inferior to the *high* (or *fine*, or *creative*, or *imaginative*) *arts*. The stock distinction between the *useful* and *fine arts* had served to ratify an analogous—often invidious lineup of distinctions between things and ideas, the physical and the mental, the mundane and the ideal, body and soul, making and thinking, the work of slaves and of free people. But now Webster's generation,

> by associating epoch-making machines like the railroad and the telegraph with science, business and wealth, was seeking an entirely new category—a distinctively novel referent—untainted by the machine's derogatory legacy of social and intellectual inferiority and hence capable of elevating the *useful arts* to a higher plane—a plane closer to that of the *fine arts*.[1]

In Marx's account, then, the hybrid word *techno-logy* filled a semantic void that existed at the end of the 19th century. Social scientists have more recently defined modern "technology" to mean, not only artifacts such as the cotton gin, the automobile, and the atomic reactor, but also the knowledge required to make and operate such devices, as well as the human practices that accompany the artifact—farming, commuting to work, and producing energy.[2] For Senator Webster, using the new word "technology" was a way to describe, not only the appearance of novel machines such as the steam locomotive, but also the large social organizations required to operate them. These technological organizations included stockholders, managers, engineers, machine workers, and maintenance workers, not to mention the always-contested contracts and assumptions that bound these actors together as an efficient workforce.[3] North Americans of that era needed a way to express their aspirations for (and concerns about) a different kind of world that was then emerging at a ferocious pace.

A primary argument of this chapter is that the term "sociotechnical" fills a similar semantic void that became apparent in the second half of the 20th century. A related observation is that the field of scholarship generally referred to as *science and technology studies* emerged to help craft words to fill that semantic void.[4] Just as Daniel Webster needed a new word to describe what he saw happening in 1847, we too need some new words to describe our growing awareness that our technological and environmental problems are also social ones.

In the STS literature, or what we referred to as *technology studies* in Chapter 1, the modern concept of technology is understood as the coevolution of our tools, knowledge, and practices in a world that is action-oriented. By *action-oriented*, we mean that technology-makers and users share the assumption that their inventions and actions will be useful in changing existing conditions, presumably for the better. A more efficient "widget-maker" will produce more profits, but so too will a better serum save more lives, or a new school better educate children. Our point is that these assumptions about the effectiveness of our action-in-the-world did not exist a century or two before Webster's speech. The cultural change to which Marx refers was, then, one that shifted our cultural focus from the fine to the applied arts, from *interpreting* conditions to *changing* them. And, if the purpose of building is now to change, in addition to representing conditions, then a building too is a technology as well as an art object or an experience. From architectural theorist David Leatherbarrow's perspective, we have shifted our attention away from "what buildings are" to "what they do" or "how they perform."[5]

In this observation, our logic is not to set up art and technology as binary opposites, which is what moderns have done, but rather to view them both through new lenses. Thomas Hughes has, for example, argued that,

> historians and sociologists of technology can . . . use the notion of style to advantage, for, unlike historians of art, they are not burdened by long-established and rigid concepts of style, such as those of the High Renaissance and the Baroque that can obfuscate perceptive differentiation.[6]

In other words, technology studies are an interpretive tool that can be applied to art and architecture as well as technology in the narrow sense of the term. Just as Daniel Webster searched for new interpretive tools in 1847, we too need new tools to consider how technologies are representations of our aspirations, just as the fine arts are technologies that help us solve problems. It is hard to overstate the impact of this cultural shift, because it now seems so neutral and natural to us.

A related, if second-order, assumption behind this shift was for people to assume that our technologies increase our *agency* in the world. By "agency," we mean the individual "ability to intervene in social life through . . . action," in spite of the structural barriers imposed by the power relations embedded in economic, gender, and class relations.[7] We telephone users, for example, tend to imagine that it is only we who have agency, because we pay our bill monthly, and that the rest of the system exists only to serve the demands we make on it. But what happens when we experience a power outage? Yes, our cell phones become useless, but who is responsible? Is it the engineer in Bangalore, who incorrectly programmed the computer? The one who underestimated wire transmission capacity from the coal-powered generator in Fayette, Texas? A lightning bolt thrown by nature? Or, might unintended agency exist within the gaps of the system itself? These possibilities serve to illustrate that it is increasingly difficult to locate the *agency* within systems as complex as contemporary telephone communications.[8] It is one thing to locate the agency afforded by a hammer, but it is something entirely different to locate the agency afforded by a massive system of digital production and consumption.

The flip side of asking who has *agency* is the question of *determinism*—what forces control, cause, or influence events, artifacts, and spaces to unfold as they do? Over time, various authors have argued that it is the natural environment that determines social change—also referred to as *environmental determinism*.[9] Others hold that it is the economy that holds such power—*economic determinism*.[10] Still others hold that it is technology that determines what we do—*technological determinism*.[11] There is also the reverse argument—that societies cause technologies, economics, or environments to change when we deem it necessary—*social determinism*.[12] History is, then, crowded with arguments that afford agency to a particular category of activity.

Architecture is but one of those categories of activity. Questions concerning *how*, or *if* designers have agency, or the inverse—the degree to which architecture itself determines social behavior—have been debated in many fields over many years. For our purposes here, however, it will be helpful to briefly examine how the question of modern agency has been treated, both in architecture and technology studies, because the comparison will provide necessary background to considering the history of standardizing and regulating the built environment in Chapter 3.

AGENCY AND DETERMINISM IN ARCHITECTURE

As we demonstrated in Chapter 1, there is significant diversity in how technology is understood by *modern* architects—meaning those who have practiced in the modern era, from the late 19th century onward. We emphasize the term *modern* to indicate that to *be* modern one necessarily associates action through technology as having consequence of a (usually) positive nature. What distinguishes modern designers from each other is where agency is thought to reside and how it works to change the world. In our investigation, we have identified five potential sources of agency: *artifacts and spaces, designers, types, users*, and *methods*. At least one of these dispositions is naïve, but others warrant more attention. We will consider each in turn, in proportion to its value to our inquiry.

Artifacts and Spaces as Agents

To see intentionality and agency in artifacts or spaces is typically referred to as technological determinism. People who see the world in this way assume that the multifarious processes of technological change occur as a Darwinesque process in which tools, materials, and systems evolve from a process of natural selection that weeds out lesser technological choices along the way. In this one-dimensional version of technological change, the assumption is that the inherent efficiency of a new tool, material, or spatial configuration will be automatically recognized by designers and builders. Furthermore, because, in the minds of determinists, well-trained designers and builders make only rational choices, the new material or system will necessarily succeed. For example, when determinists hold that the success of solar-powered buildings is "inevitable," they assume that the logic inherent in the system itself will soon become apparent to others, as it is to them, and thus determine the course of history.[13] Some advocates of the New Urbanism employ the same hopeful logic toward the deterministic character of spaces designed in accordance with historic patterns.[14] The agency of artifacts and/or spaces is a popular yet naïve assumption that ignores the complexity of how social choices concerning technology are actually made.

A somewhat more sophisticated approach is found in historian Cecil Elliott's book, *Technics and Architecture.* Elliott holds that, "successful new materials and systems soon become necessities, elevating the standards of performance by which buildings are to be judged." Unlike the naïve, popular view of technological change claimed by environmental blogger King, Elliott does not simplistically argue that new technologies succeed on the basis of some internal and inhuman logic. Rather, Elliott allows that, "governmental and economic influences determine the outcome" of some technologies, or that, "scientific discoveries or the growth of other industries may have controlled events" in the success of others.[15] Although Elliott recognizes that there is some contingency introduced by the actions of government or industry, his narrative of technological change is still deterministic—he assumes that the trajectory of a particular system might be moderately deflected by social interests, but that the inherently *asocial* logic embodied in the artifact itself will ultimately lead to success.

Architectural or spatial determinism is but a subset of technological determinism; it is a set of assumptions that contributed to the *functionalist* school of architecture that dominated modern architecture until after World War II (Figure 2.1). Perhaps the most strident exemplar of this position was Hannes Meyer, second Director of the Bauhaus. He famously held that, "all things in the world are a product of one formula: (function times economy)."[16] Meyer's extreme position was based on the Marxist hope that, not only the social sciences, but architecture too, would become scientific and thus determine the proper course of history. However, Meyer and his colleagues had only the vaguest of ideas about what that "scientific" turn might mean in practice. At the very best, it was an ideological position derived from Karl Marx's hopeful notions of inevitable social progress. By the early 1960s, by which time the failure of technological determinism was becoming apparent, this naïve assumption became increasingly challenged and discredited.[17]

More recently, a nuanced form of soft determinism has appeared that might better be called "relationalism" or "performativity."[18] By these terms we mean, not that objects or buildings consciously cause events or conditions to change, but that, once they are put in place by the application of human technology, the relationships between humans and nonhumans is changed in ways that are marginally predictable. This phenomenological perspective has support within architectural discourse[19] and within STS[20] in a manner that challenges the agency of both the engineer (with regard to technological agency) and the architect (with regard to aesthetic agency).

Perhaps the most sophisticated notion of "spatial agency" to be developed is that by French geographer Henri Lefebvre. In simple terms, Lefebvre demonstrated that each "mode of production," or type of economy—be that communism (Cuba), socialism (Scandinavia), state capitalism (Russia), liberal capitalism (the US), theocracy (Iran), or populism (Venezuela)—develops consistent social practices that materialize spaces which embody the kinds of social relationship valued by that kind of economy.[21] It is not that spaces, or the things that define them, are themselves determinant, but that the systemic power relations that guide architectural production remain in place after construction is completed. That fundamental idea has recently been expanded

Figure 2.1 "Perspective": Competition entry by architect Hannes Meyer of the Peterschule, Basel, Switzerland. 1923–1926. Meyer's approach to design was highly "objective" in the sense intended by early 20th-century science.

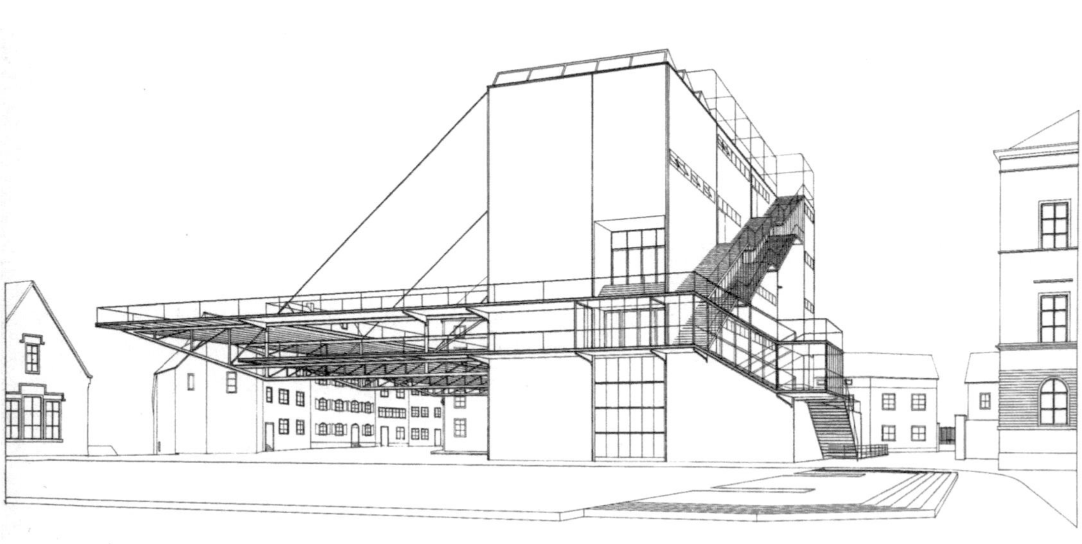

by Awan, Schneider, and Till to consider how the individual agency of designers can still operate effectively within the structural constraints imposed by each kind of economy.[22]

Designer as Agent

Most designers take up their pens and computers to make the world a better place. However, assuming that designers are the sole agents of environmental or social change is only the inverse of seeing technologies in that role. Nonetheless, society routinely assigns agency to distinguished professionals equipped with expert knowledge.[23] These gifted individuals are said to give form to buildings and spaces that, in turn, influences human experience and behavior for the better. Architects routinely ask for, and often receive, credit for the improved grades of students studying in new schools, the improved sales of retailers who have moved into new space, or the enhanced experience of viewing works of art.[24] However, rather than claim *technological* agency—that the buildings cause positive change—architects tend to claim *creative* agency for themselves, by framing the problem at hand, not in technological terms, but in aesthetic ones. Although there is empirical evidence that spatial configurations do indeed have social consequences,[25] the unfortunate tendency in architectural discourse is to credit authorship to individual designers, rather than the collaborative decision-making process. Scholars generally refer to this claim, with some derision, as the "great man" theory of history.

Some historians rely on the great man theory, not only when examining stylistic changes, but also when examining technological ones. A good example is found in Sigfried Giedion's *Space, Time and Architecture*. In that very influential book of the mid 20th century, he argued that American light wood frame construction, or the "balloon frame," was invented almost overnight by a single person when presented with three novel conditions: the market demand that followed Chicago's Great Fire of 1871; a modest budget for a church; and the availability of inexpensive extruded nails, rather than those that are hand-forged and cut. In Giedion's heroic narrative, Chicago contractor George W. Snow single-handedly invented this new building system, which replaced labor-intensive heavy timber framing, in a flash of creative insight.[26] Giedion portrayed the sudden development of the balloon frame as an example of technological innovation made possible by modern American ingenuity. In turn, this single case was used to support the aesthetic and technological agency of designers in the modern era.

Fortunately, Giedion's ideological and romantic history of modernism has been subsequently deconstructed and revised by the empirical research of Ted Cavanagh. Cavanagh convincingly demonstrates the balloon frame to be of French origin, a practice that worked its way up the Mississippi River from Louisiana to Chicago over a century or more.[27] Rather than being "invented," as Giedion claimed, the balloon frame evolved over time as a tacit practice within a local "culture of building"[28]—a term to which we will return several times in what follows. The point to be made here is that the tacit practices of French settlers were invisible to mainstream builders and architects, until they appeared useful to dominant social groups. The agency of *invention* was then granted to the Anglo contractor who made the practice visible to his peers.

In these great man narratives, the designer is granted agency that tends to suppress the complex influences, not only of broader economic and social forces mentioned above, but also of other actors on the scene. Giedion neglected to consider, for example, that the carpenters employed by George W. Snow might themselves bring useful knowledge to the job site. Ascribing so much power to individuals appears naïve, but no more so than the doctrines of technological determinism in which nonhuman technologies determine history. In the first version, asocial forces are given complete agency, and, in the second, great men are. In our view, the "hard" version of either kind of determinism is simply the modern binary attitudes of a society attempting to make sense of what is happening around it.

With that distinction in mind, we must be careful not to leave the impression that, if architects are not singular agents who control all aspects of architectural production, they have no agency at all. This is certainly not the case. We have already noted above that there is evidence to support the claim that spatial configurations designed by architects do indeed influence social behavior, even if these influences are not always consistent or fully understood.[29]

To grant the designer agency with regard to social change is an idea that emerged in the 18th and 19th centuries. In Chapter 6, we consider how codes of taste were manipulated by architects of that era to enhance the social position of their clients. By the 20th century, that limited kind of agency was to be applied more generally and in a more material than representational context by socially conscious figures such as Ernst May (1886–1970) and Mart Stam (1899–1986). The idea that architects and planners could act as agents of the masses was significantly amplified by the tradition of Critical Theory pioneered at the Frankfurt School for Social Research.[30] Most historians characterize this group as third- and fourth-generation Marxists who were left with the unenviable problem of reconciling the insights and good intentions of Marx with the horrors wrought by Lenin and Stalin. In the past six decades, contemporary Critical Theory has moved beyond Marx's historical determinism, but has retained the movement's commitment to social justice. Simply put, critical theorists hold that "the masses" lack the "revolutionary consciousness" to act effectively on their own behalf. History requires, then, movement intellectuals to act as agents on behalf of the uninformed.

Although well-intended agents of the masses have indeed designed many "good" buildings, too often the tradition of Critical Theory in the US has produced projects such as the Wexner Center for the Arts at Ohio State University by architect Peter Eisenman, who we introduced in Chapter 1. Without the sociotechnical interests of early practitioners such as Stam or May, the Wexner Center remains what philosopher Richard Rorty refers to as a "theoretical hallucination"[31]—abstract and disconnected from everyday life.

Lang, writing in 1980, generally discredits the agency of individual architects and its partner concept, architectural determinism, not because he is ideologically opposed, but because, at that time, there was very little empirical research on the topic that was credible. The status of relevant research has, however, advanced somewhat in the past three decades and is discussed below in relation to *method as agent*. Nonetheless, the idea that designers are the sole agents, or authors, of life-enhancing social change remains contested.

Figure 2.2 Eisenman Architects: The Wexner Center for the Arts, Ohio State University. The determinants of form in this and other projects by Eisenman are consciously "arbitrary," or unrelated to social or environmental context. In Dobney, Stephen. 1995. *Eisenman Architects* (p. 112). Australia: The Images Publishing Group Pty Ltd. ISBN 1 875498 21 4.

More often than not, observers from outside the profession see claims to the agency of individual designers as an example of disciplinary solipsism—meaning that "architects have emphasized their social engineering claims in an attempt to boost their self-images" and legitimize the value of architecture-as-art.[32] Until there is significantly more research available, a prospect to which we look forward, there are more satisfying avenues to consider how architects and architecture can be agents of human well-being.

Type as Agent

Associating agency with building types is a more credible approach to understanding architectural determinism, because it considers the architect to be one of many actors engaged in the social production of old and new architectural *types*. The modern concept of type has alternately been used as a method to classify both building functions—hospital, bank, house, museum, etc.—as well as building morphologies—courtyard, linear, tower, block, ziggurat, etc. The concept of architectural type may have first appeared in the early modern period studies of J.-F. Blondel (1705–1774), in which he documented the existence of 64 "genres" of architecture. The motivation to categorize "genres," or "types," of building derived, many have argued, from the Enlightenment-era practice of categorizing the flora and fauna of nature initiated by Carl Linnaeus (1707–1778) and others. The practice of cataloguing things was not, then, limited to architecture, but became an obsession unique to modern culture. It was Quatremère de Quincy (1775–1849) who first developed a theory of architectural "types" in the 1780s. In turn, his work was adopted and extended in different form by Gottfried Semper (1803–1879) in the 1830s, after which the practice became mainstream.

Nikolaus Pevsner first articulated a systematic history of building types around 1930. Rather than tell the story of architecture as the succession of building styles, which had been the dominant method well into the 20th century, Pevsner opted to tell architecture's story as the succession of uses, or functional building types. In his words, "this treatment of buildings allows for a demonstration of development both by style and by function, style being a matter of architectural history, function of *social history*" (our emphasis).[33] The significance of Pevsner's insight is a major contribution to the formation of sociotechnical codes—it is to recognize that buildings are an index of changing *social organization* as well as changing *social tastes*. Buildings are, then, technologies (as we defined this term above) designed to assist us in our efforts to make the world a better or richer place. Although other observers had certainly noted the appearance of new building types, such as railroad stations, banks, or office buildings, it had not occurred to historians before Pevsner to rigorously and systematically relate architecture to social history. This surprising oversight by architectural historians is once again an indicator of the long ties that the discipline has to art studies.

Pevsner's *History of Building Types* set out 17 distinct types, arranged from the most monumental at the top (national monuments and monuments to genius), to the least monumental at the bottom (factories). Such a hierarchy indicates that he still saw monuments as inherently superior to factories, but that he also recognized that social history modifies what it is that we build and how we build it. His thesis is that, until the early-to-mid 18th century, architectural history was little more than the documentation of the styles in which "churches, castles, and palaces" were built, with a few town halls and theatres added when deemed to be exceptional. "All that changed in the course of the nineteenth century."[34] This observation by Pevsner is to make two significant points: First, the 19th century was a time of unprecedented social change, in which it was hard to ignore the appearance of so many new social purposes and the buildings required to enable them. And, second, that architectural art was being reframed as a technology to manage, mediate, or facilitate those new social purposes. In other words, the purpose of architecture was moving away from the representation of a patron's power and tastefulness to also serving the patron's work.[35] Just as the patron's social activity changed, so must his building. Our argument is that, *the emergence of new building types is both an index of social change and a technology developed to manage that change*. The adoption of a recognized building typology by a patron is, then, to accept the social agency of that type as a tool necessary to satisfy *normal* social activities. The German theorist Ernst Neufert further developed this idea, but perhaps the most influential architect to consider typology was Aldo Rossi, along with other neo-rationalists of the 1970s and 1980s, who saw the city as a collective memory, embodied in building types, that is constructed over time by various social groups.[36]

Our primary point here is that the existence of architectural types that emerge over time—in response to changing social, ecological, and economic conditions—precedes the agency of individual designers. What designers do, then, is to modify the patron's preconception of a building type according to context-dependent conditions, such as the site and the unique organizational culture of those who will inhabit the particular project. It is helpful, then, to frame the agency of designers, not as isolated romantic heroes who manipulate only visual variables, but in the historical and highly social context of articulating constantly evolving types. This does not suggest that individual designers and firms are only undifferentiated members of the building committee, but that their contribution is to reify a way of living initially envisioned by the communities they serve.

The User as Agent

The idea that users might themselves have agency emerged from at least two sources: Reception Theory and the liberative tradition initiated by Paulo Freire. We will consider each in turn:

Reception Theory is a very interesting doctrine for our purposes, because it emerged as *rezeption theory* at the University of Constance (Germany) in the late 1960s as an internal critique of Critical Theory.[37] In the view of American reception theorist Robert Holub, "the historical essence of an artwork cannot be elucidated by examining its production or by simply describing it. Rather, literature should be treated as a dialectic process of production and *reception*" (original emphasis).[38] This is to hold that users are not the passive receivers of works by artists, but retain at least 50 percent of the power to interpret the meaning of a work and thus its cultural significance. Although Holub's research examined literature, others have used Reception Theory to examine different art forms, including architecture.[39]

In the expanded use of Reception Theory, the meaning of any work cannot be understood by reconstructing only the intentions of the architect–artist who designed the work in question. Rather, it is the gap—or, better, the dimensions of the gap—that exists between an architect's *intentions* and the *reception* provided by a public that tells us the most about any particular work. In this context, it not only what receivers have to say, but how they modify a building in the process of habitation. Although Reception Theory provides a valuable critique of the significance of works by expert designers, the concern of Reception Theorists remains focused on "meaning" and, thus, within the tradition of art studies as we defined it above.

A more radical departure from dependence on expert knowledge was developed by activist Paulo Freire in South America in the 1960s, 1970s, and 1980s.[40] Freire constructed a "pedagogy of the oppressed" that would enable the production of critical consciousness by the poor themselves, rather than its being handed down to them from above. For Freire, the role of the intellectual is not to educate the oppressed from the margins of everyday life, but to converse with them in their own space of action, so that their critical awareness of social reality can be articulated. Freire warns us that, "leaders who deny praxis to the oppressed thereby invalidate their own praxis." And, by "praxis," he means the process of reflecting on social conditions through action and on one's perceptions of those conditions. It is the responsibility of the educator, then, to nurture that questioning spirit and allow it to be expressed.[41] However, key to Freire's pedagogy is the role of action within the community. Rather than remain within the critical isolation of studio culture, as critical theorists have advocated, Freire holds that effective learning can only happen in the process of real-world experimentation.

Within contemporary architectural discourse in North America, Freire's pedagogical model has been appropriated and adapted by a new generation of activist–architects, including Bryan Bell (Director of Design Corps),[42] Sergio Palleroni (Director of the BASIC Initiative),[43] and David Perkes (Director of the Gulf Coast Community Design Studio at Biloxi, Mississippi). Perkes argues that conventional, let alone elite, practices have "a propensity to separate . . . practice from its social context." He objects to the abstract values of studio culture and argues for a mode of practice that is directly "useful to the community,"[44] rather than offering to the oppressed indirect metaphors of how modern life might be organized differently than it is. In his view, "the value that energizes a useful practice is not expertise; it is experience," where "expertise describes uncommon skills and specialized abilities that set one person, or a group of people apart from others." "Experience, on the other hand, describes skills and knowledge that come from commonly shared events or activities that form and strengthen human relationships around those activities."[45] Perkes, then, sees the role of the designer in society, not as an expert handing down veiled or abstract knowledge to an uninformed mass, but, like Freire, as a collaborator with users who are also peers, with knowledge, practices, and agency of their own.

The tradition of design in which the user becomes a coauthor of works and an agent in his/her own right has supporters in Critical Theory as well as Pragmatism.[46] However, some architects object to participatory design, because they see it as a prescriptive method that diminishes both the value of architectural knowledge and the artifacts that derive from it.[47]

Method as Agent

Assigning agency to a method of inquiry, or a design process, is a concept that originates in modern science. The scientific method, according to the *Oxford English Dictionary* is: "a method or procedure . . . consisting of systematic observation, measurement, and experiment, and the formulation, testing, and modification of hypotheses."[48] The conventional view of science is that, if you rigorously follow this method, you will either support or falsify the hypothesis being investigated and, with either outcome, move incrementally toward scientific fact. There is a very large literature that both supports and criticizes conventional science and the scientific method. Without immersing ourselves in that discussion completely, we will simply argue that, at its core, the battle is over the question of agency in science: Does agency lie in the method, or in the people who employ it? Scientists tend to prefer the first option. In their view, the process of peer review is at the heart of the scientific method and is designed to weed out individual subjectivity in favor of methodological objectivity.[49] In contrast, designers prefer the second option and reject the first, because, they hold, the highly complex variables at play in architectural problem-solving defy the capabilities of objective "observation," "measurement," "experiment," and "hypothesis testing." In lieu of empirical methods, designers tend to argue that intuition, supported by experience, produces better results.

Our position is that both extremes are problematic. Neither traditional positivist science nor traditional intuitive art provides the means, or methods, required for effective architectural problem-solving. The hybrid ground we propose derives from our analysis of typological modernism above, and here we extend that idea to support the emerging practice of evidence-based design (EBD) as a practice that incorporates the best of scientific rigor yet allows for designerly intuition. Hamilton, for example, has argued that:

> An evidence-based designer makes decisions—with an informed client—based on the best available information from credible research and evaluations of projects. Critical thinking is required to draw rational inferences about design from information that seldom fits a unique situation precisely.[50]

The appearance of EBD indicates that design culture—which is but one part of society as a whole—has taken what philosophers have called "an empirical turn."[51] By this phrase, philosophers of technology mean that, just as it is no longer acceptable, within their discipline, to sit alone in a white room and make *deductive* pronouncements without supportive evidence, it is also no longer acceptable for architects to sit alone in a white studio and *intuit* buildings they like, without supportive evidence that it will benefit both the client and society at large.[52] In this context, we should consider a building's *design* as an architectural *hypothesis* that makes claims about the consequences of building in a particular way—how much it will cost to build, heat, and cool it; what its acoustical qualities will be like; how people will experience a particular space under particular conditions. What is generally missing in architectural practice, as opposed to scientific practice, are the means to test the hypothesis (designs) in a manner that can be used as evidence for subsequent proposals by other designers. In both fields of inquiry, the evidence required will likely come from rigorous case studies that will, over time, establish bodies of knowledge upon which technology-studies scholars and designers might interchangeably draw.[53]

Above, we argued that the empirical study of building types will provide the context-*independent* evidence for designers and their clients to make more informed preliminary choices. For example, in the design of North American high schools, does the amount of natural light in classrooms influence attendance and learning by students? Given the general evidence regarding this question, the skill of designers is then required to test the usefulness of that generic evidence for a particular project, using context-*dependent* evidence gathered locally as a means of testing an emergent design hypothesis with available tools. For example, given the site orientation and other related local variables, such as insolation, average wind speeds and directions, adjacent building forms and types, can the generic norms of desirable daylighting be met, and how?

In spite of this small example, the proposal for EBD is still very abstract, and so it will be helpful to make it more concrete by at least mentioning the various methods that are emerging to discipline the agency of design teams. Building assessment systems (BASs) have emerged in response to the now well-known data related to climate change. BASs are, in general, quantitative methods designed to assess building performance in a number of dimensions, but most typically site impact and energy and water consumption. They include tools such as BREEAM,[54] LEED,[55] CASBEE,[56] SBAT Tool,[57] the Living Building Challenge,[58] DGNB,[59] or Green Globes,[60] all of which are *practice-based* inductive methods designed to transform the market.[61] These can be contrasted to the various *science-based* deductive life cycle assessment methods designed to provide valid evidence. Yet a third type of BAS is SEED—the Social, Ecological, and Economical Design network—which is the first serious attempt at measuring social equity as a dimension of sustainable design using both quantitative and qualitative evidence. The SEED Network is a group of architects and planners committed to integrating social responsibility further into the field of sustainable development, most notably through the development of an assessment and certification system that extends beyond current green building systems to include concerns of community and environmental justice. Advocating the insertion of a social element into the BAS conversations developing around the building industry, the SEED Network's mission is *to advance the right of every person to live in a socially, economically, and environmentally healthy community.*[62]

We can derive from the emergence of BASs at least three things: First, that, amid all the confusion and competition to establish reliable building performance measures, there is a growing recognition that empirical measures are not only necessary but desirable. It is not only sustainability advocates who campaign for them, but, increasingly, it is the development community—mortgage lenders, insurance companies, and real estate interests—who do so because each of these groups has found evidence that even voluntary environmental codes are in their interests. This is because meeting collective standards alleviates economic and litigation risks and thus increases contract certainty.[63]

Second, the location of agency—be it in the method or in the analyst—is not a question that will be resolved in the near future. It is highly unlikely that most scientists will immediately soften reliance on post-positivist scientific methods, or, correspondingly, that most designers will immediately soften reliance on intuition. Our own position is once again hybrid—the scientific method is, like the canon of architecture, a socially constructed system. What is important on both sides of the science/intuition divide is to recognize that both systems (attempt to) grant agency to respective, and opposed, classes of experts. This is a logic that has been developed in technology studies, to which we turn in the next section.

In summing up this section, we have argued that the five possible sources of modern agency—*artifacts and spaces, designers, types, users*, or *methods*—all share the expectation that action matters. What we build and how we build have consequences, not only for environmental, but also for social, conditions. Architecture is, then, both a technology and a representation. Where there is disagreement concerns where the agency lies. It is highly unlikely that one of these attitudes will come to dominate the others.[64] Rather, the uncertain trajectory of history will likely embody a hybrid of a few, but not all of them.[65] This is a topic to which we will return in our concluding chapter. For the moment, we see hope that the empirical and historical study of context-independent types, combined with the designerly agency required to adapt successful types to context-dependent conditions, in collaboration with users as active agents of their own future, can become the core principles of EBD.

Before we can conclude this discussion of architecture-as-technology, it is necessary to briefly review how the question of agency and determinism is treated in technology studies. We can then surmise if there is common ground between the two fields that might prove helpful in developing a ground for action and judgment in architecture.

AGENCY AND DETERMINISM IN TECHNOLOGY STUDIES

Technology studies have emerged, over the past half century or so, as a highly interdisciplinary field that has drawn scholars and activists from a variety of fields, including the philosophy of technology, anthropology, sociology, history, geography, and, increasingly, architecture and planning. What this diverse group has in common is the desire to understand how it is that societies develop and embrace the technologies that they do. The assumption behind this question is that technological choices are far from neutral or inevitable. Rather, our choices both reflect and influence a way of life.[66] For example, selecting a prepackaged heat pump to thermally condition your home, or designing your home to interact with the natural energy flows that are already there—wind, sun, shade, and water—has implications, not only for how you will live in a particular place, but also for the people who make those artifacts, as well as the places from where the materials and energy resources come. It is a complex set of variables to study, but one that can help us to locate agency in the systems of production and consumption we create. Although there are a variety of positions on the question of agency in technology studies, the two of greatest interest for our purposes are social construction of technology (SCOT) and Actor Network Theory (ANT).[67]

The Social Construction of Technology

As a group, SCOT advocates are fond of saying that our technologies might be different than they are.[68] Although most of us assume that, for example, the steam engine naturally and logically precedes the gasoline engine, and the gasoline engine necessarily precedes the atomic reactor, SCOT advocates argue that there is no internal logic within artifacts that was not put there by their makers.[69] By "makers," SCOT advocates don't refer to individual inventors, but to the social groups who, over time, incrementally construct new artifacts and systems through the agreements that they make with each other. The point is that the nature of our social agreements, and thus our technologies, is "contingent" upon changing conditions and our perception of them. The nature of a bicycle, for example, was not *discovered* by a heroic inventor, it was "socially constructed"[70] through a series of agreements made between interested parties. There is, then, no neutral and natural evolution of technologies or buildings that precede human interests, there is only the social and political process of deciding how we want to live together and with nature. From this perspective, new artifacts are popularly said to be *invented* when they come to "closure,"[71] when there is no longer disagreement in society about the form the new artifact should take. One important lesson to be learned from SCOT analysis is that technology may be shaped more by the need to preserve social and political agreements between producers, governments, and consumers than by conforming to seemingly objective science, or the problem defined by producers or consumers.[72] Technologies (including buildings) emerge, then, not from the application of pure science, but from the negotiated agreements, codes, and standards that regulate relations between producers, governments, and consumers.

From the SCOT perspective, artifacts such as buildings have no agency of their own—they are only the material reification of social agreements.[73] This is not to say, however, that the people who are most directly engaged in the social construction of new artifacts do not have agency. Hughes, for example, in his famous study of Thomas Edison, demonstrated that Edison was not so much the genius scientist who invented electricity on his own, but a very creative manager of the social agreements required to institutionalize the production and reproduction of previously isolated technologies as a workable system—the electrical grid.[74] Agency, then, derives from the ability to bind together the various resources required to build a thing through social agreements and the ability to manage those agreements as conditions change. This is a description, as any design practitioner knows, that is readily applied to architectural practice, but one that differs from the naïve notion that the agency of designers resides only in drawings and models.

In our view, then, the SCOT position with regard to technological and social change is sympathetic to, and expands, the hybrid attitude toward agency in architecture we sketched above—save the tendency of designers to overestimate their own agency.

Actor Network Theory

ANT is the second principal tradition of technology studies. Although ANT evolved from SCOT, significant differences have emerged, particularly with regard to the question of agency.

ANT practitioners argue that human agreements and objects that derive from them are hard to separate. For ANT advocates, the structure of human agreements is literally inscribed in the structure of artifacts, and the structures of artifacts limit subsequent action and agreements. We could not, for example, easily transform an elementary school into an automobile factory —the concrete floor slabs are too thin to handle heavy machinery, the ceilings are too low, and the mechanical services are undersized. Latour, in particular, argues that human agreements do not exist independently of the practices physically embodied in artifacts. Objects *do* compel practices, but the nature and quality of those practices is not entirely predictable. That logic is extended to argue that, "technological networks" are comprised not only of people, but also of the artifacts and landscapes with which people interact through action.[75] In concrete terms, ANT's claim is that the technological network that constructs a building, for example, is comprised not only of architects, engineers, contractors, suppliers, clients, bankers, and code officials, but also of saws, bulldozers, and welding torches, not to mention metals, wood, glass, concrete, and the places at which those materials were gathered. ANT advocates hold, then, that it is the sum of these human and nonhuman actors that has agency *through action*—agency is not limited to human intent. In their conversation about the "performativity" of architecture, theorists David Leatherbarrow and Ali Rahim come to very similar conclusions.[76]

Once again, there is nothing in this overly brief characterization of ANT that conflicts with the hybrid attitude toward agency in architecture we sketched in the previous section—save the tendency of designers to overestimate their own agency. In fact, designers have demonstrated themselves to be attracted to the ANT frame of analysis.[77]

However, if technology studies provide useful insights into the question of agency in architecture, there is substantive disagreement between SCOT and ANT advocates regarding the agency of artifacts themselves.[78,79] Although the disagreement is more than wordplay, we would be wise to consider it to be a family feud and take side with those who find the two doctrines to be compatible.[80] In this synthetic view, the issue is not whether artifacts such as buildings have intentional agency, but whether they modify human action. It is helpful to consider this position, because modern designers of all stripes clearly find efficacy in the idea that their works matter. Most sensible people agree, even if they can't demonstrate a correlation between the architect's intent and their own experience.[81]

ARCHITECTURE AS A SOCIOTECHNICAL SYSTEM

In this chapter, we have argued that our reason for constructing new buildings has shifted over time from being a fine art, or a system preoccupied with the problem of representation, to *also* being a technological system—a system of interrelated artifacts that helps us to realize our intentions, not only to represent conditions, or experience them, but *to change them*. Just as Daniel Webster adopted the new word "technology" in 1847 to express the aspirations of his time, practitioners of the relatively new field of technology studies have expanded that term to include the increasingly visible social dimension of our rapidly evolving technological systems—the *sociotechnical*. We then argued that architecture, no less than farm machinery or an atomic reactor, is a *sociotechnical* system, because we see in our buildings the agency required to change the conditions in which we find ourselves. What few people can agree upon, however, is where the agency for change resides: within artifacts, designers, types, users, or methods. Finally, we argue, it is unlikely that we will identify any single source of agency, because it is embedded in the long string of social agreements, artifacts, and spaces we make. It is far more likely that we will find multiple agencies within a system of buildings, spaces, designers, types, users, and methods, sometimes working in cooperation and sometimes in opposition to each other. The value of technology studies is, then, to locate the competing agencies within such a system and help us to realign them toward a common purpose—this is the process of *sociotechnical design*. To do so consciously would amount to a fundamental shift in our building culture. In Chapter 4, we will examine tools derived from technology studies that can help us to expand the boundaries of the design process. Before that, however, it is necessary to better understand the historical context in which our agreements, codes, standards, and regulations are forged. That is the purpose of Chapter 3.

Chapter 3

Standardization, Justice, and the Built Environment

> Standards are recipes for reality, or perhaps for realities. Like recipes for foods they may be well- or ill-conceived, the subject of careful analysis or of a slapdash throwing together of ingredients, and they may result in a tasty dish or one that is barely palatable.[1]
>
> (L. Busch, 2011)

> Standards and standardization are "ubiquitous but underestimated phenomena that help regulate and calibrate social life by rendering the modern world equivalent across cultures, time and geography."[2]
>
> (S. Timmermans and S. Epstein, 2010)

In everyday life, the term "standardization" is a pejorative one. Citizens of the US in particular tend to conjure up visions of uniform Soviet housing blocks or low-level corporate office cubicles when they hear it. Yet aspiring to "standards" has a ring of high, rather than low performance, as in "setting the standard" in an athletic competition. Timmermans and Epstein, cited above, "argue against any simple suggestion that standards or standardization are inherently either good or bad." "This does not mean," however,"that standards are intrinsically neutral. Standards' objectivity, universality, and optimality are hard won victories that can be heavily contested by third parties lobbing accusations of bias and politicization."[3] For example, it is not by accident that aerial photographs of the US, Britain, or Mali are so radically different. The land use patterns found in these images are the reification of informal and formal land management standards as they have developed over time. Such standards operate like "recipes for reality," as Busch claims above, or like maps—they eliminate most classes of information from the field of action, so that actors can choose between a few that are deemed worthy by the chef or map-maker. Were this not the case, the recipe or map would necessarily be as big as the world itself and, thus, not manageable.[4] Standards exist, then, to make complex tasks such as constructing a building manageable within a field of possibilities radically narrowed by experts in the field—they discipline technology using a particular set of values. In a directly political context, Brownsword holds, in "the technologically enhanced state . . . there is a danger of the Rule of Law being displaced by the Rule of Technology."[5] But, in the end, standards, like recipes and maps, can be suggested or imposed by experts from above—by government, religious authority, industrial power, by aggressive retail practices —or they can emerge from contested public talk and political consensus—as in the case of the disability rights movement (DRM), discussed in Chapter 9.

With these observations as background, the purpose of this chapter is fourfold: First, we make a distinction between spatial and material standard-making in the US, because they have similarities and differences. Second, we establish the constitutional background of historical conflicts concerning material standards that still plague us, yet offer unrealized potential. Third, we enumerate the ongoing conflicts that derive from that process. And fourth, we examine a few of the frustrations and criticisms of contemporary practitioners with regard to both spatial and material standards. This background provides the context required for Part Two of the book.

SPATIAL STANDARDS AND JUSTICE

Distinguishing between spaces and the materials used to form them is not as straightforward as it might initially seem. For example, both automobiles and buildings are artifacts that contain spaces for humans to inhabit. Buildings, in turn, form urban spaces and are thus subject to both spatial and material standards. For the purposes of this section, we will, then, limit our discussion to the question of zoning in the US, or spatial standards, not only because it is clearer, but because, unlike material standards discussed in the next section, spatial zoning in the US has been a product of public, more than private, legislation. One characteristic that spatial and material standard-making do share, however, is that they are home grown and unlike those of other nations. Although much of jurisprudence in the US derives from British, or at least European, precedents, our approach to both spatial and material standard-making is unique and thus worth reconstructing—particularly with regard to the concept of spatial justice.

Spatial justice is an emerging term often employed to critique the social and environmental structures of inequity that are physically codified into the built environment. One concrete example is the wave of "anti-homelessness" laws implemented in the 1990s throughout the US that prohibit specific uses of public space, such as sleeping on benches or sitting on curbs, so as to imply that these spaces can only be used by certain types of citizen for activities preferred by code-makers.[6] In response, advocates of spatial justice promote the recognition and reform of unjust standards to better reflect emerging societal values.

Territorial notions of justice included in the social justice literature do not explicitly grapple with the spatial dimensions of inequity in any physical sense, but, instead, focus on resource distribution in typically economic terms. For example, Edward Soja recently called for the establishment of a vision of spatial justice that transcends its typical concerns with "such related concepts as territorial justice, environmental justice, the urbanization of injustice, the reduction of regional inequalities, or even more broadly in the generic search for a just city and a just society" toward an "explicitly spatialized concept of justice."[7] Many argue, however, that Henri Lefebvre's writings from the late 1960s do just that.

For geographer–philosopher Henri Lefebvre, spaces are often given meaning by the "practico-social activity," happening in them, which he understands as a type of social discourse. Lefebvre asserts that, through the production of space, each inhabitant is demonstrating his/her "right to the city." He further extrapolates that all inhabitants have the right to participation, the right to difference, and the right to appropriation, and these rights not only give inhabitants the privilege to the use of all urban space, but also the power of decision-making about the ways in which space is produced.[8] Mustafa Dikeç builds on Lefebvre's *right to the city* concept by attempting to place it within a larger definition of spatial justice. Spatial justice, in Dikeç's terms, embraces the social construction of space as a producer and as a reproducer of inequity, rather than reducing these effects to matters of distribution—a limited but popular reading of Lefebvre. Dikeç notes that the accompanying right to difference in Lefebvre's writings might be translated better as the "right to resist/struggle."[9] Dikeç argues for a spatially informed emancipatory politics that gleans insights from the work of urban social movements.

Manuel Castells introduced the concept of *urban social movements* (USMs) to geography and planning theorists in the early 1970s to better connect spatiality and social change.[10] For Castells, USMs "emphasized the potential of urban struggles to express structural contradictions and assist in bringing about radical changes in political power . . . the extent (of which) would depend on the underlying contradictions and the ability of organizations to concretize them."[11] In *The City and the Grassroots*, Castells calls for the development of "a theory able to explain how city forms (and therefore good city forms) are produced."[12]

Although Lefebvre, Soja, Castells, and Dikeç have linked social movements to urban form, little has been written about how USMs make concrete changes to urban form. One exception is Fainstein and Hirst, who, in a survey of USMs in Europe and the United States, found most social movements to be limited in scope, localized, and—unlike the proponents of The New Urbanism—highly radical. At the end of their review, they ask if USMs can "*continue to be effective if they become connected to party organizations or professionalized staffs?*" And second, "*Does a social movement remain a social movement if its constitutive organizations participate in normal politics or administration?*"[13]

As we noted in Chapter 1, there is resistance from many critical theorists, such as Fainstein and Hirst, to connect radical change with the professional, and even institutional, realms of spatial regulation. From our estimation, however, and as we will demonstrate further in Chapter 9, the Americans with Disabilities Act (ADA) is a clear result of an institutionalized, professionalized urban social movement that was able to concretize radical values into built form. Although regulation has historically been used as a tool to preserve existing power relations, it is also one of the few venues through which radical values might be made concrete in the most literal sense. Thus, we see the oft-ignored intersections between spatial justice and spatial regulation, which have become increasingly more common during the last century, to be critical in response to

Fainstein and Hirst's questions. A historical perspective will be helpful in making this point clear.

Historians generally agree that one of the first events of spatial regulation in the US was the banning of commercial laundries (and, indirectly, the families of Chinese descent who ran them) from locating within the City of Modesto, California, in 1885.[14] What is most significant about this case is not the blatant anti-Chinese racism that motivated the action, but the fact that the "drafters used considerations related to health, safety, and general welfare to rationalize measures whose primary purpose was the maintenance and reinforcement of social distinctions and the confirmation of local relations of power."[15] This strategy by the City of Modesto is so historically significant because matters of "health, safety, and general welfare" in the US are relegated by the Constitution to local police for enforcement. The historical conflict to emerge from this distribution of power is that, although constitutional framers may have intended some form of universal justice, it was up to local authorities to interpret what that might mean in the unique time and context of their community.

Reliance upon police powers to spatially zone cities into different patterns, land uses, and densities was solidified by the making of, and challenges to, the New York City zoning code of 1916. The fundamental challenge recognized by the leaders of the "Save New York" campaign, which was formed at that time to support spatial zoning, was how to employ police power rhetoric for zoning, based on its constitutional link to the health, safety, and welfare of all citizens, while still preserving the land values of the Fifth Avenue Association of merchants driving this effort. This does not suggest that the first New York Zoning Commission did not also include empathetic social reformers who advocated for housing and sanitary infrastructure, only that the zoning process itself was dominated by elite landowners and merchants around Fifth Avenue. The concern of elites derives from the simple awareness that land value and appeal to shoppers decrease in direct proportion to the adjacency of degraded buildings and the people who inhabit them. Correspondingly, land values increase as use becomes more exclusive. It was, then, in the interest of elites, and cities that tax land in proportion to value, to spatially segregate land uses by race and class.[16]

In the early 20th century, municipalities attempted to implement racial zoning ordinances across the country—in fact, the U.S. Supreme Court declared a racially driven zoning ordinance in Louisville, Kentucky, unconstitutional by 1917.[17] New York was growing dramatically and vertically, and the Fifth Avenue merchants longed for a zoning ordinance more like the ordinances pioneered in Germany in the decade prior, which included bulk and massing stipulations. Citizens of all classes were concerned about access to air, light, and sanitation. Some had already decamped to the new suburbs, where air, light, sanitation, and compatible social conditions were more certain. We cite Fischler, who had a seat on the Zoning Commission, to reconstruct the reasoning of elite zoning advocates. They argued:

> We cannot justify more stringent regulations for dwelling in the suburbs than in lower Manhattan on the ground that light, air and comfort for the residents of the suburbs are of greater public importance than for the residents of lower Manhattan.

But if, they reasoned, sociospatial segregation of the classes could be demonstrated to benefit the *general* welfare, then judges might be swayed. The key is that "welfare" was construed by the commission to mean the natural "social sorting"[18] of society into relatively homogeneous social groups—as if class segregation was neutral and natural. Although racism had a role to play in such assumptions, it was income, or social class, that was the primary driver of "natural separation."

> The commission's reasoning proceeded in two steps: (1) The imposition of development constraints is justified because it is in the interests of health, safety and welfare; (2) The differentiation of these constraints is justified because in certain areas of the city they "impose burdens on private owners disproportionate to the public gain." Where the formal purposes of the police power did not suffice to legitimate zoning, the principle of reasonableness contributed added justification. Since government action had to show "proportionateness" of means to ends, lower standards of protection were justified in places where the cost of regulation would be too heavy. These were places where real estate owners had paid high prices for their properties—locations where the market expected high-density development to occur.[19]

Fischler argues, then, that sociospatial segregation was deemed to be "natural" by code-makers because it contributed to the general "social order," at a time when the radical change proposed by socialists threatened the pattern of everyday life. From this worried perspective, "Unequal treatment was not only permissible (by virtue of the principles of reasonableness and comprehensiveness), it was also desirable," at least in the view of property owners in New York at that time.[20] It was this kind of local, rather than constitutional, reasoning that contributed to the suburbanization of North American cities over the next century. The use of police powers to assure the welfare of the dominant classes privileged single-family homes over all other land uses. Local interpretation trumped what the framers may have had in mind.

The then secretary of commerce, Herbert Hoover, was interested in city building and saw zoning as a potential tool to protect homeowners and support business interests. Hoover created the Division of Building and Housing within the National Bureau of Standards and appointed committees to create a standard building code and to draft model planning and zoning statutes.[21] As an engineer who espoused efficiency as a fundamental standard, and as a social conservative, Hoover espoused a socially conservative agenda that would catalyze public morality by standardizing the development of single-use residential districts and resident-only neighborhoods.[22] The most powerful model developed through Hoover's committees was the Standard State Zoning Enabling Act of 1928 and its associated *Zoning Primer*. Committee member Edward Bassett, who had been intimately involved in the New York zoning campaign, advocated strongly for the inclusion of a variance process that was "judge proof"—forcing unhappy property owners to appeal to a Board of Adjustments on a case-by-case basis when they felt a zoning change caused them undue hardship. Further, if an appellant did not like the decision of the board, s/he could challenge this by a *writ of certiorari*, instead of a *writ of mandus*.[23] Writ of certiorari means that the court is only asked to judge if the board acted within its power, as granted by the Zoning Act. The reason these minutiae are so important is that together they set up a system in which property owners could not easily organize to challenge the constitutionality of zoning on any broad scale, and relegated site-by-site variance decisions to a separate board or commission of local leaders. Frederick Law Olmsted, who was also on Hoover's Advisory Committee on City Planning and Zoning, objected to the language authorizing the board because he feared its ambiguity "could lead to backdoor amendments and similar abuses."[24] Despite legitimate objection, that language was retained. By 1926, the now famous Euclid ruling by the Supreme Court[25] made sociospatial zoning a legitimate police power under the Constitution. By 1927, approximately half of the population was living in zoned spaces, and, by 1929, nearly 800 cities in the US had adopted zoning ordinances. As we will see in Chapter 10, one of these was Austin, Texas. No matter the original motives of its progenitors, the public regulation of space has been, at least so far, inconsistent with the democratic spirit of the Constitution.

The effects of zoning in the US are interpreted somewhat more generously by Emily Talen. Rather than calculated ill will toward the poor by social conservatives such as Hoover, she argues that social reformers too gradually embraced zoning as a tool to benefit the poor as well as the rich. The problem is that, "the effect of rules as well as the motivations behind them, over the course of the twentieth century, became obscured" by the intrusion of new concerns for mobility, fire safety, parking, and ad hoc problem-solving.[26] Although the diverse coalition that produced New York's first zoning ordinance in 1916 may have recognized and intended benefits for both the rich and poor, the codes and ordinances that actually became law generally forbade standards that would catalyze affordable and healthy housing—small lot sizes, higher densities, narrow setbacks, and housing *types* (as we defined that term in Chapter 2) for other than "single-families."

Although spatial codes and ordinances were developed in the public realm by local governments, in implementation they came to favor the private interests of local developers, land owners, and the "moral" class that Hoover envisioned. In contrast, the regulation of material standards was reserved for public regulation by the U.S. Constitution, but, paradoxically, material standards too were developed in the private sector. They also favor private interests over public ones.

THE U.S. CONSTITUTION AND MATERIAL STANDARD-SETTING

To our knowledge, no other nation has set forth in its constitution the need and authority to establish basic material measures. The U.S. Articles of Confederation, initially written in 1776–1777 and ratified in 1781, provided in Article 9 that, "the United States in Congress assembled shall . . . have the sole and exclusive right and power of . . . fixing the standard of weights and measures throughout the United States."[27] So important was this issue to President Washington, in his first annual message to Congress in January 1790, he stated: "uniformity in the currency, weights, and measures of the United States is an object of great importance, and will, I am persuaded, be duly attended to."[28] And to confirm that Washington was not alone on the issue of setting uniform standards, Secretary of State Thomas Jefferson, in his subsequent report to the House on July 13, 1790, "presented two alternatives: one was the placing of all divisions of weights and measures on a decimal basis, the other was 'to define and render uniform and stable the existing system.' "[29] And,

> to allay public fears and lessen the inconveniences attending the introduction of uniform standards, when determined, Jefferson recommended that they be introduced first in the customhouses, to familiarize merchants with them, then among merchants and traders in foreign commodities, and finally offered to the general public.[30]

These promises and recommendations from the Founding Fathers suggest that they saw the situation as critical. Why?

Cochrane argues that the tone of crisis invoked by Washington and Jefferson "represented a needless loss of time, effort, and money"[31] that the young Republic could ill afford. Although the new US generally used the same weights and measures that were then in use in England, in day-to-day practice they varied considerably from state to state, town to town, and trade to trade.[32] In fact, there was no *uniform* measure, thus making the collection of taxes and trading goods overly difficult or subject to fraudulent practices. Such a lack of categorical order, federalists thought, was inconsistent with the Enlightenment ideals on which the Constitution was forged.

Given the gravity lent to the situation by the framers, one would imagine that Congress would have quickly resolved the issue. Yet it was not until the fifth Congress in 1799 that even the most minor action was taken to standardize the weights and measures used at customs houses to facilitate the collection of import taxes and duties.[33] Still unresolved, the matter was again visited by President Madison in 1816, and by Secretary of State John Quincy Adams in 1821.[34] It was only in 1836 that the most meager joint resolution of Congress was reached on weights and measures to be used in commerce.[35] Although there is almost endless detail of historical interest in the long congressional battle to pass legislation that would standardize the seemingly simple matter of common measures for currency, wheat, pork, or timber across the nation, it was not until 1901 that modest legislation was achieved to establish the National Bureau of Standards (NBS).[36] Scientists in particular were disappointed at the limited scope of activity authorized by Congress for the NBS. Where scientists saw the need for precision and order, others saw government over-stepping its authority.[37]

From our contemporary perspective and assumptions, this protracted battle may seem strange indeed. But, Cochrane observes that,

> Federal reluctance to enter scientific fields and congressional agreement to keep in bounds those it perforce established grew out of the nature of the Constitution, which reserved to the individual and to the States the greatest possible freedom and the maximum opportunity for private enterprise consistent with the public good.[38]

Cochrane's explanation of the long delay in establishing what the Constitution set out as a responsibility of government is an index of anti-federalist sentiment at that time and conflict within the Constitution itself. Anti-federalists generally oppose any centralized public authority that might compete with private entrepreneurship and profit-making at the federal, state, or local level.[39] Although we tend to describe this position using other terms today, anti-federalists constitute a powerful and historically consistent segment of our society that has successfully resisted implementation of Article 9 of the Articles of Confederation. Lest we think this segment of society disappeared after 1901, consider this anecdotal current event:

In 2011, anti-federalist sentiment ran so high in the State of Iowa that its legislators urged the State to return to the gold standard of currency and thus set itself apart from the Union and federal monetary policy.[40] This small example serves to illustrate that conflict over who gets to establish standards for materials and spaces in our democratic society is far from over, even if practically settled by institutional momentum. In the realm of the construction and manufacturing industries, which brings with it significant public responsibility for the health, safety, and welfare of citizens, the situation is quite different. In the next section, we visit the federalist versus anti-federalist conflict between government experts and those in business over who should best set standards for the nation.

THE PRIVATIZATION OF PUBLIC STANDARDS

The public–private conflict over who gets to set standards and codify technologies has, over the past 250 years, largely been settled in favor of private (or industrial) interests.[41] This is not to say that the NBS disappeared. The Bureau did expand to include a Division of Buildings and Housing in 1921, the scope of research authorized by Congress expanded again in 1925, and, in 1947, yet another new division of Building Technology was authorized.[42] Expansion, however, did not mean control—the role of the NBS was reduced by Congress to be "advisory" and "educational" in service to industry. In other words, the public–private conflict was made to go away by establishing what Russell has called "industrial legislatures."[43] By this term, he refers to industry-dominated organizations that worked outside of government, but with the support and authority of the NBS, to establish voluntary and noncoercive standards to guide the production of goods and services. The story of how this came about is particularly salient to our interests in this book.

In 1918, the entry of the US into World War I necessitated a strategic level of standardization that had been previously resisted by industry and anti-federalists. But, rather than have such standards legislated by the NBS (much to their chagrin), an industry-led umbrella organization, the American Engineering Standards Committee (AESC) was established to "eliminate the duplications and jurisdictional conflicts in engineering standards."[44] That organization brought together, for the first time, smaller industrial groups from the lumber, steel, concrete, glass, and other industries to compare methods and products, establish common and interchangeable standards, and thus bring "consensus" (among producers) and closure to old disagreements.[45]

The governance of this institution was organized in such a way that it collected more dues from, and thus effectively gave more authority to, companies with higher levels of production. Although the AESC claimed to be a democratic platform for both producers and consumers, it was economically dependent on, and thereby politically driven by, large corporate interests. In the eyes of government, however, "legitimation" was granted to member industries through their participation in the AESC.[46]

In 1928, the AESC was renamed the American Standards Association (ASA), as an indication that industry groups would further represent national interests. So close was the working relationship of the NBS to the ASA that, when Congress dramatically reduced funding to the bureau in 1933, the ASA simply started paying the salaries of government employees, so that they could continue their work on behalf of the ASA and their industrial constituents while still in government laboratories.[47]

In 1946, the name of the organization was again changed to the American National Standards Institute (ANSI), a nomenclature that continues to this day. In 1981, ANSI estimated that 80 percent of the standards created and subsequently recommended by its members are eventually adopted as law by various branches of government.[48] This remarkable number is amplified by the fact that ANSI also represents the US in international standard-setting. ANSI has, unlike in any other country, effectively achieved public legislative authority as a non-governmental organization (NGO) that first represents private industrial interests. The chief mechanism for such legislative authority is the simple process of "incorporation by reference," wherein government appropriates standards recommended by second-party industrial organizations.[49]

Although this description of the governance of standard-making in the US is very brief, it does provide a reasonable picture of how anti-federalist interests present at the time of the Constitution came to establish, over time, a unique relationship with government. The scope of their control over national standards is generally undisputed, although some new standards, or recommendations for them, do begin within other agencies of government, such as the National Aeronautical and Space Administration, the Department of Housing and Urban Development, or the Environmental Protection Agency (EPA). As other observers have noted, however, the public is generally unaware of where our technological standards come from, or their significance for everyday life. As Busch argues, "Standards may become anonymous, but they are always, at least in principle, traceable to their originators,"[50] who are generally corporate.

To be clear, our concern is not that ANSI standards, and those established by member organizations, are good, bad, or somehow suspect, owing to their origin alone. Rather, our concern is that, as a nation, we have established a system of standard-making that is not accountable to the public for the social consequences of our technological choices. Although ANSI holds that "access rights" to its activities are open to "organizations and individuals,"[51] we find that its organizational structure is more accurately described as oligarchic rather than democratic.[52]

It has only been since the 1960s and 1970s that federal legislation—in the form of the Clean Air Act (1963), the Clean Water Act (1972), etc.—has begun to hold industrial standards accountable for their environmental consequences. If one believes that technological choices are routine and mundane, then yielding authority to make those inconsequential choices to practical men and women from industry makes good sense. But, if one believes that making choices about technological standards is of significant ontological and political consequence, as we argued in the previous chapters, then it is another matter altogether. This is because the practical men and women who establish our standards, presumably with scientific detachment, are in fact what Noble characterizes as the "corporate managers" of private profit. In Noble's unflattering portrait of this social group, they are deeply schooled in the ethics and culture of corporate profit-making and unlikely to be receptive to a sociotechnical understanding of their work, or toward social change in general.[53]

Realistically, then, there is no clear or established path for citizens of the US to press for the adoption of codes and standards that represent the interests of those marginal or suppressed social groups who are not able to gain access to the standard-making table. With a public road toward sociotechnical code-making effectively blocked at the national level by historical conditions, it is necessary to seek "alternative pathways."[54]

Municipal Adaptation

Although ANSI and its member organizations have significant authority to construct model technological codes, those models require review and acceptance at the state and local level before they can take effect. However, in the local review process, it is common for sometimes-significant modifications to be made. This authority derives from the same anti-federalist sentiment that restricted the NBS from centralized code-making. In other words, the constitutional deflection to "local control" also provides individual communities with the right to socialize what most engineers consider to be asocial technological codes.[55]

In the US, code-making flows in two directions, top–down and bottom–up. In the top–down version, model codes are constructed by national organizations such as the UL, the International Code Council (ICC), or the National Fire Protection Association (NFPA), under the ANSI umbrella. Based upon empirical data derived from recent catastrophic events, national experts update existing codes, which are in turn published for consideration by appropriate municipal departments, typically on a three-year cycle. In some cities such as Austin, Texas—the case examined in Chapter 10—the effects of adopting the new national standard are first considered by interdepartmental staff groups, before being presented to municipal boards and commissions charged with assessing and recommending codes relevant to the trades, such as the "Electrical Board; the Mechanical, Plumbing, and Solar Board; et cetera." These appointed citizen boards are comprised of local engineers and tradespersons (architects rarely involve themselves) who have a vested interest in technological change, but whose support is required before any proposed code change can be presented to the city council for adoption. In some cases, technology boards recommend increasing minimum standards stipulated by national and international organizations and, in other cases, they recommend rejecting new standards altogether in response to their own judgment and recent municipal focal issues.

Several respondents in our case studies noted that there are a few "leader cities," such as Seattle, Portland, and Boulder, that serve as regional testing grounds for technological and social change. Technological dispersion, then, tends to follow a hierarchy in which the technical capacity of city staff, as well as their linkages to staff in other cities, is a significant factor. Being a "leader city" requires funding municipal staff at a consistent, advanced level in order to provide staff with the expertise, time, and resources to both empirically test codes and also lobby for their acceptance at the mayor's office, the city manager, or city council. Being a "follower city" reduces both the economic burden of staff funding and the risks associated with early adoption of technologies such as those required for residential "visitability" by disabled citizens, "gray-water recycling" or the "smart-grid," all of which now attract the attention of municipal officials across the nation. Being a "leader city," then, requires an economic and political commitment to examine always-changing standards on an ongoing basis.

In the bottom–up version of code-making, *civil society*—or voluntary coalitions of citizen groups—identifies focal issues related to technological change that national and international code-makers have either missed or avoided for the reasons we discussed above. Respondents in our case studies stressed that it is essential for such civil society initiatives to emerge from "credible sources," such as universities or nonprofit organizations, that "don't have a dog in the race," as one Texan put it, to control municipal economics. A second criterion for success made by respondents is that civil society groups must find "champions" in each and every municipal department and technology board affected before attempting to influence policy at the city council level. And a third criterion suggested by respondents is that "demonstrations" of technological efficacy in the local context are far more effective than "words" in gaining supporters. Only when these criteria are satisfied do local regulators have a political mandate to construct new codes or amend old ones.[56] As in the top–down model, leader cities such as Seattle, Portland, Boulder, or Austin then influence follower cities in their region to adopt comparable technological codes.

Be it top–down or bottom–up, advocates for technological change have found considerably more success with the incremental approach long ago recommended by President Jefferson, as we noted above, than a comprehensive one. But, not only must revision of codes be "sliced up small enough" for "builders to be comfortable" with associated costs, as one respondent argued, but they must also be "strategic" in setting up subsequent innovation in a programmatic sequence that "isn't scary."

In our fieldwork, we learned, then, that code- and standard-making are complex and multi-layered processes that can be initiated at either end of the political spectrum. In the case of the DRM examined in Chapter 9, it took simultaneous action at both ends. In the case of S.M.A.R.T. Housing in Austin, Texas, examined in Chapter 10, it took aggressive adaptation of national standards and the invention of new local codes. In both cases, several conflicts surfaced that are typical in the field. In the next section, we review those as a precursor to hearing from frustrated practitioners.

PUBLIC–PRIVATE CONFLICTS OVER STANDARD-MAKING

In our field work and review of the conflicts rooted in constitutional debate, we have found not just two combatants, or relevant social groups, but four: First are those framers such as Washington and Adams who champion the role of government in establishing order, health, safety, and welfare on behalf of the citizenry. Second, "it was the scientists who sought better standards of measurement, better tools, precision instruments, and materials" in order to promote the advancement of science and international respect.[57] Third, in opposition to these two groups were proponents of commerce and industry, who argued that these are matters more wisely settled in the marketplace, by "the hidden hand" of capitalism. And certainly not last are "consumers" (whom we would rather refer to as "citizens"). It is this last group who increasingly advocated for the NBS to both protect their interests through product testing, and provide consumer information so that they could advance their own. Between these four constituencies we found seven overlapping topics of conflict, from the seemingly simple establishment of *weights and measures*, to philosophically complex questions about what can be measured. None of these is fully resolved today, but they have various degrees of interest in this book.

Weights and Measures

From a contemporary economic perspective, this conflict would seem to be noncontroversial—the conflict over basic weights and measures for currency, coal, meat, or corn has been pretty much resolved. However, as social conditions continue to change, and new controversial products—pharmaceuticals, for example—enter the market, conflict returns. How are the individual and social effects, costs, and qualities of these new products to be measured, and who will measure them—doctors, government, or insurance companies? These are not mundane questions in a democratic society, yet they are judged by private "industrial legislatures."

Government Purchasing

Perhaps the most basic reason for government to establish common measures is to level the procurement playing field. Government buys a great deal to feed the armed forces and office its workers, so it is deemed efficient by most to require a common product standard for everything from aircraft carriers to paper clips. Toward this end, most also agree that government should conduct "objective material testing," so as to provide an objective basis for procurement. However, the degree of standardization is hotly debated, because regulation that is too strict, many argue, stifles both technological innovation and competition.[58] To make matters worse, the higher goal of government efficiency is commonly subverted by the complexity of bureaucratic language, specifications, and bidding procedures used in the procurement process. Although the *process* of standardizing government purchases remains controversial, very few question the need for standards per se.

Basic Research and Patents

It is clear that the controversy concerning standardization is not rhetorically resolved, even if it has been practically resolved by increasing cooperation between government, industry, and the academy with regard to basic research. Advocates of private rights argue, as we noted above, that government should in no way compete with the entrepreneurial activities of private citizens. In their view, conducting research in publicly supported universities, and then issuing patents to public institutions to prevent competition from private enterprise, is an inherent infringement of individual constitutional rights. The controversy of who should conduct basic research, and who should be protected by patent rights, is, then, rhetorically unresolved.

Voluntary Versus Mandatory Standards

We have already established in preceding sections that, in the US, regulation of industry is generally voluntary and noncoercive. Recent international research suggests that, "there is strong evidence to suggest that voluntary measures have been instrumental in driving standards upward." This is because, we argue, individuals and groups are *enscripted* into a technical practice only when they have internalized the *generative frame* of the code. In other words, their voluntary participation is an indicator that they have come to understand, welcome, and even see their own interests in the reasoning that generated the standard in the first place. The notion of generative frames we introduce here is further defined in Chapter 4, "Frame Analysis," and will play a significant role in the hypothesis developed in Chapter 8.

Local Versus Centralized Standards

In the US, the contest between local and national jurisdictions is older than the Constitution itself and shaped the agreements forged there. In the 21st century, some observers are encouraged that the historical conflict between centralized and local control is resolving itself, and yet others are far less optimistic,[59] because standard-makers fail to recognize the degree to which their preferred, universal new standards reproduce cultural habits that are themselves unsustainable. Those who favor centralization provide evidence to demonstrate the need for commensurability between standards and technologies across space. Those who favor localization provide evidence to demonstrate the need for local adaptation and "buy-in," or the reframing of the generative rationale for regulation. If both are correct, then a hybrid process may prove successful, as it has in our case studies. Hybridizing will, however, require backing away from the ideological conflict that has confounded standard-making for all of this nation's history. This issue resurfaces in the cases studied in Chapters 9 and 10.

Consumer Protection

The old NBS inevitably found itself caught between the interests of producers and consumers, and both groups expected government to take their side. Where producers thought increasing private-sector profits—which directly increase taxes and indirectly increase public services—was the government's responsibility, homeowners thought protecting citizens from substandard products was the government's primary responsibility.

From the consumer perspective, one result of subsequent government inaction has been the creation by civil society of an increasing number of testing, certification, and labeling NGOs. As food and other products have become increasingly industrialized, it is virtually impossible for consumers to know what it is they are buying.[60] In the absence of government testing and certification, a reliable authority is demanded by an increasingly vulnerable public.[61] So, just as standard-making was privatized *in favor of industry* in the early decades of the 20th century, standard-making *in favor of consumers* is being privatized in the 21st.[62] This is a major conflict of our time and one that will not be quickly resolved. It is one, then, that is central to the concerns of this book. This conflict appears in both the case studies examined in Chapters 9 and 10 and takes a central role in our conclusions in Chapter 11.

One final category of measurement controversy derives from the concerns of consumer advocates.

What Should be Measured?

We have already introduced above the notion that trying to decide *what* to measure and thereby standardize can in itself be controversial. For example, in an earlier era, the measurement and standardization of time was highly controversial.[63] In contemporary debate concerning global sustainable building practices, Adshead and her colleagues have put their finger on a particularly important contemporary controversy. They found that the many BASs now available—including BREEAM, LEED, Green Globes, the Green Mark, Energy Smart, EEWH, and various life cycle analysis (LCA) tools—all measure, and therefore create, standards for different things.[64] On the surface, this might be a simple matter of scientific debate, determining what variables are *dependent* and *independent*. It only takes a light scratch in that surface, however, to recognize that the debate is very substantial indeed. Should we, for example, measure social equity as a dimension of sustainability, as well as the consumption of energy, water, and nonrenewable resources? And if so, how will we measure that variable? This latter question introduces the need to establish "standards of practice,"as opposed to standards for things, which was itself controversial until 1914–1915, when the NBS first adopted them.[65] These are controversies that are far from being resolved, but that are central to the concept of sustainability[66] and to the sociotechnical standards investigated in Chapters 8–10.

THE CONTEMPORARY CRITIQUE OF STANDARDS AND CODES

From the perspective of design practitioners—planners, urban designers, architects, and landscape architects—there is a "crisis of regulation" in everyday practice. The fact that anti-federalists have generally won the battle for minimal government in the United States does not mean that there is a regulatory vacuum.[67] As Imrie and Street have documented, the reverse is true. In their view of both the United States and the UK, regulation has both proliferated dramatically and become "decentered." By this term they mean that standard-making has been appropriated, not only by industrial groups such as ANSI, as we demonstrated above, but also by the insurance industry and mortgage lenders.[68] All of these groups have established generally conservative technological and administrative standards in their own interest, to reduce risk, enhance real estate resale value, and thereby stabilize market certainty. It is these risk-adverse values that frequently prohibit the use of new "sustainable" technologies.

In this context of privatized standards, one of the eight areas of conflict we enumerated above dominates all the others in the minds of practitioners—that is, central versus local control—the very same binary conflict with which constitutional framers struggled. This conflict influences contemporary practitioners in at least two primary ways: through the *abstraction* and *atomization* of decision-making. By *abstraction*, we refer to two related phenomena: (1.) the gradual scientization of codes that has obscured the original intent of code-makers, thus rendering contemporary codes indecipherable;[69] and (2.) the adoption of model codes by municipalities that have neither the expertise nor the resources to localize or humanize them. By *atomization*, we refer to the development of finer and finer degrees of disciplinary specialization among design practitioners, accompanied by the increasing isolation of the disciplines in municipal decision-making.

The perceived "regulatory crisis" is, then, characterized by the fact that codes are overly abstract (hard to apply), and that the authorities that manage them are increasingly atomized (hard to locate). A strategy that may contribute to easing the situation is *experimentation*.

Experimentation

Ben-Joseph has recognized that standards delineate not only what is acceptable to build, but also what is not. In a world that is increasingly litigious, this means that "building-to-code" is not only a strategy to protect the health, safety, and welfare of citizens, it is also a strategy to avoid corporate litigation and financial loss. Codes become obdurate, then, because they are "black boxes" that contain agreements that hold the interests of code-makers.[70] Few are more aware of this issue than individuals working in municipal governments. Because they build and maintain a great deal of public space, municipal managers and attorneys are keenly aware that buildings and public spaces are what Imrie and Street call, "risky objects," meaning that they attract code-based conflict.[71] Ben-Joseph's observation is that risk avoidance by cities tends to keep the lid on the black box, or that cities are very reluctant to experiment with local modification to model codes. The prior reference to *leader* and *follower* cities now takes on a slightly different complexion.

Ben-Joseph practically recommends that leader cities might band together and self-insure their experiments, thus avoiding conflict with the powerful insurance industry. Mayors of large cities, owing to their fiscal scale, have greater flexibility in this regard. By directly engaging cities in the testing and experimentation of life-enhancing codes, the gap between abstract and concrete conditions, or the gap between rule and effect on the ground, might be narrowed.[72] The municipal liability problem is a serious one that, once again, returns us to the public–private conflict embedded in the Constitution.

In sum, this chapter has focused on the long and not very productive opposition between federalist and anti-federalist claims regarding standard-making that are embodied in the U.S. Constitution. In our concluding chapter, we will return to this issue, but also expand on these observations to recommend that a mechanism be found to create municipal *spaces of experimentation*.[73] By this term, we suggest that real cities and real citizens be engaged in the process of code- and standard-making, rather than only "corporate managers" from the private sector and/or government employees of the National Institute of Standards and Technology (NIST). This is to say that experts, no matter their organizational affiliations or ideological assumptions, are never in a position to make technological choices that benefit citizens most.[74] Nonetheless, the observations of this chapter will contribute by bringing to light the controversy over who gets to make technological and spatial standards in the United States. The kinds of code that are available to whoever wins that struggle are the subject of Part Two.

Part Two

A Taxonomy of Codes

Introduction

In Part One, we introduced the idea that architectural judgment would benefit by relying, not only on lenses forged in art studies, but also on those forged in technology studies. In this effort to broaden the basis of interpretation, codes of technology, in addition to codes of taste, would also become standards of public goodness. In mundane terms, this is, of course, already the case—no building can be constructed without complying with hundreds if not thousands of technical codes. The problem is, however, that we moderns—meaning those of us who assume technology will automatically make our lives better—imagine our technical codes to be simple matters of safety and efficiency, not substantive matters of ontology or politics. The potential benefit of elevating public talk concerning technology is twofold: First, judgment would focus on the nonvisual as well as the visual competency and consequences of design, and, second, the criteria for judgment could more readily be held accountable to democratic processes. In support of this shift, we argued that existing technical codes, whether we intend them to be or not, are both an index of emergent social values and a strategy to enforce those values. This is to hold that the conscious move to include technical codes in judgment criteria, not only aesthetic ones, will make architectural production and its consequences more transparent.

In this second part of the book, we propose that it is necessary to understand the kinds of technical code that already exist, and the values embodied in them, before we can propose to democratize them. Another way to say this is that the purpose of this middle part of the book is to deconstruct prevailing types of code, so that we can later reconstruct them in more democratic fashion. In our investigation, we have found that four types of technical code have developed over time—*tacit, sumptuary, economic*, and *sociotechnical*. These were briefly defined in the General Introduction, but will be more rigorously defined in the chapters that follow. They are not periodic, which would suggest that the appearance of the second replaces the first, but spatial as well as temporal—types of code appear in different places at different times. They are, then, geo-historical types that have rather porous boundaries. To make matters just a bit more complex, not only do code types develop differently across time and space, but we also categorize them as "ideal types," by which we mean that they are logical constructs that are coherent in ways that actual human practices rarely are. In the real world, codes are commonly hybridized to fit the messy and ever-changing conditions of the city. This is why we refer to our list of categories as "taxonomic"—a way of classifying phenomena that avoids some of the complexity of actual conditions. Our taxonomy is, then, best understood as a heuristic device rather than a scientific fact. Coming to grips with the constant change or evolution of cities also suggests that societies continue to develop various new strategies of code-making to articulate and enforce evolving social values.

In the first chapter of this section, we discuss *frame analysis* as the primary analytic tool that we use to understand how code-makers interpret the world around them and construct codes to modify social behavior and the conditions that they produce. Different social groups interpret codes, artifacts, and spaces through different technological frames. This is to say that codes materialize the way that code-makers interpret and manage the world. Understanding the frame of interpretation employed helps us to understand how the code does or does not work through action.

In the following chapters of this section, we examine *tacit*, *sumptuary*, and *economic* codes by asking eight related questions:

1. What is the *strategy* used by the code in question to modify human behavior? Are codes embedded in social norms, or are they formally written prescriptions, incentives, or open-ended performance standards? Characterizing the strategy employed by code-makers helps us to understand the relationship of the means used to the ends anticipated by code-makers.
2. Using historical and empirical methods we ask: How do different kinds of code regulate and thus realize particular *artifacts*? The assumption behind this question is that codes play an active role in shaping the exemplar selected.
3. We then perform the same examination with regard to *spaces* as well as artifacts. For example, prescriptive economic codes typically require a stair (an exemplar artifact), and the turning radius for a wheelchair (an exemplar space), to have very precise dimensions. Examining concrete examples of artifacts and spaces helps us to understand how codes influence both, often in unexpected ways.
4. We also characterize the consequences catalyzed by the selected examples. Consequences are not always congruent with the intentions of code-makers, and so it is instructive to estimate if, and how, they differ.
5. By characterizing the intentions of code-makers we necessarily ask: What *frame* did code-makers inhabit when they rewrote the script of interaction between humans, artifacts, and spaces? This concept is fully defined in Chapter 4.
6. How do the exemplar codes actually work to modify human behavior in the specific examples selected? Our approach is, then, inductive.
7. What is the kind of authority required to implement the kind of code in question? Condemning a person to death for wearing the wrong color of cloth requires, for example, a very different kind of political authority than does issuing a parking ticket for parking one's car in the wrong space. Understanding the type of authority embedded in any particular code reveals the nature of power relations in the spaces regulated.
8. And, lastly, the final question employed asks: Where does the authority to enforce codes reside? Although precise locations are often difficult to ascertain, the exercise helps us to understand the nature of the authority in question.

We use these questions to interrogate the first three code types, but not in a rigid order. Because they overlap, we allow a few to dominate our analysis of particular examples and others to take a back seat.

Tacit codes are examined in Chapter 5 and are generally understood to be the unspoken or implicit rules of practice and behavior we all carry around in the back of our heads but rarely, if ever, examine critically. How we build a fence around our back yard or what kind of food we bring to a Fourth of July picnic are practices subject to tacit rules that impose limits on our choices. What makes this investigation particularly interesting, at least for our purposes in this book, is that it requires us to critically examine the commonly accepted distinction between vernacular architecture—which most of us understand as a collection of tacit or unspoken craft practices—and modern architecture—which most of us have been taught to understand as the fully self-conscious production of art. Our findings are that the words "vernacular" and "modern" are ideological and, thus, no longer very helpful. Just as, from time to time, we invent new words to describe new conditions, we should also retire other words from use because they no longer adequately describe conditions. In this case, the word "vernacular" overstates the unconscious obduracy, or inflexibility, of local building cultures, and the term "modern" overstates the degree of consciousness found in avant-garde studio cultures. Stated inversely, this is to argue that the values embedded in modern studio cultures are no less tacit than those found among "self-builders" in Brazil—a reference to which we return.

Sumptuary codes are examined in Chapter 6. This archaic term derives from the same root word as consumption and refers to the medieval practice of regulating clothing and buildings as systems of signs that signify class distinctions. Some colors, for example, could be worn only by members of a specific class of subjects, so as to make their presence and rank immediately known to anyone present. Although most people assume that such practices disappeared long ago, we find that sumptuary codes are still very much with us, if in more subtle form. And, although they are historically a method of privileging some classes of people over others, we also find that sumptuary coding might become a positive method of distinguishing, or honoring, members of society who practice sustainable consumption.

In Chapter 7, we investigate economic codes, which we define as those regulations, laws, or ordinances designed to stimulate economic activity by standardizing products and practices across previously isolated geographies, or by motivating practices or projects deemed desirable by code-makers. Economic codes generally employ a mix of strategies that alternately prescribe minimum standards, incentivize desired standards, or allow development teams to propose new construction methods on a performance basis. All three strategies seek to promote the economic interests that are vested in both sides of the regulatory process. It is hardly surprising that, in contemporary Western society, economic codes are the dominant mode for regulating the built environment.

Each of these code types is investigated theoretically and through concrete examples that demonstrate how they do and do not work to satisfy Mumford's criteria of "knowledge and judgment" that serve "human benefit." Our investigation of each of these code types helps us to answer the political questions posed above—how are codes socially constructed, and in whose interest?

The final ideal type of code to be investigated, sociotechnical, is the topic of Part Three of the book. By reserving this type for last, we do not suggest that sociotechnical codes are a more recent arrival, or that history favors codes of this type. We do, however, favor sociotechnical codes ourselves, because we find them to be inherently democratic. Supporting that claim requires, however, that we first deconstruct tacit, sumptuary, and economic codes.

Chapter 4

Frame Analysis as a Practical Tool

In Chapter 2, we argued that technology studies provide us with practical tools to locate the competing sources of agency that exist within a system such as the construction industry. In Chapter 3, we sketched the history of standard-making, in which competing agents vie to standardize or regulate our technological practices. In this chapter, we examine a tool appropriated by technology studies, frame analysis, that helps us to identify and locate the agencies that operate within any system. As we argued in Chapter 2, the ability to make a difference in the world is generally collective rather than singular. Sociologist David Brain puts it this way:

> Professional work is not just a matter of esoteric knowledge, but involves a distinct mode of judgment. What distinguishes professional work is not that professionals (individually) possess knowledge and authority, but that they (collectively) construct the grounds on which they can exercise a certain kind of judgment, and make a point of it.[1]

Max Weber may have been the first to recognize that the process of modernization is synonymous with standardization—the process through which we discipline the making of things in such a way that they become interchangeable. The meat packing industry of Chicago was a progenitor of mechanical standardization in the late 19th century, quickly followed by Henry Ford's motor works. Weber, however, was concerned that, in social systems, it was people, not just things, who would be held to a single standard through the development of the bureaucracies and institutions of the modern state.

Two decades after Weber's initial concerns were articulated, Michel Foucault was among the first to extend this logic as a systematic critique of modern institutions. Foucault held that the only reason for the "disciplines" to exist was "to increase both the docility and the utility of all the elements of the system." In *Discipline and* Punish,[2] and elsewhere, he suggested that modern institutions successfully reproduce themselves in a two-step process: first, by imposing rules on an initially unwilling population and, second, by making it attractive for some of that population to internalize the rules as their own. The quotation from contemporary sociologist David Brain, above, makes a related argument: that architects and other professionals "construct the grounds on which they can exercise a certain kind of judgment."[3] This is to argue that all professionals, including architects, tend to frame the problem at hand in a manner that requires their unique expertise to solve it—in a word, disciplinary *solipsism*. However, solving problems is not done in a vacuum; rather, it requires a particular organizational hierarchy that conforms to social as well as technical codes.

A logic derived from the typology of codes developed in what follows is that it is a short step from Weber, Foucault, and Brain to understand building codes in the same way. Building codes of all kinds are institutional rules for using the new tools invented, presumably, to make life better. Although we may resist watering the lawn only one day each week via a municipally controlled computer, because our sense of propriety is offended, we gradually internalize those rules as part of our building culture. Ben-Joseph[4] argues that we internalize rules and codes, not so much by being rewarded, but by forgetting the reason for their making in the first place. Put in anthropological terms, we might say that tacit practices are continually replaced by self-consciously adopted new technologies and codes to regulate them, which, eventually, become tacit practices as well. In this technological drama, our social capacities merge with the material capacities of our tools, because it is both convenient and obedient to do so.[5]

In Part Three, we expand upon this line of reasoning to argue for an emergent type of code that we describe as "sociotechnical." It is not that sociotechnical codes are entirely distinct from the tacit, sumptuary, and economic codes we discuss in this part of the book, but that sociotechnical code-makers consciously reframe technological standards as being also social ones. Rather than ignore or suppress the social consequences of our technological choices, sociotechnical codes integrate our material and social intentions for change. In this context, we hold, technological codes are not a simple matter of technological safety or economic efficiency.[6] Rather, all codes are both an index of changing social values and, at the same time, a strategy to enforce those values, as Weber, Foucault, and Brain anticipated.

Before we discuss the types of code that already exist, it will be helpful to define a key term woven into our assertion that "sociotechnical code-makers consciously *reframe* technological standards as being also social." If codes can be reframed, it stands to reason that we must first articulate what it means to *frame* social practices in the first place, before we can make a case for *frame analysis* as a tool with which to analyze the development of sociotechnical codes. A brief comparison of "frames" to the related concepts of "social values," and what Bourdieu called "fields," should be helpful.

Social values, or a value system, refer to an internally consistent set of beliefs, morals, ethics, or principles that individuals hold in common with members of a social group. Some values, such as being a "social progressive," are self-consciously held and can be articulated. Federalists in the United States, for example, share a value system that derives from their foundational belief in regulation as a desirable and necessary activity of government. Other values of the system, however, are tacit or unconsciously held. A possible example might be a vague preference for sports that are less violent than football. Values are, then, best understood as abstract moral codes, not necessarily related to space.

In contrast, what Bourdieu refers to as a "field of cultural production" is "understood as the system of objective relations between . . . agents or institutions and as the site of the struggle for monopoly of the power to consecrate" or set apart the values and products of a particular social group as somehow superior.[7] Owen and Dovey have put the concept to good use in their examination of sustainability as an emergent value in the *field of architecture*. They found that growing acceptance of the concept and projects that embody such values, by practitioners and academics, has generated a struggle for professional dominance between architect–artists, who rely on the "art defense" to support their authority in the field, and architect–scientists, who rely on the "eco defense," or the authority of nature and science.[8] In this context, "fields" are not only physical offices of professional practice, but also cultural spaces of activity in which social groups compete for ideas that contain their values and interests.

Different from both "values" and "fields" is the concept of "frames," which is discussed in detail in the balance of this chapter. To begin, we can distinguish "frames" from "values" by saying that frames are not abstract principles, but tacit habits of interpreting events, conditions, or artifacts. They are patterns of making sense of experience and artifacts that are generally learned through education and/or social activity with a social group. For example, students in schools of architecture generally learn to interpret designs, not on the basis of social values that may be embodied in them, but on the basis of formal characteristics preferred by the group, or school. Likewise, we can also distinguish "frames" from "fields" by saying that frames are not social spaces of struggle, but modes of interpretation.

Although these terms are related, there are helpful differences. With these distinctions in mind, we can examine different kinds of frame.

INSTITUTIONAL FRAMING

Many observers assume that the contemporary literature regarding "frame analysis," or more simply "framing," began with Foucault's critique of institutional rule-making. His well-known study of 19th-century prisons, particularly the *Panopticon* devised by the English utilitarian, Jeremy Bentham, is a case in point. What interested Foucault about prisons, and later hospitals, is how social practices, and the power relations that order them, are transformed or amplified by space. He held that meaning of events is always bound by the frame, or interpretive context, in which they occur. He also held, however, that frames are in a constant state of evolution, except at those unfortunate moments in history when local politicians are able to temporarily fix meaning for their own purposes. Ultimately, Foucault's position is that all frames bind observers, even if temporarily, to provisional meanings that are equally true. His was a particularly relativistic and dark view of the injustice constructed by modern institutions.

Elsewhere, we have found fault with Foucault's version of postmodern relativism and his dystopian view of any claim to "progress,"[9] and so, rather than repeat that argument here, it will be more helpful to recall the work of Erving Goffman, who produced what many still find to be the definitive work on the subject. Although Foucault and Goffman were contemporaries, reaching their peak of production in the mid 1970s, they were certainly not equally well known. We will return to the relationship between these two figures after setting out a brief summary of Goffman's thesis.

Goffman's Thesis

Goffman received his doctorate at the University of Chicago, where he subsequently taught, and when the influence of the Pragmatists John Dewey and George Herbert Mead was still very strong. To say that Goffman was himself a Pragmatist may be appropriate, but unnecessary, because his work was often said to be beyond easy classification. It will suffice to say that Goffman's work was always based on very fine-grained observation of human behavior in changing social contexts. In the first pages of his final major work, *Frame Analysis: An essay on the organization of experience,* Goffman cites William James' argument, taken from "The Perception of Reality," that there is not one world, but many subworlds, each with "its own and special style of existence."[10] He then appropriated the sense of the term "frame," originally developed by Gregory Bateson, to suggest that frames are "provinces of meaning," or a code that "informs and patterns all events that fall within the boundaries of its application." In this context, Goffman argued that, "the view that one person has of what is going on is likely to be quite different from that of another."[11] Trial lawyers, for example, have ample evidence to verify this claim. Witnesses to a street robbery or an automobile accident will report competing accounts, not only because they experienced the event from a different spatial point of view, but because they experienced events through a different frame of interpretation. The same can be said of buildings and landscapes—what is beautiful to one is ugly to another.

In Goffman's view of North American social life, "strips of experience," or the ordinary activities of everyday life, are not interpreted through a frame that exists in one's head, but are experienced and cognitively organized inside of a primary frame, or "schemata of interpretation," that one inhabits along with a particular social group. "A primary framework is one that is seen as rendering what would otherwise be a meaningless aspect of the scene into something that is meaningful." Our frames, then, not only help us to make sense of "what is going on," but also help us to "guide our doings"—to direct our actions within the frame. In architectural education, for example, students at Notre Dame (which teaches classicism) and at Columbia (which teaches modernism) learn to adopt opposing frames of interpretation. Frames are, then, also used by social groups to judge the actions of individuals within the group. However, primary frames are not singular. Rather, Goffman holds that social groups have a "cosmology," or "framework of frameworks" (classicism vs. modernism) that we should understand as a "belief system" in which experience is perceived and ordered.

A second major concept permits an even finer grading of events. Goffman argues that situations, and the frameworks they evoke, are "keyed"—as in music—by the presence of recognized objects such as a child's toy, or conventions such as a military uniform or a man wearing a bowtie. And, as in music, the key selected transforms the framework and its meaning. A good example would be the critiques held in schools of architecture. Although the primary frame is judgmental, as it would be in the world of business, the "studio crit" is keyed as a trial run, an opportunity for students to practice their presentation skills and receive helpful criticism. This is not to say studio reviews lack seriousness or consequence, only that judgment is layered, or "laminated," with other meanings and limits for acceptable action. And, importantly for the context of our consideration of sociotechnical codes, social practices may also be transformed by "rekeying," adding another layer to serial experience, as when a studio instructor behaves badly by being either too harsh in his/her judgment of a student's work, too enthusiastic, or introducing criteria for judgment outside the tacit values of the group.[12]

If "keying" can transform a situation, so can "fabrication," or the purposeful construction of a frame within a controlled social group. A faculty of architecture, for example, could self-consciously agree to frame studio reviews in the context of beauty, economy, or sustainability, so that students would inculcate that way of interpreting what it means to judge works of architecture. Although Goffman considers most fabrications to be negative social engineering, or "exploitive," in that they induce "a false belief about what is going on," we allow for positive fabrications that allow for new, life-enhancing opportunities. In either case, those who accept fabricated frames of interpretation can be said to be "contained within the fabrication" for a short or very long duration.[13] The implicit rules of segregation in the United States that still haunt some southern landscapes are a good example of a large-scale fabrication that might be productively transformed. The more layered interpretation becomes, the more we can speak of a condition's "structure," its multiple layers of transformation and retransformation.

Complex framing structures can be alternately poetic or confusing. Frames can be, not only vulnerable to misframing by psychotic or otherwise delusional individuals, but also "ambiguous," and thus misread—as in the two cases analyzed in Chapters 9 and 10. In such cases as these, we generally ask specialists to clear up any ambiguity about frames through objective analysis.[14] For example, when one social group sees homeless individuals in their city as victims of economic and medical conditions, and the other sees them in a negative moralistic framework, professionals, acting in a semi-official capacity, are typically asked to clarify such matters. The role of the professional in society, particularly designers, is to act as the custodian of institutional agreements, so that the rest of us can get on with our work without having to modify our primary frameworks and the relationships they portray as natural.

In the context of fundamental frame disputes, social institutions exist, then, to maintain standards through maintaining the clarity of dominant primary frames. Foucault and Goffman can agree on at least this much. When fundamental frame disputes persist over very long periods, as in both of the cases studied in Chapters 9 and 10, the normal modus operandi is for the minority frame to be suppressed, as Foucault taught us to expect. Goffman, however, suggests that it is also possible for a "seeing through" to occur. By this term, he means that a misreading can be "cleared," but that to claim "a frame is clear is not only to say that each participant has a workably correct view of what is going on, but also, usually, a tolerably correct view of the others' views, which includes their view of his view."[15] A good example of clearing a fundamental frame dispute might be when advocates of affordable housing come to "see" the justifiable fears of opponents, and when opponents come to "see" the justifiable hopes of advocates. This definition of "seeing through," or transforming, a fundamental frame dispute is also a good definition for "social learning," a topic we will return to in Chapters 9 and 10, where we test frame analysis and social learning as a way forward. For the moment, however, we will accept this to be a reasonably accurate summary of Goffman's thesis. However, before proceeding to a discussion of technological frames, it is necessary to briefly test Goffman's thesis through other lenses. We will start with Frederik Jameson and then turn to Ian Hacking for their dissimilar appraisals.

Critique and Counter-critique of Frame Analysis

In simple terms, Jameson's critique of frame analysis as a method of analysis is that it focuses only on the micro-scale of human interaction and thereby fails to account for how local relations are influenced by macro-scale structures of political economy, race, or gender. Jameson, then, adopts a position that reflects Foucault's concerns.

However, if Jameson dismisses frame analysis as hopelessly mired in the unreality of subjective bourgeois judgment, and lacking in an appreciation of historical structure, Ian Hacking offers a far more synthetic analysis. By looking through existential lenses, or frames, Hacking argues that the difference between Foucault and Goffman is a matter more of method than of substance.[16] That task is made easier by the fact that Foucault and Goffman both published influential books (*Histoire de la folie* and *Asylums*, respectively) on what Goffman called "total institutions"—prisons, hospitals, boarding schools, merchant ships, etc.—in the same year, 1961. Hacking's thesis, unlike Jameson's, is that Foucault and Goffman, taken together, offer complementary halves of a single, coherent system of analysis.

Hacking characterizes Foucault's archeologies as "'top–down', directed at entire 'systems of thought'." Foucault's study of how the institution of the "penitentiary," or place of penance, emerged is a good example of analysis that is historical and structural. In contrast, he characterizes Goffman's sociology as "'bottom–up'—always concerned with individuals in specific locations." His study of waitress behavior in and out of the dining room is a good example of the analysis of individual conformity to institutional expectations. In the end, Hacking demonstrates that both figures were trying to understand the same thing—the relationship between individuals and social institutions. Hacking's observation is that, although they simply used very different methods to do so, they arrived at sympathetic answers. Of primary interest to Hacking is what he refers to as the "looping effect," or "the ways in which those who are classified, and are altered by so being classified, also change in ways that cause systems of classification to be modified in turn."[17] If, for example, an individual is classified by society as an architect in one context, or alternately as a developer in another, Hacking holds that, not only does the label influence the behavior of the individual, but the individual also influences the operation of the institution where the modified behavior takes place. In short, people learn how to behave appropriately in the social context they inhabit, yet also transform those settings. In terms that Goffman adopted later, we both live in and influence our "frames"—which is to say that we "filter" both experience and subsequent action through an intersubjective set of perspectives that simultaneously enhance certain possibilities for meaning and action while also suppressing others.[18]

Hacking characterizes his own work as "standing between the two men," not to mediate their differences, but to demonstrate that works of Foucault and Goffman with regard to frame analysis are not only complementary, but also best understood from a middle ground, halfway between Foucault's abstractions and Goffman's face-to-face encounters. Elsewhere, we described such an epistemic position as "meso-analysis," neither macro-level analysis of grand structures, nor micro-analysis of individual choices, but taking a middle position so as to appreciate both.[19] In this project, we again adopt the procedures of meso-analysis and here apply it to the relationship of individuals to institutions, and vice versa, in the case studies that follow in Part Three. It is our perspective toward design professionals from the middle ground that allows us to argue in favor of a second category of framing—in addition to the institutional—that was not anticipated by either Goffman or Foucault—the "technological."

TECHNOLOGICAL FRAMING

Joining the grand structures of global economics and the intimate engagements of everyday social life are technologies. It was Karl Marx who observed that we humans act upon nature through technology to move history forward, to (presumably) make our lives better.[20] However, as we argued in Chapters 2 and 3, choosing a technology is not a simple matter of efficiency, but a matter of how we choose to live with regard to nature and to each other. Our technologies are, then, in the very middle of everything—they cut across and through institutional frames and so disrupt power relations by requiring us all to jump on the "technological treadmill" that drives capitalist societies.[21]

We also argued in Chapter 2 that we North Americans tend to be technological determinists—meaning that we interpret technological events, such as the appearance of the iPhone 5 or smart thermostats, as neutral and inevitable events. This is to say, we cannot imagine that history might have been different than it has turned out—that we might have chosen other tools to reify our (un)conscious social aspirations. In Goffman's terms, we have "projected" our technological frames into our lifeworld of ever-accelerating material consumption, so that the appearance of these new artifacts only confirms our expectations for the unfolding of history and for the built world.

Frame Analysis in Architecture

The application of frame analysis to social and technological change has been one way that STS scholars have challenged the American predisposition to technological determinism. Dutch social scientist Weibe Bijker is one of the first to employ the concept in analyzing the world of design in his seminal 1995 book, *Of Bicycles, Bakelites and Bulbs*.[22] Bijker was also, with Eduardo Aibar, one of the first to apply frame analysis to architecture and planning in their 1997 study of city planning in 19th-century Barcelona.[23] In that analysis, Aibar and Bijker reconstruct the public battle for influence between architects, who served the political and aesthetic interests of the nobility, and the new "sanitarians," or engineers, who served the rational and democratic interests of public health—a concept that was, at that moment, emergent not only in

Spain, but throughout Europe. The proposals of the architects emphasized *grandes avenues* that linked foci of institutional power in the manner of the *ancient regime.* In contrast, the proposals of the engineers emphasized new systems of public infrastructure—sanitation, water supply, fire protection, public transportation, hospitals, and hygiene. In other words, architects and engineers framed the problem at hand very differently. Fortunately for the citizens of Barcelona, history records the winner of this long battle to be engineer Ildefonso Cerda (Figure 4.1).[24] Although both of these studies have important lessons for our own project, a slightly later study by Bijker and Bijsterveld is most directly salient.

Bijker and Bijsterveld begin their analysis of the Netherlands' *Vrouwen Adviescommissies voor de Woningbouw* (Women's Advisory Committees on Housing, or VACs) by simply stating that housing can be understood as a "socially constructed technology."[25] Making this claim without considerable backing was made easy because the authors could demonstrate that this is how housing was understood by the 19th-century "material feminists," who conceptualized the idea of public housing that subsequently took deep root in the Netherlands. "For them, the house was a technology to enhance the economic emancipation of women."[26] That goal did change over time to reflect the changing values of Dutch society as a whole; however, the idea that housing is a technological means to realize evolving social goals did not. Given that historical background, the contemporary existence of VACs

Figure 4.1 Street Cross-section Derived From Ildefonso Cerda.
The section illustrates Cerda's very early integration of building services and public sanitary infrastructure.
In *Cerda: The Five Bases of the General Theory of Urbanization.* Edited by Arturo Soria y Puig (p. 297). Barcelona: Electa.

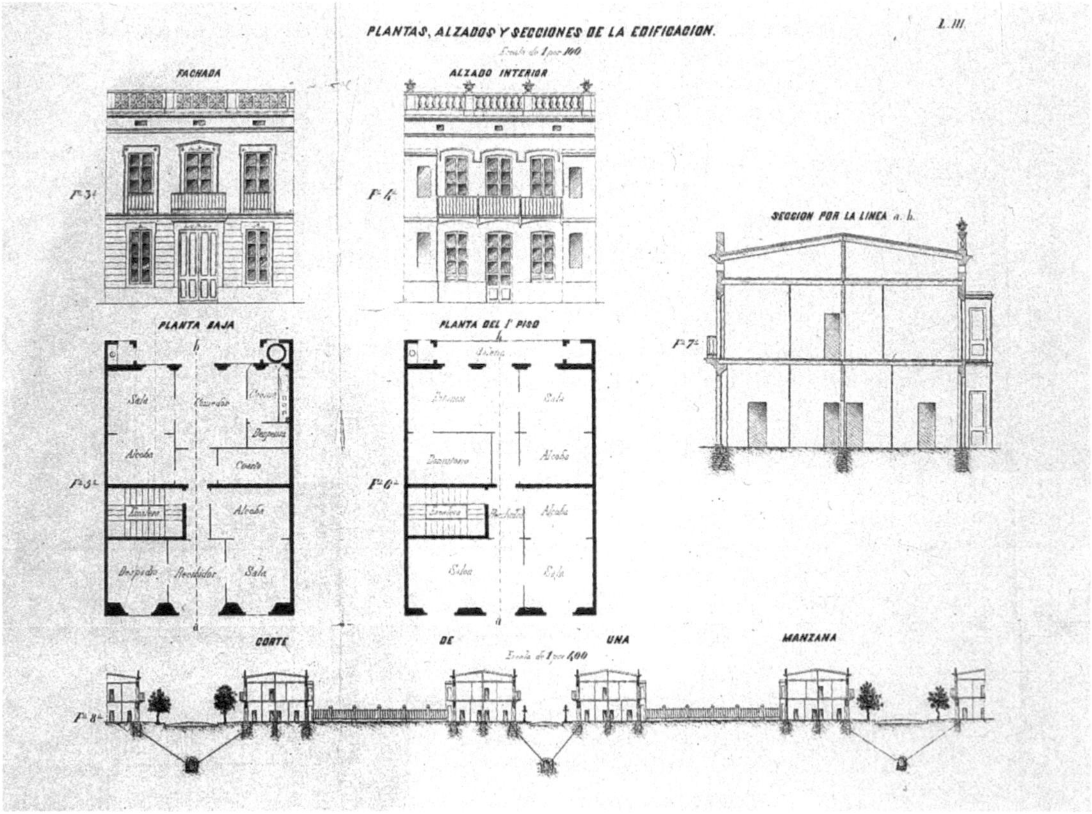

provided an ideal context for Bijker and Bijsterveld "to study the relationships between technology, gender, and power."[27]

In simple terms, the VACs evolved as a state-sponsored institution, staffed initially only by volunteer "housewives," to improve the quality of public housing. The charge given the advisory committee relied on the explicit understanding that women have "non-expert knowledge" with regard to practical matters that is valuable to the state, and thus to citizens as a whole. It did not mean, however, that housewives at that time were considered the social or professional equals of the male-dominated housing policy sector, or of the equally male-dominated design and construction industry. There were, however, emergent and culturally specific conditions that challenged the status quo of 19th-century gender politics.

The late 19th and early 20th centuries in the Netherlands were dominated by three competing, yet sympathetic, discourses: that of the same sanitarians who were at work in Barcelona (who advocated for public health and hygiene in growing cities), that of the modern or functionalist movement in architecture (who advocated for rational planning and the industrialization of housing), and that of the feminist efficiency movement (who advocated for labor-reducing designs for the home). "'Housing' thus meant very different things for different *relevant social groups* at more or less the same time" (our emphasis).[28] The term "relevant social groups" is defined elsewhere as those who "influence the creation, the demand for, the production, the diffusion, the acceptance, or the opposition to new technologies."[29] Where the male-dominated policy and construction spheres tended to concern themselves with "abstract" variables of an economic or aesthetic nature, women self-identified with the practical needs of everyday life—how to bathe the baby, how to wash the clothes, how to gather food, and so forth. In spite of these differences, there was enough overlap in the interests of these relevant social groups, and the generally "reformist" attitude of the time, to provide adequate support for the VAC mission to get under way. The VAC women responded to the challenge, perhaps unconsciously as well as consciously, by developing a highly rational *advisory* role that advocated for small, incremental changes, on a project-by-project basis, through the use of checklists, design standards, and the innovative narrative strategy of "walking through plans" with their male counterparts as a method to test design with regard to the concrete everyday needs mentioned above. In was through such strategies that the VAC women sewed together the three dominant discourses of the time.

"One way of summarizing the advisory committee's position is to say that their goal is not to promote buildings for women, but that buildings for all sexes can benefit from their specific experiences as women."[30] In spite of their advisory role, over the decades that followed, the VACs managed to accumulate considerable power to influence design and construction decisions. They did so by building their own technical expertise, but not by taking credit for their many successes, nor by being confrontational and "going public"—thus exposing their male colleagues to public criticism. Rather, they accrued power by investing in their relationships with the men with whom they necessarily worked. "Viewed in this way, 'power' is a more summary concept that serves to describe in one word a situation that can only be understood as the result of a long chain of complicated interactions."[31]

In their analysis of the success enjoyed by the VACs, Bijker and Bijsterveld introduce two terms that will prove helpful in our own analysis of code-making and the North American case studies. First, they adopt, and build upon, Goffman's concept by arguing that a "technological frame,"

> structures the interactions among members of a social group, and is similar to Kuhn's "paradigm." A high inclusion in a technological frame means that an actor interacts, acts, and thinks to a great degree in terms of that frame—the actor is quite central to that technological frame. A low inclusion means that an actor only employs the vocabulary, values, aims, techniques, and so forth of that frame to a limited extent—she or he is rather marginal.[32]

In this definition, architects tend to "have no life outside their frame"—they have a "high inclusion" rate of participation in that frame, meaning that they are likely to interpret events in only one way that is considered professionally "pure" by colleagues.[33] The flip side of a high inclusion rate is that participants are unable to imagine radical change within the system of which they are a part. In effect, they are trapped or, as Goffman would say, "contained," within the frame.

In contrast to most architects, VAC women have a "low inclusion" rate, meaning that they can pick and choose from whatever frame is helpful at the time. This distinction allows the women to become what others have called "code-switchers"—individuals capable of adopting the "external vocabularies" of others (the abstract and quantitative vocabulary employed by engineers and architects as one example, or the legal and policy vocabulary of civil servants as another), while at the same time maintaining and developing their own "internal vocabulary." The most significant capacity gained by code-switchers is the ability to imagine the radical change of any frame, including their own. Their linguistic flexibility is, then, a strategic advantage. Some will argue, of course, that code-switching is only opportunism or relativism of the kind employed by savvy politicians. In some cases, this may be so. That observation, however, doesn't challenge the effectiveness of the strategy or the existence of the pluralistic insight. In the next section, we will return to the idea of code-switching in the more positive sense of *integrating* frames. For the moment, we recognize that there is a "paradox" in low versus high inclusion in any particular frame, which is that *the ability to imagine radical change can only occur to individuals with low rates of inclusion.* The problem is that individuals with low inclusion in a social group generally have little power within the group to implement it. Conversely, those who do have power are generally unable to imagine change that would threaten their worldview and interests.

The second related concept introduced is "semiotic power structures," by which the authors mean that the VAC women were skilled in developing individual relationships with their male counterparts that were anchored in broader cultural norms of collaborative behavior, which, in turn, established "an obligation for housing corporations and architects to consult the committees." Through work at the level of "micropolitics" in neighborhoods and cities, the existing power structure was changed "without wholly overturning it."[34] It was not only with men, however, that the committee women invoked broader semiotic structures. In meeting with more radical feminists within the community, and/or with women architects, they spoke and acted in ways that would conjure common modes of interpreting conditions and thus create person bonds that could prove helpful in the future.

So far, we have identified three technological frames in this story of Dutch public housing: the abstract economic frame of policymakers, the abstract aesthetic frames of designers, and the practical domestic frame of VAC members. There is, of course, a fourth frame, which is that of residents themselves. Bijker and Bijsterveld document a case in which future residents of a housing block were directly involved in making substantive design decisions, but who still became unhappy when they experienced what they had participated in designing. The point made is that user participation is not necessarily successful if participants have no " 'objective' knowledge" of the consequences of their choices. Indirectly, their observation suggests that the real value of the advisory services provided by the VACs is to represent the concrete interests of residents from being overshadowed by either the illusion of participation or by the abstract interests of professionals, male or female.

The authors conclude their analysis with two warnings that are particularly relevant to our own investigation and interests. First, Bijker and Bijsterveld hold that it is difficult to generalize on the basis of the Dutch experience, because that case uniquely depends on the local political culture of the 1950s and the status of middle-class women. Second, analysis of historical conditions and the self-conscious production of new ones are very different projects. Were analysis of events in the past and action proposed for the future so seamlessly joined, managing social change in the manner envisaged by classical Marxists might yet be, for better or worse, a possibility. This is an important issue to which we shall return in Part Three.

Since the analysis of technological framing was introduced to the broad world of design by Bijker and others two decades ago, the practice has moved into many other fields, including information systems,[35] engineering ethics,[36] and architecture,[37] if to a lesser extent. In a particularly influential 2001 article, British sociologist Simon Guy and architect Graham Farmer employed frame analysis to classify seven competing discourses within the then still-emergent field of sustainable architecture. The point of their analysis was to, first, demonstrate that "sustainability" was far from being a single coherent concept and, second, argue that pluralism in the realm of ideas is a good, rather than bad, thing.[38] Among many insights, Guy and Farmer observed that a primary disagreement among the seven discourses of sustainable architecture has to do with what is, and isn't, included in the system being designed. Whether or not "social equity" is to be considered part of an architectural or environmental system is still, more than a decade later, the most visible dispute over the boundaries of architectural problem-solving. This conflict is front and center in both of the North American cases investigated in Part Three.

A more recent use of frame analysis in the related field of sustainable development is by Leach, Scoones, and Stirling, who argue, like Guy and Farmer, that social equity must be included within the system boundaries and frames of sustainability. For these British authors, system framing is the foundational set of assumptions that structure the possibilities we construct to move history—however faulty our efforts may be—in one direction or another. Of course, the system boundary of sustainable architecture is not the only place where ambiguity and dispute occur. In one of the case studies that follow, for example, code-makers in Austin, Texas, were reluctant to include within their technological frame concerns other than the traditional variables of "health, safety, and welfare." Including environmental concerns in their frame of interpretation was initially resisted. The edges of their frame were subsequently expanded, however, through the long process of public talk. Although environmental variables are now seen through the frames inhabited by code-makers in Austin, social equity is still a concept that disrupts long-standing institutional agreements. This is a theme to which we will return in Chapter 8.

SUMMARY

In sum, we have argued that *institutional* frames (those that condition our interpretation of social events) and *technological* frames (those that influence our interpretation of how things work) are necessary concepts to grasp the significance of what we call *sociotechnical codes*. These are codes that aspire to consciously integrate life-enhancing social and technological change for specific groups. Being able to identify the institutional frames employed by particular groups—say, famous architects—helps us to understand the degree to which they are bound by their relationships to the institutions in which they operate. And, in turn, identifying the institutional frame of a group such as the American Home Builders Association helps us to place its agency—its capacity to change things—within the broader system of the construction industry.

With these tools in hand, we can now turn our attention to the types of technological code that frame and materialize the built world.

Chapter 5

Tacit Codes in Traditional and Modern Building Cultures

Tacit *knowledge* is generally understood to be that which is embedded in cultural practices—it is knowledge that is difficult for individuals to articulate, because we carry it around in the back of our heads; it is not formally codified in the modern sense. Tacit *codes* are similar, but should be understood as a subset of tacit knowledge. Tacit *building* codes are, then, a third-order subset—they are the "rules, procedures, and habits" that discipline how we build, or what Davis refers to as our "building culture."[1] Although tacit codes of all kinds may be unspoken, they still "frame" acceptable behavior, as we discussed that concept in the previous chapter, and thus regulate what we can and can't do in predictable ways.

The tacit codes of building are far from universal—they characterize a people in the same manner as does language. The primary difference is that habits of building are embedded in our material practices, whereas habits of speaking express and organize those practices. For example, when 19th-century New English farmers needed to enclose space to protect their animals from the harsh winter, they would build an addition to their "big house, little house, and back house," or move an existing building and attach it to that linear composition and call it a "barn." The purpose of attaching several buildings together was more about creating a warm microclimate on the south side than to provide sheltered circulation from one to the other.[2] By comparison, 19th-century farmers in the Southwest would build a "cowshed" at some distance from the house that might serve as a windbreak as well as storage area. These very distinct agricultural practices evolved over time, as did the language that describes them. Just as the language is different, so is the way of building and using what is built.

Tacit codes are generally associated with vernacular architecture, which most of us take to mean the unconscious and unchanging traditions of building handed down from generation to generation in premodern societies.[3] The term "vernacular" is itself "an invention of the 19th century"[4] and appeared at about the same time as its twin term, "modern" architecture. In this chronology, the vernacular is understood by those who use the term to include all that is unmodern (bound by context), or as the antithesis to the modern thesis of progress and change (free of context). To state it inversely would be to say that the implicit assumption of moderns is that the vernacular "has no real future"—that it is of interest only to antiquarians or those with a penchant for categorizing the past.[5]

In contrast to this popular view, Bernard Rudofsky, in his influential 1965 exhibition and book *Architecture Without Architects*, clearly argues that anonymous builders of the past and present, just like trained architects, are "collective authors" and "designers" in the modern sense of those terms. Rudofsky recognizes, however, that the popular view is supported by most historians, who understand vernacular builders to be unconscious makers, one step above beavers and ants, rather than conscious designers.[6] Where Rudofsky does agree with conventional historians is that they both hold that "Vernacular architecture . . . is nearly immutable, indeed, unimprovable, since it serves its purpose to perfection." In this chapter, we will agree with Rudofsky on the first point—that anonymous builders are conscious designers, as are modern architects—but disagree on the second—that vernacular architecture is perfect, fixed, or unchanging. Although Norberg-Schulz[7] accepts the thesis that vernacular or tacit codes are unchanging, major figures in the field such as Oliver,[8] Rapoport,[9] and Davis[10] do not. The field is thus split in a way that requires a bit more investigation.

THREE DISPOSITIONS TOWARD TACIT BUILDING CODES

In order to demonstrate how the distinction between *vernacular* and *modern* architecture is ideological, rather than factual, it will be helpful to characterize three groups of architects: *orthodox moderns*, *romantic moderns*, and *romantic anti-moderns*. Our argument is that nearly all architects in the modern era fall into one of these categories, or a hybrid derived from them. Although these groups disagree about core values of modernity itself, they share a common view of vernacular makers as naïve and fixed in time by rigid cosmology. We briefly characterize them in turn.

Orthodox Moderns

Orthodox modern practitioners tend to embrace *science* as the way to enlightened progress. This is a view of what it means to be modern developed by such philosophers as Descartes, Locke, and Hegel. An architect exemplar of this position is Hannes Meyer, the second Director of the Bauhaus, from 1928 to 1930. Meyer and his "Left Column" colleagues, as they referred to themselves, embraced a Marxist view of science as including both architecture and the social sciences as tools of human liberation. In this context, they envisioned a science of architecture that could overcome the traditions and mysticism of societies they could characterize as *pre*modern. Meyer argued, for example,

> building
> all things in this world are a product of the formula: (function times economy).
> all these things are, therefore, not works of art.
> all art is composition and, hence, is unsuited to achieve goals.
> all life is function and is therefore unartistic.[11]

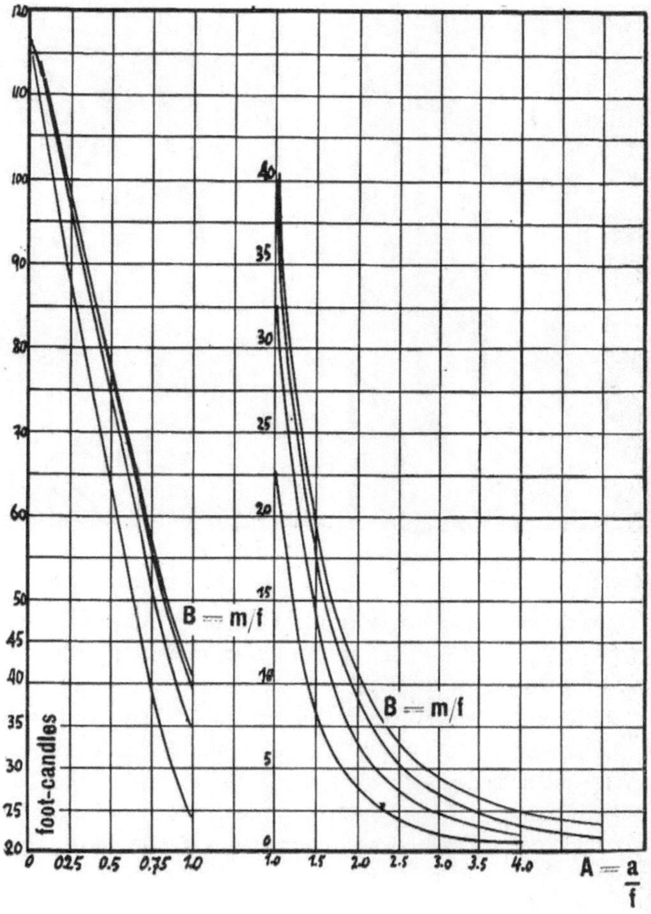

Figure 5.1 "Theoretical Illumination Curves for Windows Inclined at 60 Degrees." Hannes Meyer Architect. In his Peterschule project of 1923–1926 (Figure 2.1), Meyer attempted to calculate the amount of illumination provided by the window pattern. This is a very early use of empirical data to make design choices, rather than aesthetic preference tempered by experience. In Schnaidt, Claude. 1965. *Hannes Meyer* (p. 21). Teufen.

The orthodox modern disposition, less some of its strident politics, became embedded in the Environmental Design Research Association (EDRA), founded in 1968. Some have even argued that the contemporary sustainable design movement is only an extension of the scientific disposition of orthodox modernism.[12]

Romantic Moderns

The group we refer to as romantic moderns tends to embrace *art* as a path of liberation rather than science.[13] The possibility of a romantic disposition in the modern movement emerged in the late 18th century as a reaction to the urban conditions brought about by the industrial revolution. In the 19th century, literary figures such as Byron, Goethe, and Holderlin led the movement in Europe. In lieu of promoting the rationality of science and industrialization on behalf of liberating humanity, romantics imagined a future governed by intuition, individual self-realization, and self-expression in which individuals could overcome both the codes of repressive tradition (mass subjectivity) and reductive science (mass objectivity). However, like the orthodox moderns they challenged, romantics too understand their role in history as overcoming the traditions and mysticism of premodern cultures fixed in the past.

Figure 5.2 House by Henry van de Velde. This composition by van de Velde is both modern in its approach to craft and romantic in its recuperation of history. In *Belgium Art Nouveau*. 1994. Text by Pierre Loze; photographs by François Loze. Snoeck-Ducaju & Zoon.

An architectural exemplar of this tradition is Henry Van de Velde, an organizing member of the *Deutscher Werkbund*, founded in Munich in 1907 to modernize German craft practices. According to van de Velde, "the artist is a burning idealist, a free spontaneous creator."[14] The German Romantic Movement, which so influenced van de Velde and his colleagues, sought a synthesis of art and science as they imagined it had existed in the Middle Ages. Although that misconception has been long abandoned, the romantic ideal of the genius artistic creator is still very much alive today in heroic figures such as Frank Lloyd Wright or Frank Gehry.

Romantic Anti-moderns

The third group, romantic anti-moderns, reject the very idea of modern Enlightenment progress, yet embrace art—as do romantic moderns—as the way to authentic Being and self-fulfillment. The philosopher Isaiah Berlin later referred to this movement as the "counter-Enlightenment."[15] The project of Enlightenment is characterized by them as the dark side of modern hubris—in their eyes, the very concept of modern Enlightenment is a view of reality so mechanistic and reductive that authentic Being is lost in the scientific process. This group sees its role in history as finding a way out of modernity without attempting the impossible task of overcoming the forces of overcoming.[16] Richard Wolin has linked this strand of postmodernism to the counter-Enlightenment.[17] Exemplars of this disposition include architects such as Mike Reynolds in the United States and the "back-to-the-land" subculture he serves.

What these three dispositions have in common is that they all see vernacular makers as naïve and unconscious, or as units in a collective organic community that is *context-bound*. We mean by this term that all three groups understand tacit codes to bind vernacular builders very tightly to local ecological and cultural contexts. Although many figures straddle these three dispositions, our purpose in developing them is to bring to the surface some dominant conflicts within modern architecture that remain too infrequently challenged.

Figure 5.3 Earthships, Taos, New Mexico, 1996. Mike Reynolds Architect. Built from recycled bottles and earth-based materials, Reynold's "Earthships" are a re-enchantment of the landscape and an alchemical critique of modernity.

By characterizing vernacular designers as rote makers who unconsciously reproduce conservative social orders, each competing modern disposition hopes to distinguish its own significance by comparison. In other words, its disposition is ideological rather than being based on sound observation. In the first instance, if orthodox moderns claim that the masses can overcome superstition only through science, they must discount the rationality and efficacy of tradition to be logically coherent. In the second instance, if romantic moderns claim that individuals can overcome superstition only through experiencing the expressive vision of artists, they may admire vernacular artifacts, but must discount tradition as unconscious. And, in the third instance, if romantic anti-moderns see the dark side of the Enlightenment, they must resist the forces of overcoming modernity without falling back into yet another unsupported superstition to be coherent. In contrast, our argument is that contemporary empirical research has demonstrated all three dispositions to be mistaken.

Latour has made a similar argument by insisting that the distinctions between premodern and modern consciousness are much overrated. In his view, modern self-consciousness has served more as a convenient excuse to exploit natural resources than as a characterization of how we actually live. In short, Latour holds that, "we have never been modern," or free from organic context, even if we think we have been.[18] Stated in architectural rather than philosophical terms, Davis likewise holds that, "No strong boundary exists between the vernacular and the nonvernacular—all buildings are a part of a continuous web in which such distinctions have little meaning."[19] And, not to be ignored, editors Umbach and Huppauf, supported by contributors Stanford Anderson, Kenneth Frampton, and others, make two sympathetic points: First, the vernacular and the modern are not "mutually exclusive," and, second, that, just as we have never been modern, the vernacular has never been "timeless."[20] Two brief empirical examples, followed by a third, help to make our point:

The Case of Folk Housing in Middle Virginia

In Henry Glassie's classic study of 18th- and 19th-century folk housing in Middle Virginia, he observed that,

> The builder did not plan in a vacuum; the process of design was constricted and driven by the context that held him. In the concrete artifact is written the tense of conflict of what the designer could do and what he had to do.[21]

Glassie goes on to distinguish "context" as being of two types: the immediate local, or "particularistic," physical context, and "the abstract context of mind." It is this latter kind of lived context that:

> serves to control and prod the competence so that the things generated out of it will fit into their particularistic context—so that the house will protect its inhabitants from the weather and project the image that its maker desired. . . . It relates the object being composed in the designing mind to the maker's view of himself and to human, natural, and supernatural forces that exist beyond him.[22]

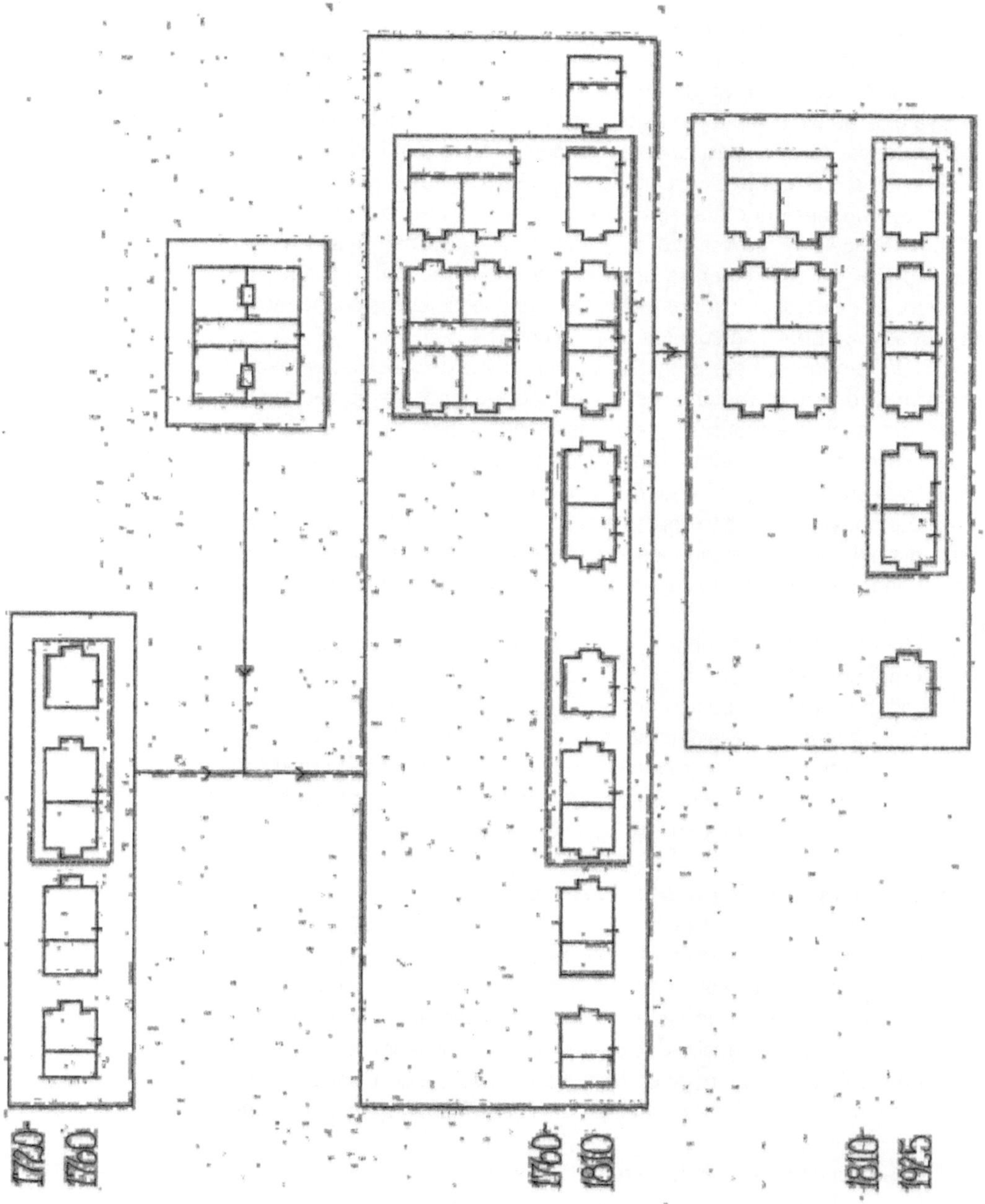

Figure 5.4 House Patterns of Middle Virginia. In this drawing, Glassie is tracing "Evolution of architectural competence. The diagram includes plans of all the forms in the repositories of the three different phases. The statistically important forms are enclosed by broken lines." In Glassie, Henry. 1975. *Folk Housing in Middle Virginia* (p. 110). The analysis demonstrates the compositional constraints embodied in the building culture of Middle Virginia.

Today, in lieu of using the term "abstract context" as Glassie did, we prefer to say the *cultural context* of a work holds the "structures in the thought of the artifact's maker." It is these structures, as Glassie puts it, that bind the designer to a palette of choices deemed reliable by his community. This is to argue, as we did in the previous chapter, that vernacular makers, just like modern ones, inhabit a particular technological frame that holds the values common to the social group of which they are a part. The frame of interpretation inhabited by the designer manages the interaction between the various individuals engaged in the making of artifacts (like houses) or spaces (like streets), as well as the materials used in their construction. The intriguing evidence found by Glassie is not only that an individual builder is bound by tacit codes, but also that building cultures share a code.

Our argument here is that all cultural contexts, not just vernacular ones, attempt to restrict the choices of designers to those embodied in the dominant ethos of the group. Or, as Glassie put it directly, "we find that important buildings can be interpreted as displays of the values we value—grandeur, perhaps, or originality—while unimportant buildings display values that we have not yet learned to appreciate."[23] Another way to make the same point is to hold that our categories—such as the distinction between the vernacular and the modern—tell us more about the category-makers than the things categorized.

Modern societies, unlike traditional ones, tend to be made up of multiple competing groups of category-makers, rather than ethnocratically pure ones. Although it is the disposition of some cultures to bind practices more restrictively than others, Glassie demonstrates that tacit building codes do not limit builders to rote-making, as moderns tend to claim. Rather, tacit designers in all societies are free to innovate within a tested set of practices and patterns and to contribute to that ever-evolving body of knowledge.

The Case of Modern Vernacular in Brazil

In a second empirical study of tacit codes, Fernando Luiz Lara has observed that, where the North American middle classes have largely rejected modern architecture as alien to their values, South Americans, particularly middle-class Brazilians, have embraced it. In his effort to understand how such conflicting receptions transpired, Lara decided to examine how knowledge about modern architecture reached Brazil's middle class. He was surprised to discover that "the dissemination of design knowledge" in Brazil followed an unexpected path.[24]

Cultural elites everywhere tend to assume that knowledge follows only a downward, "intradisciplinary" path, from expert (artist–architect), to practitioner (practitioner–architect), to client (patron), to maker (contractor–builder). As in our discussion above that distinguished three dispositions toward tacit codes, elites who expect knowledge to flow only downward make two mistaken assumptions: First, modern architecture is the project of enlightened consciousness that is distinct from, and critical of, normative or vernacular practices. Modern architecture can, in this view of history, be produced only by educated elites who take on the project of educating normal people. Second, elites assume that those at the end of the knowledge chain, contractors, are capable only of rote-making—meaning that they build either within the context-bound traditions of their society, or they build as they are told by self-conscious designers and/or clients. Lara's fieldwork, however, turns this chain of knowledge dissemination on its head by documenting that it has been uneducated builders who forcefully adopted the technical vocabulary of Le Corbusier's "Dom-Ino frame" and, over time, developed façades and plans that are visually and intellectually consistent with international modern architecture.

Of particular interest, Lara tells us that, of the more than 600 "modern" houses he has documented, all were products of "autoconstruction," by which he means informal collaborations between middle-class families and builders *without* involvement by architects. The phenomenon is, then, a case of *modern* "Architecture Without Architects." In the terms we developed above and in the previous chapter, it is fair to say that Brazilians, particularly in cities such as Belo Horizonte, have constructed a dominant technological frame in which knowledge flows uphill as well as down. It is not surprising, then, that there is contested ownership of modern architecture in Brazil. Lara documents that, rather than congratulating autoconstructors as collaborators in the modern project, Brazilian architects and scholars tend to label the modern vernacular as "primitive or deviant" by comparison with their own work.[25]

At issue here is who owns modern *intentionality*? In the literature of *reception theory*, it is not possible to determine the meaning of a work by understanding only the articulated intentions of the artists. Rather, meaning can only be determined by understanding the degree to which there is a gap

Figure 5.5
"Autoconstruction" at Aglomerado da Serra, Belo Horizonte, Brazil. An example of modernist concrete-frame architecture conceived and produced not by architects, but by the informal sector.

between artistic intention and reception by a community of users.[26] Lara has already established that the gap between the intentions of modern architects in North America and the reception by middle-class home builders is very large indeed. The meaning of modern architecture in South America is, in contrast, measured by the relatively narrow gap between intention and reception.

Andrew Jamison takes this observation one step further in arguing for what he calls "cognitive praxis," by which he means the ability of community users to integrate the worldview assumptions, or cosmology, of artist–architects such as Le Corbusier with their own practices through action and the appropriation of technologies such as the Dom-Ino frame.[27] In such cases, the appropriation of art or technology by community users tends to produce useful hybrid types, rather than singular objects of distinction—hence the conflict over who owns modern intentionality.

Lara's analysis demonstrates two related points: First, vernacular builders have appropriated modern architecture in three dimensions: technologically, as an aesthetic expression of a liberated future, but also as a way of living that is consistent with the tacit codes of their past—their own evolving cosmology. By comparison, the second point is that most Brazilian architects and scholars have adopted modern architecture in a single dimension: as a mode of personal expression, without the politics of human liberation as envisioned by Hannes Meyer, who we discussed above. There is little doubt that Brazil's modern vernacular is a hybrid of global and local, formal and tacit influences. But there is also little doubt that it is a creative and innovative response to changing conditions. In our own view, it is not very helpful to expend time and energy considering whether it is trained architects or vernacular builders who are the rightful heirs of the modern project, or which set of projects are deviant. It is helpful, however, to consider how tacit codes evolve and contribute to a sustainable world of hybrid possibilities.

In summarizing this section, the empirical scholarship of Glassie and Lara challenges the assumptions of the dispositions held by orthodox moderns, romantic moderns, and romantic anti-moderns. In both Middle Virginia and Brazil, vernacular knowledge and the tacit codes that discipline it are far from static. Rather, they evolve through trial and error as conditions change. What is to be derived from this brief analysis is twofold. First, Horkheimer and Adorno warned us more than a half-century ago that Enlightenment claims to human liberation through technology are prone to becoming ironic, as anti-moderns have also claimed.[28] They meant by this that, in lieu of liberating "the masses," the arrogant assumptions of orthodox and romantic moderns generally fail to recognize the agency of the uneducated—their capacity to liberate or build for themselves. Another way of saying this is to hold that modern architecture has a blind spot. In characterizing the building practices of some groups as vernacular, or tightly controlled by unconscious tacit codes, we assume—mistakenly—that our own are fully conscious and Enlightened.

The second lesson to be learned from this analysis is that architects might serve the unfinished modern project more successfully, not by rejecting tacit codes as primitive and contrary to the predetermined trajectory of history as we have, but by learning how to decode tacit knowledge, so that it might contribute to the production of sustainable cities. To make this reasoning concrete, in the balance of this chapter, we examine a 20th-century case of

Brazilian architecture to demonstrate the existence of a third possibility—one that we describe as *context-rich* design thinking. This third possibility avoids the false opposition between context-bound and context-free design thinking that is assumed by both moderns and anti-moderns.

A CASE OF CONTEXT-RICH DESIGN THINKING IN SÃO PAULO

Before we can introduce the case of the Sport and Leisure Center of Pompeii (SESC), which serves the poor citizens of a central industrial neighborhood in São Paulo, it is necessary to at least sketch the context into which architect Lina Bo Bardi inserted what we consider to be a *context-rich* design. By this term, we mean a design that is neither bound by tacit codes nor entirely free from them, but one informed by a substantive understanding by the architect of the codes that precede her.

Geographer Henri Lefebvre has argued that each "mode of production"—capitalism, socialism, theocracy, oligarchy, etc.—produces a different kind of space that is uniquely suited to serve the dominant values of the society.[29] The qualities of such spaces are, of course, further modified by cultural and ecological variables, but, in all cases, human power relations are alternately limited and/or amplified by the social construction of space. This is to argue that the interpretive flexibility of architects, although substantial, has limitations set out by the social agreements that precede them.

A relevant way to demonstrate this point is to compare Brazilian cities—which were colonized by Portugal and settled by a rich mixture of Africans, Muslims, and northern Europeans—with cities in the rest of the Americas, influenced primarily by Spain. In Spanish municipalities, the organization of space was predetermined by the 1573 *Spanish Orders for Discovery and Settlement* (commonly referred to as the Law of the Indies), which required a central square, or *zocalo*, bounded orthogonally by the church, garrison, and municipal structures. The distribution of residential and farming lands beyond the zocalo was similarly predetermined by central governmental authority, as was the disposition of natives. In contrast, Portuguese cities "showed little of the elegance and trim geometry which characterized Spanish cities in the new world. [. . .] The Portuguese, also, were less concerned than the Spaniards with establishing abroad the metropolitan symbols of Imperial prestige."[30] Without a predetermined and abstract spatial pattern that related local power relations to those of the colonial court, or an agenda for ordering the lives of natives, Brazilian cultural landscapes emerged more directly from local political and economic conflicts, as well as ecological conditions. In this context, we can understand Brazilian cities as *landscapes of conflict*, rather than landscapes of abstract power relations. It was into this conflict that architect Lina Bo Bardi inserted herself when she emigrated from Italy in 1946.

Lina Bo Bardi

The architect Lina Bo Bardi was comfortably born in 1914, in Rome, and graduated from architecture school there in 1940. Her education was guided by the conservative rationalist principles of that time, which were supported by Mussolini, and so, upon her graduation, she left Rome for the more progressive climate of Milan. There, she worked primarily as a design journalist and, in 1944–1945, was Deputy Director at *DOMUS*, one of the leading international architecture and design journals of the time. Others have described her rise in Milan's design culture as very successful, particularly in Leftist political circles.[31]

Shortly after the war, she met and married Pietro Maria Bardi, a self-educated art dealer, collector, and socially well-connected fascist, who was a personal friend to Le Corbusier and other major figures in the world of high art and architecture. When Bardi was invited by a Brazilian media baron to visit São Paulo, the couple accepted, assuming they would stay a few months. What they found, however, must have captured their imagination, so that they quickly established themselves in Brazilian design journalism and culture and never returned to Italy, except for brief vacations. In 1950–1951, Bo Bardi built her first project, now referred to as "the Glass House," for herself and her husband—a clear reference to Le Corbusier's Maison Dom-Ino system, and what some have called "an International Style tree-house."[32] Before long, Pietro Bardi became the Director of the Museum of Art of São Paulo, and, as many might expect, Lina Bo Bardi was somewhat later commissioned by her husband and his influential colleagues to design a major new museum for the city. The trajectory of this art-world narrative would seem headed to a very successful, upper-class shelf. There was, however, a turn along the way—a turn catalyzed by the reception given to this Italian woman by Brazilian architects, and, in reverse, by her own reception to the conditions she found in Brazil.

According to her younger collaborator, Marcello Carvalho Ferraz, Bo Bardi and her husband were received socially and respected intellectually by the leading Brazilian architects of the period as "international persons with a novelty." In the 1950s, Lina was, for example, invited by Niemeyer to design furniture for his Alvadorada Palace at Brasilia, but she was never received by him or his colleagues as a peer. Established architects in São Paulo were even less receptive. Esther da Costa Meyer observed, as did many, Bo Bardi was not only a foreigner, but a woman in a man's professional culture.[33] Although there is no direct evidence of gender discrimination, no one on the scene at the time was surprised that she was never invited to teach at the University of São Paulo (FAU). In the first two decades of Bo Bardi's career in São Paulo, she did build a few projects other than her own house and developed expertise in what we now call "historic preservation." For Lina, however, that genre of work brought with it intense political questions, informed by her reading of the Italian socialist Gramsci. Following his intellectual position, she came to challenge the dominant meaning of "Culture," with a big C, as a field of production dominated by elites.

After more than 20 years in Brazil, Bo Bardi was invited to teach, but not at FAU. Rather, she was invited by the president of the University of Salvador in Bahia, in the north of Brazil, inhabited by a very different population of African and native groups, as well as by Europeans. Her apprentice Ferraz confirms that Lina had already developed an "anthropological vocation," by which he meant that her double outsider status as a woman and a foreigner made her "sensitive to perceive cultural differences." That identity was amplified by her increasingly interdisciplinary reading and interest in figures such as Levi Strauss, who visited Brazil at about that time. It was no surprise, then, when she accepted the offer to teach at Salvador from 1958 through 1963, where she became, as Lima holds, a key intellectual leader [in related regionalist movements] such as *Tropica lia* and *Cinema Novo*. These groups shared practices of cultural hybridization as they candidly integrated different aesthetic form, both from modern and traditional background, vernacular and industrial, mass and educated cultures, merging political nationalism with international artistic movements.[34]

This was an intense period of intellectual development for Bo Bardi, in which she began to employ "anthropology as a tool of analysis,"[35] in addition to her considerable analytic skills as an architect. Although she had built almost nothing in the first decade of the military dictatorship that took power in 1964, the political thaw that began in the mid 1970s opened an opportunity for experimentation founded on what she learned in Bahia.

SESC—Pompeii

Our interest in Bo Bardi's design for SESC has less to do with interpreting its formal characteristics than with her intentions, the design process employed to realize those intentions, and its reception by users.

In 1976, at the age of 62, Bo Bardi received the SESC commission from the Social Services Trade Association of São Paulo, the purpose of which was to serve the recreational and community needs of the low-income workers of Pompeii, one of the city's early industrial neighborhoods that emerged along one of the canals that cut through the city. The site actually straddled the canal and retained two horizontal buildings of a former steel-drum factory built in the 1920s. In simple terms, the project program was to include sport facilities as well as theaters, restaurants, a library, and facilities for the arts. In broader terms, the program was to preserve a local culture, with a small "c," threatened by changing economic conditions. By that time in her career, Lina had articulated her mature intentions for practice as the making of *arquitectura pobre*, or "simple architecture,"[36] by which she may have meant that, "architecture should embrace and value human life, especially those lives rejected by dominant groups."[37]

The design process she adopted to implement her intentions was indeed novel, especially in the context of mainstream Brazilian practice. Rather than restart her office in a fashionable location, Bo Bardi occupied a very modest house adjacent to the site and hired two interns, Marcelo Ferraz and Andre Vainer, to assist her in a design process that would last for 5 years. And, rather than begin the demolition of the existing structures, as was expected by her client, she took the time to observe how these abandoned buildings had already become informally inhabited by the community for "soccer games, weekend barbeques, cub scout meetings, a playhouse, and a theater environment that were very popular."[38] Lima cites Bo Bardi as saying that the existing structures needed only to be "cleaned up and maintained," and her work was "just to add a few things like a reflecting pool, a fireplace, and some furniture."[39] An examination of her drawings (Figure 5.6) suggests, however, that there was also considerable architectural analysis into which her "anthropological analysis" was integrated. The design process was, then, not one of expressing abstract values from a distance, but of documenting how a functioning community had appropriated available space and then facilitating those existing patterns.

Bo Bardi was, then, exercising a very different kind of judgment than other Brazilian architects of the period.[40]

Figure 5.6 Drawing for SESC, 1976–1981, São Paulo, Brazil. Architect, Lina Bo Bardi. Bo Bardi's drawing is an analysis of people's use of space, not the abstract qualities of that space.

Although her client was initially skeptical of her "anthropological" approach, they eventually embraced a design proposal that evolved from years of meeting with the design team. During this extended conversation, the "clean-up" process, involving as many as 300 workers, was being directed daily by Bo Bardi and her interns, so that detailed new information about construction details and the "lived space" of the complex was constantly being introduced to decision-makers, who included community members as well as staff. In addition to the leisure facilities housed in the existing factory buildings, the design team eventually proposed to stack the sport facilities in two adjacent and newly constructed towers that straddled the canal with bridges, thus introducing what locals now refer to as their "beach." As seen in Figure 5.7, the towers are a significant departure from her earlier Corbusian vocabulary and freely mix a hybrid of international "brutalism" and vernacular references with the industrial forms of the existing buildings.

As for the community reception, a local taxi driver who has lived in the neighborhood since SESC opened in 1984 reported that the area "would be dead" without it. The "old people," he said, come here to play guitars and sing. He and his daughter swim at SESC every week, his wife goes to the opera, and they all go to the dentist there. He enjoys the food and a "pub." In short, he said, "I'm comfortable at SESC." Although this taxi driver did not articulate exactly why he felt "comfortable" there, Bo Bardi's intern, Ferraz,

Figure 5.7 Photo of the SESC Towers and "Beach," 1976–1981. São Paulo, Brazil. Architect, Lina Bo Bardi. As in Bo Bardi's analytic drawing of spaces in use (Figure 5.6), her design of the "beach" reflects existing patterns of use.

suggests that it is because Lina understood how to make the place "accessible," not in the simple sense of being physically accessible to the disabled, but in the more complex sense of being "psychologically accessible." Our way of restating this claim is to say that Bo Bardi and her collaborators were able to decode the tacit knowledge and codes of the community through observation over time, and then they were able to employ that new knowledge in the reconstruction of "simple architecture."

It is impossible to say with any certainty how Bo Bardi understood São Paulo's landscape of conflict. Nor is there any evidence—other than the recollections of her collaborator, Marcelo Ferraz—that documents the methods of "anthropological analysis" used by the design team. Having reconstructed the available evidence, however, it is reasonable to hypothesize that SESC succeeds in its mission because it operates as a cosmological map of the city—

one that is psychologically accessible to those who live in Pompeii, if not to the elite architects who found the project to be somehow deviant from the abstract aesthetic principles of modernism. In our view, the design and its success in the eyes of locals derive from Bo Bardi's ability to decode and use the "vernacular," as elites refer to it, rather than overcome it.

Bo Bardi's Frame of Interpretation

In Chapter 4, we discussed "frame analysis" at length, and it will be helpful to return to those concepts here as a way to understand Bo Bardi's relationship to two groups: first, her relationship to her institutional client for SESC, and, second, her relationship to the professional culture of architecture in Brazil.

From her collaborator, Marcelo Ferraz, we understand that her client—meaning the administrators of SESC—were initially resistant to what he characterized as her "anthropological approach" to design. SESC operates many facilities, not only the one at Pompeii, and can be understood as a sophisticated client, or one that has long experience in dealing with architects. This is to say that their expectation of what architects produce and how they produce drawings and specifications were conditioned, or framed, by prior experience. The point here is that Bo Bardi was willing, and able, to invest the time to reframe her client's understanding of architectural process, not in words, but through action. She did so by engaging the site directly, managing the "clean-up" herself, and introducing information and knowledge about the rich context of the existing environment that is not ordinarily part of architectural thinking. Rather than adopt the posture of a heroic artist–author, she adopted that of a *knowledge-worker*.

The second relationship that can be better understood through frame analysis is that between Bo Bardi and the professional community of Brazilian architects. Above, we suggested that Lina was unlike members of that group because she was both a woman and a foreigner. It was Ferraz who observed that her double outsider status gave her cultural insights that other architects lacked. This is to say that, unlike Bruno Zevi who was also an Italian immigrant to Brazil, she had a "low inclusion rate" in the high-art frame through which other architects interpreted the world. Said in reverse, she had the imagination to see what radical change might look like in São Paulo, because her own interests were not at risk through change. In contrast, the male leaders in the field could not imagine a world in which the aesthetic abstractions of their discourse were not dominant. She was, in short, a code-switcher—a designer with the capacity to make environments accessible to multiple groups. Although the professional community of Brazilian architects has generally ignored her as somehow unmodern, that assessment is beginning to change.

In this context, Lima's recent assessment of Bo Bardi is that, "She was less loyal to modernist aesthetic principles than she was to a modernist conception of modernity."[41] This is to say that her way of interpreting the world embraced the Enlightenment project of human liberation, but not the ossified aesthetic codes of the international style. In other words, her mode of interpreting events clearly rejected two of the three frames with which we began this chapter—the romantic modern (architecture as artistic expression) and the romantic anti-modern (architecture as authentic dwelling).[42] She comes closest to the third frame, the orthodox modern (architecture as science), but challenges that perspective in two ways. First, she embraced the radical social science of anthropology over conventional science and engineering. Second, as a consequence of the first insight, she embraced rather than rejected local codes. Her view of the world was to see through the false dichotomy between *context-bound* and *context-free* design thinking. Rather than inhabit that dichotomy, she fabricated a mode of design thinking that was *context rich*. Put into concrete rather than theoretical terms, our understanding of Bo Bardi's mature intentions is that she gave up seeing herself as an artist–author, which is still the dominant frame through which architects fashion their identities. This may explain why, after so many years of hard work, she chose not to attend the opening ceremony of SESC. In lieu of that heroic frame, Harding coined the term "valuable stranger," which may describe how Bo Bardi saw her role at SESC–Pompeii—as a skilled professional whose job was to help the members of the community make informed choices about their relationships to each other and to the landscape of conflict that they inhabit. This is a theme to which we will return in Chapters 8 through 10.

SUMMARY

Our brief summary of tacit codes is collected into Table 5.1. In general, we found that the strategy of tacit codes is to embed social values in the day-to-day practices of the community in a manner that appears neutral and natural. Two examples of an artifact embedded with tacit social values are the wooden house technologies of Middle Virginia documented by Glassie, and the concrete house technologies appropriated by contemporary vernacular builders in Brazil from modern architecture.

A good example of a space embedded with social values is the SESC canal-side landscape designed by Bo Bardi and her collaborators in São Paulo. In all three cases, the interpretive frame employed by builders is cosmological, in that artifacts and spaces literally reconstruct the universe of the community in miniaturized material form. The way material forms work to embody social values is by ordering the bits, pieces, and social process of building in the everyday world.

Table 5.1 Characteristics of tacit codes

Strategy	*Practice-based*
Exemplar artifacts	Wood technology in Middle Virginia
	Concrete frame technology in Brazil
Exemplar space	SESC community center
Exemplar consequence	Characterizing the "vernacular" as unconscious and unchanging suppresses relevant local knowledge, but bringing unrecognized building cultures to consciousness may lead to positive civilizational change
Frame	Cosmological
How they work	By ordering the material and social processes of building
Type of authority required	Ethnocratic
Location of authority	Local community

In general, the kind of authority required to conceptualize and implement tacit codes is *ethnocratic*, by which we mean the unspoken authority found in homogeneous cultural groups. Eighteenth- and nineteenth-century Middle Virginia is such a case, but modern conditions in Brazil are far from homogeneous. Rather, the favellas of modern São Paulo, in particular, are ethnically very diverse. In this case, the type of authority required to forge new tacit codes is a hybrid, yet common, understanding of the shared landscape and the conflicts that shape it.

The social movement initiated by the Workers' Party of Brazil is, in our view, the new authority that has fostered such tacit code-making. However, as must always be the case with tacit codes, the ultimate location of that authority must be the community itself. In the case of Brazil, the bringing to consciousness of "vernacular" building codes is also the emancipation of relevant local knowledge that is suppressed by the hegemony of high-style modernism and class distinction.

To be clear, social movements cannot fabricate new tacit codes without making desirable values explicit, and therefore no longer tacit. A way to resolve this seeming conflict is to argue that tacit codes remain largely unconscious, until they are challenged and replaced with codes that are consciously constructed by citizens to make the world a hybrid and better place. Our findings suggest, however, that people tend to have short memories. We forget about the conflicts that bring new codes into existence, just as we forget the reasoning for the existence of old codes. This is to say that tacit codes are replaced by consciously constructed ones, but those gradually become tacit again, as history moves forward, and society adapts. However, far from being a failure, the gradual adaptation to new laws is a fundamental indication of human ability to govern behavior and consciously construct positive "civilizational change."[43] Put a bit differently, this is to argue that the development of good habits is far more effective than the legislation of powerful laws. It is this observation that requires us to examine what we refer to as economic codes in the next chapter.

Chapter 6

Sumptuary Codes, Taste, and Distinction in the Built World

In simple terms, contemporary sumptuary codes regulate the perceived status of an individual in a social context. The example of a uniform is the easiest way to introduce the idea. Military officers, for example, can be identified, not only by the color of their uniform and the style of its tailoring, but also by medals and emblems that indicate the individual's rank and achievement. The primary purpose of uniforms is to make rank, and thus authority to take certain kinds of action, legible to people in that particular social system and thus maintain the order of command in constantly changing contexts. Individuals from other systems, or of different ranks, are prohibited from wearing the same uniform. As in the military, similar customs are practiced in religious orders, among academics, and less formally in the international world of business. However, because we tend to think of these *dress codes* as a matter of contemporary style, we forget their cultural origins and how the same principles operate in other fields, such as architecture.

The word "sumptuary" is an archaic one and derives from the Latin pertaining to "regulating or limiting expense." In the medieval societies of Europe, Japan, and China, sumptuary codes regulated, not only the dress of all classes of people, but also architectural representation and material construction systems. Sumptuary codes are, then, those that regulate, not only the appearance of individuals, but expenditures related to *consumption* made by those individuals—how lavish or large their houses might be, for example. Uniforms can be thought of either as a visual license to consume community resources or as a warrant and responsibility to preserve them.

The antonym of con-sump-tion is, of course, sumpt-uous, which pertains to "splendor suggesting great expense." In contemporary society, we generally understand "consumption"—as in devouring meat, or burning wood to keep warm—as making a commodity disappear for personal benefit. In this limited meaning, the idea that society should limit the consumption of certain items by its members has been with us since the Bronze Age and was well known to the Romans.[1] However, the Latin root word of consumption also links the concept to "taking" and "distribution."[2] In this second or expanded meaning, we can also relate consumption to "taking-together," "taking-in," or "buying" an item, not just devouring it. Some forms of consumption, such as filling a backyard swimming pool, for example, are correctly related to large amounts of *entropy*—the amount of chaos and disorder present in a system. By filling the pool to entertain ourselves, the hydrological system as a whole is disrupted, thus reducing the ecosystem services provided to maintain system balance. Other forms of consumption, such as when we "take in" a movie, can be associated with minor amounts of entropy. Yes, some energy per capita is consumed in screening films, but this is minor by comparison with the energy required to fill and maintain a private swimming pool. The regulation of consumption can, then, be more or less effective in decreasing entropy by carefully selecting what practices are regulated.

In this chapter, we argue that consumption is an evolving concept that is related to the modern concepts of *expression* and *distinction*. In other words, *what* you take in and *how* you do so are related to self-expression in a manner that medieval Europeans or Asians would not have readily understood. In those prior worlds, individual identity and expression simply did not exist in the same way that we experience them today. Modern self-expression is a tool for distinguishing oneself in society. Although overconsumption—a bigger car, house, or ring—is a common way for some contemporary individuals to distinguish themselves from others, it is not the *only* way. Our argument is that it is conceptually, if not practically, possible to weaken the link between consumption and high-entropy social practices such as flying private jets or building a 25,000 square foot house for a family of four when 2,500 square feet, or even 1,500, would suffice. Contemporary sumptuary codes might, then, prove to be a useful tool in working toward a sustainable level of consumption in a way that will also satisfy understandable human needs for self-expression and distinction. The key to moving in this direction will be to differentiate between sumptuary codes of the past (which are inherited tools for maintaining a class-based social order) and sumptuary codes of the future (which might be tools produced through collective reasoning, so as to maintain both a social *and* ecological order). Making this argument requires some background.

OVERVIEW

According to Hollander, "Sumptuary laws are rules designed to inhibit specific consumption practices on the part of all or some segments of society."[3] In his analysis, Hollander has also recognized that sumptuary codes can be both positive (meaning that you *must* consume an item) or negative (meaning that you must *not*). The modes of consumption that various societies have selected to regulate (the width of sleeves, for example), and their methods of regulation (monetary fines, banishment to the galleys, or even death), may indeed appear very strange or extreme from our contemporary perspective and by contemporary standards, and yet each contributes to understanding the long evolution of coding consumption.

In what follows, we examine three related forms of sumptuary code in anticipation of applying the concept to contemporary regulation associated with sustainable, or low-entropy and just, development.[4] Many observers have characterized the condition of unsustainability as simply the overconsumption of resources or, conversely, the overproduction of greenhouse gases, and thus any social tradition of limiting consumption by some or all of society is directly related to the project of sustainable development.[5] In our analysis of this tradition, we argue, as have others, that the dominant mode of sumptuary coding seeks to maintain the legibility of social classes by *explicitly* restricting the material consumption of various commodities on the basis of class rank. We extend that reasoning, however, to argue that the modern concept of taste is but an *implicit* sumptuary code that regulates and relates aesthetic to material consumption. By *aesthetic consumption*, we mean the taking-in or the buying of "beautiful" artifacts and experiences. Such artifacts and experiences could embody significant amounts of entropy, but not necessarily. That is the core question to be investigated—how might modern sumptuary codes link self-expression and distinction to low-entropy consumption, or what Thorpe refers to as "alternate modes of wealth."[6]

In our research, we have found that there is a continuum of evolution in which the archaic sumptuary codes of medieval Europe and Asia are conceptually linked to the 18th-century French concept of *convenance*, to the 19th-century "pattern books," and finally to contemporary form-based codes (FBCs) on which we touched briefly in Chapter 3. FBCs have, we find, evolved as a hybrid version of sumptuary coding that presents interesting and unexpected possibilities for developing more democratic, low-entropy, socio-technical codes for the architecture of the future. Before making that argument, however, more background is required, and, because the three traditions of coding consumption are far from equal in their significance, we will begin by briefly describing the more obscure and work toward the dominant tradition, before relating these to FBCs.

TWO MINOR TRADITIONS IN SUMPTUARY CODING

Historians and analysts who have studied sumptuary codes document how they have been used to protect local economies and conserve community resources.[7] Our observation is that each of these traditions continues to exist in contemporary societies and has relevance to the broad topic of sustainable consumption in architecture.

Protecting Local Economies

Hooper argues that Elizabethan sumptuary codes related to fashion design, or couture, were, at least in part, economically driven.[8] These were, in contemporary language, "localist" in their intent, by which we mean that they were intended to protect local economies against foreign competition. Freudenberger, for one, has argued that there is a dimension of social equity in locally inspired sumptuary codes, because they were intended to indirectly protect the weak by first protecting those who employed them.[9] Likewise Howard, in his history of Elizabethan and Jacobean architecture, argues that the central government of Tudor and early Stuart England was perpetually concerned with the visual appearance of towns so as to "create a sense of urban well-being that would encourage trade and commerce." Out of such concern for the appearance of order, the owners of derelict buildings were fined, as were those who dressed inappropriately. Although there seems to have been no explicit or written sumptuary code for Elizabethan buildings, as there was for fashion, the same rationale and means were used to regulate the

(a)

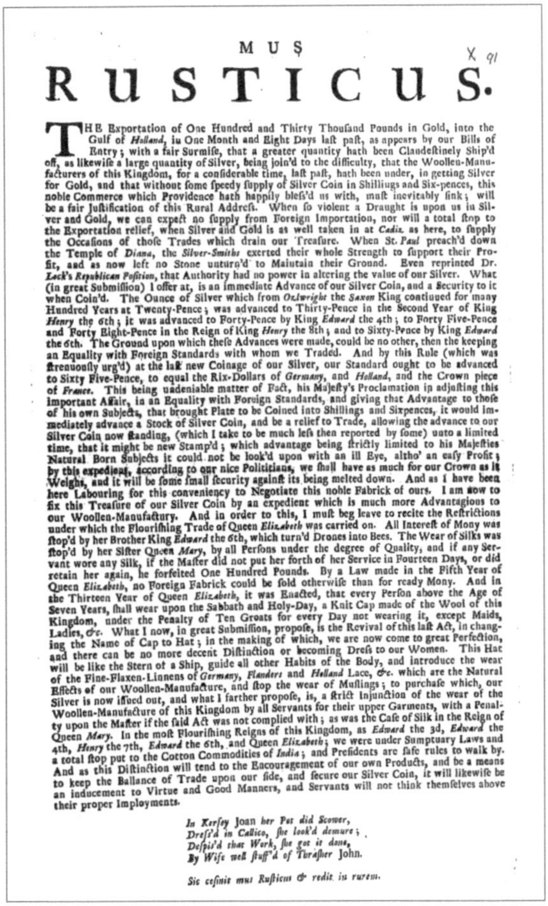

MUS

RUSTICUS.

THE Exportation of One Hundred and Thirty Thousand Pounds in Gold, into the Gulf of *Holland*, in One Month and Eight Days last past, as appears by our Bills of Entry; with a fair Surmise, that a greater quantity hath been Clandestinely Ship'd off, as likewise a large quantity of Silver, being join'd to the difficulty, that the Woollen-Manufacturers of this Kingdom, for a considerable time, last past, hath been under, in getting Silver for Gold, and that without some speedy supply of Silver Coin in Shillings and Six-pences, this noble Commerce which Providence hath happily bless'd us with, must inevitably sink; will be a fair Justification of this Rural Address. When so violent a Draught is upon us in Silver and Gold, we can expect no supply from Foreign Importation, nor will a total stop to the Exportation relief, when Silver and Gold is as well taken in at *Cadiz* as here, to supply the Occasions of those Trades which drain our Treasure. When St. *Paul* preach'd down the Temple of *Diana*, the *Silver-Smiths* exerted their whole Strength to support their Profit, and as now left no Stone unturn'd to Maintain their Ground. Even reprinted Dr. *Lock's Republican Position*, that Authority had no power in altering the value of our Silver. What (in great Submission) I offer at, is an immediate Advance of our Silver Coin, and a Security to it when Coin'd. The Ounce of Silver which from *Ozlwright* the *Saxon* King continued for many Hundred Years at Twenty-Pence; was advanced to Thirty-Pence in the Second Year of King *Henry* the 6th; it was advanced to Forty-Pence by King *Edward* the 4th; to Forty Five-Pence and Forty Eight-Pence in the Reign of King *Henry* the 8th; and to Sixty-Pence by King *Edward* the 6th. The Ground upon which these Advances were made, could be no other, then the keeping an Equality with Foreign Standards with whom we Traded. And by this Rule (which was strenuously urg'd) at the last new Coinage of our Silver, our Standard ought to be advanced to Sixty Five-Pence, to equal the Rix-Dollars of *Germany*, and *Holland*, and the Crown piece of *France*. This being undeniable matter of Fact, his Majesty's Proclamation in adjusting this important Affair, in an Equality with Foreign Standards, and giving that Advantage to those of his own Subjects, that brought Plate to be Coined into Shillings and Sixpences, it would immediately advance a Stock of Silver Coin, and be a relief to Trade, allowing the advance to our Silver Coin now standing, (which I take to be much less then reported by some) unto a limited time, that it might be new Stamp'd; which advantage being strictly limited to his Majesties Natural Born Subjects it could not be look'd upon with an ill Eye, altho' an easy Profit; by this expedient, according to our nice Politicians, we shall have as much for our Crown as it Weighs, and it will be some small security against its being melted down. And as I have been here Labouring for this conveniency to Negotiate this noble Fabrick of ours. I am now to fix this Treasure of our Silver Coin by an expedient which is much more Advantagious to our Woollen-Manufactury. And in order to this, I must beg leave to recite the Restrictions under which the Flourishing Trade of Queen *Elizabeth* was carried on. All Interest of Mony was stop'd by her Brother King *Edward* the 6th, which turn'd Drones into Bees. The Wear of Silks was stop'd by her Sister Queen *Mary*, by all Persons under the degree of Quality, and if any Servant wore any Silk, if the Master did not put her forth of her Service in Fourteen Days, or did retain her again, he forfeited One Hundred Pounds. By a Law made in the Fifth Year of Queen *Elizabeth*, no Foreign Fabrick could be sold otherwise than for ready Mony. And in the Thirteen Year of Queen *Elizabeth*, it was Enacted, that every Person above the Age of Seven Years, shall wear upon the Sabbath and Holy-Day, a Knit Cap made of the Wool of this Kingdom, under the Penalty of Ten Groats for every Day not wearing it, except Maids, Ladies, &c. What I now, in great Submission, propose, is the Revival of this last Act, in changing the Name of Cap to Hat; in the making of which, we are now come to great Perfection, and there can be no more decent Distinction or becoming Dress to our Women. This Hat will be like the Stern of a Ship, guide all other Habits of the Body, and introduce the wear of the Fine-Flaxen-Linnens of *Germany*, *Flanders* and *Holland* Lace, &c. which are the Natural Effects of our Woollen-Manufacture, and stop the wear of Muslings; to purchase which, our Silver is now issued out, and what I farther propose, is, a strict Injunction of the wear of the Woollen-Manufacture of this Kingdom by all Servants for their upper Garments, with a Penalty upon the Master if the said Act was not complied with; as was the Case of Silk in the Reign of Queen *Mary*. In the most Flourishing Reigns of this Kingdom, as *Edward* the 3d, *Edward* the 4th, *Henry* the 7th, *Edward* the 6th, and Queen *Elizabeth*; we were under Sumptuary Laws and a total stop put to the Cotton Commodities of *India*; and Presidents are safe rules to walk by. And as this Distinction will tend to the Encouragement of our own Products, and be a means to keep the Ballance of Trade upon our side, and secure our Silver Coin, it will likewise be an inducement to Virtue and Good Manners, and Servants will not think themselves above their proper Imployments.

In Kersey Joan *her Pot did Scower,*
Dress'd in Callico, she look'd demure;
Despis'd that Work, she got it done,
By Wife well stuff'd of Thrasher John.

Sic cesinit mus Rusticus & redit in rurem.

(b)

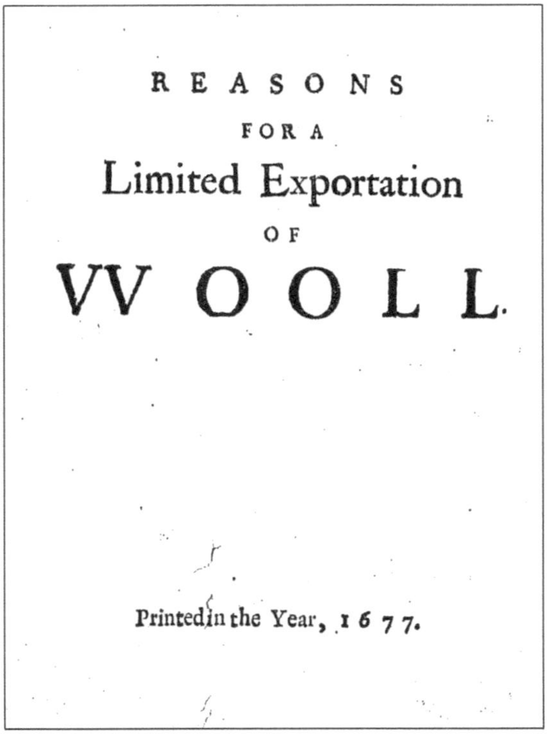

REASONS
FOR A
Limited Exportation
OF
VV O O L L.

Printed in the Year, 1677.

Figure 6.1 Seventeenth-Century Sumptuary Codes: (a) This "broadside" appeared on the streets of London about 1680 to announce a proposed code that would restrict the making and wearing of sumptuous attire. (b) Cover of *Reasons for a Limited Exportation of Wooll*. 1677. Copy from Henry E. Huntington Library and Art Gallery.

appearances of architectural order. The point is that commerce requires a setting that befits the dignity and seeming prosperity of the community.

Although the *localist* movements of the 21st century—those that work to protect local economies and cultures from foreign competition—employ very different language, the issues at stake remain much the same.[10] Restrictions of production, consumption, spending, and investment to within the geographic community are sumptuary codes of long standing and are linked to the concepts of appropriate technology,[11] regionalism,[12] and the practice of organic farming, which is by definition *local*.[13] Protecting local economies is, then, one dimension of sumptuary code-making.

The Conservation of Community Resources

Jared Diamond's somewhat controversial book, *Collapse*, uses 17th-century Japan as a case in which centralized authority sought to conserve local resources so as to avoid the kind of ecological collapse suffered by the civilizations of Easter Island, the Maya, the Norse Greenlanders, and the Anasazi. Following the devastating *Meikeki* fire of 1657 in Edo—what is present-day Tokyo—successive shoguns, according to Diamond's narrative, recognized the potential for the massive rebuilding effort to catalyze ecological disaster and invoked Confucian principles to develop "an official ideology that encouraged limiting consumption" of wood and other forest resources. Although Diamond does not refer to this "ideology" as a sumptuary code per se, it strongly resembles Hollander's definition above. In 1666, Diamond holds, the shogun issued a proclamation "warning of the dangers of erosion, stream siltation, and flooding caused by deforestation, and urging people to plant seedlings." And "by 1700 an elaborate system of wood management was in place 'specifying who could do what, where, when, how, how much, and at what price'."[14] Many writers, particularly Ishikawa, have held that Edo culture was a prescient example of the modern concept of sustainability.[15]

Although both of these traditions of sumptuary coding are related to contemporary concerns and conditions, they are obscured by the dominant tradition and can be reconsidered as useful only after we assess the largely ineffective use of sumptuary codes to either invent or preserve class distinctions.

THE DOMINANT TRADITION OF SUMPTUARY CODING: PRESERVATION OF CLASS DISTINCTION

The most common use of sumptuary codes is to preserve traditional distinctions between the social classes. These sumptuary discourses are a principal concern of governance[16] and embody a particularly conservative view toward social and technological change.[17] Lim and Hunt each argue that sumptuary codes tend to be recuperative—meaning that they are constructed as a means to retain the "recognizability" of social groups, most often when they are threatened by rapidly changing conditions.[18] The aftermath of war and the emergence of capitalism are two such destabilizing events. In the aftermath of World War II in Europe, for example, once readily available commodities such as gasoline and cigarettes became rare, and thus very expensive. These basic commodities became rare because the war had disrupted production. In the same period, once rare luxury commodities such as Renaissance art became available at low cost in both North and South America. These once rare commodities became relatively plentiful because theft by soldiers created an artificial supply. In such cases, threatened groups tend to intervene politically to reestablish "systems of social distinction" through the rationing and/or redistribution of goods.[19] The purpose of rationing goods is often that the preservation of unequal power relations depends on maintaining cultural proprieties.

In our review of sumptuary codes, we have found five things that elites have historically attempted to regulate in order to preserve the legibility of the classes: honorific artifacts,[20] manners,[21] food,[22] fashion, and architecture. For our purposes here, the last two—fashion and architecture—are most relevant, and so we will limit our discussion to them.

The aphorism that "architects are but tailors to the rich" is commonly taken by architects as demeaning, because they see their discipline as the more demanding and significant of the two. Yet, historically, it is accurate to say that tailors and architects did serve the aristocracy in very similar ways—by creating for their patrons artifacts deemed beautiful by society—a designation that distinguished the relative tastefulness of patrons and thus elevated their standing within society. Architects and tailors were not themselves taste-makers, but provided the raw material required for aristocrats empowered by birthright to judge (and thus produce) good taste. In this context, we should understand "taste" as the acquired disposition to differentiate the beautiful from the ugly and the capacity to appreciate excellence.[23] In the following section, we consider the sumptuary codes controlling architecture and fashion design in both the medieval and Renaissance periods, in order to illustrate how these systems of regulation reinforced the dominant social order by providing a visual guide to class and status.

Medieval Sumptuary Codes for Fashion

Sumptuary codes may have first emerged in medieval Europe from the *córtes* held in Valladolid, Spain, under the rule of King Alfonso X, *El Sabio* (the Wise) in January of 1258.[24] Alfonso's sumptuary code precedes that decreed by King Edward II of England by only 69 years, and so it is reasonable to argue that the matter was not limited to the Spanish court. The Spanish restrictions concentrated on the colors, materials, and styles of both clothing and jewelry that could be worn in public by all classes of individual. Likewise, Hooper[25] documents somewhat later English proclamations of 1574 and 1588 that restricted the type and amount of cloth that might be used in any article of clothing for a particular class of English subject (as in Figures 6.2 and 6.3).[26]

The clear intent of these codes was to make one's social station (and thus breeding) publicly apparent. As moderns, we tend to think of elaborate public consumption or display as hedonistic—a private and self-indulgent demonstration of excess. However, for the aristocracy of the European late Middle Ages and early Renaissance, elaborate public consumption was understood to be a necessary practice by which social rank was adjusted, within the stratum to which one was born, according to one's consumptive skill.[27] Maintaining the clarity of the language of consumption was, then, a political responsibility of the state related to the maintenance of social order. In this late-medieval context, we can understand that the distinction given to aristocrats derives first from birth, but must be maintained by their overconsumption

Figure 6.2 *British Costume During XIX Centuries (Civil and Ecclesiastical)* (p. 248). Ashdown, Mrs Charles H. 1910. London and Edinburgh: T.C. & E.C. Jack. Sumptuary codes are explicit laws, or implicit social codes of taste, that render the social rank of individuals legible to society and the state. In this case, the "velvet breeches" on the left and the "cloth breeches" on the right demarcate social rank.

Figure 1. Men's Apparel

None shall wear in his apparel

- Silk of the color purple, cloth of gold, or silver tissued, nor fur of sables — under the degree of an earl.
- Cloth of gold, silver, or tinsel satin; Silk, cloth, canvas or any stuff in any apparel, that shall be mixed or embroidered with any gold or silver — under the degree of a baron.
- Woolen cloth made out of the realm, saving in caps only; Velvet (crimson, carnation, or blue); Scarlet cloth; Furs of (black genets, or lucerns); Embroidery, or tailor's work, having gold, or silver, or pearl therein, nor any enamel, musk, ambergris, agate, or any other precious stone, in chain, button, or aglet. Nor any doublet, jerkin, or other apparel of any stuff perfumed — under the degree of (A knight of the Order, one of the Privy Council, or a gentleman of the privy chamber.)

Figure 6.3 Sumptuary Specifications for Elizabethan Men's Apparel (Partial). "A 'sumptuary chart' that details what clothing English males were permitted to wear in the late 16th century, upon pain of legal penalty." Reproduced from Whigham, Frank. 1984. *Ambition and Privilege: The Social Tropes of Elizabethan Courtesy Theory* (pp. 164–165). The text is based on Hughes and Larkin. 1580. *Tudor Royal Proclamations*, Proclamation 646 (2.458–461).

of resources—a practice that was generally detrimental to the community as a whole.

Of course, the more successful such codes were in associating individuals with desirable status, the more tempting it was for individuals of lesser distinction, as well as their tailors and wig-makers, to transgress through creative interpretation of the code. The width of a sleeve might be creatively tapered, or a color blended to blur its legislated meaning. As we argued in Chapter 3, the process of codification is always one of coding and interpretation, reinterpretation, and counter-coding, ad infinitum. The problem of enforcing sumptuary codes was, then, difficult from the very beginning. Queen Elizabeth I of England (1533–1603), who had a particular penchant for public order, issued the Surveillance Statute of 1554, which both established a monetary fine for each day that offenders publicly falsified their station and rewarded the whistleblowers who reported transgressors to the authorities.[28] Not to be outdone, Freudengerger reports that, a century later, Louis XIV of France (1638–1715) imposed the penalty of death or banishment to the galleys for transgressing sumptuary codes related to fashion under his rule.[29] The regulators of the *Ancien Régime* took matters of representing one's social position very seriously indeed. The severity of the penalty should be understood as an index of just how seriously the social order of the time was threatened by popular unrest.

Medieval Sumptuary Codes for Architecture

Sumptuary codes that regulate architecture are no less venerable or significant to the societies in which they emerged. In 7th–10th-century China, for example, Knapp describes how sumptuary regulation, employed during the Tang, Ming, and Qing dynasties, contributed to the standardization, modularization, and stylization of Chinese houses. Like their European counterparts, Chinese sumptuary laws were established to preserve class distinctions, but viewed through a Confucian value system. In the 14th century, during the Ming dynasty, officials of different ranks were permitted dwellings of certain size, defined by the number of bays and purlins they contained—those of a lower rank could have up to three bays and seven purlins, and those of a higher rank could have up to five bays and nine purlins. These units of dwelling size were determined by the dimensions of timber available and, thus, linked patterns of hierarchy, consumption, and inhabitation to forestry practices. Wood joinery (Figure 6.4), like the social bonds it metaphorically represented, was also regulated by sumptuary codes. However, although penalties for transgressors existed, Knapp argues that enforcing rules was not as crucial as simply having them.

In Asia, Europe, and the New World,[30] such provisions were intended to preserve the sociopolitical and ethical–religious order. According to Shively,[31] even if the Asian examples were not as strict as their European counterparts, which were enforced by penalties, they affected the consciousness of citizens.

Renaissance Sumptuary Codes for Architecture

In Western architecture, the Renaissance period can be similarly associated with sumptuary coding. Simply put, our argument is that European codes of taste and propriety, particularly the French concept of *convenance* (or *bienséance*), are also codes of consumption by another name.[32] However, if medieval European sumptuary codes and the Asian examples cited above were *explicitly* stated laws, enforced by aristocratic political power, Renaissance sumptuary codes of taste tended to be *implicit*.[33] They were, perhaps, more effective by being implicit, because they harnessed the emergent bourgeois desire to achieve social distinction.

For example, 16th-century French courtier Philibert de l'Orme (1514–1570) held that, "by hiring a good architect, one could avoid being ridiculed because of an ill-designed or unfinished building."[34] Rather than being

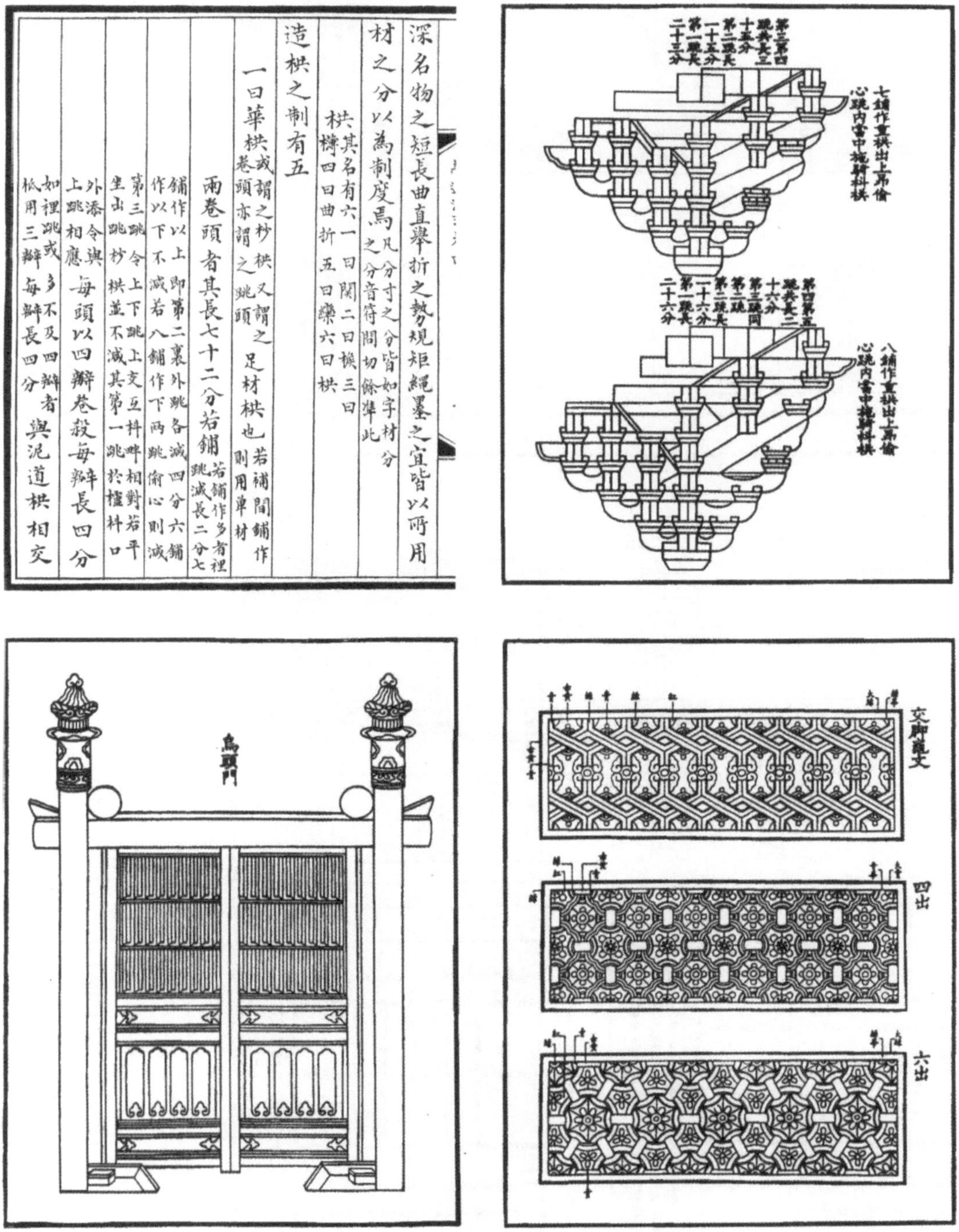

深名物之短長曲直舉折之勢規矩繩墨之宜皆以所用
材之分以為制度焉凡分寸之分皆如字材分之分音符問切餘準此
栱其名有六一曰閞二曰槉三曰欂四曰曲枅五曰欒六曰栱
造栱之制有五
一曰華栱或謂之杪栱又謂之卷頭亦謂之跳頭足材栱也若補間鋪作則用單材
兩卷頭者其長七十二分若鋪作多者裏跳減長二分七
鋪作以上即第二裏外跳各減四分六鋪作以下不減若八鋪作下兩跳偷心則減
第三跳令上下跳上交互枓畔相對若平坐出跳杪栱並不減其第一跳於櫨枓口
外添令與上跳相應每頭以四瓣卷殺每瓣長四分
如裏跳減多不及四瓣者祇用三瓣每瓣長四分與泥道栱相交

Figure 6.4 An Architectural Code: Yingshan Ling, 600–900 AD. Source: Guo, Qinghua. 2005. *Chinese Architecture and Planning: Ideas, Methods, Techniques* (p. 92). Stuttgart: Edition Axel Menges.

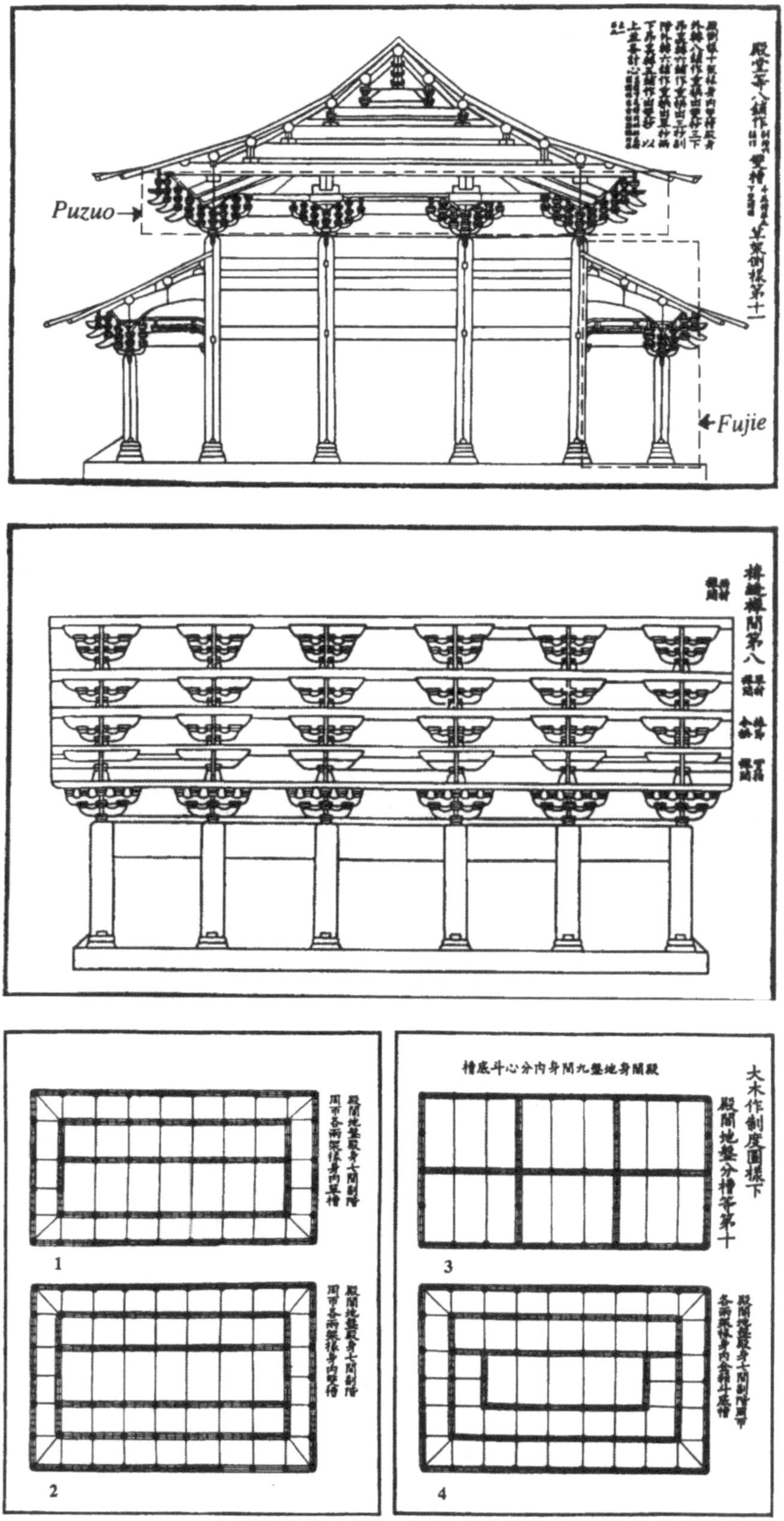

Figure 6.5 Coding Status in Construction: Yingzan Fushi, 1145. Qing Dynasty. Although the precise meaning of this drawing is difficult to interpret, scholars suggest that the social stature of an individual at court could be determined by counting the number of bays and purlins in his house. Guo, Qinghua. 2005. "Chinese Architecture and Planning: Ideas, Methods, Techniques." In *Architectural History* 41, 1993:10. Stuttgart: Edition Axel Menges.

fined monetarily, sent to the galleys, or beheaded, transgressors of that era would be disciplined and punished by social isolation. De l'Orme's characterizations of the "good architect" and the "bad architect" are depicted in Figures 6.6 and 6.7. Looking back from the 20th century, Foucault observed that it was through such social mechanisms of "discipline and punishment" that some subjects of the realm adopted codes of consumption, taste, and behavior as their own, because it was in their interest to do so.[35]

By the mid 17th century in France, during the reign of Louis XIII (1601–1643) and that of his more famous heir, Louis XIV (1638–1715), the sense of architectural propriety derived from the Middle Ages and Renaissance was beginning to be associated, not with society in general, but with the interest of the national state, embodied by the Crown. A concrete example of this shift was the establishment of the French Royal Academy of Architecture in 1671. This new authority was "explicitly charged with the standardization of expressive and practical architectural codes," so as to satisfy the Crown's ambition to become the singular seat of cultural authority in the realm. In addition to the Royal Academy of Architecture, similar institutions were established for literature, painting, and other disciplines. What is most significant for our purposes is that the system of French academies established reasoning as the basis of code-making, rather than the benign acceptance of ancient authority. It was the construction of codes of taste on the basis of reasoning, rather than heredity, that ironically gave to the arts, including architecture, some autonomy from religion and politics.[36] Just as Diderot and his authors wrote the world's first encyclopedia in this era, designers were simultaneously compiling architectural knowledge. It was through this process that a new "expert class" was first established.[37]

It was in the context of the Royal Academy of Architecture that Charles Perrault (1628–1703) made his significant contribution to architectural code-making. Perrault's *Ordonnance for the Five Kinds of Columns After the Method of the Ancients*, published in 1683 (Figure 6.8), established the French Crown as the source of architectural authority. In Perrault's ordinance, each class of activity, or type of social occasion, required a different composition derived from the orders. For example, the Paris Opera House, built in 1669 under the reign of Louis XIV, required a very different composition of signs than did the east façade of the Louvre, built at about the same time. Picon has argued that, by publishing his *Ordonnance*, or code, Perrault hoped to normalize, or institutionalize, taste as a rational directive of the state.[38] Like others who followed him, Perrault assumed (with some hubris) that his code would maintain the status of rational architectural expression above the realm of mere fashion. However, in lieu of stability, Perrault's code ironically opened the door for others to also reinterpret the ancients for their own time constituency—a pattern that repeats itself.

Perrault's rational code was strongly linked to the concept of *convenance*. The term is typically translated as "suitability" or "appropriateness," but evolves over time, as does society itself. *Convenance* was, then, a contested and transitional concept. In the early part of the century, courtier Michel de Fremin, in his memoire of 1702, defines the term by saying,

> I have one more word to say about what I mean by *convenance* for the condition of those for whom the building is built, it is the science

Figure 6.6 "The Good Architect," Etching by Philibert de L'Orme (1515?–1570). 1568. "The good architect stands in a flourishing garden, has many hands, is surrounded by classical and new buildings alike, and is familiarizing young people with his scientific discipline." In *Le premier tome de l'architecture de Philibert de l'Orme* (p. 131). Paris: Fédéric Morel.

Figure 6.7 "The Bad Architect," Etching by Philibert de L'Orme (1515?–1570). 1568. In contrast to Figure 6.6, "The bad [architect] wanders bereft of hands and eyes through a barren landscape with a Medieval castle," unable to serve the patron class. In *Le premier tome de l'architecture de Philibert de l'Orme* (p. 131). Paris: Fédéric Morel.

Figure 6.8 *A Treatise of the Five Orders in Architecture, to Which is Annex'd a Discourse Concerning Pilasters.* 1722. Perrault, Claude (1613–1688). London. Printed for J. Senex and R. Gosling [etc.] 1722. 2nd ed. Plate 1. Using the correct order to articulate the social status of the building patron, or activity to take place therein, meant the difference between public praise and ostracism. Perrault's claim is, then, that it is only the ability to define good "taste" possessed by the architect that saves the patron from false judgment and ridicule. Text from the Preface, p. X. "'Tis certain, then, that there are some beauties in architecture, which are positive, and some that are only arbitrary, though they seem positive through prejudice, from which is very difficult to guard ourselves. 'Tis also true that a good judgment is founded on the knowledge of both these beauties; but it is certain, that the knowing of arbitrary beauties is most proper to form what we call right Tast[e], and 'tis that only which distinguishes true architects from those who are not so."

x **The PREFACE.**

otherwiſe, without prejudice to the other Graces, would have produc'd an ill Effect, had they been alter'd. Juſt as when a man is paſſionately in love with a Face, tho' it has nothing perfectly beautiful but the Complexion, yet he cannot help thinking the Proportion too, ſo agreeable, that he knows not how to believe, any Change thereof could render it more charming: foraſmuch as the great Beauty of a Part making him love the whole, the love of the whole neceſſarily includes that of all the Parts.

'Tis certain, then, that there are ſome Beauties in Architecture, which are poſitive, and ſome that are only arbitrary, tho' they ſeem poſitive through prejudice, from which it is very difficult to guard our ſelves. 'Tis alſo true, that a good judgment is founded on the Knowledge of both theſe Beauties; but it is certain, that the Knowledge of arbitrary Beauties, is moſt proper to form what we call a right Taſt, and 'tis that only which diſtinguiſhes true Architects from thoſe that are not ſo; becauſe common Senſe alone is ſufficient for knowing the greateſt part of poſitive Beauties; nor is there any great difficulty in judging that a large Fabrick of Marble, wrought with great Nicety and Exactneſs, is handſomer than a ſmall Building of rough-hewn Stones, where there is nothing exactly level, ſquare, or perpendicular. It requires no very great Ability in Architecture, to know that the Court of a Houſe ought not to be leſs than the Chambers, that the Cellars ſhould not be lighter than the Staircaſes, and that Columns ought not to be thicker than their Pedeſtals. But good Senſe can never inform us, that the Baſes of Columns ought to have in Height, neither more nor leſs, than half the Diameter of the Column; that the Modillions and Dentels, in Pedaments ſhould be perpendicular to the Horizon; that the Dentels ought to be under the Modillions; that the Triglyphs ſhould have in Breadth half the Diameter of the Column, and that the Metopes ſhould be preciſely ſquare.

It is alſo eaſy to conceive that all theſe things might have had other Proportions, without Offence to the moſt exquiſite and delicate Senſe; and that it is not here, as in the Conſtitution of our Bodies, which, when diſorder'd, may be dangerous, tho' the ſick perſon knows not the degrees of thoſe Qualities which make it ſo: for to be diſpleas'd or pleas'd with the Proportions of Architecture, we muſt be inſtructed by a long Obſervation of the Rules, which Uſe alone has eſtabliſh'd, and of which, good Senſe could never have given us the leaſt Knowledge: as in the Civil Laws, there are ſome

> of avoiding anything that does not suit the dignity or the status of the master; when this precept is not followed, there occurs an *inconvenance*, which consists in forgetting one's condition and rejecting the rules of modesty and prudence.[39]

The emphasis in de Fremin's memoire is directly related to how skillfully architects represent the social status of the patron, at a time when the norms of the French aristocracy were being threatened by both the *nouveaux riches* and the early rumblings of the coming revolution. As in the older concept of sumptuary codes, the purpose of coding architecture in this way is to prop up and reinforce a social system of order that was already crumbling.[40] *Convenance* was a social convention, or code, that worked to regulate the transition of a Renaissance-era society at the beginning of the 18th century to an Enlightenment-era society by the end of the century.

In his *Social Critique of the Judgment of Taste*, Bourdieu makes a similar observation in holding that Enlightenment, or modern codes of taste that emerged in the mid 18th century, "are a practical mastery of distribution which makes it possible to sense or intuit what is likely (or unlikely) to befall, and therefore to befit, an individual occupying a given position in social space."[41] Such skill is "practical" because it is highly unlikely that the distribution of goods, or of social distinction, will be other than that dictated by dominant social groups. Modern taste is, from roughly the Renaissance onward, to have a "sense of one's place" in the world, no matter what one's status happens to be.[42] In this sense, what Bourdieu refers to as "class habitus" makes a virtue of necessity. Class habitus is the acquired competence to encode and decode social situations that classify both people and their practices, in order to instruct subjects to act "appropriately."[43] The concept and practice of *convenance* is, then, paradoxically linked to both the feudal concept of hereditary superiority and the Enlightenment-era concepts of rationality and social progress.

In these examples and others, the sumptuary coding of both fashion and architecture worked to render people and the buildings they inhabit recognizable within a shared, or at least commonly understood, system of social distinction. Sumptuary coding in fashion and architecture has had, then, two important functions: First, such codes seek to make power relations in the city "legible" and thus manageable.[44]

Implications of Medieval and Renaissance Sumptuary Codes

At this point in our analysis, we can make two other related claims, based on the work of the historians and analysts who have studied medieval and Renaissance sumptuary codes: First, sumptuary codes with a negative orientation tend to be ineffective.[45] As we argued above, not only are the ever-accelerating cycles of coding, interpretation, and recoding very hard to enforce, but enforcement itself becomes something of a parlor game for urbane consumers of taste.[46] In this context, Beebe cites an 18th-century London stage character as saying, presumably accompanied by hearty audience laughter, "I don't care for it, now [that] it is not prohibited."[47] And second, historians and analysts tend to agree that, in the cyclical battles waged to prop up failing social orders, architects tend to be on the conservative (and generally losing) side.

In this context, systems of classification are scenes of struggle between social groups seeking to "transform the categories of perception" and, thus, turn them to their own advantage.[48] One's ability to do so, however, is inevitably limited by one's position in the class structure, which is but one reason why architects tend to associate themselves with the interests of the patron class and further distance themselves from the less studied tastes of the middle class and the poor. This is an issue to which we will return more than once, because it is central to our concerns in this book.

If subjects of the law can so easily subvert sumptuary codes, then it is not likely that they would be reproduced. Yet, as we have already observed, sumptuary codes continuously reappear in new forms, even if unconsciously reproduced.[49] Beebe makes two related observations that are particularly helpful: The first is that, in contrast to the Elizabethan or Edo societies discussed above, competitive consumption in contemporary society uses different means that, in turn, transform ends. Modern sumptuary codes, or taste, are driven less by the desire to maintain or prop up power relations within an established hierarchy than they are by the desire to achieve the satisfaction of individual distinctiveness, or what Thorpe and others refer to as "positional consumption"[50] —keeping up with the Joneses. In other words, the nature of the distinction sought by individuals has evolved.

For example, in dressing this morning, none of us could conceive of donning the habit of a Nobel Laureate, because there is no commonly understood dress code for that rank in society that would be different from, say, an assistant professor. We did, however, dress with some care so that we could represent how we are both like some of the people we will meet during the day, but also different from others. It is a matter of social affiliation and distinction. With such intentions in mind, we might understand that, in contemporary life, "A society's sumptuary code is its system of consumption practices, akin to a language (or at least a set of dialects), by which individuals in the society signal through their consumption their differences from and similarities to others."[51] At the most superficial level, individuals signal to each other by branding themselves—L.L.Bean, Louis Vuitton, or Hermès. At a more substantial level, individuals signal their social station by inventing personal attitudes toward color, shape, or hair. This revised definition of a sumptuary code is but a short distance from Lynes' 1954 definition of taste. For Lynes, "Taste is our personal delight, our private dilemma, and our public facade."[52] Taste is, then, a matter of relational "being" in modern society. In this contemporary context, then, Beebe's argument is that sumptuary codes, or taste, have evolved to be as much *ontological* as they are *political* in orientation. They continue, however, to link aesthetic to material consumption.

Beebe's second observation distinguishes between the "absolute" and "relative utility" of an artifact. Absolute utility refers to how well a new raincoat, for example, keeps out the water when it rains, as it might have this morning as one of us walked to the train. Relative utility, however, refers to how the raincoat performs *socially* in relation to the outerwear worn by other members of society.[53] One of us experienced this relative functionality while standing on the train platform admiring the elegantly versatile and seemingly inexpensive raincoat worn by a middle-aged man. From our perspective, it was the man's good judgment that distinguished him, not his explicit rank, nor our knowledge of how much he spent on his coat compared with our own. We admired his good taste, not because he signaled sumptuousness, but because he signaled the kind of elegant simplicity that we associate (rightly or wrongly) with low-entropy consumption.

From these observations, we can construct a twin proposition: first, sumptuary codes are not about to disappear any time soon, because it is only human to desire affiliation with some social groups and distinction from others. This is especially true as a matter of social psychology in an increasingly global society. And second, contemporary sumptuary codes might, we hold, be further rationalized by the processes of democratization. Achieving distinction in society might be uncoupled from both inequity and overconsumption or high-entropy practices. Before doing so, however, it is necessary to demonstrate how later forms of sumptuary codes, pattern books in particular, have evolved as a form of taste and regulation.

PATTERN BOOKS, CONSUMPTION, AND TASTE

A method of sumptuary coding common to both tailors and architects is the publication of "pattern books" by well-known practitioners (Figures 6.9 and 6.10). Pattern books for English tailors emerged by the 16th century, but in this section we limit our interest to the North American architectural pattern books that emerged in the late 18th century, because they are most salient to contemporary issues related to sustainable development. Our argument in this section is twofold: first, that North American patterns books have evolved as sumptuary codes that focus more on regulating aesthetic rather than material consumption. In this context, 19th-century pattern books retained the political intent of earlier societies to distinguish between the social classes for political purposes, but weakened or suppressed the direct link to material consumption and ecological sustainability. By comparison, contemporary pattern books are politically less restrictive, if not yet fully democratic. And second, pattern books have evolved in three overlapping phases that we characterize as *pedagogical*, *populist*, and *form-based*. As we hinted above, the continuing evolution of sumptuary codes in general, and pattern books in particular, opens up surprising possibilities for coding the future.

Pedagogical Pattern and Stylebooks

Although the American Revolution loosened the yoke of political and economic domination by European aristocracy, it did not immediately free us from cultural domination of the hierarchical codes of taste embodied in the neoclassical orders. Well after 1776, even the most strident patriots tacitly assumed that we would learn civilization from our most distinguished citizens, both by example and through their books. Architectural historian Dell Upton has provided the most compelling analysis of the first phase of pattern book-making—which we term *pedagogical* because of their instructive value—by further subdividing their development into two subgroups: pattern books per se and "stylebooks."[54] Both were intended to teach citizens of the young nation how to build tastefully, and thus improve the related aesthetic and moral conditions of our emerging democracy. The first group of books, "pattern books," was aimed at practitioners, and the second group, "stylebooks," was aimed at citizens themselves. Between 1797 and 1860, nearly 200 architectural pattern books were issued

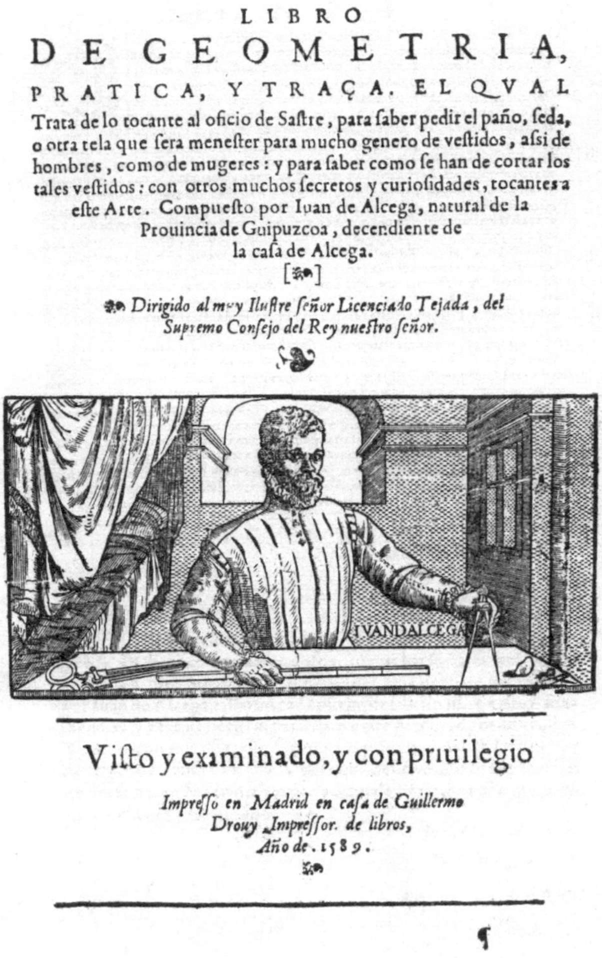
LIBRO
DE GEOMETRIA,
PRATICA, Y TRAÇA. EL QVAL
Trata de lo tocante al oficio de Saſtre, para ſaber pedir el paño, ſeda, o otra tela que ſera meneſter para mucho genero de veſtidos, aſsi de hombres, como de mugeres: y para ſaber como ſe han de cortar los tales veſtidos: con otros muchos ſecretos y curioſidades, tocantes a eſte Arte. Compueſto por Iuan de Alcega, natural de la Prouincia de Guipuzcoa, decendiente de la caſa de Alcega.
Dirigido al muy Iluſtre ſeñor Licenciado Tejada, del Supremo Conſejo del Rey nueſtro ſeñor.

Viſto y examinado, y con priuilegio
Impreſſo en Madrid en caſa de Guillermo Drouy, Impreſſor de libros, Año de. 1589.

Figure 6.9 *The Tailor's Pattern Book*. Juan De Alcega. 1589. To hold that "architects are but tailors to the rich" is to observe that the authority of both professions relies on rendering the patron tasteful in public. *Facsimile*. 1979. With translation from the Spanish by Jean Paine and Cecilia Bainton. Introduction and notes by J.L. Nevinson. Bedford, UK: Ruth Bean.

by North American presses—a very substantial number by comparison with other publishing genres.[55]

Pattern books served to educate designers and builders about the neoclassical orders of architecture, as they were defined by British and French authors of the time, as well as other very practical matters. However, these books also served to stimulate public discourse concerning the nature of professional knowledge and taste in a democratic society. Upton productively narrates the competition between two categories of early architects: the first personified by Asher Benjamin (1773–1845), the North American-born author of the first known Pattern Book, *The American Builders' Companion* (1797), and the English-born Benjamin Latrobe (1764–1820), architect of the Capitol and many other prestigious commissions of the time. The central issue that divided the two camps was not a matter of class affiliation per se, but was a disagreement about the nature of professional knowledge in a democratic society. Upton carefully debunks the popular myth that native-born master carpenters (Benjamin) were of a lower class than European-born gentlemen

Figure 6.10 Benjamin, Asher. 1811. *The American Builder's Companion; or, A System of Architecture, Particularly Adapted to the Present Style of Building. Treating: Practical Geometry. The Origin of Building. Of the Five Orders of Architecture. Of Their Particular Parts and Embellishments, and of Their Application. Also Very Fully on Stairs. On the Pland and Elevations of Houses, for both Town and Country. On Churches, Courthouses, &c. On Sashes, Sash Frames, Shutters, Doors, Cornices, Base and Surbase Mouldings, Architraves, &c. &c.* 2nd ed. Corrected and Enlarged. Charlestown: Printed by Samuel Etheridge, Junior. Plate 21, Cornices. Plate 54, Plan and Elevation for a House which is Intended for a Country Situation. Pattern books like that by Benjamin distributed the authority of good taste to aspiring architects and builders. Each architectural element contributes to the meaning of the whole. The composition as a whole communicates appropriateness, or *convenance*, to the "situation." That term is, however, not a reference to geography, but to one's social "situation" or place within society.

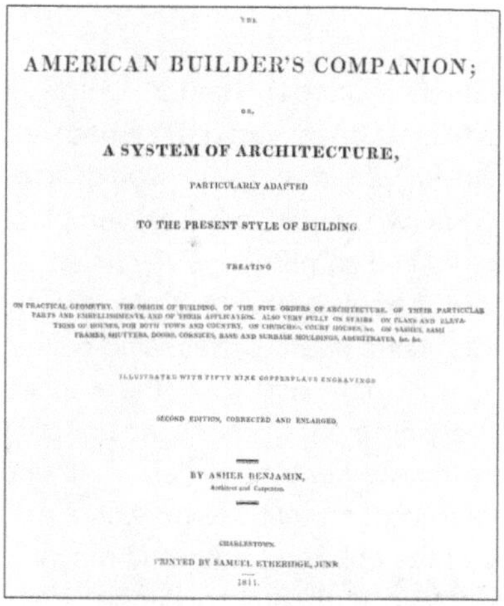
THE

AMERICAN BUILDER'S COMPANION;

OR,

A SYSTEM OF ARCHITECTURE,

PARTICULARLY ADAPTED

TO THE PRESENT STYLE OF BUILDING

TREATING

ON PRACTICAL GEOMETRY. THE ORIGIN OF BUILDING. OF THE FIVE ORDERS OF ARCHITECTURE. OF THEIR PARTICULAR PARTS AND EMBELLISHMENTS, AND OF THEIR APPLICATION. ALSO VERY FULLY ON STAIRS. ON PLANS AND ELEVATIONS OF HOUSES, FOR BOTH TOWN AND COUNTRY. ON CHURCHES, COURT HOUSES, &c. ON SASHES, SASH FRAMES, SHUTTERS, DOORS, CORNICES, BASE AND SURBASE MOULDINGS, ARCHITRAVES, &c. &c.

ILLUSTRATED WITH FIFTY NINE COPPERPLATE ENGRAVINGS

SECOND EDITION, CORRECTED AND ENLARGED.

BY ASHER BENJAMIN,

Architect and Carpenter.

CHARLESTOWN:

PRINTED BY SAMUEL ETHERIDGE, JUNR

1811.

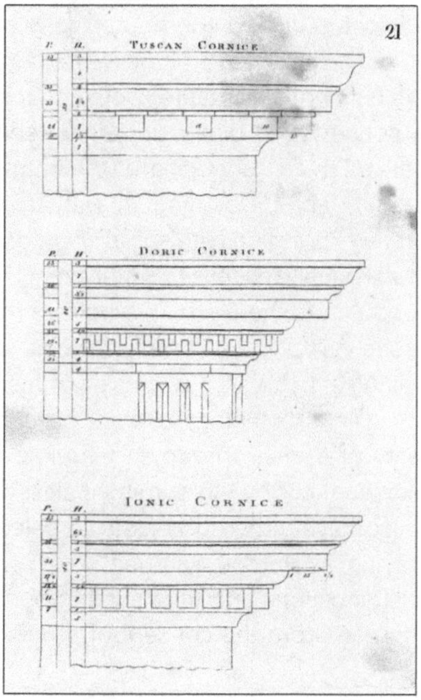

architects (Latrobe). Rather, Upton demonstrates that both gentlemen and native craftsmen worked at both ends of the designer–builder spectrum. However, where Benjamin would base a democratic architecture on experience, or what we would now call empirical standards, "Latrobe insisted on the superior and comprehensive *character* of his acquired architectural knowledge, asserting that it was qualitatively and quantitatively distinct from both his clients' taste and the practicing builders' experience"[56] (emphasis added).

In the end, then, the architectural knowledge favored by Latrobe was not very different from the idea of *convenance* proposed by French academics more than a century earlier. That kind of abstract knowledge was based on the assumption that design was a practice distinct from, and superior to, that held in the building trades and mechanical arts. In effect, Latrobe embraced an aristocratic form of knowledge, free of practical context. As we argued in Chapter 2, Latrobe followed the tradition of Palladio. However, without access to the aristocratic tradition of superior breeding to back his claim, Latrobe had no independent ground to support the special "character" of his knowledge. Upton holds that "Latrobe's professional vision has never been completely realized in the United States."[57] We agree, and further suggest that skeptical North American farmers, merchants, and businessmen of the 19th century and after were reluctant to subjugate their own ability to reason and choose tastefully to a source of authority that had no legitimacy in a democratic and highly practical society. Although the first group of pattern books to appear may have influenced other designers and builders who aspired to social and artistic autonomy, they did not influence middle-class clients as intended—to accept the authority of architects as rational master tastemakers.

What Upton refers to as "stylebooks" began to appear in the late 1830s. Titles such as John Buonarotti Papworth's *Rural Residences* (1832) and Andrew Jackson Downing's *Cottage Residences* (1842) were directed, not at designers or builders, but at citizens themselves. In attempting to teach or influence the public taste directly, 19th-century designers and critics generally participated in, and contributed to, what many have characterized as the conservative social reform movement of the time—one that included a highly moralistic notion of taste. Downing's stylebooks demonstrate particularly well the conservative dimension of stylebooks as sumptuary codes.[58] As did the elites of 7th-century China, 13th-century Spain, 16th-century England, and 18th-century France, Downing, in *The Architecture of Country Houses*, links architectural expression with social *character*, a term that still designated social class, cultural origin, and religious affiliation. Speaking in the plural, as a North American of good taste, he held, "we believe much of the character of every man may be read in his house. If he has molded its leading features from the foundation it will give a clue to a large part of his character."[59]

"Character," used in this context, should be understood as the moral quality of a man or woman who knows his/her place within the hierarchy of society set out by the dominant class (Figure 6.11). Good character is revealed by also having the good taste to select the correct style in which to build—it is having, as Bourdieu argued, the "social competence" to decode and encode social situations and thus act appropriately or with *propriety*—a term derived, of course, from the concept of property.

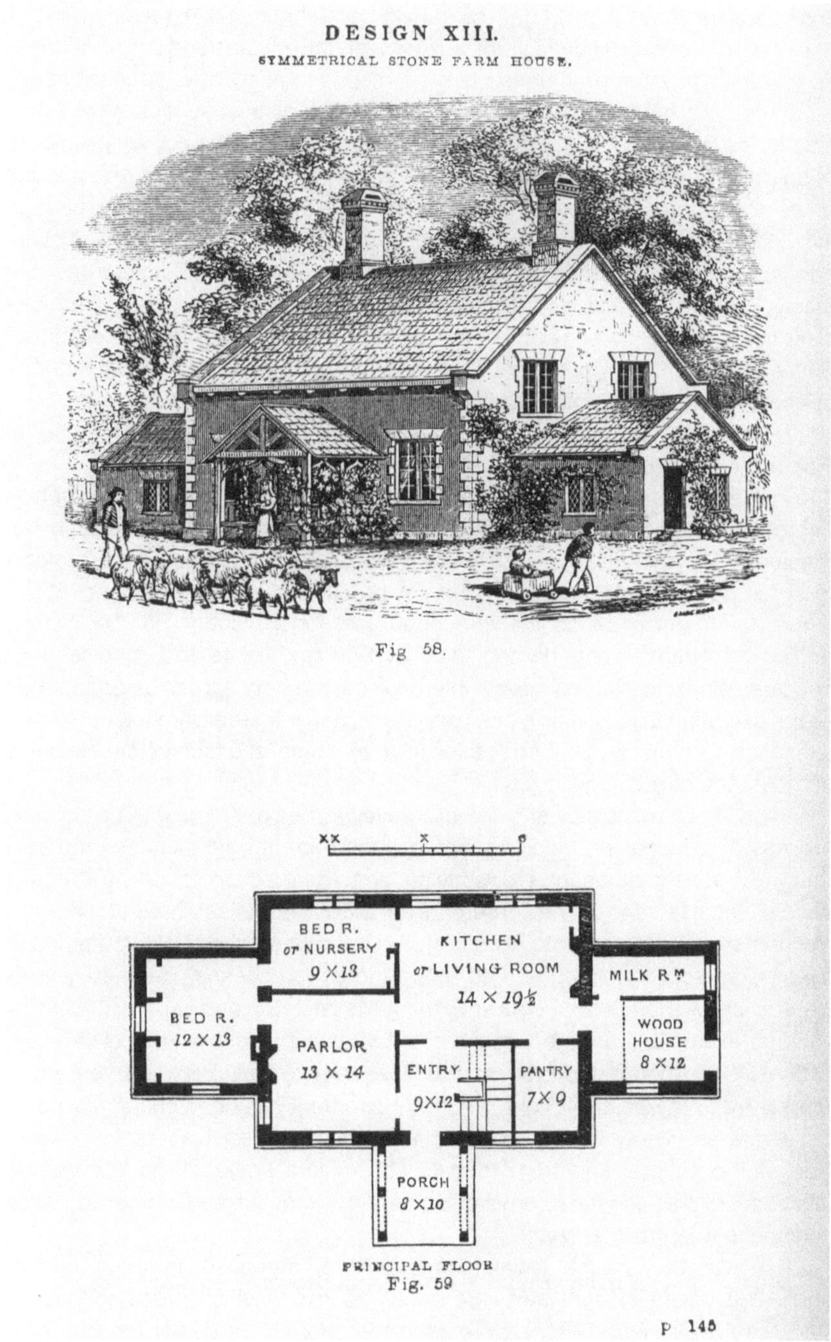

Figure 6.11 Design XIV, "Symmetrical Stone Farmhouse." In Downing, Andrew Jackson. 1969[1850]. *The Architecture of Country Houses; Including Designs for Cottages, and Farmhouses, and Villas, With Remarks on Interiors, Furniture, and the Best Modes of Warming and Ventilating.* For Downing and his followers there was an appropriate form, material, and color for each station of society.

In his analysis of pattern books and stylebooks, Upton reached two conclusions: First, in appropriating thoroughly familiar forms from history, architects of the young nation imbued selected forms with the authority of professionalism and then passed them on to an emergent middle class. In other words, architects made the weight of history available to everyday people in a manner that it had not been previously. Second, Upton concluded, with considerable irony, that, in lieu of stabilizing architectural expression in the new nation in a manner consistent with conservative tastes and social values—as Perrault had attempted before him—the opposite occurred, "pattern books reinforced the notion that novelty and [individual] distinctiveness were desirable in the appearance of a building."[60] Pattern and stylebooks were, then, a bridge between the tacit use of traditional architectural form and the popular or aesthetic consumption of architectural style as a novelty—as a path to individual distinctiveness. If, through codifying good taste in pattern and stylebooks, architects thought that the social and built worlds would become more stable, predictable, and tasteful by educating designers, builders, and middle-class homebuilders, then our project was ironic, because the opposite occurred. Education did not prop up the already rejected aristocratic social order; it opened the floodgates of populism.

Populist Pattern Books: Catalogs and Magazines

The idea that every man might have "good taste" emerged only with Jacksonian democracy in the United States—a period that began with the election of President Andrew Jackson (1767–1845) in 1824 and lasted until the regional disagreement over slavery could no longer be avoided—sometime after 1850.[61] If the Jeffersonian period that preceded Jackson's election can be characterized as a gentlemanly democracy, in which the values and good taste of educated elites dominated most public choices, the new era can be understood as the rise of populist values historically associated with the Democratic Party—expanded suffrage, public participation in governance, and faith in the reasoning competence of ordinary citizens.

Populist politics should not, however, be conflated with democratic process or Left-leaning ideology. Rather, populism is better understood as a rhetorical style that appeals directly to emotional action taken by "regular people" against entrenched interests of elites. Populism has, at different moments in history, erupted from both the radical Left and Right and tends to bypass established parties and institutional processes deemed overly hierarchical. Although the Populist Party of the late 19th and early 20th century was, for example, a Southern coalition of Left-leaning poor whites, blacks, and Latinos,[62] the populist quality of the 21st-century Tea Party Movement is equally far to the political Right. Neither movement has been characterized by observers as overtly tasteful or rational. Rather, populist leaders from either side of the political spectrum tend to accumulate power through rhetorical tactics that are long on promises but short on detail about how idealized conditions might be realized.[63]

In the era of Jacksonian populism, emphasis in the world of publishing began to shift away from "stylebooks," which prepared middle-class families to work with architects in the appropriate design of their new home, to the publication of two new genres: magazine plans and catalogs. Rather than targeting men, as did the publishers of pattern books in an earlier era, magazines targeted women, both as decision-makers and guardians of American domesticity. *Godey's Lady's Book* (Figure 6.12), for example, published over 450 cottage and villa designs between 1846 and 1900 that were intended to inspire "Mrs. Consumer" to assemble the innovative design for the family home, based on the recommendations of pioneering domestic

Figure 6.12 *Godey's Lady's Book*, January 1850. In the January 1850 edition of this popular magazine, a previously unpublished poem by Park Benjamin informed readers that "The *vulgar* rich need to carefully select charities so as not to betray their station in society."

crusaders such as Catherine Beecher and Orson Fowler. Beginning in 1885, the very influential *Ladies Home Journal* joined the cause for every American family to own its own home.[64]

Certainly the most well-known and successful popular catalog was that produced by Sears, Roebuck & Company, beginning in 1908 (Figure 6.13). The catalog was, however, far more than a collection of house designs from which customers could choose. Rather, it was a vertically integrated industry that collaborated with customers on the design of their home.[65] Although Sears did purchase house designs from architects early in its history, over time the company developed designs internally and published them without reference to authors.[66] This is not to say that authorship was appropriated by "salespeople" and homeowners themselves, but that "authorship" in the traditional sense of sumptuary encoding by "authorities" (architects) had become irrelevant. In the place of representing one's place in society through the expertise of others, North Americans were entering a period of solidarity between producers and consumers—a period that well-educated elites would see as a period of bad taste.

The difference between a pedagogical pattern book and a populist catalog is that the earlier books presented a narrative or pedagogical lesson

$657.00 PAYS FOR ALL THE MATERIAL

TO BUILD THIS SIX-ROOM BUNGALOW.

For this price we furnish the Mill Work, Lumber, Building Paper, Eaves Trough, Mantel, Hardware and Painting Material. By allowing a fair price for labor this bungalow can be built for $1,466.00

WE WILL FURNISH YOU THE PLANS, SPECIFICATIONS AND BILL OF MATERIALS ENTIRELY WITHOUT COST, AS EXPLAINED ON PAGE 1.

MODERN HOME No. 126

Please examine the floor plan illustrated here below and note the exceptionally convenient arrangement of this house. Every room in the house is light and airy, the ventilation is perfect. Both bedrooms adjoin the bathroom. Has a large, spacious reception hall which leads to a large living room and kitchen. The living room, which is planned to be used as a dining room and living room, is equipped with a beautiful rustic open fireplace. The arrangement of the kitchen is very convenient and it has a large, spacious cupboard which serves as a pantry. This modern home is of the 20th Century Queen Anne style. The finish or trim throughout is made of the finest grade of yellow pine in natural finish; the mill work and other material is of the best selected quality. Hardwood doors and finishing if desired at a small advance in price.

The arrangement of this house is as follows:

Reception Hall	10 feet by 10 feet 9 inches
Bedroom	13 feet 6 inches by 10 feet
Bedroom	13 feet by 10 feet
Three Closets.	
Kitchen	11 feet by 13 feet 6 inches
Large Living Room	27 feet by 13 feet 6 inches
Front Porch	25 feet by 8 feet 10 inches

Excavated cellar, 12 feet by 24 feet. Height of basement from floor to ceiling, 7 feet. Height of ceiling, 10 feet.

To appreciate this wonderful value that can be built for less than $1,500.00, compare this house with any house in your neighborhood of similar size and construction which costs between $2,500.00 and $3,000.00. The extremely low cost we name is made possible by our furnishing most everything necessary to construct this building at less than wholesale prices. We guarantee the quality to be absolutely the best.

If this style of architecture appeals to you be sure to send $1.00 temporary deposit for our building plans for this Bungalow No. 126, and we will send you the complete set of plans and apply the $1.00 deposit as cash on your order for mill work amounting to $10.00 or more, thus making the plans cost you nothing.

Complete Hot Air Heating Plant, for soft coal, extra	$ 67.00
Complete Hot Air Heating Plant, for hard coal, extra	70.00
Complete Hot Water Heating Plant, extra	106.67
Complete Steam Heating Plant, extra	143.97
Complete Plumbing Outfit, extra	120.21

BOOK OF MODERN HOMES —53— Sears, Roebuck & Co., Chicago, Ill.

Figure 6.13 Sears Modern Homes Mail Order Catalog, 1909–1913, Home No. 126. The Sears Catalog of "modern homes" presented homeowners with choices, not pedagogy.

about *how* and *why* to make tasteful choices appropriate to one's social station. In contrast, catalogs such as Sears & Roebuck's and magazines such as *Godey's Lady's Book* are but a list of possibilities *from which* to choose. Populist catalogs and magazines presented to North American families a kit of parts from which they could choose architectural plans and elements *that they would themselves compose*. It is hard to overstate the significance of this cultural shift in agency. Rather than adopt the vernacular patterns of housing that evolved over time within "building cultures,"[67] as had 18th-century home-builders, or seek out the expertise of an architect, as did elites, middle-class North American consumers of the Jacksonian era and later demonstrated themselves to feel perfectly comfortable in making material and aesthetic choices on their own, without the "superior reasoning" of either tradition or architects to guide them. Contrary to the intention of early pattern-book authors, however, middle-class North Americans tended to mix and match from these early sources as they wished.

If we understand sumptuary codes of taste as those that are imposed from above, then it is appropriate to say they were weakened, or seriously challenged, in the Jacksonian era and after. This does not necessarily mean that judgments concerning individual distinctiveness disappeared, but that distinctiveness came to be judged by the popular standards unleashed, at least in part, by architects, beginning with Perrault, if not Palladio. The new standards did not derive from French or English interpretations of the neoclassical orders, but from the everyday experience of middle-class North Americans (Figure 6.14). Those experiences were not, however, what Asher Benjamin had in mind at the turn of the 19th century, when he argued for an empirical, or experience-based, foundation to North American professional knowledge. In our concluding chapter, we will argue that Benjamin's hope for the production of democratic professional knowledge has yet to be realized, but that our proposal for a system of sociotechnical codes and evidence-based design moves in that direction.

The argument that follows in the next section is that the reappearance of pattern books that promote traditional design aesthetics in the 20th century, which are self-consciously modeled on the works of Downing, and others,[68] is a middle-class response to the populist economics and bad taste of "consumerist architecture"[69] and the "commercial vernacular"[70] embraced by 20th-century citizens of modest means. No landscape embodies the rudeness of populist bad taste more than the sprawling subdivision (Figure 6.15).

Form-based Codes

In Chapter 3, we characterized New Urbanist FBCs as the attempt by late-20th-century architects to transform the regulation of urban forms and spaces from a disconnected and dysfunctional collection of prescriptive technical requirements to a unified approach for urban design based on spatial and formal quality. The appearance of FBCs, and the 20th- and 21st-century pattern books that illustrate them, however, is not an entirely new phenomenon. In our view, FBCs continue the legacy of sumptuary coding in general, and 19th-century pedagogical codes in particular. FBCs are a reaction to the increasingly commercial nature of North American populism, which enabled the "bad taste" embodied in the commercial landscapes of the late 20th century or the equally distasteful high-style works by "starchitects."[71]

As is the case with sumptuary codes in general, one reason for the reappearance of pedagogical pattern books is to recuperate, through the reeducation of middle-class decision-makers, lost conditions that presumably existed at a preferred moment in history. For the advocates of FBCs, that preferred moment is almost any time before the emergence of European modernism and the commercialization of the American landscape—a time in which there was, according to Witold Rybczynski, "a collective wisdom and a shared consensus about what constituted good architectural manners."[72] In a word, having "good architectural manners" is to have *convenance*, or what might be better described today as decorum.

"Form-based codes" is a term initially coined by Carol Wyant and has been generally accepted by members of the Congress for New Urbanism (CNU) as a suitable name, or descriptor, for their primary stylistic index.[73] It is fair to say that the activity of form-based code-making became, not only a professional service, but a significant social movement in North America sometime before the turn of the 21st century. By "social movement," we mean a constellation of individuals and organizations voicing collective claims against specific institutions.[74] In this case, the specific institutions being challenged are municipal code-makers. The organizations and individuals who affiliate

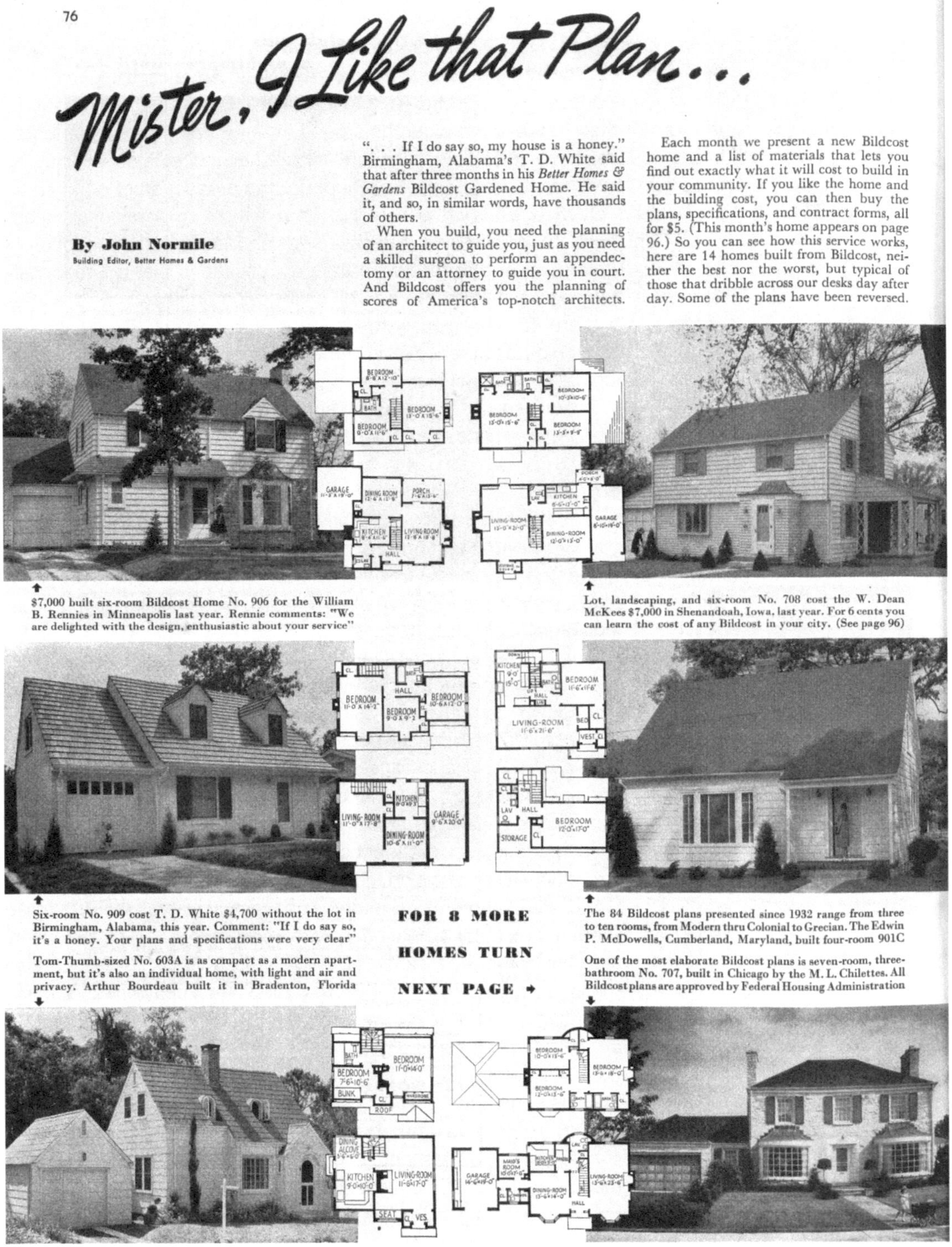

76

Mister, I Like that Plan...

By John Normile

Building Editor, Better Homes & Gardens

". . . If I do say so, my house is a honey." Birmingham, Alabama's T. D. White said that after three months in his *Better Homes & Gardens* Bildcost Gardened Home. He said it, and so, in similar words, have thousands of others.

When you build, you need the planning of an architect to guide you, just as you need a skilled surgeon to perform an appendectomy or an attorney to guide you in court. And Bildcost offers you the planning of scores of America's top-notch architects.

Each month we present a new Bildcost home and a list of materials that lets you find out exactly what it will cost to build in your community. If you like the home and the building cost, you can then buy the plans, specifications, and contract forms, all for $5. (This month's home appears on page 96.) So you can see how this service works, here are 14 homes built from Bildcost, neither the best nor the worst, but typical of those that dribble across our desks day after day. Some of the plans have been reversed.

$7,000 built six-room Bildcost Home No. 906 for the William B. Rennies in Minneapolis last year. Rennie comments: "We are delighted with the design, enthusiastic about your service"

Lot, landscaping, and six-room No. 708 cost the W. Dean McKees $7,000 in Shenandoah, Iowa, last year. For 6 cents you can learn the cost of any Bildcost in your city. (See page 96)

Six-room No. 909 cost T. D. White $4,700 without the lot in Birmingham, Alabama, this year. Comment: "If I do say so, it's a honey. Your plans and specifications were very clear"

Tom-Thumb-sized No. 603A is as compact as a modern apartment, but it's also an individual home, with light and air and privacy. Arthur Bourdeau built it in Bradenton, Florida

FOR 8 MORE HOMES TURN NEXT PAGE →

The 84 Bildcost plans presented since 1932 range from three to ten rooms, from Modern thru Colonial to Grecian. The Edwin P. McDowells, Cumberland, Maryland, built four-room 901C

One of the most elaborate Bildcost plans is seven-room, three-bathroom No. 707, built in Chicago by the M. L. Chilettes. All Bildcost plans are approved by Federal Housing Administration

Figure 6.14 Normile, John. "Mister, I Like that Plan." In *Better Homes & Gardens*. 1940. December:76. At this time, *Better Homes & Gardens* was still offering architect-designed *Buildcost Homes*. Each month, a new model and a new architect were introduced, along with a complete bill of materials for local estimating.

Figure 6.15 "Ready. Set. Design." The Exercise of Popular Taste. 2012. In a contemporary web-based advertisement, Meritage Homes tells viewers "Choices for flooring can be vast, but your tastes, lifestyle and budget will help narrow them down."

themselves with the FBC movement include, not only professional architects, urban designers, and planners, but also developers, activists, contractors, public policymakers, and ordinary citizens.

As in any social movement, however, the advocates of FBCs are not a monolithic group. Some explicitly see themselves as inheritors and revivalists of the long tradition of classically inspired coding that begins with Vitruvius (1st century), and includes Alberti (15th century), Serlio (16th century), Palladio (16th century), as well as the French architects mentioned above—Perrault and Boffrand (18th century)—not to mention the American pattern-book makers—Benjamin and Downing (19th century).[75] This first group of FBC advocates—we will call them social conservatives—generally continues the project of sumptuary coding, which is to develop *tasteful places*. By this term, we mean places that stimulate consumptive behavior of a preferred kind—fashionable shopping districts, gated communities, and second-home communities.[76] In contrast, other advocates of FBCs—we will call them social progressives—see themselves as reformers of the "public realm" and as self-conscious advocates for greater public participation in decision-making.[77] The mission of this second group is directed more to the future, rather than to the recuperation of past social orders, through the will, as Talen puts it, to "substitute something for a consensus about urban form that no longer exists."[78]

In this evolutionary context, it is historically important to recognize that the movement as a whole was initially conceived in the 1970s as "neo-traditional town planning," before it became known as "the New Urbanism" in the 1990s, or FBCs after 2000 (Figure 6.16). These name changes are significant, because they provide an index of how movement participants have chosen to identify themselves within the larger society of which they are a part, and to change that identity as the movement has evolved. It would be surprising at this stage of evolution for the movement to suddenly ossify.

Figure 6.16 Duany Plater-Zyberk & Co. Form-Based Code for Middleton Hills, WI. For the advocates of FBC, good taste is neither crassly commercial nor high style.

In the final section of this chapter, we argue that the further evolution of FBCs is already happening through the integration of competing frames.[79] CNU co-founder Duany has himself recognized the convergence of FBCs with environmental concerns, even if he is unclear about which discourse will dominate the merger.[80]

POSSIBILITIES FOR INTEGRATING FRAMES

In Chapter 4, we reviewed the concept of "frame analysis" as an action-oriented method of investigation that might contribute to making desirable social and technological change. We now return to that proposal in the more concrete context of sumptuary codes. At the beginning of this chapter, we distinguished between the dominant tradition of sumptuary coding, which is to render class distinctions legible for political purposes, and three minor traditions that developed to regulate consumption. Our closing argument is that sumptuary codes in general, and FBCs in particular, might become, not only more just, but also more effective, by first uncoupling historic links (conscious or unconscious) to class favoritism, and, second, reclaiming two of the three minor traditions that are part of their history—the protection of local economies and the conservation of community resources. Above, we argued that archaic sumptuary codes distinguished elites on the basis of birth and maintained their distinction by celebrating practices of maximized consumption to the *detriment* of the community.[81] Here, we will argue that contemporary sumptuary codes might distinguish citizens on the basis of their reasoning and maintain their distinction by celebrating practices of minimized consumption to the *benefit* of the community. The variables remain the same, but the reason for distinguishing individuals is reversed. The contemporary case of the San Antonio Water System illustrates this possibility.

Over the past several decades, the City of San Antonio, Texas, has experienced several periods of serious water shortage that have threatened both the security of citizens and the economic growth of the region. As a partial response, in October of 2010, the city implemented a steeply graduated water-rate plan to significantly raise water costs for over-consumers. Perhaps equally significant is that a front-page newspaper article announcing implementation of the plan identified, using clearly delineated maps, areas where water consumption was high for the previous year. In other words, public officials used the negative technique of *public shaming* to identify those citizens who wasted a scarce community resource. More positively, the front-page article also provided profiles of three "smart consumers," along with details about how they conserve water, thereby distinguishing them among their peers. In the context of this public conversation, being "smart" is not associated with either "going without" (being poor) or class privilege (being rich enough to waste resources and money). Rather, being smart is associated with reasoning and action that benefits oneself *and* the community.

San Antonio's water-rate system is, then, both a sumptuary and sociotechnical code that has reframed water conservation as a distinguishing practice in the community. Although this single sociotechnical code will not solve San Antonio's substantial water problem, it is an incremental step that will help to secure the regional economy and conserve essential community resources. The implications for landscape and architectural design, as in Figure 6.17, are significant. We mean by this that designs that incorporate changed social habits related to gardening (in lieu of lawn maintenance) and water harvesting (in lieu of turning on the faucet) have far more substantial implications for socially constructing life-enhancing places than the abstract content of historic forms that the advocates of structuralism in design imagine to be universal.

Figure 6.17 San Antonio Xeriscape and Water Catchment System. Brackenridge Park, parking structure; Lake/Flato Architects. In projects such as this one, conservation, rather than consumption, has become a source of expression.

We are sure that it is not lost on the reader that these two practices—protecting local economies and conserving community resources—are synonymous with the practices of sustainable design and development. There is, then, the opportunity for the advocates of both movements— FBCs and sustainable development—to expand their influence by integrating frames, as suggested in Chapter 4. Although there is some history of antagonism by FBC advocates toward environmental concerns,[82] just as environmentalists have criticized FBCs,[83] the appearance of new books such as that by Douglas Farr[84] and projects such as High Point in Seattle,[85] which marry both sets of values, is a very encouraging sign that code integration is already happening. In sum, the characteristics of sumptuary codes are abbreviated in Table 6.1.

Table 6.1 Characteristics of sumptuary codes

	Sumptuary codes
Strategy	Restricting or enhancing consumption
Exemplar artifact	Pattern book, magazines, and catalogs
Exemplar space	Rodeo Drive
Exemplar consequence	Seeking distinction in society is historically associated with high-entropy consumption, but it might be reframed as related to low-entropy consumption
Frame	Hierarchical
How they work	By catalyzing behavior appropriate to one's social rank
Type of authority	Aristocratic
Location of authority	Dominant classes

We conclude this chapter by arguing that archaic sumptuary codes, designed to restrict or enhance consumption by some members of society, have evolved to be more just, if not yet fully democratic. The key to catalyzing the evolution of these codes will be to better understand the social psychology through which individuals and social groups are distinguished in society in positive, life-enhancing, and low-entropy ways, rather than through negative, life-diminishing, and high-entropy ones. It is not likely or desirable that we will rid society of "good taste," because that is one way by which modern people distinguish and delight each other. It is, however, desirable that we reframe good taste and self-expression, not through hereditary privilege or manipulation by the market, but through collective rational judgment, first exercised in the era of Enlightenment by Perrault and others. Contemporary collective reasoning, however, will necessarily link social order to ecological order so as to sustain the community as a whole.[86] Through our analysis of sumptuary codes, we foresee a storyline in which sumptuary codes might also become sociotechnical ones. However, before we can construct that possibility, it is necessary to first reconstruct the development of economic codes in the next chapter.

Chapter 7

Economic Codes and the Civic Economy

> In proposing the co-construction of technology and modernity . . . we emphatically reject the idea that either technology or modernity alone can be used as a template to "explain" each other.[1]
>
> (T.J. Misa, Philip Brey, and Andrew Feenberg, 2003)

In arguing that "technology and modernity" are "co-constructed," Misa et al. emphasize that being "co-constructed" does not mean that one phenomenon explains or is caused by the other. Rather, the authors hold that the phenomena emerged at about the same time and in response to the same evolving social values and material conditions. We add to this pair of variables the emergence of capitalism. Our point in making this observation is not to dive deeply into modernization theory, but to argue that modernity, technology, and capitalism are three basic dimensions of contemporary Western culture that cannot be comfortably separated—they have all been "co-constructed" over several centuries by humans in pursuit of their own interests. However, as "critical constructivists,"[2] Misa et al. would not hold that these three variables are constant across cultures or time, only that they are particularly important in Western culture, from the Renaissance onward. There is nothing inevitable or unchanging about them—history might have been different than we know it.

In this chapter, we examine what we refer to as *economic codes* as formal constructs that have emerged along with modernity, technology, and capitalism. Economic codes derive from what Jeremy Bentham referred to as *civic economy*. By this term, he distinguished between the particular rights of entrepreneurs and the general right of the community as they depended on economic growth and stability. For example, an individual mill owner might become very rich by employing children to operate looms, but the general health and welfare of workers as a class of people might be jeopardized by the practice, thus weakening the economy as a whole. A related argument in favor of Bentham's proposal is the recognition (very unpopular at the time) that preventative care for the poor would benefit society as a whole.[3]

We find that economic codes have two primary characteristics that derive from utilitarian thinking: First, they regulate artifacts and spaces primarily to enhance what code-makers, both private and public, perceive and determine to be the common good. The central element of advancing the common good in a capitalist market economy is to create codes and standards that foster economic growth and profitability.[4] This should not suggest that social groups other than private-sector code-makers themselves do not also benefit economically. As we argued in Chapter 3, in the United States, private code-makers from industry (under the umbrella of ANSI) have been legitimated by Congress to act as managers of the common good. At the very least, the public benefits from economic stability. At best, it benefits from improved health, safety, and welfare.

Second, the economic interests of code-makers coevolve with modernity, technology, and capitalism. Economic codes are inherently modern because they are tied to modern notions of efficiency, and they are inherently capitalist because they are tied to modern notions of profit and entrepreneurial risk. Economic codes are, then, those that are inherently linked to, and co-constructed with, the concepts of efficiency, risk, and profit, as well as the civic economy. Economic codes optimize efficiency and profit, minimize risk, and promote the civic economy.

Tacit and sumptuary codes, which we investigated in the two previous chapters, employ a single strategy to develop and enforce evolving social values. Economic codes, however, employ three distinct strategies: *prescription*, *incentive*, and *performance*. We will examine each of these strategies in turn.

PRESCRIPTIVE ECONOMIC CODES

Prescriptive codes are those that lay down exact specifications for making a class of artifacts or spaces. In the case of artifacts, codes that regulate construction materials, as well as plumbing, mechanical, or electrical systems, in buildings are typical examples. Examined in detail, prescriptive codes are themselves of two kinds: First are those that derive directly from civic economy as we defined that term above, and second are those that seek to establish universal standards.

Civic Economy

The concept of *civic economy* is an attempt to balance the particular interests of capitalists with the general interests of the economy as a whole. In the hands of Bentham's principal assistant, Edwin Chadwick, these insights were the basis for proposing the first general building code for Britain. A good historical example that employs utilitarian reasoning concerning artifacts is legislation that denied London citizens the right to build thatched roofs on their homes and thus prevented, at least in theory, another Great Fire like that of 1666.

With regard to space, the contemporary civic economy can be said to be also served by regulation of *floor area ratios* (FARs)—a concept we also discussed in Chapter 3. Such regulations limit the volume of building that can be placed on any property in a particular zone and thus mold urban space, control access to sunlight, and mediate scale in relation to other buildings and shade on adjacent spaces and buildings. A FAR of 3.0, for example, would allow three times as much building floor area as the property area and thus allow a multistory building. Typically, height limits and set-back requirements are also used to further regulate the mass of what might be built and the urban spaces

Figure 7.1 *The Great Fire of London*, depicting September 2–5, 1666. Author unknown. Codes regulating construction methods commonly derive from catastrophic events.

that result. In this way, massing, zoning, and other codes serve to assure the owners of adjacent properties that their investment is (relatively) safe from being devalued by incompatible uses.

A very interesting, if ironic, case of such prescriptive coding is the Miami Beach mixed-use project designed by Herzog and de Meuron at 1111 Lincoln Road, which was completed in 2010. In Miami Beach and elsewhere, FAR ordinances limit building mass of various building types, but not that of the parking garages required by code to serve them. The assumption of code-makers is that the two "programs" would be separate structures, and that it is the number of cars parked that is important, not the mass necessary to house them. To take creative advantage of this prescriptive code, the architects wove parking together with high-end retail venues on six floors, thus creating a new building type—one described by a member of the design team as "a merger of architecture and infrastructure."[5] The resulting ramp-like collection of shops is used by runners, bikers, as well as shoppers, as an urban auto-oriented park.

What is to be learned from this case is that urban planners presumed that they could limit the amount of retail space that could be built on the site by prescribing limits to land use, mass, and height, assuming a conventional relationship of retail to parking. What happened, however, is that the architects had the intellectual capacity to reframe the letter of the law in a way that

code-makers couldn't, thus gaining the developer, not only more retail space, but a novel and marketable experience for shoppers and pedestrians alike.[6]

A generalizable lesson drawn from this case is that prescriptive codes, more than other code types, invite subversive and/or creative interpretation—code-makers and code-users forever embrace in a technological tango that, in part, determines the form and use of buildings and urban space. In the place of this ironic and life-enhancing example, there are millions that creatively subvert the intentions of code-makers in very destructive ways. If the intent of codes is to enhance the civic economy, prescription is a well-intended but unreliable method.

Figure 7.2 1111 Lincoln Road, Miami Beach, FL. Herzog and de Meuron Architects. Although prescriptive codes attempt to limit design choices, they are vulnerable to creative subversion.

Universal Standards

In Chapter 3, we reviewed the political process through which standards for spaces and materials were established in the United States. Here, we argue that, once universal standards were finally implemented, they should be understood not only as a technological issue, but also as a way to amplify the exchange value of what is regulated. For example, it is easy to understand that economic exchanges are made more quickly and more efficiently when a pound of 16 penny framing nails are made the same size, weight, and strength in Chicago as in New York. Without a common standard, the established habits of wood-frame construction in one city would have to be laboriously reconsidered with each purchase of material from the other. Carpenters would have to calculate how many nails at what spacing are required to hold a 2 × 4 safely in place, rather than assemble a frame using only tacit knowledge.

Building contractors typically argue that it is clearly in the economic interest of the nation as a whole to prescribe building product specifications to

Figure 7.3 Nails, Knives, and Miscellaneous Relics, Published 1898 [1946]. The standardization of nail shapes, sizes, and head types is linked to the standardization of lumber and the human practice of carpentry.

protect home buyers from shoddy construction practices. However, it is also clear that building contractors may benefit as much or more than homeowners, because product standardization allows contractors to practice their craft over a greater area, thus increasing competition and, at least through the lenses of neoclassical economic theory, reducing costs to homeowners and enhancing profits for contractors.

In the case of standards for spaces, the NFPA's Life Safety Code provides relevant examples of prescriptive codes that standardize spaces. Based on historical and empirical evidence derived from catastrophic events, NFPA specifies that corridors in specific building types—homes, schools, offices, or stadia—based on estimated "occupant loads," must have minimum widths to ensure that, in the event of a fire, occupants can exit safely. Such basic safety standards are fundamental to the concern for citizens in a democratic society. However, although citizens certainly benefit from codes when catastrophic events occur, insurance companies, attorneys, banks, and the construction industry also benefit every day from such regulation. They do so by establishing, along with government, limits to the economic risk inherent in building public structures. Without such regulation, the potential risk of various kinds of litigation would be too great. Our point is not that a minimum 6 foot 0 inches corridor width in an elementary school creates certainty that no children will die in a fire, but that this spatial code establishes precedent for accountability and enough contract certainty that, if the prescription is followed, architects and contractors cannot be sued when children do tragically die from fire.

Both kinds of prescriptive economic code—those that seek civic economy and those that seek universal standards—see the built environment as an assembly of technological objects and spaces in which the relationship

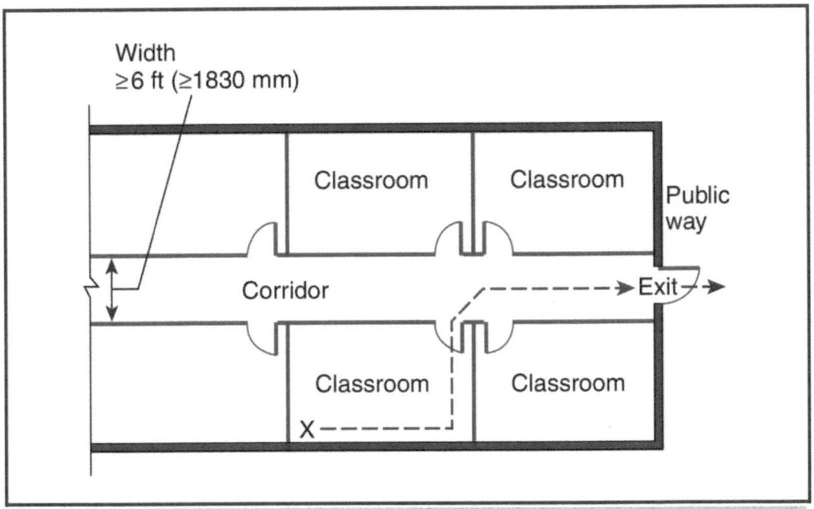

Exit door width and corridor width relationship. Because operational features of the occupancy, in addition to the occupant load, are considered in determining required corridor width, the corridor may be wider than the exit door serving the corridor. In this example of a new school, the corridor is required by 10-2.3.2.1 to be 6 ft (1.8 m) wide as a minimum, and wider only if it serves more than 360 persons. The exit door is required by 5-2.1.2.2 to be 32 in. (81 cm) wide as a minimum, and wider only if it serves more than 160 persons.

Figure 7.4 National Fire Protection Association Specification for Corridors in Schools. The NFPA standard for a minimum corridor width of 6 feet in elementary schools established not only a reasonable degree of safety for children, but also a standard of liability in the market.

between humans and their environment is ordered at a distance, by experts. Understood in this way, code-makers assume that their own agency can be transferred to nails, roofing materials, corridors, or parking garages—that is, regulated artifacts and spaces can act in the place of code-makers themselves. The social values of code-makers—their "scripts"—are then "transcribed, inscribed, or encoded" into the technical artifact or space.[7]

The principal problem with prescriptive codes is, however, that code-makers—perhaps owing to their training—tend to be unaware of the complexity of the systems they hope to regulate. Simply put, prescriptive codes tend to have unintended consequences. In his study of the door closer, for example, Latour notes the subsequent production by room inhabitants of wood wedges to keep doors open and thus subvert the fire marshall's intention. Similar observation can be made about increasing requirement for minimum volumes of fresh air in school classrooms after the first oil embargo of the 1970s. Introducing fresh air in cold climates also meant increasing fuel consumption to heat the air, and so industrious building managers took it upon themselves to block air intake louvers, which, in turn, precipitated degraded air quality and a large number of unhealthy buildings, sick children, and related lawsuits. There is, then, a frequent gap between the intentions of code-makers and the consequences of codes, because the social and environmental components of systems are poorly understood by regulators.

Prescriptive codes work, of course, only if there is an authority behind them as pervasive and relentless as the mechanical door closer. At the scale of the city or nation, it takes a highly centralized "command-and-control" form of government, like the one advocated by Chadwick and the utilitarians, to maintain standards upon which the civic economy depends. However, just as Bentham's 19th-century contemporaries saw prescriptive codes as overly invasive, so do 21st-century anti-federalists. It is not only political conservatives who are skeptical of the effectiveness of prescriptive codes, but also those progressives such as Jane Jacobs and Lewis Mumford who objected, for example, to the categorical rigidity of single-use zoning in modern cities. Jacobs, in particular, criticized technocratic zoning of her beloved New York as an authoritative practice akin to "placing a grid over this profusion of unknowable possibilities."[8] Contemporary conservatives object to the intrusion of prescriptive codes on principle, because they retard innovation by individuals, but progressives also object to them when they lack responsiveness to context.

Prescription, then, is not always the tool of totalitarian states attempting to order an unwilling populace. As we discussed in Chapter 3, in the first era of standardization in North America (1900–1930), many manufacturing groups came to exist (under the umbrella of what is now ANSI) with the sole purpose of standardizing their own products so as to avoid standardization by government, but also to market their products more widely. The American Institute of Steel Construction (AISC), organized in 1921 with a mission to "make structural steel the material of choice,"[9] is a good example of this practice. Prescriptive codes can, then, be self-imposed and enforced as an offensive strategy to gain new territory, or a defensive strategy against "outside" control.

In general, we can best describe the kind of authority required to legislatively prescribe the characteristics of artifacts and spaces as *technocratic*. In a technocracy, power is gained by individuals with specific training to solve a particular class of problem. In the United States, material code-making is, at best, quasi-democratic. Although the process is officially open to public comment, it is practically dominated by technocrats from industry.[10] It is certainly true that the empirical process of refining codes over time does improve them from a purely technological perspective. It is also probably true that most material code-makers see themselves as managers of the public health, safety, and welfare. It is unlikely, however, that the existing system of prescribing material standards will quickly become fully democratic, because it is unlikely that prescriptive code-makers will promote beneficial technological change on their own.[11] As an example of the worst case, Mussolini gained popular support by "making the trains run on time." However, as we will see in Chapter 10, technocratic code-making also has a long history in North America, particularly in southern cities such as Austin, Texas, where citizens adopted a city-manager form of municipal government in order to, in their view, depoliticize technological choices.

Locating technocratic authority should, one would think, be an easy matter of opening the code book and reading the names of the authors and publishers. In reality, however, it is far more complex, because technocratic authority is a tacit as well as explicit part of our culture.[12] As we argued in Chapter 3, code-making has become a complex enterprise that involves, not only NIST and ANSI, but also international economic interest groups (corporations), federal agencies, state legislatures, municipal governments, and increasingly the banks, insurance companies, and mortgage lenders that prescribe various conditions.[13] In general, all of these groups work in concert to advance global efficiency, reduce economic risks, and maximize profits. On the other hand, prescriptive codes do provide consistency and reliability, without which society could not function equitably. Table 7.1 summarizes the social values inscribed in prescriptive economic codes.

INCENTIVE-BASED ECONOMIC CODES

In lieu of perennially unpopular prescriptive strategies to develop and enforce economic codes, North American and EU regulators of all kinds have increasingly adopted a second strategy—*incentive*. The most common example of incentive coding is for municipal governments to offer real-estate developers a "density bonus" if they will also include in their projects facilities such as public parks, which the city has no funds to build, but for which there is popular demand. This is an economic trade-off that has two sides: On the one hand, the developer can construct a building taller than the previously legislated limit and, thus, improve efficiency and profit by creating additional salable or rentable space on a fixed area of property. On the other hand, citizens get a public space, but one that is more crowded and has diminished sunlight. Figure 7.5 illustrates a case in Manchester, UK, where developers were given a very large density bonus adjacent to an architecturally significant historic district—a trade-off that is generally very unpopular in the city. In the UK, as in the US, it is mostly left to the market, not to communities, to decide if the trade-off of commodities is commensurate.

A second type of economic incentive strategy works in reverse. Many cities have constructed significant infrastructure and/or public spaces in order to increase adjacent land values and thus attract developer-funded projects of a desired type. One much emulated project is the River Walk in San Antonio, Texas. Initially conceived in the 1920s and 1930s, this project has been so successful that a second phase, begun in 2008, has extended the River Walk pedestrian space, thus stimulating significant private development and correspondingly increasing municipal property tax revenues.

Table 7.1 Characteristics of prescription-based economic codes

Economic codes	
Strategy	Prescription
Exemplar artifact	Nails
Exemplar space	Building corridor width
Exemplar consequence	System complexity is misunderstood, which leads to unintended consequences
Frame	Command and control or self-regulation
How they work	By relocating human agency
Types of authority	Technocratic
Location of authority	Industry, as well as international, federal, state, and local authorities

Figure 7.5 The Beetham Hilton Tower, Manchester, UK. Ian Simpson Architects. Although this section of Manchester has been nominated as a World Heritage Site, municipal government provided economic incentives to construct one of the tallest residential buildings in Europe here.

Figure 7.6 The River Walk in San Antonio, Texas. On left, February 1966, downstream from Jones Street Bridge. On right, November 2012. The River Walk is one example of municipal investment that stimulates desired private investment.

The frame of interpretation that defines the relationship between cities and developers in both incentive-based examples is *entrepreneurial*. In the first example of Manchester, developers accepted all the economic risks inherent in realizing this large, complex project. However, just as the developers of Beetham Hilton Tower accepted all of the economic risks, a few elected officials symmetrically accepted all the political risks inherent in trading social "goods" and "bads." An oft-cited problem with this model is that such an arrangement too often ends up shifting environmental risks and social "bads" to those underrepresented groups not present at the negotiating table.[14] In the second case of San Antonio, the city did take on economic risks by first creating the political will to realize the project in the interest of citizens. That investment paid off by giving the city far more control in attracting the kind of development preferred by citizens. Both developers and municipalities are rewarded (or punished) in proportion to the risks they take.

The kind of authority required to keep the deal-making in operation at city hall is, of course, the form of liberal–capitalist governance North Americans in particular have embraced. Another problem with this arrangement has been best described by "regime theorists," who have empirically documented how the mutual economic interests of municipal officials and real-estate development can work against the interests of citizens.[15] Particularly in North American cities, such as those in Texas and New Hampshire, that are entirely dependent on property taxes to fund city services, the problem is acute. Without encouraging new development that is profitable to developers, municipalities cannot collect enough tax revenue to provide services to citizens. The only alternative would be to raise taxes, which is anathema to contemporary officials who are popularly elected. The kind of authority required to employ incentive-based codes is a capitalistic form of democracy in which the environmental and political interests of citizens take a backseat to abstract economic growth.

Locating incentive-based codes has historically been easier than locating prescriptive economic codes, at least in the United States. This is because most of the deal-making has gone on at city hall. Increasingly, however, incentive-based codes are created by insurance companies that will, for example, lower your homeowners' insurance policy premium if you install a residential sprinkler system, or raise it if you don't. The situation is made more

Table 7.2 Characteristics of incentive-based economic codes

Economic codes	
Strategy	Incentive
Exemplar artifact	Beetham Hilton Tower, Manchester, UK
Exemplar space	River Walk, San Antonio, Texas
Exemplar consequence	Trade-offs of public and private goods
Frame	Entrepreneurial
How they work	By rewarding risk-takers
Types of authority	Capitalistic
Location of authority	Municipal

complex by the fact that, in the United States, land-use regulation varies by state, but, after 1926, it is generally controlled by municipal governments.[16]

In sum, the social values that characterize incentive-based economic codes are as illustrated in Table 7.2. Although incentive-based codes have been used productively in unique contexts, it is difficult to understand them as "durable" codes rather than "fiscal maneuvers." Economist Michael Oden, for example, sees incentive economic codes "as symptomatic of a decline in civic solidarity, responsibility, and the public sector."[17]

PERFORMANCE-BASED ECONOMIC CODES

The third and increasingly popular strategy employed in constructing and enforcing economic codes is a *performance*-based strategy.[18] Rather than prescribe the exact size, shape, and technical qualities of artifacts or spaces that can be made, or introduce economic incentives designed to attract those qualities, performance-based codes specify only the outcomes to be achieved—*if* they meet or exceed basic prescriptions.[19] Although it is tempting to imagine that performance-based codes are a recent innovation tied to the development of capitalism, they were used as early as the 5th century AD by Julian of Ascalon in his planning treatise for Byzantine Palestine.[20] The frame of interpretation that relates designers, owners, and builders to authorities in this strategic scenario is what we call *consequential*, and, to make this relationship more concrete, we will use as an example the design of the Genzyme corporate headquarters in Cambridge, Massachusetts, designed by Behnisch Architekten of Stuttgart, which was completed in 2007.[21]

Fire protection codes for office buildings focus a great deal of attention on the evacuation of smoke from corridors and stairs, because more deaths are caused by smoke inhalation than by the fire itself. In this context, the Genzyme building presented a particularly difficult challenge, because its design included a large interior atrium that, left unventilated in the event of fire, would surely contribute to the loss of life. This case is of interest to us because, rather than follow prescriptive codes on how to design office atriums, the design team (which included Buro Happold engineers and climate engineer Matthias Schuler) asked city officials to consider an alternative design that would prove, they argued, not only more beautiful and more energy efficient, but also less costly.[22]

The design team's claim is illustrated in Figure 7.7—the central atrium is an irregular void that jogs through 12 floors of the building and is accentuated by floating interior gardens. The atrium is, in effect, a massive light well that draws natural light from seven rooftop heliostats that track the sun and redirect it to opposing mirrors. The light is then diffused through a filter of prismatic louvers and drawn down into interior work spaces, with the help of a 10-story chandelier made of thousands of mirrors. This "light enhancement system" was designed in collaboration with Austrian lighting consultants Bartenbach Lichtlabor and allows for 75 percent of work spaces to receive natural light.[23] In addition to radically reducing the need for artificial lighting in work spaces, the atrium also functions as a heat reclamation system in winter and a solar chimney in summer.

As is the case increasingly in cities with sophisticated engineering staff of their own, Cambridge code officials had the authority, through adoption of the International Building Code (IBC),[24] to accept the performance-based alternative to prescribed standards, on the condition that the designers' computer simulations of smoke evacuation would be physically tested in the completed building before an occupancy permit would be issued. In fact, the completed building exceeded fire code requirements and ultimately received the first LEED Platinum rating issued by the U.S. Green Building Council (USGBC). This case illustrates that the consequentialist frame embraced by the owner, designers, contractors, and city officials was successful because it rewarded the creativity and experimental thinking of all parties involved.[25] The members of the design team are quick to point out that their experience in the design of this project was a highly collaborative one that was as much about the research of sustainable technologies appropriate to a particular climate and cultural context as it was about architectural space and aesthetic experience.[26]

There are two related arguments that are helpful in interpreting the Genzyme case—one regarding *context-based learning*, and the other regarding *collaborative learning*. With regard to context, Dewey argued that, "analysis is but a process of abstraction, leaving us . . . know[ing] almost nothing about the actual activities and processes."[27] In this passage, the emphasis is on "the actual activities and processes" that take place in Cambridge, Massachusetts. This suggests that designers should not separate analysis of abstract phenomena such as smoke evacuation—calculated in cubic feet per minute—from the local, historical, and social context of judging what is equal or superior to the universal prescriptive standard. In concrete terms, this means that the local fire marshall judged the design proposal submitted by the design team, not only on the basis of the abstract engineering principles spelled out in the IBC, but also on the basis of her long experience with, and understanding of, the capacity of city fire fighters, inspectors, and building managers. Her concerns were not only theoretical, but also practical and contextual. Useful knowledge is, then, "context rich."[28] From within this frame of interpretation, knowledge that isn't useful in a particular situation is, for the city fire marshall and others, not knowledge at all.

Regarding collaborative learning, Dewey held that *successful* inquiry is most often experimental and takes place within a community, rather than in the isolation of the scientist's laboratory or architect's studio.[29] By community, he intended any group of people involved in solving mutual problems, which

Figure 7.7 Genzyme Headquarters, Cambridge, MA. Behnisch Architekten. The ability to use a performance-based code, in lieu of the standard prescriptive code, allowed the architects to make significant design innovations.

inevitably include real-world economic constraint. That definition would include all those engaged in the design, construction, regulation, operation, and management of the Genzyme offices. Although Behnisch Architekten are regarded as the designers of the project, by the architects' own reflection, they were but one party in a community of learners.[30] For our purposes in this book, we have found that, "norms emerge as the *by-products* of experimental inquiry."[31] Not only do participants in the community of learners come away with new knowledge, but successful experimentation by one community influences the experiments conducted by others. The recognition of the project granted by the USGBC and other influential groups made the building a new norm to be emulated by practitioners elsewhere. The collective learning about performance-based codes that *took place* in Cambridge is already changing our building culture as a whole, and for the better.

Performance-based codes are not, however, a panacea—there are two significant problems in determining exactly how judgment about alternative processes is to be made and by whom. First, in the case of Genzyme, the corporation was in an economic position to risk having the design team spend a great deal of time investigating alternative designs and technologies. In Cambridge, as in most cities, it is the applicant who is responsible for providing engineering proof that the proposed alternative is equal or superior to the prescribed norm. This process can be very expensive.[32] Such expense makes the use of performance-based alternatives virtually impossible for citizens of modest means. The same logic applies to small cities of modest means that do not have the personnel or expertise to even consider performance-based alternatives. There is, then, an inherent injustice in how code-makers and cities have implemented the performance-based strategy. As an abstract idea, it has great potential, but its implementation is antithetical to the possibilities found in context-based and collaborative learning.

The second problem inherent in performance-based codes derives from the first. Our current system of judging alternative technologies or spatial configurations relies entirely on negotiation between credentialed experts. Although many argue that this process is only prudent, it also privileges expert knowledge over the local knowledge embedded in communities. In *The Public and its Problems*, Dewey argues that, "A class of experts is inevitably so removed from common interests as to become a class with private interests and private knowledge, which in social matters is not knowledge at all."[33] If citizens of modest means are effectively excluded from proposing and/or employing performance-based technological or spatial alternatives, and experts are oblivious to actual conditions, the likelihood that genuinely new knowledge will be produced is significantly diminished.[34]

One possible "work-around" for both of these problems is found in the format of "community benefit agreements." These relatively new tools have been pioneered by the Partnership for Working Families and is best understood as an enforceable contract between groups who have competing interests in a particular project—developers, owners, environmentalists, environmental justice advocates, abutters, community groups, etc. Through a formal negotiating process, interested groups may negotiate, not only design, but also performance criteria that are measured pre- and post-development. Should

Table 7.3 Characteristics of performance-based economic codes

Economic codes	
Strategy	Performance
Exemplar artifact	Genzyme Corporate Headquarters, Cambridge, MA
Exemplar space	Genzyme atrium
Exemplar consequence	Creative problem-solving that is inequitably distributed
Frame	Consequential
How they work	By rewarding creativity
Types of authority	Pragmatic
Location of authority	Municipal

performance fail to meet negotiated levels, the owner is required to comply. This tool provides protection against the empty promises of dishonest developers and encourages social leaning by all parties.[35] Although it is not a tool appropriate for all cases, because it is site-specific and can be expensive, it is a civil society strategy that anticipates the certification movement discussed in Chapter 11.

The type of authority required to make and enforce performance-based codes is *pragmatic*, and such authority is necessarily local enough to participate directly in judgment about public matters. There are, however, significant problems in how cities implement their potential. On the basis of this analysis, we can characterize performance-based economic codes as illustrated in Table 7.3.

At the onset of this chapter, we argued that economic codes have been co-constructed by humans in pursuit of their own interests, as technology, capitalism, and modernity itself have emerged in Western societies. In sum, we now argue that the strategies of prescription, incentive-, and performance-based assessment are all in service to the economic advancement of both code-makers and those they presume to manage. In our investigation, we did find that most people resent prescriptive codes, because they leave no alternative for creative action and assume that builders at any scale are incapable of sound judgment. We also found that most people favor those incentive codes that serve their own interests. People tend to resent, however, those incentive codes that favor only the interests of others. And, with regard to performance codes, we found that nearly all the people we interviewed favored this strategy, except those who are economically excluded from participation. Anti-federalists favor performance codes because individual human creativity and entrepreneurship are rewarded. Federalists favor them because experimental communities can be built through the process of local, collaborative problem-solving. However, we also found that people of all persuasions tend to think of economic codes in the narrow contexts of efficiency, risk, and profit. Turning this finding on its head is to say that very few people are able to recognize economically based codes as socially constructed norms that embody changing social values.

Economic codes in general can be characterized as illustrated in Table 7.4.

Table 7.4 Characteristics of economic codes

Economic codes	*Strategy*		
	Prescription	*Incentive*	*Performance*
Exemplar artifact	Nails	Beetham Hilton Tower, Manchester, UK	Genzyme Corporate Headquarters, Cambridge, MA
Exemplar space	Building corridor or room	River Walk, San Antonio, TX	Genzyme atrium
Exemplar consequence	System complexity is misunderstood, which leads to unintended consequences	Trade-offs of public and private goods	Creative problem-solving inequitably distributed
Frame	Command and control	Entrepreneurial	Consequential
How they work	By relocating human agency	By rewarding risk-takers	By rewarding creativity
Type of authority	Technocratic	Capitalistic	Pragmatic
Location of authority	International, federal, state, and local authorities	Municipal	Municipal

This partial taxonomy is helpful only to the degree that it aids us in recognizing the ideal types of economic code that exist. In practice, ideal types are always muddied by local contexts and generally fused together as hybrids. These ideal types do, however, help us to understand the opportunities for, and obstacles to, judging architecture that we introduced in Part One. The taxonomy also sets up the introduction to the fourth ideal type, *sociotechnical* codes, which are the topic of Part Three.

Part Three

Sociotechnical Codes as Both an Index and a Tool of Change

Introduction

In our General Introduction, we briefly defined "sociotechnical codes" as those that self-consciously seek to make simultaneous and symbiotic changes in both the technical and social realms. This is to say that sociotechnical code-makers understand that any technical code *also* has social as well as environmental consequences, whether we intend them or not. If we accept the empirical evidence in support of this claim, it suggests that code-makers should design codes to have technical as well as desirable social and ecological impacts. It also suggests that citizens should hold them accountable to do so.

In our introduction to Part Two, we further argued that all technical codes are both an index of social change and a method of enforcing such change. This is to say that, even when code-makers have no intention of making social policy, they do so inadvertently, because technologies are always linked to social practices in ways that are sometimes subtle but at other times blatant. In this context, our examination of *tacit*, *sumptuary*, and *economic* codes in Part Two of the book demonstrated how all technological codes must be understood as sociotechnical systems. In our investigation of prescriptive economic codes, for example, we argued that the manufacture of standard nail sizes transfers the agency of code-makers, not only to anyone who swings a hammer, but also to insurance companies, bankers, and home buyers. In this case, society as a whole is systemically affected by technological intervention. In this final part of the book, we demonstrate empirically how certain technical codes, those that we refer to as *sociotechnical*, operate to affect specific social groups, either positively or negatively.

The first case examined is the DRM in the United States. Although disability rights advocates still argue that there are many barriers remaining to achieving full equality for disabled citizens, it is reasonable to argue that this movement is an exemplary case of sociotechnical change and deserves additional study in this context. Although some scholars have argued that exemplary or extraordinary cases hold little relevance for ordinary life, Flyvbjerg has thoughtfully argued the reverse, in holding that:

> One can often generalize on the basis of a single case, and the case study may be central to scientific development via generalization as supplement or alternative to other methods. But formal generalization is overvalued as a source of scientific development, whereas "the force of example" is underestimated.[1]

The DRM in the United States serves, then, by force of example as a highly successful case of sociotechnical code-making.

Our second empirical case—affordable housing in Austin, Texas—has not been quite as successful as the national DRM, yet serves this study well by comparison, if not always by example. By examining the historical evolution of affordable housing in three phases—the City Plan of 1928, the S.M.A.R.T. Housing code of 2000, and the subsequent Alley Flat Initiative (AFI)—we are able to demonstrate how key variables change over time, how the outcome of one controversy sets up conditions for the next one, and how attempts to resolve public controversies through code-making become embedded in the built environment itself. Taken together, the two case studies demonstrate a relationship between *technological frames*, *relevant social groups*, and what we refer to as the *focal events* that drive local history. Before defining these terms, however, it is necessary to explain the structure of what follows.

Given the research assumptions of the co-authors, which generally follow those of grounded theory,[2] it would be appropriate to tell the stories of the selected cases and allow the theory to develop from those stories. Although we have employed this structure elsewhere, we find that it does not always serve the reader. In this project, we have followed the opposite structure, which is to set out the theory first, in Chapter 8, which will then be followed by telling the stories of the DRM in Chapter 9 and then affordable housing for Austin in Chapter 10. Our hope is that presenting the evidence after the theory allows the reader to appreciate the story more fully.

We should also tell the reader up front that our research intention is *action-* or *change-oriented.* By this term, we mean that any hypotheses that arise from our analysis are intended to be tested, not only by sound reasoning, but also by action being taken to reconstitute the topics investigated.[3] The chapter should be understood as both an analysis and a *design*. Herbert Simon has defined this thorny term by arguing that,

> Every one designs who devises courses of action aimed at changing existing conditions into preferred ones. The intellectual activity that produces material artifacts is no different fundamentally from the one that prescribes remedies for a sick patient or the one that devises a new sales plan for a company or a welfare policy for the state. Design, so construed, is the core of all professional training: it is the principal mark that distinguishes the professions from the sciences.[4]

We expect that architects and other designers may find this broad definition of design to be overly inclusive. If *everyone* is a designer, architects may reason, it only degrades the value of the expert knowledge they have worked so hard to master. We think this is not the case, and, in the concluding chapter, we will expand on the theme to argue that code-making may be a more powerful form of design than the elegant articulation of a single object. Before doing so, however, the following three chapters will provide the evidence required to make that claim relevant to design practitioners and others.

Chapter 8

Social Groups, Technological Frames, and Focal Events

Sociotechnical codes differ from *tacit*, *sumptuary*, and *economic* codes primarily in the conscious intention of code-makers to change social conditions, either positively or negatively, for specific social groups through technological change. An oft-cited example of this kind of change is the standardized design of 19th-century textile looms to fit the small stature of children, so that they could be employed in textile mills at lower cost to mill owners (Figure 8.1). A more positive example would be the late-20th-century safety code requirement to install higher and less porous safety rails on balconies to prevent children from falling through them (Figure 8.2). Both technologies were designed specifically to alter conditions for children as a distinct class of people.

However, the intention of code-makers might also work in reverse, to change the technologies needed by first coding new social practices for specific groups. A positive example of this type would be the municipal requirement for homeowners to recycle solid waste, which in turn catalyzes not only new waste-stream technologies and new kitchen cabinet designs, but also the creation of new material resources for manufacturing. A less positive example would be coding by homeowner associations that prohibits the hanging of laundry outside. In this negative example, homeowners are prohibited from erecting clotheslines, and thus indirectly required to purchase a clothes dryer and consume the energy required to run it. In both cases, homeowners are the target population of regulation.

In this chapter, we argue that there is a consistent and predictable relationship between three primary variables: First are the *relevant social groups*, a term we defined in Chapter 4 as groups of people who compete to "influence the creation, the demand for, the production, the diffusion, the acceptance, or the opposition to new technologies."[1] This term derives generally from *social identity theory* and attempts to explain how individuals perceive their membership of various social groups that may be political, professional, recreational, or social in orientation.[2] Second are the *technological frames*, also defined in Chapter 4, through which these social groups interpret the world. And third are the *focal issues* that drive policy-making. Focal issues

Figure 8.1 "Girl Standing Between Looms." Location: Fall River, MA. Photo by Lewis Wickes Hine, 1874–1940. Published: June 21, 1916. By adapting the scale of adult-sized looms to the smaller stature of girls, engineers and owners could reduce labor costs and increase profits.

are defined here as public conflicts that tend to dominate public consciousness and obscure other issues that compete for attention, because they touch core tensions or identities in the community. Although these three variables are modified by the economies and cultural politics of particular places, we find the relationship between the variables remains pretty much the same from place to place. To make our reasoning clear, we will further define, or revisit, each of these specialized terms, after we set out the analytic approach that led us to this hypothesis. We recognize that this chapter is rather technical, and so, for the casual reader, the terms developed here are also condensed as a glossary that follows Chapter 11.

ANALYTIC APPROACH

Our analysis of sociotechnical code-making derives from comparing the two cases investigated in the following two chapters. In reconstructing the making of sociotechnical codes, we used a mixed-method approach, with some variation between the two cases as conditions required.[3] Overall, we used eight methods of gathering and interpreting data. First, because much of the critical work of the DRM is well catalogued in oral histories and archival documents at the University of California at Berkeley's Bancroft Library, archival research served as the main source for primary data for this movement. Second, we conducted semi-structured interviews—2 related to disability rights, and 29 related to affordable housing in Austin. These interviews were subsequently transcribed and dissected into topical categories of text through digital means

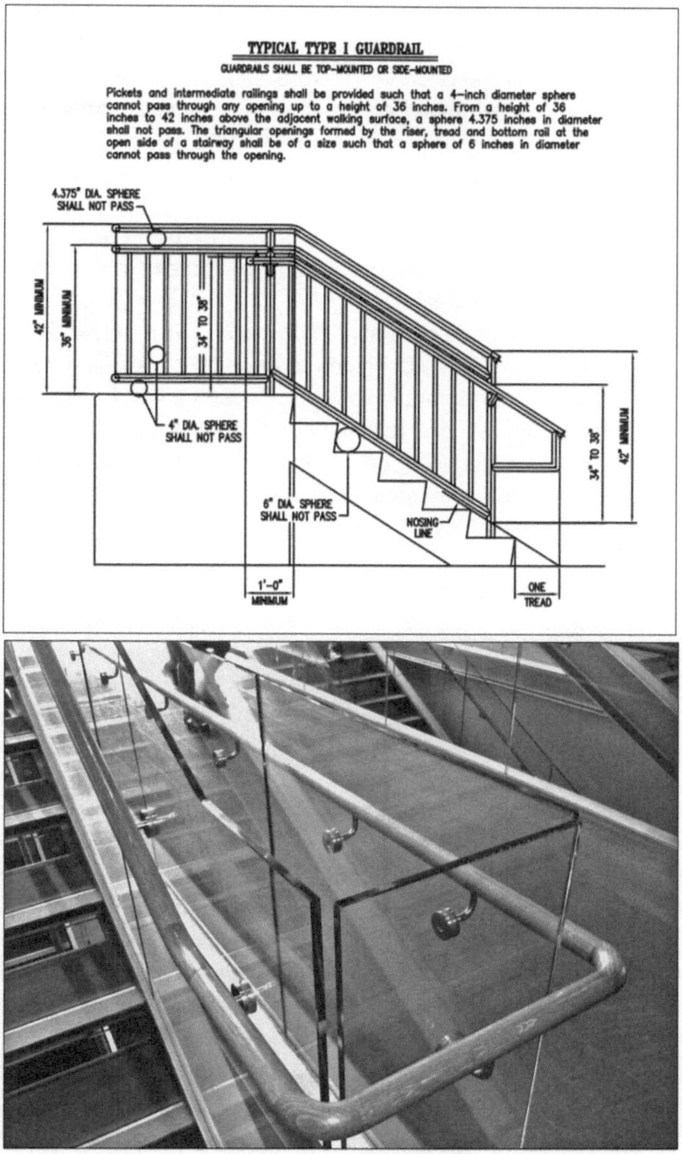

Figure 8.2 Contemporary Regulation for Handrails (above) and a Creative Interpretation of That Regulation at the Elizabeth Gardiner Museum, Boston, MA. Renzo Piano Workshop (below). The negative example of coding technology for specific social groups illustrated in Figure 8.1 can be contrasted by this positive example, where children are prevented from falling through railings.

that helped us interpret how our respondents understand and/or participated in code-making. Third, in the Austin case, we installed a heuristic exhibition about "alley flats" at City Hall and used that event as an opportunity to hold a public opening and two focus groups, with a broad spectrum of community stakeholders. Next, we were "participant observers" at meetings related to both cases. We have also been active, through the Austin Community Design and Development Center (ACDDC), in developing housing that is both affordable and accessible. Fifth, we facilitated a discussion between the Real Estate Council of Austin (RECA) and the Austin Community Housing Development Organization Roundtable about code-oriented impediments to affordability and accessibility in Austin. Sixth, as University of Texas faculty members, we also engaged students in the design and building of alley flats—small, affordable, sustainable, and accessible infill housing units. And last, we conducted archival research and a lengthy secondary literature search related to affordability, sustainability, and accessibility. Each of these methods contributed to our understanding the storyline, or the structure of code-making, nationally and in Austin. In sum, our hypothesis can be stated as four linked and sequential sub-hypotheses:

1. *Relevant social groups* interpret *focal issues* from within shared *technological frames*.
2. Technological frames are said to be *generative* if they catalyze action intended to improve conditions for a particular social group.
3. Generative frames are said to be *regenerative* if they transform, realign, and/or expand relevant social groups through action.
4. Regenerative technological frames are said to be *successful* if they produce codes that materialize built environments that, in turn, enhance the agency of relevant groups.

These are highly abstract propositions that require each specialized term used to be further defined and then backed by evidence to make them useful.

RELEVANT SOCIAL GROUPS

In the technology studies literature, the term "relevant social groups" is commonly used to describe the two sides of the neoliberal economy: *producers* and *consumers* of technologies, goods, and services.[4] The assumption in distinguishing producers from consumers is that they have different and often opposing interests—producers want to optimize profits, and consumers want to minimize costs. Each of these groups has, in turn, subgroups. One can imagine the consumers of telephone services—to continue the example used in Chapter 2—being divided into subgroups of payphone users, landline users, digital users, smartphone users, bluetooth users, and so forth. Likewise, producers can be divided into subgroups of circuit-makers, software designers, hardware designers, assemblers, etc. And what about satellite makers and launchers, relay station tower makers, and the almost infinite number of subgroups that influence public policy, the law, and the business of telephoning? In Chapter 2, we recognized that, in complex technological systems such as telephone communication, it is increasingly difficult to locate the *agency*, or ability to make a difference, within the system. Any discussion of relevant social groups, then, must recognize how the actions of both the producers and consumers of technologies are enhanced or limited by the agreements embodied in the technologies themselves. How is the agency of a social group, or artifact, affected, and how is it *relevant* to a particular focal issue?

A second issue that deserves attention with regard to *relevant social groups* is that the term seems to imply homogeneity (that actors are of a single kind) and constancy (that they always act in the same way). In our fieldwork, however, we found neither. Rather, we found that individuals could self-identify with one group at a morning staff meeting and another at an evening meeting of the PTA. This is particularly true when architects, for example, work directly in heterogeneous groups of people with different kinds of training (as they do at city hall), rather than in homogeneous groups comprised only of architects (as they do in firm offices). This is to say that, not only are social groups dynamic, but also individuals come and go from groups as their attitudes and surrounding conditions change. Relevant social groups are, then, dynamic and heterogeneous, rather than constant and homogeneous, as they have been portrayed by some researchers.

In our analysis and interviews concerning the DRM, we found six relevant social groups: *grassroots advocates, the business community, the welfare reformer community, the medical community*, and *the legal community*. The interaction between these groups is narrated further in Chapter 9. Using similar methods in our analysis of affordable housing in Austin, we found five distinct relevant social groups there: *neighborhoods, the environmental community, the development community, the knowledge community*, and *the professional community*. The interaction between these groups is narrated further in Chapter 10. One significant finding from both cases is that relevant social groups are, like types of code themselves, best understood as *ideal types*, which are logically coherent, rather than as human beings, who rarely are. Relevant social groups hold individual agents as members only as long as the frame of interpretation embraced by both the group and the individual is "aligned."[5] Over time, people get burned out or enlightened, or are attracted to other movements or practices. Likewise, movements themselves shift in response to changing leadership and conditions. In the case of making socio-technical codes, rather than tacit, sumptuary, or economic ones, an essential logic of the group is that there is an explicit association between social and technological change. For example, this observation holds true for anti-violence groups as much as for the National Rifle Association—both relevant social groups understand the very existence of weaponry influences day-to-day social practices, but they interpret the nature of that influence differently—through different frames. This observation requires that we revisit the concept of "technological frames."

TECHNOLOGICAL FRAMES

As we defined them in Chapter 4, *frames* organize our perceptions of the events that take place around us, as well as how we expect people to behave as events unfold. In the introduction to Chapter 4, we also distinguished between institutional and technological frames. With that distinction made, in this section we limit ourselves to reconsidering how technological frames operate to bind relevant social groups to a common interpretation of the built world.

Our finding is that agents act upon the world through the technological frame they inhabit. Some individual agents are completely contained within a single frame in which they are influential. An influential national politician might make a good example of what we refer to as an *enframed agent*. In such cases, agents tend to be blind, or at least resistant, to competing interpretations of reality, because their ranking in the group depends upon their apparent commitment to it and their leadership in advocating for the ideas shared by the party to which they are affiliated. Other agents are, however, able to integrate, switch codes, or employ the language, tools, values, and frames of other groups, without being wholly contained within them. *Code-switchers*,[6] as we defined them in Chapter 4, tend to be visitors to many groups—tolerated but, most of the time, not very influential, because they are not perceived to be fully committed to the values or interpretations of that particular group.[7] A university professor engaged in interdisciplinary research and teaching in several academic units at a single campus might make a good example of a code-switching agent. Our point in making this distinction between enframed agents and code-switchers is not to argue that the latter are doomed to failure and the former to success, but that the process of gathering resources, or constructing an influential network, is more complex and difficult for those wanting to reach beyond the boundaries of established frames. Both kinds of agent—those who are enframed by a particular interpretation of reality and those who switch between multiple frames—were present in both of the selected cases.

We also found that, in their relevant social groups, both enframed agents and code-switchers interpreted what is going on in their cities through three kinds of technological frame: *supply-side*, *demand-side*, and *effect-side*. We will examine each of these in turn.

The Supply-side Technological Frame

Advocates of what is routinely referred to as *supply-side economics* argue that economic growth can best be created by reducing obstacles, in the form of taxes or regulation, to producers. As a result, producers will, supply-siders argue, be able to provide consumers with lower-cost goods and services. A supply-side technological frame embraces this economic view, which depends in turn on defining the social system in question in a simplistic, linear, and narrow fashion.

Using the supply of electricity to the City of Austin as an example, one respondent put it this way: "electrical utilities exist only to supply consumers with highly reliable power at the lowest possible rate." The system of production and consumption of electricity is understood through this respondent's frame as a one-way flow in which oil, coal, or natural gas are transformed at a predictable cost by utilities and supplied to consumers in usable form. For their part, autonomous consumers rationally determine for themselves what use of energy is in their best interest—be it running air conditioning to keep the house at a comfortable temperature, heating water, or turning the TV on or off. From the producer's perspective, it seems perfectly rational to give reduced rates to large-volume consumers such as industrial consumers, or homeowners with swimming pools, because the producer's overhead costs per unit of consumption are reduced, thus stimulating more consumption and increased overall profits. This simplistic frame of interpretation relies upon keeping the unconsidered effects of production out of the accounting system, thereby reducing risk. External effects, such as degraded air quality and attendant health care treatment, are either denied or treated as problems to be shouldered by related, overlapping systems.

The same linear, one-way logic is consistently applied by supply-siders to housing. Making housing more or less affordable depends on the cost of four primary variables: the cost of land, the "hard" costs of construction, and the "soft" costs of administrative labor, as well as financing debt service. Only recently has a fifth variable—the annual cost of energy use and maintenance—been elevated as a relevant variable in the system of housing construction and finance.[8] As one respondent argued, "both the land development code and market drivers tend to make us think of housing as [autonomous] units rather than as components of a larger whole, or a community." From that perspective, *all* houses are understood by supply-siders as *units of consumption*—they sit at the end of a linear system of production that exists only to enable private consumption by residents, rich or poor. The only distinction between rich and poor consumers would be the amount of consumption, and thus preferential rates accumulated.

Similar supply-side reasoning is also applied by some to "the problem of disability." In this frame, disabled individuals are perceived to be the consumers of services more than commodities. For instance, supply-side reasoning was the main argument for the widespread institutionalization of persons with physical or mental disabilities in the 19th and 20th centuries. From the government's perspective, a portion of the population requiring a certain kind of care would be most efficiently treated from centralized facilities. In this argument, the "disabled" consumer required services that were too costly to provide effectively in a distributed fashion, and thus the only rational way to give these consumers the services they required was to build large-scale government facilities where resources could be pooled to ensure that all the residents would receive the best care available to them at the lowest level of risk.

In sum, we can say that, seen through a supply-side frame, electricity, houses, or people with disabilities have been perceived to be autonomous *units of consumption*, large or small, instead of parts of a larger and more complex urban ecology. This view is rejected as overly simplistic and self-serving by those who embrace a *demand-side technological frame*.

The Demand-side Technological Frame

Advocates of demand-side economics argue that the unwanted external costs of production, such as degraded air quality, can only be avoided by reducing system-wide demand by all consumers. According to one respondent, changing what is going on in Austin through the demand-side frame requires that, "you reduce the demand, not just supply electricity [to meet] the demand, but you attack the problem by reducing the demand." But she also recognizes that, "the demand-side is viewed by the supply-side as the one that doesn't generate money." For a business, even a publicly owned one, the problem of reducing demand while maintaining revenue levels is a paradox, at least to supply-siders. Although many supply-side advocates agree that improving air and water quality may be desirable, they do not agree that those improvements should come at the cost of reducing revenue production by the utility, which would only increase taxation, because profits are plowed into the city's general fund, thus keeping taxes artificially low. For demand-siders, as one respondent put it, "That's where all the action is," because it gets at the core problem—the shortsighted definition of profit and risk.

From within the demand-side frame, the seeming paradox of selling less power, yet maintaining, or even increasing, revenues is only a paradox if you maintain the rigid boundaries of the existing power supply system and fail to see and take advantage of what advocates call "network effects." If, in the eyes of another official, you expand utility system boundaries by adding "information technology and intelligence to the old, dumb, one-way electron delivery system," it will become possible to "decouple revenues from volume, maximize value rather than price, be proactive as opposed to compliant, be connected rather than isolated, and integrated rather than incremental." Such an expanded system would "facilitate [two-way] conversations, at first between customers and the utility and eventually between buildings."

This perhaps overly optimistic view of technological change depends on the economic integration of "market externalities" into the system as potential income streams. In another respondent's perspective,

> We have a very narrow view of what price means and we make our electricity system cheap at the expense of making our health care premiums expensive . . . or, we make the price of gasoline cheap, at the expense of making our taxes higher to pay for the national security apparatus to protect the flow of oil. And so it's very expensive, we just pay for it in different columns.

But how, supply-side advocates legitimately want to know, can this integrated, highly complex form of accounting be made clear enough to make informed individual decisions? The risks involved are substantial. Even more important, they ask, who will control the accounting and the flow of promised savings? Ultimately, Austin's demand-side advocates, like the supply-side advocates on the other side of the room, hold that it is a matter for autonomous consumers to account for themselves. It is a matter of individual behavior. To date, however, no new "business model" has appeared that answers the difficult questions asked by supply-siders.

Supply-siders and demand-siders agree on at least one thing—that decision-making for a smart, integrated energy system will best be distributed to rational consumers who will choose, with the aid of smart technologies, to use electricity when it is very inexpensive, rather than at peak demand periods, when it is very expensive. Where they differ is in who has the right, the capital, and competence to take such risks. As we argued above, supply-side advocates tend to think that high volumes of consumption should be rewarded by lower rates through a positive sumptuary code. For demand-side advocates, however, the reverse is true—those who consume more should pay at the higher end of a graduated rate, and those who consume less should be rewarded for doing so with a lower rate, through a negative sumptuary code. It is this difference in reasoning that leads to opposing views about housing itself. Where supply-siders reason that it is up to the autonomous family unit to seek out efficient housing on its own behalf, demand-siders reason that it is in the interest of the community as a whole to create affordable housing, because it would reduce system-wide demand, not only for energy, but also for transportation, health care, and related social services. Supply-siders see risks to themselves, and demand-siders see risks to the system.

A demand-side technological frame is also used by some to interpret the world of disability rights. Where energy and housing are a matter of distributing goods, disability advocates are also concerned with the distribution of services. For instance, the welfare reform community employs a demand-side frame to support the claims of advocates of both spatial and programmatic accessibility. Welfare reformers argued that, although the upfront costs of such change would be significant, the government could not afford to continue keeping persons with disabilities out of the educational system and the workforce. For these demand-side thinkers, the costs of financially supporting uneducated and unemployable disabled persons, instead of giving them the opportunity to access the services and programs that might lead to self-sufficiency, were too great for the government to continue to bear.

In both cases—the DRM and housing in Austin—supply- and demand-siders tend to interpret events ideologically, through a priori frames of cause and effect. Those citizens who interpret technological change from within the supply-side frame tend to prefer the status quo to the uncertain risk inherent in change of any kind. They understand, from long experience, how narrowly defined system boundaries and assumptions of simple linear causality serve their own interests. Conversely, they also understand that technological change tends to upset vested interests. In their view, the stability upon which wealth production relies is put at risk by social, cosmological, and technological change. The politics of technology are, then, filtered out by the supply-side frame of interpretation, because those who inhabit that frame have allegiance to how that system has served them in the past.

In contrast, those who inhabit the demand-side frame cannot catalyze technological change fast enough. They are equally convinced that benefits will flow in all directions, even if they have yet to demonstrate exactly how. They are certain, however, that a new "business model" will be found in the future. For this group, the politics of technology are, then, filtered out by allegiance to a utopian and uncertain future. In this limited context, supply-side advocates can be generally understood as *technophobes*, or technological skeptics who avoid risk, and demand-side advocates can be understood as *technophiles*, or technological enthusiasts who embrace risk. A third group in our case studies, however, interpreted events through what we refer to as the effect-side frame, which is neither technophobic nor technophilic.

The Effect-side Frame

For those who inhabit the effect-side frame, technologies are neither good nor bad in essence. Rather, their value depends on who is affected by change, how they are affected, and when. In our fieldwork, we found that those who inhabited this effect-side frame tended to share two characteristics: First, they tended to be the most vulnerable to change of any kind in the present, because they were often poor. And second, they were not particularly invested in either the supply- or demand-side frame. They were, although no individual used the term, practitioners of the *precautionary principle*.[9] This is to say that effect-siders recognized the risks inherent in either allowing conditions to remain as they were or embracing new and, to them, untested technologies. In short, effect-siders in our cases were code-switchers—meaning that they had the ability to see how the storylines constructed by the advocates of the other two competing frames could be alternately helpful or harmful. The level of risk varies depending upon local conditions.[10] More important, however, is that effect-siders could see that the storylines constructed by supply- or demand-siders historically failed to include their interests, either in the short or long run. Another way to say this is that both supply- and demand-siders tended to interpret technological events ideologically from an overly negative or overly positive perspective. Effect-siders, however, tended to be prudent and to wait for evidence to inform their interpretation of the risks embodied in change.

A final point to be made about these three technological frames is that, although they are interpretive dispositions, they can also catalyze action. In the hypothesis articulated above, we stated that technological frames can be said to be *generative* if and when they inform group activity. The appropriate question to ask here is, "what causes an interpretation by an individual or social group to generate action?" We found that it is a provocative "focal issue" that can serve this function.

FOCAL ISSUES

In the long experience of one Austin municipal planner,

> every city has something that is their perceived crisis of the day. It might be a police issue, or it might be an issue with solid waste, or it might be an issue with growth and development, or water/wastewater . . . you know, something that has floated to the top as a problem. And then all the other things are seen in reference to where that central problem, or set of problems, is.

From this practiced perspective, cities everywhere are unique primarily in the issues that focus, or fail to focus, the attention of relevant social groups. Planners of several persuasions also report that the issues that "float to the top" tend to be event-driven.[11] For example, the Federal Fair Housing Act of 1968, which banned racial advertising for home sales and rentals (i.e., "whites only"), catalyzed public attention throughout the south on "secondary dwelling units," garage apartments, or alley flats. Like elsewhere in the region, the public attention given to the issue in Austin resulted in zoning codes that banned "garage apartments in single-family neighborhoods," so as to avoid forced racial integration. One respondent offered that when such galvanizing events occur, "city government . . . will step in and say, 'OK, this has got to stop [so] let's think about how we're going to do this.' So, there's a positive way to get there and a not so positive way to get there." Our finding is that, over time, cities socially construct a culture, or schema of "ways to get there," of seeing, or not seeing, particular kinds of problem, and of acting in consistent patterns.

We have, above and elsewhere, argued that the evolution of focal issues in any city is best understood as a "storyline," or a trajectory of related events, in which narratives and counter-narratives constructed by competing social groups vie to attract supporters and thus reframe interpretation of the next event on the horizon.[12] The dominant storyline of the DRM is a tale of inclusivity and grassroots empowerment—the rallying cry, "nothing without us, about us, is for us," maintained the cultural space for subplots within the movement to slowly align around a broad, rights-based definition for the movement that saw disability, not as a medical condition or affliction, but as an environmental limitation.

By contrast, the dominant storyline of Austin has been the weaving together of environmental issues with those related to digital technology, environmental protection, music, rapid population growth, and gentrification.[13]

It is the relative success of competing storylines that moves decision-making and history forward, if not always to the place imagined by storytellers. This is to argue that no single focal issue can be understood in isolation from the long and competing storylines of which it is, or becomes, a part through the process of frame alignment.

FRAME ALIGNMENT

The idea that competing frames of interpretation could be "aligned" was initially developed by Snow, Rochford, Worden, and Benford. That idea is also supported by our case studies in two other dimensions: the fabrication of common language and of action. We will examine each in turn.

Explicitly following Goffman, whose work we examined in Chapter 4, Snow et al. contribute to the development of frame analysis by linking together the social psychology of individuals with structural and organizational factors related to social movements, in precisely the way that offended Frederik Jameson, as discussed in Chapter 4. Like the meso-level analysis employed by Hacking, Snow et al. view social movements from the middle ground between grounded individual motivations and the abstract limitations imposed by broad social structures. In coining the term "frame alignment," they mean the degree to which "the interpretive orientations" of individuals come to be "congruent and complementary" with the values and beliefs articulated by specific social movements.[14] Their argument is that the efficacy and staying power of social movements depend on the ability of movement leaders to align the stated values and beliefs of the movement in question with the ever-changing interpretive frames of individuals. The relationship between the two, they hold, is always a dynamic rather than static one.

Snow et al. argue that the interpretive frames of individuals can be self-consciously aligned with those of movements, and thus attract adherents, through four related but distinct processes. The first of these, *frame bridging*, refers to the linking of ideologically congruent but structurally independent frames. Elsewhere, we have demonstrated that the organic food and green building movements emerged from discourses generally isolated from each other by barriers of class and politics. When the focal events of the mid 20th century—the environmental devastation of Love Canal near Niagara Falls and the burning of the Cuyahoga River in Cleveland—related public health issues to those of building, it became possible for activists to "bridge" barriers and, thus, construct hybrid social groups.[15]

The second mode of alignment, *frame amplification*, refers to the "clarification and invigoration that bears on a particular issue." A good example, told in greater detail in Chapter 10, involves the 1928 plan for the City of Austin. Black and Latino citizens are painfully aware of how that plan employed the provisioning of infrastructure, such as roads, streetlights, and schools, to effectively segregate the city. When community activists in the late 1990s employed that same frame to interpret the planning practices of the latter era, the frame was "amplified," "clarified," and "invigorated," because citizens could use it productively to interpret contemporary events that influenced their lives directly.

The third, *frame extension*, refers to enlargement of a group's "adherent pool" by claiming ideological beliefs related to a sympathetic group.

In the DRM, its frame was, for example, successfully extended to include returned war veterans, as well as persons living with AIDS or struggling with substance abuse issues. The same pattern of extending the group's adherent pool is being used by housing advocates in Austin, by linking affordable housing to environmental issues through coding and economic incentives for energy efficiency. Extending their frame in this direction has brought environmentalists into the adherent pool of housing advocates.

Fourth, *frame transformation*, refers to the jettisoning and "reframing" of old values "in order to garner support and secure participants."[16] In the world of green building, for example, the hippie doctrine of "back-to-the-land" was over time transformed—some would say co-opted—from an overtly romantic ideal into "sustainable development" and "green business."[17] In that process of transformation, the business community, the insurance industry, and other mainstream social groups saw new opportunities that were relevant to their interests and, thus, adopted that emergent frame of interpretation.

These four modes of frame alignment are not nested or successive strategies required for movement-building, but alternative modes of mobilization. The authors take pains to demonstrate that, to be successful in mobilizing social forces, it is not enough to know that frame alignment can be fabricated by movement leaders. This is because activists come and go for many reasons—successful fabrication on one front is met by dissolution on another. Successful social change, they argue, has less to do with changing opportunities than with the ability of groups to consciously align and realign frames as opportunities evolve. Their thesis is that, once someone has constructed convincing frames of interpretation, large-scale changes in society can be achieved through frame alignment and realignment. In the cases studied, we found that all four modes of aligning frames appeared. This claim will become concrete in the chapters that follow.

Integrating Language for Sustainability

A second useful expansion of frame analysis that is supported by our case studies is directly related to sustainability and architectural practice. In Denmark, social scientists Dammann and Elle were asked by their government to study which sustainability indicators should be used to develop public policy related to a variety of building types, including housing, schools, daycare, offices, and institutions. The motivation for the study was the observation by government officials that, when they brought relevant social groups within the building industry together, they were unable to "speak a common language" and, thus, make coherent policy recommendations. The assumption of government officials was that a common language, or common understanding of the variables at play, must be constructed between relevant social groups before "closure" can be reached for public policies about which environmental indicators should be used to evaluate a building's sustainability. The researchers argue that some "multilingual actors," or *code-switchers* as we prefer to call them, may already be able to appreciate multiple technological frames, but these individuals are in very short supply. Given that shortage, the government determined that the purpose of the study was to ascertain if a common language, and thus a common policy, might be "fabricated," in the sense proposed above by Goffman.

In answer to the research question initially put to them by government, the researchers concluded that it was highly "unlikely" that a common language would emerge on its own anytime soon. The interpretive conflict between the four documented frames was seen by the researchers as too great to be quickly overcome. In lieu of finding a common language, they found three alternative "scenarios" as more likely outcomes. In the most likely of these, politicians, scientists, and laypersons are able to agree on appropriate indicators based on a more scientifically robust LCA, but architects would become marginalized—at least until they are dragged back into agreement by the "gravitational pull" of the building industry.

For our purposes in this book, it is important to emphasize that the researchers found architects to be the relevant social group with the least capacity to switch codes, or consider the technological frames of other relevant social groups with whom they must work, and so contribute to the fabrication of a common language and coherent public policy. This is a pattern that we also found in our selected cases. That characteristic is hardly a ringing endorsement of the discipline.

Finding Language Through Action

Above, we argued that technological frames are not only interpretive dispositions, but that they generate action when provoked by focal issues. Here, we extend that logic by arguing that generative frames become *re*generative when the action taken transforms, realigns, and/or expands the group in question. This is to say that, through the collaborative experience of acting together, individuals find new language, new interpretations, and new self-reflection that regenerates or "transforms" the group.

This piece of the hypothesis is supported by Tarrow, who argues in favor of what he calls "collective action frames."[18] Like Snow et al., Tarrow's interest is to consider frame analysis as not simply a tool for the analysis of existing conditions at a distance, but also as a tool for social action designed to change those conditions. This is a quite radical proposal, one that fundamentally erodes the traditional distinction between science, understood as the analysis of past conditions, and design, understood as the act of proposing new ones.[19] This point informs our introduction to the cases studied in Chapters 9 and 10.

Collective action frames, according to Tarrow, McAdams, Klandermans, and other notable social movement scholars, form through the claim-making negotiations of social movements. These frames connect the constellation of relevant social groups organizing in response to specific focal events. Klandermans notes, however, that the "transformation of social issues into collective action frames does not occur by itself. It is a process in which social actors, media, and members of a society jointly interpret, define, and redefine states of affairs."[20] Collective action frames are cognitive maps—lenses through which issues and ethics can be crafted and refined to encompass a broad range of perspectives. Tilly also notes that, because of the reductive processes required to generate a cohesive storyline on which the media and other associated groups can build successful campaigns, these frames do not always represent the democratic accumulation of social values. He cautions, however, that social movements are only successful when they democratize social institutions through the genuine expression of underrepresented voices in the public realm.[21]

For at least the last decade, and for Bijker somewhat longer, there has been an increasing desire to turn technology studies away from the traditional project of theory-making and toward the betterment of everyday practices.[22] Tarrow has contributed significantly to that redirection through his development of the concept of collective action frames, but his reasoning for doing so is not what most might reasonably expect. Following Dewey, his logic is not that intellectuals have a moral obligation to act on behalf of their communities; rather, he argues that it is only through action in-the-world that social scientists, architects, or anyone else will begin to grasp how the seemingly endless number of variables will interact in the complex conditions of the city. This is an epistemological position, more than a purely ethical one—it is to say that scientific analysis and democracy are not separate and distinct practices, but one and the same way of life. It is to hold that *action is inquiry*, or, turned inside out, it is to hold that *science is politics by another name*. The same logic applies to architecture: Artistic expression in the built environment and democracy are not separate and distinct practices, but one and the same way of life.

In this intellectual context, then, the process of finding common norms, codes, and values requires the alignment of interpretive frames through cycles of action, experimentation, and reflection generated by relevant social groups, who interpret focal issues through ever-evolving frames. It is only *action* toward a common goal, we now argue, that allows us to recognize the value of our neighbor's perspective—a realization we are not likely to reach through the parsing of words and images alone.

In the case of the DRM, for example, radical action catalyzed a common language around a broad rights-based frame during the protests of resistance to the passing of Section 504 of the Rehabilitation Act of 1973. After President Carter wavered on his promise to implement the radical rights-based language within Section 504, movement advocates of all persuasions and backgrounds rallied together to protest in April 1977. This diverse group occupied the California office of the Federal Department of Health, Education, and Welfare for almost a month, until the government would agree to full implementation of the Act's stipulations. This successful protest was a defining and unifying moment for the larger DRM and it galvanized an interpretive vocabulary that is still used today. Cooperative action, then, *regenerated* factions within the movement to employ a common frame of interpretation.

In the case of S.M.A.R.T. Housing in Austin, Texas, action catalyzed a common language in the acronym that identifies the code itself: S.M.A.R.T. stands for *safe*, *mixed-income*, *accessible*, *reasonably priced*, and *transit-oriented*. The fabrication of the code was also a fabrication of a coalition of previously isolated groups. This cooperative action also regenerated the movement—at least for a little while. A second regeneration was in the making in 2012.

Both cases have contributed to the fabrication of storylines, tentative still, that align multiple frames of interpretation, regenerate social movements, and contribute to the production of life-enhancing built environments.

SUMMARY

So far, our argument has been that, unlike tacit, sumptuary, or economic codes, sociotechnical code-makers self-consciously associate social and technological change. They also understand that individuals interpret the focal issues of their city from within a frame shared by a relevant social group of which they are members. Where supply-siders tend to filter out politics by framing technological change as generally bad, demand-siders do so by framing technological change as inevitably good, independent of immediate context. It is only the effect-siders who seem to grasp that the consequences of technological change are context-dependent. This is to argue that power relations become codified in particular municipal contexts in accordance with the dominant storylines of the city. Put more simply, this means that cities have, not only different histories and traditions, but also a variety of government structures—strong or weak mayor, city council or city manager, town meeting or voting precincts. Each of these variables works in a different way to discipline how formal codes are legislated. In one respondent's view, technological codes are the "scar tissue" left from the battles over the alignment and realignment of technological frames in the public talk about focal issues. Codes materialize built space over time in a manner that changes, for better or worse, the agency of particular social groups. The last element of the hypothesis is to argue that successful socio-technical codes, meaning ones that positively enhance conditions for specific groups, emerge through regenerative action.

To make these abstract claims more concrete, we have constructed Table 8.1 as a preview of the following two chapters, in which we tell the stories of the DRM in the United States and S.M.A.R.T. Housing in Austin, Texas.

In both cases, the supply-side frame is dominant, or the most commonly used mode of interpreting focal issues; the generative frame that catalyzes collective action is demand-side; and the regenerative frame that results from action is effect-side. Before we can consider the implications of this pattern, it will be helpful to hear our two stories in more detail.

Table 8.1 Dominant, generative, and regenerative frames of the selected cases

	Dominant supply-side frame	*Generative demand-side frame*	*Regenerative effect-side frame*
The disability rights movement	Disability is a medical problem most efficiently treated by experts in a centralized facility	Disabled people are unjustly excluded from public life and/or involuntarily incarcerated. Accessibility measures are an investment in social stability	Disability is an environmental problem that affects every citizen at some point in his/her life
S.M.A.R.T. Homes	Poverty is a social problem that is most efficiently treated by providing housing and other services to the poor in centralized facilities	People of modest means are unjustly put at risk by the cycles of urban investment and disinvestment. Affordable housing is an investment in social stability	Affordable homes are a necessary and productive investment in distributed, sustainable infrastructure

Chapter 9

Coding Disability

A Case Study of Frame Integration

> We must learn to have pride in who we are. I'm very proud of being a disabled person. I didn't choose it, but I'm proud as hell that I've been able to do what I have with my life. And I'm getting prouder all the time as I look out and I see you and thousands of other disabled people joining us and saying, "We are not going to take it, it's time we got involved and turned this around." No one else will do it for us. If we have learned one thing from the civil rights movements in the United States it's that when others speak for you, you lose. When you aren't powerful or at least perceived as being powerful, you will gain very little success. We are not begging for our rights, we're demanding our rights. We're not going to sit out and wait for them; we're going to sit in the streets if that's what it takes.[1]
>
> (E.V. Roberts, 1983)

The United States DRM was one part of a wave of civil unrest inspired by the civil rights movement (CRM). The first generation of DRM leaders watched in appreciation as the CRM constructed a language of constitutional rights to support their claims. They also watched, and learned, from the intrastate nonviolent demonstrations, the sit-ins, and the freedom rides from which the new language emerged.

Unlike many other movements that fed on the legacy of the CRM, such as the women's movement, the anti-nuclear movement, and the environmental movement, the DRM movement began with humble hopes—framing its cause outside the realms of civil rights as an independent living movement that asked only for the option to live outside of institutional walls, inside which many were unwillingly committed. It is a mistake, however, to imagine that the disabled initially conceived of themselves as a coherent social group. The intensely diverse social groups within the DRM—including the blind, the deaf, the mentally disabled, the terminally ill, and the wheelchair bound—had very different needs and thus could not initially see how their interests might overlap. This humble, fractured disposition kept the movement from mobilizing as quickly as other contemporary groups. Although the language of the Civil

Rights Acts of 1964 and 1968 did not include people with disabilities as a protected class, by the 1970s, DRM leaders began to understand that their constituencies might also be entitled to inalienable rights that they could not yet access. Within the next decade, the DRM reframed hopelessly fractured groups into the most persuasive societal force to influence architectural regulation in the 20th century.

In this chapter, we posit that the ADA of 1990, which emerged from the DRM, is an exemplary sociotechnical code. It was through a series of collective actions that the DRM developed a unifying frame that coalesced a wide spectrum of internal stakeholders and catalyzed federal legislation. It is important to note, however, that we are not arguing that the ADA and subsequent Acts have completely eradicated the spatial and programmatic injustices to which the DRM was reacting. There are weaknesses and limitations to that legislation that keep DRM advocates busy, still fighting for basic rights today. What is remarkable about the DRM is the process of frame realignment that allowed disparate social groups to agree upon a highly complex, hybrid conception of rights. It was their ability to hybridize ideas and realign interests that fused social and technological concerns into one comprehensive set of regulatory standards. We argue that this movement, better than any other in contemporary U.S. history, successfully reframed its cause to include the interests of all people—to redefine disability as an environmental and architectural limitation of the nation, rather than a medical condition of individuals.

In order to support this claim, we follow the theoretical structure established in the previous chapter. After reconstructing the origins of the movement, we first lay out the primary relevant social groups contributing to this storyline, before identifying the technological frames and focal issues around which the dominant narratives of the DRM were woven. The chapter then concludes with two sections that consider how a common language was constructed through action, and how access to public life was realized.

ORIGINS OF THE MOVEMENT

When asked to include the interests of the disabled in the Civil Rights Act of 1964, the refusal of civil rights activists to cooperate was explained away by arguing such language would dilute the power of the bill. For those fighting for the provision of rights to be contingent, not on race, religion, national origin, or, by 1974, gender, the additional association with disabled persons was seen as political suicide. After all, people of color and women had spent centuries trying to uncouple their social status from that of the disabled. A common cry of suffrage campaigns asked, for example, why women should be classed with "idiots, lunatics, persons under guardianship, and felons?" This is but one of countless examples employed by historian Douglas Baynton as evidence of the "cultural power of disability to discredit."[2]

That social restrictions were placed on the disabled is not exactly new. Historically, although people with disabilities were not always physically segregated from the general population, many subpopulations were limited in their civil liberties. For instance, whereas the Old Testament advocated for the removal of physical barriers for the blind and deaf, the Romans' Justinian Code —which served as the legal foundation for many European nations through the 18th century—prevented persons with mental disabilities from marrying.[3]

The first U.S. immigration law of 1882 prohibited entry to "any person unable to take care of himself or herself without becoming a public charge," and it is this notion of economic dependency—of becoming a public charge of the state—that institutionalized the notion that persons with disabilities are not entitled to rights and choices in their manner of living.[4] Nonetheless, before the second industrial revolution, most families historically assumed the responsibility of caring for all their family members with pride.

Institutionalization, or the systematic physical segregation of persons with disabilities into asylums, rather than the traditional household-based system of care, became a popular solution for providing aid to those requiring supportive services in the 19th century. Many disability rights scholars argue that the process of industrialization and the "commercialized existence" perpetuated by the capitalist market system brought on this societal shift from internal familial support systems to the outsourcing of familial care-giving.[5] In a capitalist, mechanized society, many social differences were reframed as inefficiencies to be cured, as we argued in the previous chapter, by supply-side mechanisms.

James Scott's notion of the "legible" cityscape provides a useful lens to understand this desire for socio-spatial control. Legibility, for Scott, is a process of reduction and simplification, meant to make complex, multifarious systems, such as the provision of social services, more manageable by authorities. This "synoptic view of a selective reality," however, tends to avoid, or sometimes suppress, the margins of society and space.[6] Simply put, if there are problems that the state doesn't want to see, because they are uncomfortable or seem to challenge the existence of ideal conditions, they are made to disappear into spaces where they can be controlled. Although many political scientists would argue that governing a landscape as large as the United States renders the occasional myopic generalization necessary, it is often the minority populations constituting the margins of society that are most in need of careful and sensitive consideration.

By segregating those in need of supportive services from the general population, minor difference was transformed into "disability" through institutionalization. Geographer Rob Imrie understands this social construction of disability to be uniquely "linked to the creation of the built environment, both those environments which seek to serve people with disabilities (e.g. the special schools) and those which effectively exclude them."[7] The widespread institutionalization of persons with disabilities in the United States only heightened the growing misconception that this population was intrinsically dependent—out of sight, out of mind.

It was not until major figures personalized this minority, such as Helen Keller with her stories of struggle and triumph over both deafness and blindness, that the 19th-century industrial paradigm began to break down. Keller was a charismatic social reformer who spoke eloquently about the oppression and alienation of persons with disabilities perpetuated through the built world. Her 1903 autobiography served to begin a shift of social consciousness for the early DRM, much in the same way that *Silent Spring* later served to popularize the tenets of the environmental movement.

Paradoxically, Keller's stories of triumph over the challenges presented by deafness and blindness more deeply impacted the social perception of disabilities than did the four successful terms of President Franklin D. Roosevelt (FDR). FDR was elected president of the US 11 years after he lost the use of his legs to polio. FDR managed to keep his disability relatively hidden from popular culture, as some polio patients did learn to walk again, and his strength as a leader allowed most citizens to assume that he must have been "cured."[8] The media perpetuated this illusion, rarely capturing FDR in his wheelchair, while widely publishing photos of the president during his daily swim.

This personal experience with paralysis did impact FDR's policies to some extent. The focus of his efforts, however, remained primarily medical in nature. In his first term as president, FDR helped to start the National March of Dimes, to fund research and rehabilitation services for polio survivors. FDR's involvement, although always presented in terms of his generosity as a benefactor, instead of as a disabled person, helped lead to the development of the polio vaccine.[9] Roosevelt also argued for universal care for the physically disabled, which was a radical notion at the time, comparing it with universal education for all citizens.[10]

The president did not, however, see equality in hiring practices as a fundamental right for the disabled. In fact, the League of the Physically Handicapped actively petitioned Roosevelt to end discriminatory hiring practices in the Works Progress Administration. After conducting a national survey that demonstrated the gravity of the issue, representatives from this group slept on the lawn of the Washington Monument in hopes of discussing these findings with the president's staff.[11] However, regardless of the personal connection FDR might have felt to their cause, the disability rights activists' efforts were largely ignored.

Not until the early 1950s did a society accustomed to life without accommodations for people with disabilities begin considering the notion of reintegration. With injured soldiers returning from World War II requiring wheelchairs to participate in the promises of the GI Bill, the University of Illinois developed a program specifically geared to disabled students as early as 1948. The university's newly founded Division of Rehabilitation Education Services developed a sports program and an accessible paratransit system for the few wheelchair-inaccessible portions of the campus to ensure that all students had a rich, barrier-free educational experience.[12] Once the necessary independent living provisions were developed for these student–veterans, the university slowly became more accepting of a variety of disabilities. In 1962, the Guy M. Beckwith Living Center, a dorm operated for and by students with severe disabilities, opened its doors.

Despite these novel forays into reintegration, institutionalization was still a reality for most people with disabilities in the United States. With the system so embedded into North American culture, the problem of transitioning the generation of citizens growing up in hospitals to independent life confounded everyone. In 1958, New York City's Goldwater Memorial Hospital chose one resident, Anne Emerman, as a test case for deinstitutionalization. After graduating from high school, Emerman defied all odds and graduated from Columbia University with a Master's in social work and later became the director of the mayor's Office for People with Disabilities in New York City.[13] She was the first of many former institution residents to leave the hospital system and become a leader of the growing social movement.

Although disability was still thought of as a problem of medical care rather than of rights, early leaders such as Keller and Roosevelt contributed to a widening of the myopic perspective traditionally used to view the treatment of disabled persons. The paradigm shift required for the government to alter its management system for disabled persons from the legible, but socially segregated, practice of institutionalization to the messy, but spatially just, practice of reintegration should not be underestimated. This first generation of activists, raised in a world of segregation, empowered the evolving movement to reframe its claims from a language of medical needs to a language of rights.

This brief background to the movement provides the context required to tell the rest of the story from the perspective of individuals and groups.

RELEVANT SOCIAL GROUPS

In our analysis and interviews concerning the DRM, we found six relevant social groups: grassroots advocates, as well as the medical community, the legal community, the welfare reform community, and the business community. Although grassroots advocates of spatial and programmatic accessibility synthesized their campaigns before the enactment of the ADA, the agendas of movement leaders and the methods of demonstration employed for each social group largely remained distinct. As the movement gained momentum, four other relevant social groups began to emerge. First, institutionalization spurred the engagement of the health care industry with the dialogue about disability rights. Second, disability rights law sprung directly out of the legalese of the CRM, but the DRM only engaged professionals who personally identified with the cause as their lobby. Third, as the status of the movement rose in public opinion, elected officials interested in welfare reform began to understand that providing spatial and programmatic access to public jobs and services might alleviate the "public charge" or burden of disability. And fourth, once it became clear that ramps and other spatial and programmatic accommodations would be required of businesses that benefited from public funds, the business community became a major force within the discussion of disability rights. Before we can understand the technological frames that these social groups assumed, the nature of each relevant social group deserves a bit more explanation.

Grassroots Advocates

The grassroots claims of the DRM emerged from two separate, but highly related, campaigns: one for spatial accessibility and one for programmatic accessibility. Those advocates who saw physical barriers to accessing public transit, commercial buildings, university campuses, and other publicly funded places as the major hindrance to equal rights championed spatial accessibility. This relevant social group came out of the anti-institutionalization factions of the DRM. Alternatively, those advocates who saw programmatic barriers to accessing employment, social services, and other public goods as of paramount importance to the movement adopted the rights-based language more naturally than those indebted to the independent living moniker. Certain subcultures within the movement—the physically or mentally disabled, for example—saw their struggle as distinct from other types of disability. As evidenced by the adoption of Helen Keller as a national icon, the deaf and blind communities often benefited from preferential treatment by the public. A patchwork of cultural frames delineated activists from one another within the early part of the movement, but, once disability was reframed in more holistic terms, DRM activists began to see how spatial and programmatic accessibility, as well as the rights of specific subcultures of disability, might be overlapping causes.

The Medical Community

The medical community was the first relevant social group, outside the movement activist network, to become heavily involved in the movement discourse. Institutionalization allowed for the consolidation of medical services for persons with disabilities, and many health care professionals adopted "separate but equal" arguments, as in the pre-civil rights era, to make the case for why institutionalization benefited persons with disabilities more than it harmed them. Of course, within this group were also compassionate, thoughtful health care professionals, in addition to self-serving bureaucrats, who understood the limitations of social and physical segregation for the institutionalized. What almost no one in this social group shared with DRM advocates, until much later in the movement, was personal experience as a person with a disability, and, because of their commitment to the medical or political communities they served, the members were generally unable to see possibilities for radical change.

The Legal Community

The dispassionate arguments of the medical community might have been unthinking, at least through the eyes of the disabled themselves. The slogan that defined the ethic of the movement—nothing without us, about us, is for us—would seem to disallow others to speak on its behalf. This slogan came out of South Africa and quickly became the primary rallying cry for movement advocates of all persuasions. Simply put, no lawyer without a personal affiliation to disability was permitted to represent the movement in negotiations. This created a unique legal community to buttress the movement. As the movement matured, many advocates within the first generation of deinstitutionalized university students gravitated towards a career in law or politics for just this reason.

The Welfare Reform Community

Welfare reformers, who were commonly conservative politicians interested in limiting government spending on social services, became unlikely allies for DRM lobbyists, because both groups had an interest in increasing the independence of people with disabilities. Although the motivations and approach were often quite different, these two interest groups saw how their interests might overlap and sought out shared solutions. The ability of grassroots advocates to extend their frame of interpretation to a previously hostile group has much to say for their political sophistication.

The Business Community

Business leaders, however, were often greatly afraid of the hidden costs of federally mandated architectural regulations, and that social group was an outspoken opponent of those arguing for legislation to mandate barrier-free commercial spaces. Of the relevant social groups involved in the DRM dialogue, the business community and, earlier on, the medical community, had the most to lose from substantive change, and thus they were typically the most stagnant in their conceptualization of how things might be different than the status quo. If we understand the business community as a technological network that includes the buildings it owns and operates, then it is easy to understand how such an enormous system would be resistant to change.

In hindsight, it seems perfectly natural that social groups related to the legislative construction of disability rights can be categorized in this fashion. These categories, however, were far from clear at the beginning and only emerged through action.

TECHNOLOGICAL FRAMES

Although the relevant social groups that emerged in the conflict over disability rights now seem unsurprising, the hybridity of the technological frames employed by the movement's leaders is. Few movements have been able to so successfully fuse, or exploit, conflicting interpretations of reality into one holistic frame. Before we discuss how this fusion took place, however, we must first understand the frames of other relevant social groups to see how, historically, less powerful grassroots advocates eclipsed these more stable and powerful frames.

The Supply-side Frame

In the previous chapter, we defined the supply-side frame as seeing economic growth created only through reducing obstacles, in the form of taxes or regulation, to producers. Producers, or in this case service providers, will then be able to provide consumers with lower-cost services. And, as we discussed earlier in this chapter, the medical community, the business community, and sometimes the welfare reform community maintained the most static stance toward the rights claims made by the DRM leaders because, we found, that members of those three groups tend to interpret conditions through the supply-side frame.

The resistance shown by the medical community also exemplifies its members' status as enframed agents, which we define in Chapter 4 as actors who are blind, or at least resistant, to competing interpretations of reality, because their ranking in the group depends upon their apparent commitment to their peers and their leadership in advocating for shared ideas. The main obstacle to success for enframed actors is that they become so embedded in a particular manner of interpretation that it limits their ability to participate in the creation of new, collaborative solutions that include their interests.

During the early phase of the DRM campaign, the medical community adopted enframed supply-side reasoning to make the case for the practice of institutionalization. From its perspective, "disabled" consumers required services that were most efficiently and effectively delivered through a consolidated center of care. These actors understood the financial and logistical investment already made in the institutionalized care industry and could not imagine how dissolving the system could improve care. Nor could they comprehend how another solution, which bore significant new, upfront costs, might be worth the financial and political risks. Nor could these same actors clearly see where they might lie in a new hierarchy of power relations. As a result, they were not eager to assist in the dismantling of a program in which they had significant influence.

Although members of the business community were far from enframed in the medical definition of disability, they found common cause with institutions, only because they saw economic burdens being shifted to them. Together, they made a powerful lobby.

The Demand-side Frame

In the previous chapter, we defined the demand-side technological frame as seeing the unwanted external costs of production, such as degraded air quality, as being avoided only by reducing system-wide demand. In this case, such reasoning requires that as many disabled people as possible be released from institutional care. Although the least compassionate actors simply argued for unmanaged release of inmates, more compassionate conservatives recognized that release would necessarily be accompanied by the innovative resources and new home-based technologies to allow the disabled to care for themselves. In the end, most demand-side actors could see such a strategy as reducing demand on resources.

The welfare reform community, made up of elected officials and government workers, employed this demand-side frame to support the claims of grassroots advocates of both spatial and programmatic accessibility. Conservative welfare reformers argued that, although the upfront costs of such change would be significant, the government could not afford to continue keeping persons with disabilities out of the educational system, the free market economy, and thus the workforce. For these demand-side thinkers, the costs of financially supporting uneducated, and thus unemployable, persons were too great for the government to continue to bear.

As DRM strategies matured, movement leaders were able to make the demand-side frame of interpretation accessible and attractive to a number of influential people in the medical community, thus moving some of that group from a supply-side to a demand-side mode of interpreting events that were unfolding on a daily basis.

The Effect-side Frame

In the previous chapter, we defined the effect-side technological frame as seeing technologies as neither good nor bad in essence. From within this frame, the value of a technology, including its organizational structure and day-to-day practices, depends on who is affected by change, how they are affected, and when. DRM grassroots advocates, and the legal community that served their interests, came to inhabit this frame, even if they did not at the beginning.

DRM advocates watched as the CRM's national power dissolved, and its leaders responded with calls to action that spoke of a broadly framed, effect-side approach to movement advocacy. DRM leaders understood that both the medical community and the welfare reform community, or the demand- and supply-side arguments posited within the movement dialogue, did not entirely capture their interests. They also understood that, although quality health care provision was critical, social segregation would never suffice as a

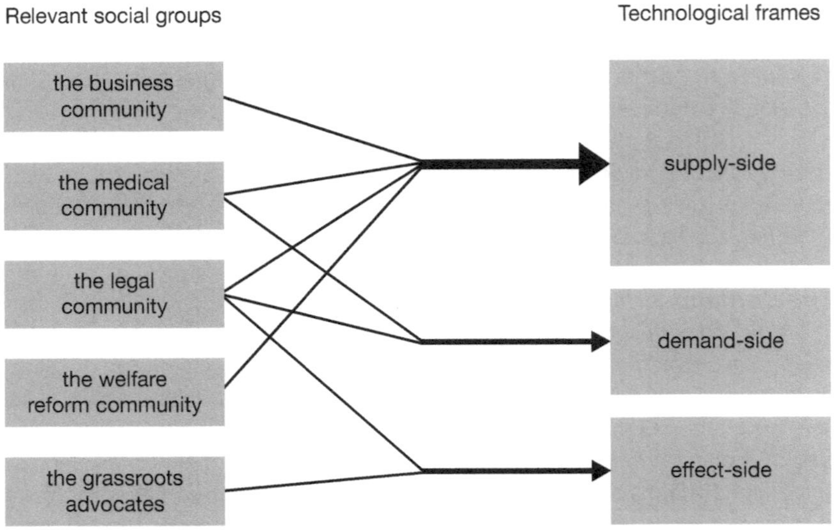

Figure 9.1 Relationship of Relevant Social Groups to Technological Frames, 2008.

venue to provide such care. And, although they wanted independence as a people, welfare reform was also a dangerously reductive lens through which to conceptualize that independence. Nevertheless, instead of dismissing these powerful social groups as prejudiced or myopic, DRM leaders participated in a delicate, but open, process of translation that allowed for new technological solutions, both home-based and institution-based, to be proposed and debated until it was clear that their effects would be just. In the process, they brought others with them.

Figure 9.1 summarizes how the five relevant social groups affiliated with the three technological frames over time.

Frame Integration

This tapestry of technological frames is predictable, considering the latent interests of each group. What was extraordinary, however, was the ability of the DRM leadership to switch codes, or understand, with empathy, the technological frames of other competing and sometimes hostile social groups.

To emphasize its frame-switching capability, it is helpful to compare the DRM with the larger CRM of which it is a part. It is not uncommon for successful social movement leaders to gain enough status within the political structure that they too become enframed by group visions. The CRM is an example of this tragic phenomenon. The CRM had four major organizations that led its advocacy efforts: the National Association of the Advancement of Colored People (NAACP), the Student Nonviolent Coordinating Committee, the Southern Christian Leadership Conference, and the Congress of Racial Equity. At times in the early growth of the movement, each of these organizations gained enough financial and political support to exert great influence over the movement trajectory, and all of the "Big Four" organizations continued to vie for movement leadership throughout the 1960s. Leaders of the Big Four, however, each became enframed by their need to maintain their organization's status within the broader movement and their position regarding appropriate organizational relationships with the government, and their desire for political power clouded the motivations for their decisions and often superseded CRM goals. This infighting over organizational authority and ideological purity only served to weaken all four organizations.

By 1970, only 15 percent of movement protests were organized by the "Big Four," whereas these aforementioned groups organized over 80 percent of movement events in 1961.[14] After the assassinations of President Kennedy (1963) and Dr. King (1968), as well as the passing of the Fair Housing Act in 1968, the centralized structure of the CRM was replaced with a "ghetto-bred generation (of movement organizations) with reputations no larger than a single city or neighborhood or even a particular block."[15] Without the shared vision of a collective frame, and the shared experience of collective action, this once united movement could not organize enough political will to continue fighting for national standards that would advance its goals for civil rights.

In contrast to the CRM, the DRM resisted ideological purity. The process of translation, of code-switching, between slightly divergent but potentially overlapping stakeholders to pave an open path toward a just end proved to be a delicate and complicated endeavor. The methods employed by the DRM to consolidate its identity by integrating multiple frames of interpretation also became the major focal issues that drove the movement, and thus laid the foundation for future leaders to continue down that path after the first generation of advocates retired.

FOCAL ISSUES

> Who are the disabled? In addition to the familiar disabilities associated with congenital factors, birth trauma, disease, and mental illness must be added the great number associated with industrial injury, major and chronic illness, stress and advanced age. It is no exaggeration to say that almost every one of us will feel the effect of a disabling condition, temporarily or long term in our lifetime.[16]

In the previous chapter, we defined "focal issues" as the problems that galvanize public talk and policy-making in particular places, or, as one respondent put it, they are problems that "float to the top" of public consciousness. Two major focal issues drive the dominant narrative of the DRM. First, the definition of disability itself is a critical storyline within the movement; and, second, the dogmatically inclusive mantra of the movement—nothing without us, about us, is for us—colors the backdrop of the entire movement's drama. Both of these focal issues were made visible by the work of the DRM leader, Ed Roberts.

Defining Disability

In the earlier years of the DRM, the cause was alternately known as Civil Rights for Disabled People or the Independent Living Movement. At the age of 14, Roberts was cast into these previously unknown groups by polio. He subsequently became paralyzed and dependent on an iron lung. He attended most of high school by phone, until he taught himself glossopharyngeal breathing so that he could attend his final year of high school in person. This technique involves the swallowing of air, which allowed Roberts to survive without the iron lung for brief periods of time. He was determined to pursue a degree in political science at the University of California at Berkeley, despite being told by the administration "we tried cripples, and they don't work."[17] After successfully suing the university, Roberts was housed in the Berkeley Infirmary at Cowell Hospital, because the dorms were not accessible and could not accommodate his 800 lb iron lung (Figure 9.2). However, his lawsuit made national news, and other disabled students empowered by his story soon joined Roberts. This growing group of disabled students was at least partially responsible for organizing the People's Park demonstrations on campus in 1964, and they were empowered by the energy displayed by leaders during these events. Roberts recalls his participation in early free speech demonstrations as primary to his development as a civil agitator:

> John Hessler (another Cowell resident) and I used to roll right up to the front of the demonstrations and stare down the police. What could they do? When they threatened to arrest us, we just asked them, "How are you going to get us in there? Do you have an iron lung in your prison?" That's one drawback of the Americans with Disabilities Act I guess, because they didn't have accessible jails back then, which meant they didn't arrest us.[18]

Roberts had a wonderful sense of humor and, in his speeches, he shared his own struggles in a candid and personal, but inclusive, way—humanizing the greater movement to the point where his calls for unity seemed like the only reasonable path. After his graduation from Berkeley in the late 1960s, Roberts created the Disabled Students Program at Berkeley, which attended to common needs of wheelchair-bound students, such as accessible housing, wheelchair repair, and attendant care. Roberts and his colleagues also started a political group called the Rolling Quads, who worked toward making Berkeley a barrier-free campus. He would later point to this spatial agenda as pivotal to the greater paradigmatic change that took place as the movement gained momentum. "Over a period of years, we literally transformed the U.C. campus and the City of Berkeley. We changed the architecture and we changed attitudes."[19] Berkeley became the literal testing ground for many techniques that would later constitute the spatial regulations mandated in the ADA. It was through this process that movement leaders came to understand the power of spatial metaphors in achieving the parallel goals of physical access and social acceptance of persons with disabilities.

Nothing About Us Is for Us Without Us

In 1972, Roberts expanded his horizon beyond campus boundaries to create the first Center for Independent Living (CIL) in Berkeley—a group organized by and for people with disabilities. In that role he quickly became an international leader. From the post, Roberts was able to spread his message, the contextualized version of which is quoted at the opening of this chapter—when others speak for you, you lose. It is this underlying theme of grassroots leadership that empowered an international movement of profoundly oppressed people to overcome this stigma of dependency.

> My experiences in Berkeley taught me a number of invaluable lessons. One of our most critical strategic decisions was to join forces with persons with other types of disabilities. . . . We enlisted the support of deaf students, blind students, and students with epilepsy and others. We quickly learned the value and strength of coalition politics. As the years went by, our struggle moved from city to county to state to national politics. We found that we also had many common issues with the elderly and began to form coalitions. We knew that institutionalization made no sense either for a disabled or elderly person. We knew that the medical model based on illness made no sense. We knew we had to move toward models based on human potential.[20]

Although universities such as the University of California at Berkeley were quickly learning how to accommodate and even support their physically disabled students, it was unclear how these students would avoid reinstitutionalization after college, because of all the barriers to independent living that still existed off campus. The amelioration of some of those obstacles was Roberts' goal when he and his colleagues founded the first CIL in Berkeley in 1972. The by-laws stated that at least 51 percent of staff and board members had to be disabled persons, although their definition of disability was already quite broad. Roberts "saw CIL as a model for joining all the splintered factions of different disability organizations . . . this was the vision we had for the future of the movement."[21] The CIL definition of disability related to a self-help mentality, working to replace the perception of people with disabilities as dependent with one of empowerment. Within a few years, the CIL was providing peer counseling, job development, health maintenance, and legal assistance —even offering a degree program focused on the psychology of disability.[22] This model was quickly replicated in other major cities across the globe, with over 400 CILs founded worldwide by 1995.[23]

Figure 9.2 Local Reporting of Acceptance to Berkeley by Ed Roberts. From the *Burlingame Advance*. Burlingame, CA.

25,000 . . . But Just One Like Ed

ED ROBERTS . . . A "FIRST" FOR MARCH OF DIMES
Burlingame resident—and his iron lung—are enrolled at U.C.

There are more than 25,000 students on the University of California campus in Berkeley, but only one like Ed Roberts, 23, son of Mr. and Mrs. Verne Roberts, 116 Bloomfield Road, Burlingame.

In fact, his case is so unusual that university officials tentatively describe his attendance as "experimental" and have announced that only one such individual will be accepted at this time.

Ed, who was stricken with bulbar polio at the age of 14, sleeps in an iron lung in his second floor room at Cowell Memorial Hospital on campus. He goes to class in a wheel chair. Unable to move any part of his body but his head, he must depend upon others to bathe, feed, dress and care for him. Even his class notes must be taken by an assistant.

It is believed this is the first time in the 25-year history of the National Foundation—March of Dimes that a polio victim so severely involved has uprooted himself to this extent.

The move meant that an iron lung had to be transferred to Cowell Hospital from Fairmont Hospital to supplement the lung kept at Ed's home for use during school vacations.

It meant special training for the staff at Cowell. It meant hiring two attendants—Chuck Taylor, who has the day shift and takes him to class, and Charles Buff, who works evenings, gives Ed his tub bath and puts him in the iron lung, where the polio victim spends 12 to 14 hours each night.

All costs involved in Ed's attendance at Cal are borne by his family or outside agencies such as the Vocational Rehabilitation Service, which is underwriting the cost of tuition, books, and supplies; National Foundation, the iron lung, and the Burlingame Rotary Club, which is helping toward the cost of attendants.

Ed is intelligent and determined. He already has proven his ability to cope with college by attending College of San Mateo, where he completed a two-year liberal arts course in three years with a grade point average of better than 3.2. He is majoring in political science at Cal, hoping to receive his degree in three years.

Later? Maybe law school.

Ed manages to remain outside the iron lung during the day by "frog breathing," a method of gulping air. His progress in this area has been by degrees. After five or six months in the iron lung following his illness, he began staying out one second, two seconds, finally a minute.

In February, 1953, the entire Verne Roberts family was stricken with polio. His parents and three brothers quickly recovered with no paralysis, but Ed's case was severe. He was at Community Hospital a year, and at Children's Hospital in San Francisco about nine months before he was allowed to go home for a year. He was in and out of Fairmont Hospital in San Leandro five times.

How does he like Cal? "This

(Please see Page 4, Col. 7)

One important wing of the Berkeley CIL housed its Disabled Paralegal Advocacy Program. This legal aid program grew into its own organization, the Disability Rights Education and Defense Fund (DREDF), by 1979. The DREDF operates for the DRM much like the NAACP functioned for the CRM, working to defend and expand the rights of its constituencies. DREDF staff often served as the lawyers for major disability rights cases and acted as consultants on every case that dealt with these issues. When federal policy issues became points of contention for the movement, as will be discussed in the next section of this chapter, leaders of the DREDF also helped organize related campaigns to protest or protect certain legislation. As the more professionalized wing of the movement, the DREDF was heavily involved in the organizing of interest groups and the drafting of legislation, but left the more radical protests to its grassroots partners.

One such radical group, Americans Disabled for Attendant Programs Today (ADAPT), made national news in 1978 for its employment of non-violent civil disobedient protest methods to block the Denver bus system from operating until authorities agreed to make the system more accessible. Today, there is a city plaque at the demonstration site honoring these fearless protestors.[24] Members of this group employed what they referred to as non-violent "street fighting tactics" to make their points, often climbing out of wheelchairs and laying their disabled bodies on the street as dramatic gestures to heighten the issues and to garner the media attention necessary to change the public's minds. Groups such as ADAPT saw themselves as outside of the mainstream DRM, not only because of their radical demonstration tactics, but also because of the more severely disabled population for which they advocated. Yet, in the end, the CIL often trained future members of ADAPT as well, and, not surprisingly, the stages of their approach—"letter writing, followed by demonstrations, and lawsuits only as a last resort"—were basically the same as those of their mainstream brethren.[25] In fact, it was the shared experience of demonstration between many different activist groups within the movement that finally solidified their presence as a unified collective.

It was these two focal issues—the self-conscious redefinition of "disability," and organizing a community that could say with conviction, "nothing about us is for us without us"—that set the stage for collective action, not in institutions, but in the streets.

FINDING SHARED LANGUAGE THROUGH ACTION

> Disability is not so much the lack of a sense or the presence of a physical or mental impairment as it is the reception and construction of that difference. . . . An impairment is a physical fact, but a disability is a social construction. For example, lack of mobility is an impairment, but an environment without ramps turns that impairment into a disability . . . a disability must be socially constructed.[26]

Because this movement was, at once, both intensely spatial and pervasively cultural in its goals, physical occupations of space were highly successful demonstration techniques. These demonstrations served, not only to illustrate in very real terms the physical barriers to equal access that existed, but also to personalize the issue with human faces and, most importantly, to put people with different types of disability into a singular space to realize and then act out their shared values. The innately spatial quality of this movement also provides a base to link this movement with the inherently spatial and architectural focus of this book. In these final sections of this chapter, we chronicle the progression of the Architectural Barriers Act (ABA) that led to the adoption of the ADA, not only to understand the spatial dimensions of this movement more clearly, but also to illustrate how these physical demonstrations served to codify movement values for advocates through the act of participating in collective action.

As we noted earlier in this chapter, when waves of injured veterans returned from World War II ready to utilize the educational benefits promised to them by the GI Bill, university campuses first began grappling with the issue of architectural accessibility. The U.S. Veteran's Administration published a set of construction criteria for universities receiving funds under the GI Bill, although the implementation of these criteria was never enforced. Based on research conducted by the Easter Seals, in partnership with the University of Illinois, the first nationally recognized accessible design standard—ANSI A117.1 Accessible and Usable Buildings and Facilities—was released in 1961 and served as the basis for subsequent related legislation.[27]

Gaining traction from recent civil rights legislation and the rising number of disenfranchised veterans returning from the Vietnam War, the first major legislative victory for the DRM was the ABA of 1968.[28] ABA required that buildings built with federal funds be accessible to persons with disabilities, but this only addressed facility accessibility, not programmatic accessibility.[29] Often, there was no way to regulate these buildings or to provide their designers with training to ensure proper application of the Act's requirements. In short, the legislation had no "teeth." When an attempt to add disabilities to the interest groups protected under the Civil Rights Act in 1972 failed, some legislators postulated that this language could possibly be tacked on to another bill. However, no one, including DRM advocates, saw this as a viable possibility at the time, and no lobbying was done to that effect.[30] In 1973, however, the legislature passed the Rehabilitation Act to address the ABA's gaps in implementation, and the stance that disabilities be treated as a medical concern instead of a problem of rights was assumed in every section of the bill but one—Section 504.[31]

Much to the surprise of disability rights advocates, who had not explicitly requested such language to be put into the bill, wording for Section 504 came, almost verbatim, from Title VI of the Civil Rights Act of 1964. The wording deemed that,

> No otherwise qualified individual with a disability in the United States, as defined in section 705(20) of this title, shall, solely by reason of her or his disability, be excluded from the participation in, be denied the benefits of, or be subjected to discrimination under any program or activity receiving Federal financial assistance or under any program or activity conducted by any Executive agency or by the United States Postal Service.

When later asked, congressional aides and movement leaders could not recall who inserted the civil rights language into the bill.[32]

The Ford administration quickly realized the potential impact of Section 504, estimating that its compliance would take billions of dollars to administer. Implementation of the regulation stalled until the Carter administration took office. In his campaign, Jimmy Carter had made promises to the DRM. However, Carter and his new Health, Education and Welfare Department (HEW) director, Joseph Califano, further stalled the signing of the regulations once they understood their scope. At this point, the American Coalition of Citizens with Disabilities, a newly formed "coalition of coalitions," made the signing of these regulations the focus of their efforts.[33] Three hundred people took over Califano's office in Washington, DC, but were denied food and access to telephones, and the protestors left within 28 hours (Figure 9.3). Simultaneously, at the nexus of the DRM in San Francisco, hundreds of severely disabled protestors held their ground at great risk to their health, occupying the regional offices of the HEW for 25 days.[34] Roberts, then state director of rehabilitation, came and spoke in support of the protest—remarking on the widespread support from outside civil rights groups such as the Black Panthers, who brought an Easter dinner for the protestors during their occupation:

> Many of you here have championed for black rights, women's rights, Chicano rights, senior citizens' rights and others. We share common enemies—discrimination, fear, ignorance and the basic reluctance on the part of the establishment to extend us our rights because it would be too expensive. Strong 504 regulations could permit us to attend any university or college, and to use every program or agency supported by federal funds. It would literally open doors for employment, education, and recreation; without it we are second-class citizens, living on the fringe of society, unable to participate, and devalued.

Figure 9.3 Demonstrators in Front of the Washington, DC, HEW Building in 1977.

Historian Joseph Shapiro refers to this event as the "political coming of age of the disability rights movement . . . a mini-Woodstock," where people with different disabilities were forced to not only join together, but also to actually live in close proximity for a month and survive together.[35] Participants fell in love and found self-worth, and the collective identity that had only been discussed in theory was created through action during their occupation. On April 28, Califano signed the regulations, and two days later the newly solidified DRM marched in the streets chanting, "We have overcome."

The backlash against these regulations experienced around the country was profound. Enforcing disability rights legislation meant higher costs for business owners, a more difficult pill to swallow than the cost-saving measures resulting from integration during the CRM. Despite the backlash, two other major successes were won in the years just following the ratification of Section 504. First, the Education for All Handicapped Children Act of 1975 guaranteed the right of children with disabilities to attend public schools in an integrated environment, to the greatest extent possible. Second, Congress awarded the federal Department of Rehabilitation Services funds to operate CILs across the country.

This network of CILs served to empower and educate thousands of disabled citizens, but their reliance on federal funds also diluted some of the organizations' advocacy power. This situation strongly paralleled the earlier funding and advocacy predicament of the CRM. Community Development Corporations, initially funded by the federal government to be vehicles for urban empowerment for the disenfranchised, found themselves in economic complicity with municipal governments, and limited by them, in the early 1970s. However, unlike the fracturing CRM, the DRM's primary organizations were able to work together to resituate their roles to best support the greater movement goals in the face of this new challenge. In 1979, the DREDF left the Berkeley CIL and became its own national entity in order to fill these advocacy gaps. When the Reagan administration threatened to weaken Section 504 regulations in 1981, the DREDF mobilized 40,000 citizens to write letters to the White House in protest.[36] Not only did these protests raise the awareness of then Vice President George H.W. Bush, the terms "reasonable accommodation," "reasonable modification," and "undue burden" were introduced into the legal debate that would continue in the courts until the enactment of the ADA in 1990.

The Reagan administration was a quiet time for the DRM, with several critics claiming during those years that 1978 was the peak of the movement.[37] Enforcement of Section 504 was inconsistent at best, and the Department of Justice, which was in charge of ensuring compliance, did not further the implementation of these regulations. For instance, in *Grove City College v. Bell* (1984), the Supreme Court ruled that only entities directly receiving federal funding (in this case, a single university department, instead of the entire campus) had to comply with Section 504 regulations.[38] In addition, the implications of the bill presented an enormous learning curve for disabled activists, and so the DREDF held workshops to train advocates on how to help enforce 504 regulations. As a result of the efforts of the 1970s DRM participants, the next generation of disabled activists was educated in a public school system to which their predecessors never had access. These children grew up in a world where ramps, curb cuts, and accessible bathrooms were not only tangible goals, but also civil rights to which they were entitled. By the late 1980s, these young activists reenergized existing advocacy groups to enact the movement's watershed legislation to date, with a more aware George H.W. Bush now in office.

Because many activists felt frustrated with the spotty enforcement of Section 504, a team of leaders from the National Council on the Handicapped began arguing for further legislation in 1983. In 1988, a comprehensive bill entitled the Americans with Disabilities Act, "prohibiting discrimination on the basis of handicap," won the endorsement of presidential candidate George H.W. Bush and several members of Congress, but it died at the session's end. Redrafted in 1989 by staff of Senators Edward Kennedy (D–MA) and Thomas Harkin (D–IA), with the help of a committee of disability rights attorneys coordinated by the DREDF, the new version of the bill omitted requirements for the retrofit of older structures and/or higher standards for insurance companies, but expanded the regulations regarding public accommodations and public transportation. The DREDF also coordinated the lobbying efforts of roughly 75 national advocacy organizations. Deborah Kaplan, the executive director of the World Institute for Disability at the time, saw the movement's cohesion as pivotal to the political successes of the early 1990s—"Passing the (ADA) was a real lobbying effort that brought together every part of the disability movement: blind groups, deaf groups, people with AIDS, independent living centers, ADAPT, everybody unified."[39]

Evoking the more expansive frame for the DRM, espoused by Roberts decades before and solidified during the Berkeley 504 demonstration, movement leaders garnered endorsement for the bill from over 180 national organizations. Around the country, persons with disabilities sent diaries chronicling the struggles of their daily lives to their representatives in Congress. Congressional attempts to weaken the bill were met with organized phone campaigns or protests.

> Coalitions . . . developed between the AIDS lobby, women's organizations and "grey power," while, more recently their lobbying for civil rights legislation for disability has sought to interlink a radical, left, politics, with the social and political concerns of the right-wing in America.[40]

ADAPT coordinated a Wheels of Justice march on Washington that included a short occupation of the Capitol rotunda. Efforts to remove antidiscrimination protection for HIV-positive food handlers drove the director of the DREDF to tell White House staff that she would rather let the bill die than to pass a version of it that excluded rights for those with HIV/AIDS.[41] No less significant in the endgame conflict, during the congressional hearings before the ratification of ADA, conservative senators employed right-wing economic logic, moving away from a pure rights argument to a hybrid frame based upon supply-side reasoning and welfare reform.

On July 26, 1990, President George H.W. Bush signed the ADA, which "prohibits discrimination in private employment, public accommodation, and telecommunications," into law. The ADA definition of disability is based on the one provided in the Rehabilitation Act of 1973, and thus also draws language from the Civil Rights Act of 1964. DREDF cofounder Mary Lou Breslin acknowledges that this sort of federal legislation did not just materialize on its own, but was pulled from a myriad of state laws and pushed through by the strength of the entire civil rights community:

> It's not like somebody just dreamed up the idea of applying civil rights coverage to all these entities, because a few states had done some of it already. If you looked at all the states and took all the best practices and policies and cludged them all together, you came up with about 60 percent of what the ADA was about. This was a process; it's not like the ADA hatched out of somebody's head full-blown. It was a complex process that built on experience over time.[42]

The ADA sat at the apex of a pyramid that was socially constructed over decades—some were the bricks of past triumphs in the state legislatures, and some were issues still plaguing the daily lives of thousands of citizens. Concepts upon which the ADA was built came from the everyday experiences of clients at the CIL, lobbyists with the DREDF, radicals at ADAPT, alcoholics, AIDS patients, clergy members, the institutionalized, and the elderly. In a defining moment for the DRM, Reverend Harold Wilke, a movement leader and one of the first American parish ministers with a severe disability, accepted the pen with which President George H.W. Bush signed the bill with his foot, as he had no arms (Figure 9.4).

Figure 9.4 Signing of the Americans with Disabilities Act, 1990. Rev. Wilke is in the top left of the picture.

And this Act had teeth. With the financial and judicial support of the federal government behind it, implementation of the bill was a realistic goal for advocates, regardless of the immediate costs it might impose on the business community. For the first time, the DRM was able to successfully push its argument beyond the limits of trade-off theories, positing disability rights as a moral imperative that superseded market deficiencies and created socio-technical space for new solutions to develop.

ADA legislation may have been incremental, but it fundamentally altered the urban form of the United States. It established accessible design standards, including curbs, ramps, sidewalks, workplace accommodations, elevators, and restrooms, for all publicly funded nonresidential spaces. The architectural design and construction industries now consider these accessibility standards to be commonplace, and the costs of building more accessible places have lowered as building habits change. The "cognitive praxis,"[43] or new forms of knowledge-making and popular understanding, of the DRM has been accepted into the spatial purview of the United States and fundamentally altered the nation's building culture. Public buildings and other commercial locales, which were relatively simple spaces from which to remove architectural barriers, now typically conform to the standards mandated by the ADA without question. Less physically pliable spaces, such as underground rail systems and spaces falling within the private residential sphere where the ADA was originally considered "unreasonable," have proved to have more obdurate technological momentum.[44] True to their proactive and flexible nature, DRM activists now work aggressively to equalize these spaces as well.

REALIZING ACCESS

The movement still advocates for disability rights through political lobbying, through civic education, and through the formation of strategic alliances that combat forces of normative prejudice from different angles. On a basic level, the local realities of enforcing abstract mandates still keep disability rights advocates busy.[45] A national campaign led by a group called Concrete Change continues to fight for small, but significant, spatial changes in the form of "visitability" standards that provide access to residential properties not covered under the ADA. Working with accessibility-oriented community design centers, Concrete Change identified three simple architectural changes that could be made in every home to make them accessible for visitation by a person with disabilities. These small changes do not require large infrastructural alterations or monetary commitments, but are more of an educational hurdle for the building industry to overcome. Many cities have begun to incentivize or even mandate visitability standards in new residential properties within the local building codes, but efforts to alter building codes in this manner often are met with formidable resistance from the residential construction and real-estate lobby. The case of S.M.A.R.T. Housing studied in the next chapter is a typical example.

One mandate upheld by the ADA, but still spotty in terms of enforcement, is accessible public transit. Although elevators have been built into the New York City subway system, for instance, their poor upkeep makes them an unreliable and sometimes even terrifying way to utilize the public transit system. In 2008, one of every six elevators and escalators in the New York

City subway system remained out of service for more than a month, and two-thirds of the elevators broke with someone trapped inside.[46] The transit authority willingly admits that this is primarily a maintenance staff training issue, more than an issue with the technologies themselves. Another way to say this from a sociotechnical perspective is that maintenance and staff habits are a part of the technology, not a separate issue.

In fact, technological solutions to solve access-associated architectural issues have become quite advanced since the ratification of the ADA. Technologies developed in accordance with the "subversive rationalization" of social movements coevolve with the movements that precipitated them.[47] Coevolution implies more than just a causal relationship between the social movements and the technologies they create.[48] In this cyclical model, technologies and societies operate in a continuous state of reflective coevolution in their optimal relationship. In the case of the DRM, the movement leaders continue to remain active participants in this dialectic between society, technology, and policy.

Based on recent sociotechnical innovations, over a decade after the ADA ratification, a proposal was put before the administration of President George W. Bush that refined and updated the ADA to heighten regulations for courts, theaters, swimming pools, golf courses, and other public venues. On the one hand, the U.S. Chamber of Commerce claimed that these amendments would be onerous, and, on the other, DRM advocates claimed them to be insufficient. The chief of the disability rights sector of the Justice Department, John L. Wodatch, resolved the dispute in saying: "Disability is inherent in the human condition. The vast majority of individuals who are fortunate enough to reach an advanced age will benefit from the proposed requirements."[49] The ADA Amendments Act went into effect on January 1, 2009 and served to recodify the DRM regenerative frame.

The most effective strategies for the DRM continue to be related to the movement's aptitude for coalition building. A significant example is the rocky relationship of the DRM with the CNU, which champions the front stoop—a prominent architectural barrier—as part of the quintessential American housing typology. In spite of initial conflict, the DRM and the CNU have now become unlikely allies.[50] DRM advocates strongly critiqued the hagiographic view of the front stoop, as well as other inaccessible housing design features supported by the CNU. Eleanor Smith, founder of Concrete Change, asked that visitability standards at least be presented as an option in CNU rhetoric, focusing on the zero-step entrance (Figure 9.5) and an accessible half-bathroom on the first floor of any multistory residence as easy, inclusive alternatives to the CNU aesthetics. CNU leaders responded positively to the critique, and, within a few years, an antagonistic relationship became an alliance against urban sprawl—a pattern of development also not suited for persons who do not drive. This alliance produced new language, with advocates from both camps making joint presentations on the importance of developing "lifelong communities"—educating practitioners interested in the ethics of either group on the importance of "designing for a pluralist population."[51]

This is not to say that every project built in the style of New Urbanism is now fully accessible and well conceived—even those that attempt to do so. For instance, ASSIST was the first community design center in the nation to

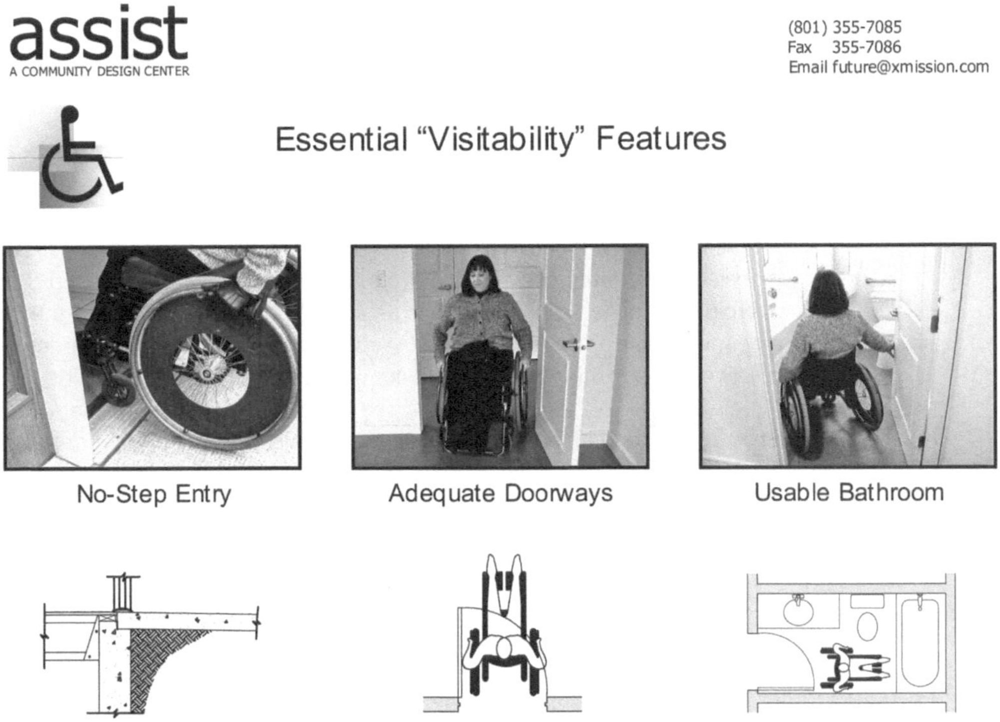

Figure 9.5 Visitability Standards. Developed by ASSIST and Concrete Change.

specialize in design for physically disabled persons. ASSIST recently developed a relationship with a New Urbanist builder in Utah who is interested in accessibility standards, primarily because of their appeal to the aging population. As a result of discussions with ASSIST, the builder agreed to make all of the model homes for the next New Urbanist development visitable. There was little discussion, however, about exactly how visitability capabilities would be addressed in the community. Figure 9.6 documents a wheelchair-bound architect at the grand opening of this New Urbanist community. Upon inquiring, the architect learned that, if he wanted to enter the home, he needed to travel down the block and enter the house from the alleyway behind it. Although that dishonorable approach to accessibility was not what the DRM had in mind, the acknowledgment of its perspective constitutes an enormous victory for the DRM. This sort of inclusive development of hybrid rhetoric opens the door for new, spatially just movement initiatives.

The DRM has been successful for two parallel reasons. First, it resisted the hubristic tendencies of many special interest groups. The various constituencies of the DRM privileged the greater mission over the agenda of any specific organization or definition of disability. Ed Roberts ingrained his philosophy of unification into the wide spectrum of early DRM leaders through his infectious rhetoric:

> When I was fourteen, I got polio. When the doctor took my parents aside, my mother asked, "Will he live?" The doctor looked at her

Figure 9.6 Mere Technical Compliance With ADA Does Not Provide Socially Equitable Access.

> and said, "You should probably hope he dies, because if he lives he will be nothing more than a vegetable for the rest of his life." Well, I'm here today as an artichoke. You know they're a little prickly on the outside with a big heart and I'd like to call on all the vegetables of the world to unite.[52]

The doctrine of inclusion posited by Ed Roberts was operationalized during the 504 protests and upheld by future generations during the ADA ratification campaigns. This ethic strengthened, expanded, and legitimized the movement at every turn. For instance, by never abandoning its allies in the AIDS lobby during the final hours of the ADA negotiations, the DRM was able to prove its solid commitment to the cause and continue to build from a platform of inclusivity in future struggles.

Second, its leaders were inclusive and receptive to the multiple frames of interpretation required to construct a just sociotechnical code. Rather than employ a single frame derived from their own personal experience or a single political strategy, they assembled a more expansive frame of action that spoke to the collective will of the public. This strategy is not opportunism, but a genuine understanding that people with different experiences, or a "situated perspective,"[53] add valuable knowledge to an ever-changing urban project. In other words, leaders learned to avoid ideological purity and thus garnered a broader political base. When the DRM engaged right-wing economists to make arguments about why the federal government could not afford to keep people with disabilities out of the job market, this expansive overlaying of various frames of understanding created an evocative web of reasoning for the ratification of ADA. The recent alliance of Concrete Change and other visitability-oriented organizations with the CNU offers a powerful example of the sort of hybrid, open approach to coalition-building that provides for the creative reinventing of spatial frameworks—these, in turn, allow new opportunities to emerge from the dialogue.

By resisting the hubristic urge to essentialize the movement into one or two specific disabilities, such as deafness or paralysis, disability rights advocates were able to cast their inclusive web so broadly that it touched every citizen's sensibilities. Through the engagement of both grassroots radicals and savvy lobbyists, of militant protests and persuasive rhetoric, of right-wing economists, social service providers, and liberal clergymen, a richer platform from which to argue for paradigmatic change was built. DRM activists drew from their daily struggles to climb a set of stairs or to utilize their city's public transportation system. But, from these singular experiences, a litany of regulatory stipulations fused together that created a holistic framework for an accessible built world.

The spatial universality of physical accessibility was a source of strength for the DRM, because it could be convincingly animated through action. Employing an inclusive, rights-based strategy and drawing from the transformative power of collective action, disability was reframed as an environmental limitation instead of a medical handicap. That process was materialized through the sociotechnical coding of the built environment. In the next chapter, the case of S.M.A.R.T. Housing in Austin, Texas, sociotechnical code-making follows a similar pattern but responds to different focal issues.

Chapter 10

Coding Affordable Housing

A Case Study of Frame Transformation

The second case of sociotechnical code-making to be examined is S.M.A.R.T. Housing in Austin, Texas. "S.M.A.R.T." is the acronym for housing that is *Safe, Mixed-income, Accessible, Reasonably priced*, and *Transit-oriented.* That combination of descriptors derives from public talk in the city of Austin over almost a century. Although not quite as successful in scope or resolution as the ADA discussed in the previous chapter, the structure of its storyline is similar—relevant social groups interpret focal events in the city through competing technological frames. One leadership group aligned the frames of several others to produce a technical code that, in turn, regenerated the built environment in a manner that benefited the urban ecology as a whole, as well as a particular group of citizens. Although the abstract structure of both cases is similar, progenitors have their own way of telling their story that highlights differences as well as similarities. The case of S.M.A.R.T. Housing is told, then, in the way it was reported to us, in three distinct phases that, so far, stretch over 90 years and include the City Plan of 1928 (which established a sociotechnical context), the S.M.A.R.T. Housing code of 2000–2010 (which generated an alternative), and the AFI of 2005 onward (which still struggles to regenerate frames and conditions). Each phase tells a part of the story.

THE CITY PLAN OF 1928 AND ITS LONG SHADOW

> "We are definitely working to prevent what happened in Clarksville," Byron Marshall says, referring to the current resistance against gentrification in east Austin and its parallels with the trendy west Austin neighborhood where only a very few founding black families still remain to hold the ancestral memories of the first freedom town west of the Mississippi.[1]

Austin has not always been a city spatially segregated by race, ethnicity, and income. In the 19th century, minority neighborhoods were dispersed throughout the city. Former slave Charles Clark, for example, founded Clarksville in central west Austin in 1871, one of the first freedmen's communities west of the Mississippi. By the early 1900s, however, economic and social pressures led many African–American and Mexican–American families to settle just east of the original boundary of the city, East Avenue, which is now Interstate Highway 35.[2] As early as 1925, one University of Texas student noticed that the east side of town seemed to be the "most desirable" place for Mexican–Americans to live in Austin as, "this (was) the only community in which Mexicans (were) found to own their homes," because, the student reasoned, "the land is cheaper and the Mexican can feel a greater security as to a permanent home, because it is not so likely that he will be driven out in the wake of business expansion."[3] The reason land was so much cheaper on the east side was because it was downstream and prone to flooding, making it less desirable for development by more wealthy groups (Figure 10.1).

Although some minority families independently chose to live on the east side in the early 20th century, the 1928 City of Austin Plan, completed by the engineering firm of Koch and Fowler, codified the emergent pattern of incentivized segregation. With the stated interest of preventing "slums," Austin's 1928 City Plan (Figure 10.2) proposed the creation of "a negro district," which provided incentives for minorities to relocate to the area east of East Avenue, where they would be offered "separate but equal" infrastructure —water, electricity, sewers, paved streets, schools, and playgrounds. Implementation of the spatial plan meant that minority populations would no longer be provided with infrastructure if they chose to live in other parts of the city,[4] effectively coercing minority dislocation. The plan also overlaid a new industrial zone to encourage industrial development in the same spaces reserved for minority populations. Although many families resisted being put out of their homes in central Austin, most eventually succumbed to pressures from the city and developers to relocate to the east side. In 1968, the remaining African–Americans of Clarksville unsuccessfully protested the construction of Highway One, and 26 additional families lost their homes.[5]

As Austin's African–Americans and Mexican–Americans relocated east, they set up strong communities of their own, spatially and culturally separate from each other. Generally speaking, 7th Street divided east Austin, with the African-American population settling northward, and Latinos establishing the region southward. According to former Austin Mayor Gus Garcia, since the 1920s, white elites deliberately manipulated these two groups through policies that supported their segregation along 7th Street.[6]

Regardless of the negative effects of segregation in Austin (and within east Austin), most of these minority cultural enclaves formed internal support systems, working with one another to create the best life possible on the forgotten side of the city. Thriving communities with rich cultural traditions grew and prospered east of Interstate Highway 35 (I-35). As Charles Urdy, who grew up in east Austin, described life in his segregated community, "What you had was doctors and educators and entrepreneurs . . . people from all walks of life, living in your neighborhood. There were role models everywhere, people who were an example of how to live . . . and how not to."[7] Thus, the spatial segregation established by the Austin 1928 City Plan has indirectly contributed to enclaves of strength, creativity, and resilience in east Austin (Figure 10.3).

Figure 10.1 Map of Historic Austin, 1839. The City of Austin was conceived as a geometric replica of Philadelphia, the City of Brotherly Love, situated between two creeks.

For the multigenerational minority families still rooted there today, east Austin's story continues to be a complex tale of oppression, racism, and spatial segregation, as well as resilience, cultural pride, and sense of place. De jure segregation ended in the city years ago, but de facto spatial segregation by race, ethnicity, and income persists. After 2000, in the face of new economic pressures created by an expanding downtown area and environmental politics, east Austin neighborhoods struggle to maintain their community's cultural fabric.

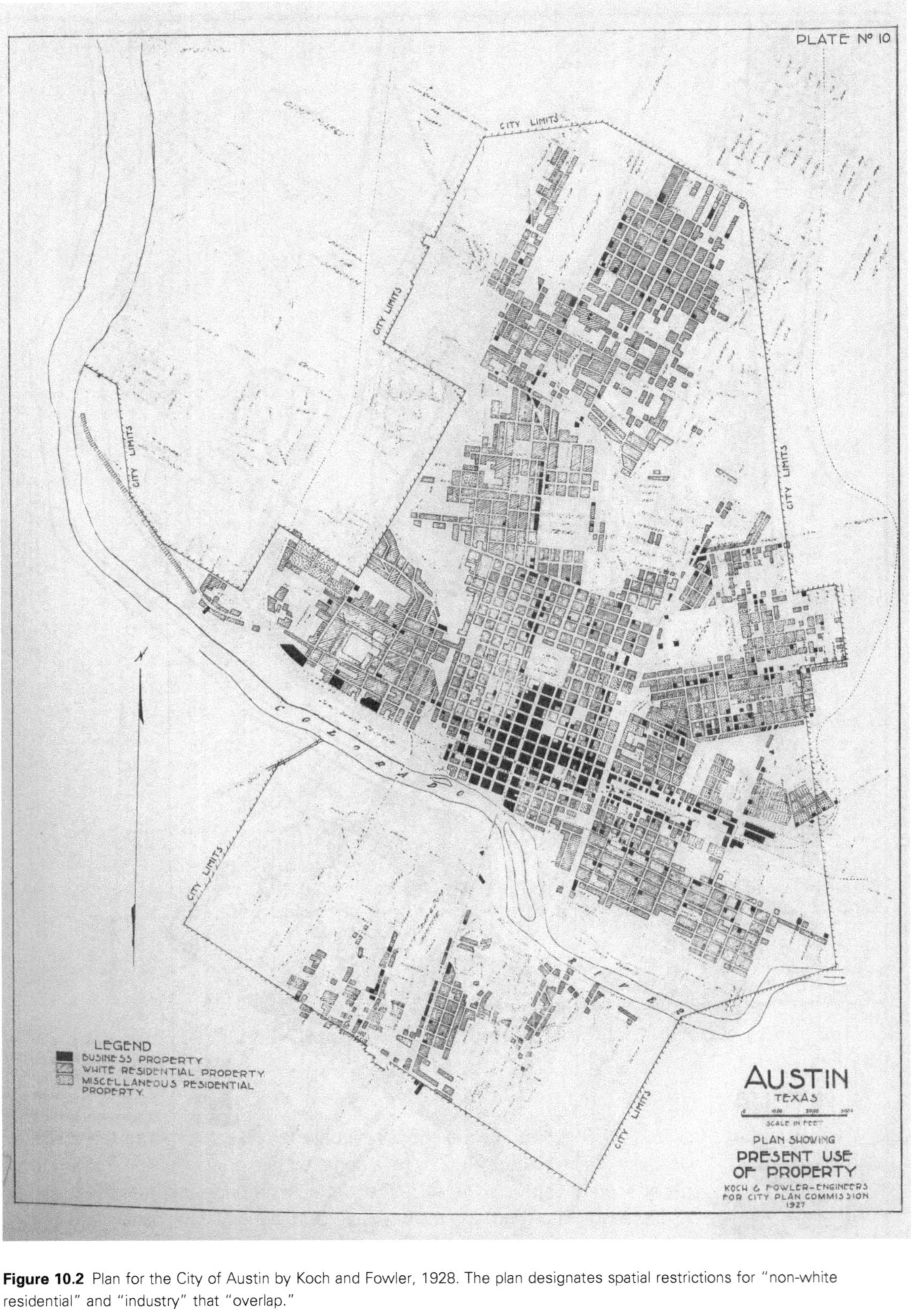

Figure 10.2 Plan for the City of Austin by Koch and Fowler, 1928. The plan designates spatial restrictions for "non-white residential" and "industry" that "overlap."

Figure 10.3 A Typical East Austin Bungalow. Although Austin's stock of early 20th-century bungalows follows patterns typical of eastern and northern cities, they are frequently overlaid with Latino motifs such as a strong or hot color palette.

Demographic patterns from the United States Census (2010) continue to show the line of segregation along I-35, dividing Austin into east and west (Figure 10.4). From the perspective of early 20th-century code-makers, the 1928 City Plan has proven to be a very effective sociotechnical code indeed. Affluence—and Austin's white majority—is concentrated on the west side, whereas African–American and Latino populations live on the east side. Today, Clarksville is a quaint, historic neighborhood tucked into the west-side hills of downtown Austin and bears little resemblance to the original African–American community, apart from a handful of original businesses and an impressive set of historic landmarks.

Unfortunately, not only has Austin continued to be a segregated city, but its African–American population has declined relative to its total population, and the Latino population struggles to stay rooted in the east part of town as property values rise. In 1860, almost 40 percent of Travis County's population was African–American; however, this population constitutes less than 9 percent of the county's citizenry today, as families move further away from the city in search of affordable housing. And, despite continued high rates of home-ownership among Latino families in east Austin, rising property taxes and heightened development pressure from the expanding downtown area threaten the stability and permanence of both minority communities.

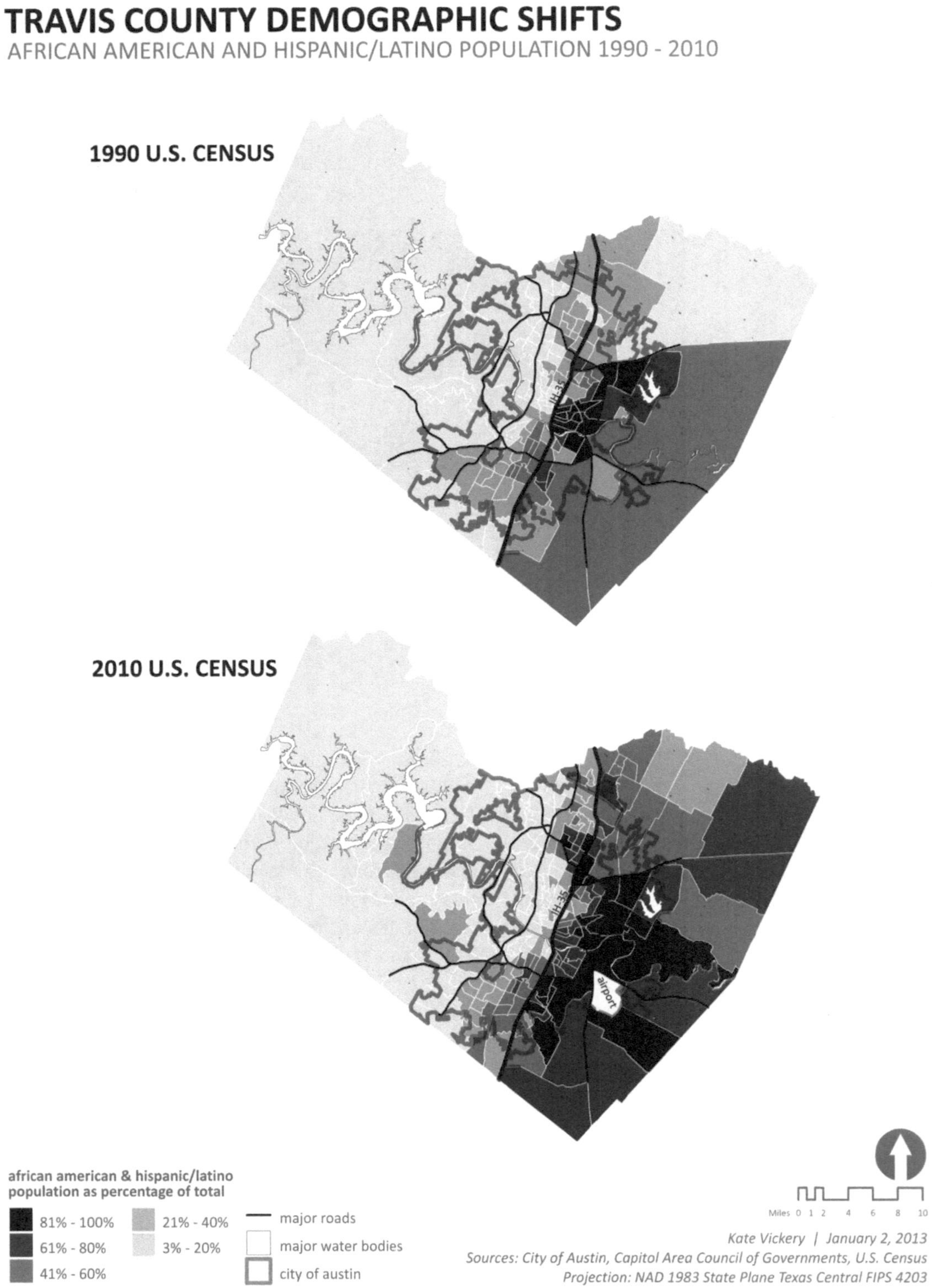

Figure 10.4 Travis County Demographic Shifts: African–American and Hispanic Populations 1990–2010. Demographic data from 1990 and 2010 clearly indicate that African–Americans and Latinos are moving from central east Austin to the periphery.

Environmental Justice and Environmental Activism in East Austin

Austin's 1928 City Plan zoned east Austin as a mix of industrial, "miscellaneous residential," and "unrestricted" spaces, and, consequently, any residents living in the "negro district" were forced to live in proximity to industrial sites (see Figure 10.2). Although many of the industries that located in east Austin's industrial and unrestricted districts have since left, their former sites have become what we now refer to as "brownfields." Examples include the Decker Creek Power Station and Holly Power Plant (demolished in 2012), both of which are considered undesirable urban infrastructure elements, built in the 1960s to serve the city as a whole, but the negative effects of which were only experienced on the east side of Austin.

A brownfield is defined by the EPA as "a site, or portion thereof, which has actual or perceived contamination and an active potential for redevelopment or reuse." An EPA survey of Austin contaminants carried out in 1992 found that, of the 26 landfills and dumpsites in the area, 20 were located in east Austin.[8] These contaminants not only affect the health and quality of life in general of east Austinites, but also discourage businesses and other organizations from locating to, or investing in, the area. Thus, unemployment is higher, and services have generally been more limited—with fewer grocery stores, quality health care facilities, employment or training opportunities, etc.

In the early 1990s, east Austin's citizenry began to organize against these injustices and form coalitions to fight further pollution. In 1991, PODER (People Organized in Defense of the Earth and her Resources) was formed, "to address the social, economic and environmental impacts" of these polluting industries in east Austin.[9] This organization empowers minorities to combat pollution in their community and has successfully cleaned up many of the contaminated sites plaguing east Austin. For instance, in 1993, PODER forced a 35-year-old, 52-acre fuel storage facility to shut down in the area. Unfortunately, partly because of hard-won improvements made to the environment in east Austin, the ecological and health problems plaguing the neighborhood were replaced with problems of another kind—gentrification.

A Sprawling City—Smart Growth in Austin and Contested Development Priorities

In 1998, the Sierra Club deemed Austin one of the fastest growing and most sprawl-threatened cities in the country.[10] The organization claims that, since 1990, on average over 1,000 people move to the city each month. Sprawl, defined by the Sierra Club as "to spread out or develop haphazardly," has become a major issue in and around the city. According to Swearingen, "The perception—whether real or imagined—among many Austinites has been that new buildings, new people, and a new culture were becoming a dominant and invasive force."[11] For relatively affluent white environmentalists on the west side, the forces of invasion were even richer Californians coming to work in the high-tech industry who lacked local environmental consciousness. Even worse, they threatened "old Austin's laid back way of life." In retaliation, old Austinites from many different neighborhoods vowed to "Keep Austin Weird."[12]

In 1990, 700 citizens rallied together at an all-night public hearing to contest a massive development project proposed along Barton Creek. Winding through the western part of the city, this watershed houses Austin's main water supply, the treasured Barton Springs swimming hole, and habitat for the Barton Springs salamander, a protected endangered species. The creek and its watershed are an ecologically sensitive region, important to Austin's water quality and cultural identity.[13]

From the momentum of this citizen activism, the Save Our Springs Alliance (S.O.S.) formed in 1991 (the same year as the formation of PODER) to push forward new development restrictions to effectively protect water quality and the watershed's sensitive ecosystem. After significant campaigning and political maneuvering by these activists, in 1992 Austin passed the S.O.S. Ordinance that limits impervious cover and requires other measures to prevent pollution in southwest Austin. Although the S.O.S. Ordinance seemed to be a dramatic success at the time, the dedicated environmentalists who supported it are generally disappointed with its inability to halt suburban development, despite the fact that large portions of the city were deemed "undevelopable" after the S.O.S. Ordinance came into effect.

In 1997, Austin developed the Smart Growth Initiative (Figure 10.5), which clearly articulated the manner in which the city should grow. S.O.S. had an influence on the city, and two zones were subsequently identified in the future growth plan: the *Desired Development Zone* and the *Drinking Water Protection Zone*. Not surprisingly, the newly cleaned-up east Austin was to be reshaped by an incentive code designed to encourage redevelopment and higher density, while development on the west side was disincentivized altogether. Once again, we should understand the Smart Growth Initiative as a sociotechnical code through which water-quality protection was used as the technological context to catalyze social changes—wittingly or not.

Unlike through the abstract lenses of expert planners, east Austin is seen by its residents, not as a blank slate ready for development, but as a place of character, vitality, and rich culture—where families have lived in their modest bungalow-style homes for generations. Residents of this side of town are just as hesitant to encourage new development in their area as those in the west, but for different reasons. Accordingly, once the city instituted its Smart Growth Plan and began funding redevelopment projects on the east side, the recently empowered advocates fighting to clean up their community began to see their property taxes rise and the composition of their neighborhoods change once again.

Communities in Crisis

"There needs to be a twelve-step program for white gentrifiers like me," says Mark Rogers, executive director of Austin's east-side Guadalupe Neighborhood Development Corporation (GNDC).

> Let me tell you what it's like to grow up a middle-class white person in America. When you're a middle-class white guy like me, you grow up thinking the system is on your side. You believe that the police are there to protect you; that the City Council works for you; and if you don't like something you can change it. . . . White people who move into this area [the east-side] feel they can make changes using a system that works for them. I will say there is a disturbingly

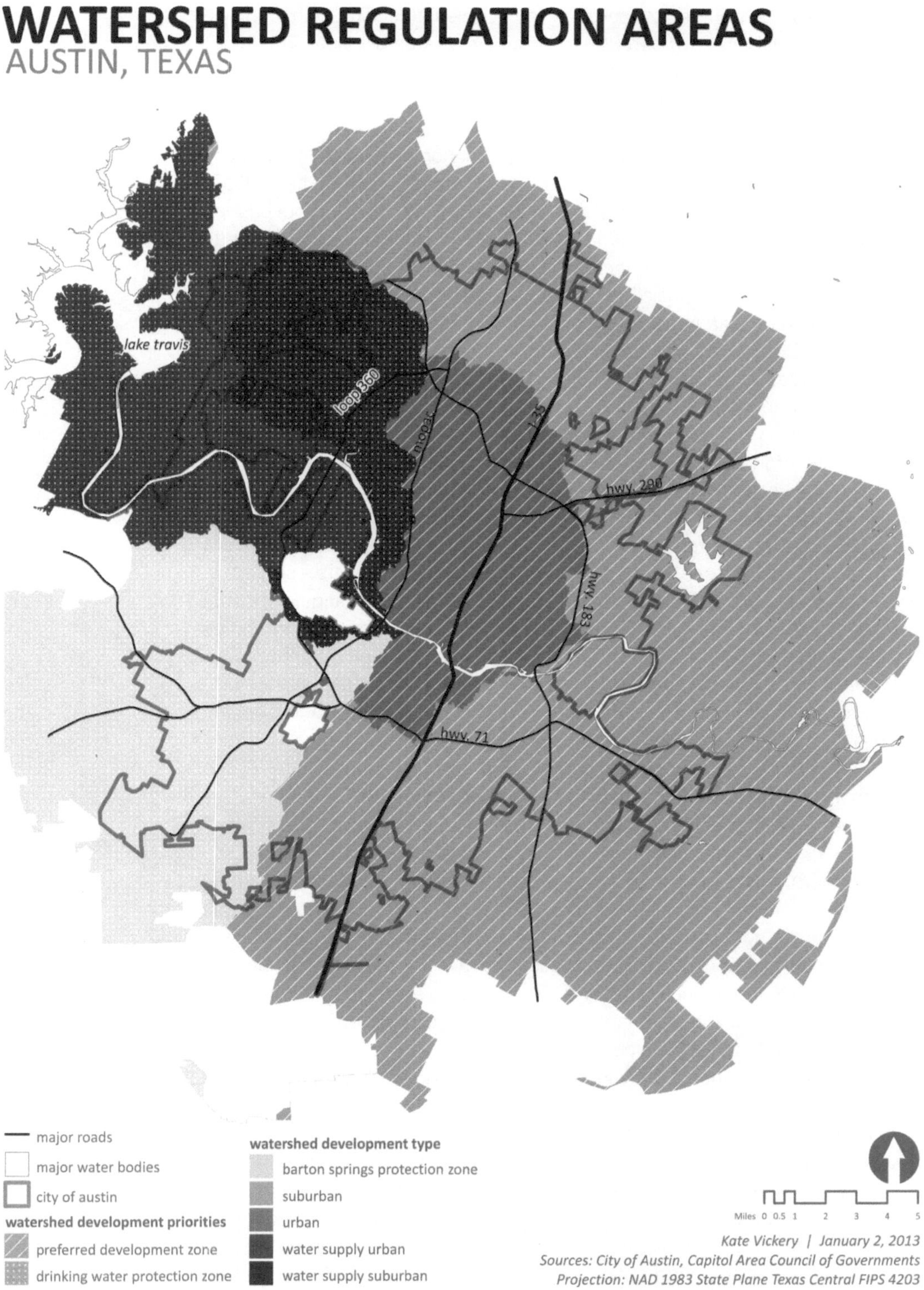

Figure 10.5 City of Austin Smart Growth Zone, May 2003. The Smart Growth Zone was constructed to avoid development impacts on the delicate Edwards aquifer to the west. It also forced development to the city's east side, where minority populations had been directed by the Plan of 1928.

> disproportionate number of white people influencing neighborhood associations over here. But they are very often the ones who don't mind giving up their Saturdays to come to meetings and work on a project to push it through.[14]

Gentrification, or "the process by which higher income households displace lower income residents of a neighborhood," began in east Austin in the 1990s.[15] Since new types of development began to seep into these impoverished neighborhoods, longtime homeowners felt the effects of this change. Property taxes in the area, for example, increased 123 percent from 1998 to 2004—a mere 6 years.[16] This is especially significant for a community, according to the Census, whose median household income in 1999 was a modest $23,348.

As land values increase and property taxes rise, many of the families who were forced to settle in east Austin in the name of "separate but equal" utility provision in 1928 are again being pushed farther out of the city to find adequate housing they can afford. Density is being touted as east Austin's answer to its affordable housing problem, but many residents feel that densification will strip the community of its unique, historic charm. To many residents, the term "density" is synonymous with bulldozed homes and high-rise development. Many development projects in the area threaten to change the character of east Austin neighborhoods, and their residents—similar to Austinites on the west side of town—strongly resist this change. With the historic patterns of exploitation experienced by east Austin communities conditioning their interpretation of what is happening to their neighborhoods and community today, new developments are perceived as simply another form of injustice, even when efforts are made to include residents in the planning process.

East Austin is a rich and complicated place, shaped by interrelated webs of political, cultural, economic, social, and environmental influences. This context presents interesting challenges to those seeking to build a "sustainable" Austin—a city that advances environmental protection, social equity, and economic urban development by protecting existing natural and cultural resources. As the stories presented above show, different social groups within Austin frame the concept of sustainability very differently.[17] When PODER set out to promote environmental justice in east Austin by initiating zoning changes and environmental clean-ups of brownfield sites, they were fighting to protect their homes and their health, not to prepare investment opportunities for wealthier outsiders to (re)develop.

Similarly, when S.O.S. set out to preserve Austin's water quality and an endangered salamander, its members did not consciously seek to dramatically alter the life of residents in east Austin. It is, however, fair to say that the financial repercussions of rising property taxes for residents of east Austin are directly related to the disincentivizing of development in west Austin's Barton Creek watershed and the mitigation of industrial sites in east Austin. In other words, tragic, if unintended, consequences tend to emerge outside the frames of interpretation in which groups take an interest and for which they take responsibility. Thus, two different environmental frames—both important aspects of sustainability—have appeared to be at odds with each other in the context of east Austin. Environmental justice, as the progenitors of PODER recognize, necessarily includes affordable housing and community stability, in addition to the preservation of endangered species. Finding ways to maintain the eclectic spirit and the affordability, while improving the environmental quality of east Austin neighborhoods, is a challenge that anyone hoping to pursue sustainable development in east Austin needs to consider very seriously.

As the term "gentrification" became heard more and more frequently on the streets of east Austin as a way to explain what was happening to the neighborhood, the City of Austin convened public and staff groups, in 2001 and 2003 respectively, to investigate the charge and, if it were true, what it meant.[18] The conclusion of city staff, at that time, was that, if the forces of gentrification were not already at work, they soon would be, and that it was bad news.[19] To the Latino and African–American residents of east Austin, it was not a surprise to once again see the long shadow of the 1928 plan attempting to push them further east, north, or south.

THE S.M.A.R.T. HOUSING CODE OF 2000–2010

It was in this historical context that the S.M.A.R.T. Housing code of 2000 was generated. Although some people on the west side of the city were unaware of, or ignored, how sociotechnical codes had been used to shape the city, almost no one on the east side was so naïve.[20] In the more than 70 years since the City Plan of 1928 was implemented, social groups reorganized themselves, frames transformed, and focal issues evolved. It will be helpful, then, to put the variables in a contemporary context before telling the story of how the S.M.A.R.T. Housing code of 2010 was generated.

As we noted in the introduction to this chapter, the acronym "S.M.A.R.T." is itself designed to appeal to a myriad of groups with an interest in safety, mixed-income neighborhoods, accessibility, reasonably priced homes, and transit-oriented development. Such groups include insurance interests, public health officials, mortgage lenders, planners, and environmentalists, not to mention the poor and the disabled and groups who advocate for them. In our fieldwork, we found this rich mix of interests to be represented by five social groups who are relevant to code-making in the city: *neighborhoods*, *the environmental community*, *the development community*, *the knowledge community*, and *the professional community*. Each group framed contemporary focal issues through the three technological frames we set out in Chapter 8: *supply-side*, *demand-side*, or *effect side*.

Neighborhoods

As in many democracies, neighborhood organizations in Austin represent those who show up at meetings, not citizens in general, and, owing to a long history of conflict between the city and the Texas legislature concerning property rights, neighborhood organizations have become the primary unit of public planning and regulation in the city.[21] In the process, they have become politically powerful and generally conservative, if fractious.[22] One city planner, for example, characterized existing neighborhood organizations, especially those near downtown on both the east and west sides, as "generally opposed to change" and "protective of the status quo." They interpret events, then, through a classical NIMBY framework, which is the negative side of an effect-side frame of interpretation, because it tends to resist the relevance of other frames. That said, our data also indicate that many socially conservative neighborhood organizations support environmental preservation citywide.

The Environmental Community

In the experience of respondents who contributed to our understanding of Austin's environmental movement, it is historically more appropriate to refer to environmental communities, in the plural.[23] Elsewhere, we have documented the divided nature of groups dedicated to environmental preservation and action in the city, and so it is unnecessary to repeat that analysis here.[24] It will suffice to say that, on the west side, the S.O.S. has achieved a reputation for aggressive and confrontational action through the courts to protect threatened landscapes and species endangered by development of the Texas Hill Country. On the east side, PODER is no less aggressive in its actions. However, in lieu of framing nature as an abstract, spiritual, or purely ecological concept, PODER's actions are directed at concrete environmental justice issues.[25] Fortunately, this divided and polar structure has evolved, or transformed, over the past decade. New groups, such as the Hill Country Conservancy and Livable City in particular, have begun the process of bridging the old ideological fault line that divides ecological and social concerns.[26] There is, then, an emergent recognition that the environmentalism of the east side and that of the west side have something to learn from each other.

The Development Community

Like the environmental community in Austin, the development community too is plural, although less symmetrically so. For-profit and non-profit developers share a goal of producing housing units, but also have differing constituencies, motivations, resources, and capacities. In a state without an income tax, where the city's only source of income to provide necessary services is property and sales taxes, the for-profit real-estate community is very powerful indeed. Students of *regime theory* argue that local politicians are naturally attracted to those who control capital tied to land-based enterprises, because such capital is relatively immobile, rather than "footloose," as is manufacturing capital. In other words, you can't move the land itself to Asia or Mexico, which makes real-estate interests disproportionally powerful in shaping municipal interests.[27] In contrast, non-profit real-estate developers in Austin have relatively little economic capital, but they have created a considerable amount of "social capital," or "the social, political, and economic interactions that inspire trust and reciprocity among citizens."[28] We find that the social capital of non-profit housing advocates has influenced, to a modest degree, the projects envisioned and built by for-profit developers.[29] Again, there is hopeful news. The bifurcated approach to housing development, like protecting the natural environment, is also demonstrating signs of frame integration.

The Knowledge Community

In his farewell address to the nation on January 17, 1961, President Dwight D. Eisenhower warned his fellow citizens about the growing influence of "the military–industrial complex," by which he referred to the symbiotic economic interests of government, the military, and industry. Since Eisenhower made that famous observation a half-century ago, others have referred to the "university–industrial complex" and, in so doing, bring to light the symbiotic economic interests of university research programs and industrial development. For some, such as the RECA, there are only benefits to linking University of Texas research to local industrial development and municipal modernization. That symbiotic relationship, in the specific form of Sematech—the university–industry partnership that catalyzed Austin's semi-conductor and high-tech industry in the 1980s and 1990s—was the economic engine that fueled Austin's dramatic economic and population growth of that period. Consciously using Sematech as an economic model, the progenitors of the Pecan Street Project (PSP) have decided that development of a "smart grid for Austin" will be Austin's next economic engine.[30] The problem, however, is that, as usual, those who are most vulnerable to any change, especially one that would stimulate an electric utility rate increase, were initially excluded from the conversation. As with the 1928 City Plan, or the Smart Growth Initiative of the late 1990s, which imposed the Preferred Development Zone on east Austin, the progenitors of PSP and smart energy only considered those consequences they chose to, or had the ability to see. It took the Roman Catholic diocese of Austin, as an advocate for the poor, to point out that the proposed project would have early and disproportionate impact on families of modest means.[31] For east Austinites who lived through the era of Austin's rapid economic growth of the 1980s and 1990s, the Sematech legacy was not "good for everybody," as boosters claimed. Rather, Sematech was the fountainhead of capital infusion into the region that catalyzed the process of gentrification. It is not a phenomenon that will be welcomed again, at least by east-side communities, without what some Austin Energy executives refer to as "a new business plan." Like the military–industrial complex, the university–industrial complex, or the knowledge community as we call it here, is capable of visionary thinking. The problem with both is that they tend, like most technological networks, to be blind to effects assumed to lie outside their own system of interests—their own frame of interpretation. There has, so far, been only minimal frame integration between knowledge elites who inhabit a demand-side frame and those who inhabit an effect-side frame, particularly the poor. The exception to this claim is found in the relationship of the knowledge community to the professional community.

The Professional Community

What we refer to as the professional community includes a diverse group of individuals and disciplines—architects, landscape architects, planners, preservation experts, and engineers—who work both in private practice and within city government. The seemingly "objective" skills of these professionals grant them agency and identity as a group within the system of code-making. One focal issue that has defined this group is the city's decision in 2009 to externalize responsibility for reviewing technical documents for construction and certifying "as-built" conditions. Not only does this new arrangement save city staff a great deal of time (and thus money), but it also redistributes the responsibility for absorbing the cost of professional services directly to citizens, rather than indirectly through taxation. The problem is that *authority follows cash flow*—if home or business owners pay for professional services directly, rather than the city providing such services through taxation, professional objectivity comes into question. What holds professionals together as a social group relevant to code-making is their common concern for eroding objective standards on which their authority lies. In our fieldwork, we found some evidence that members of this group have already expanded their frame of interpretation to include the concerns of the knowledge community, the environmental community, and the development community. We also found, however, that professionals are resistant to the idea of self-conscious sociotechnical coding, because it appears to lack "objectivity" by being too broad in scope.

In summing up our description of relevant social groups, we can say that *neighborhoods*, the *environmental community*, the *development community*, the *knowledge community*, and the *professional community* defined the field on which the progenitors of S.M.A.R.T. Housing had to play. Housing advocates eventually succeeded in their efforts to play on this field by employing two linked strategies: First, they helped to make affordable housing the dominant focal issue of the city in the late 1990s. Demographics did most of the job, but Mayor Kirk Watson—who was also responsible for the Smart Growth Initiative that ignited the process of gentrification in east Austin—also dedicated significant resources to making those demographics visible and to countermanding the unintended consequences of his own planning policy. Those resources included a handful of individuals in key administrative positions in city government, who were particularly experienced and dedicated to the project.

Second, housing advocates carefully expanded their frame of interest to include those of each social group relevant to housing policy. For example: Housing advocates gathered the support of some neighborhoods first by reframing "affordable housing" as "S.M.A.R.T. Housing" and as "workforce housing" that would benefit teachers, firefighters, and policemen, rather than the "undeserving poor" imagined by the conservative advocates of property rights. A key component was that housing advocates gathered the support of the environmental community by discouraging greenfield development and requiring every unit of housing produced to meet Austin Energy's criteria for at least 1 star in its 5-star Green Building Program. Affordable housing became, then, linked to environmental preservation. To gather the support of for-profit developers, housing advocates gave "preferential treatment to preferred housing types." In other words, not only were fees for building permits waived, but permit review was accelerated, thus saving developers significant borrowing costs—"time is money." Housing advocates gathered the support of the knowledge community by linking housing to advanced construction technologies. And finally, housing advocates gathered the support of the professional community by raising the objective measures by which housing would be judged, thus appearing to also raise their professional authority. Through such strategic expansion of their own frame, housing advocates were able to gather the economic and social capital required to get S.M.A.R.T. Housing through the city council and on the ground.

With Mayor Watson's leadership, in 2000 the city passed a $50-million-dollar General Obligation Bond dedicated to S.M.A.R.T. Housing. In the first year after enactment, there were close to 6,000 applications filed. Although all of these did not come to fruition, between 2000 and 2010, the S.M.A.R.T. Housing code did stimulate the construction of 10,110 housing units. Of these,

4,137 were single-family units (generally built on "in-fill" lots in existing neighborhoods), and 5,973 were multi-family units (generally built on larger, undeveloped parcels or "brownfields" within the city proper, not within the extraterritorial jurisdiction, or ETJ).[32] The code did, then, add measurable density to a city that is otherwise becoming more suburban and less dense. As illustrated in Figure 10.6, the spatial distribution of these homes was not exclusively in east Austin, but clearly aimed there. Equally interesting is to look at the distribution as an overlay to the 1928 Plan (Figure 10.7), which suggests that S.M.A.R.T. Housing was consciously designed as an anti-gentrification, or sociotechnical, code.

By reframing affordable housing in a way that was attractive to other relevant social groups, housing advocates also provided families of modest means with a way to consolidate social and economic resources, pay escalating taxes, reduce their cost-of-living expenses, and remain in their neighborhood. No less important, building that number of energy-efficient houses within the central city helped to avoid building new infrastructure on undeveloped suburban land (roads, water, sewer, and electrical lines) and also help to avoid building new electrical- or water-production infrastructure (coal-fired power

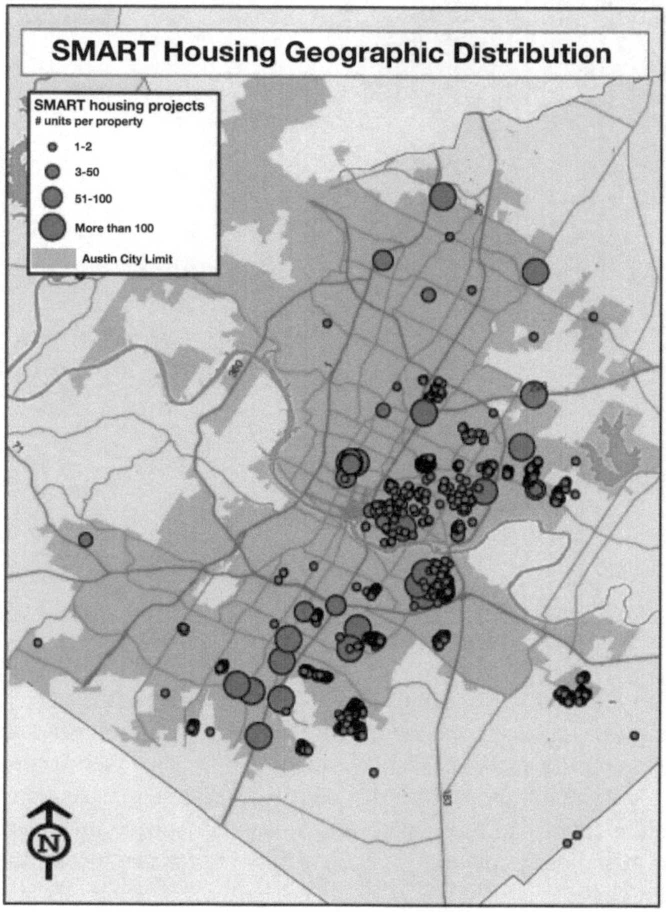

Figure 10.6 S.M.A.R.T. Housing Distribution Across the City of Austin. The spatial distribution of these homes was not exclusively in east Austin, but was focused there.

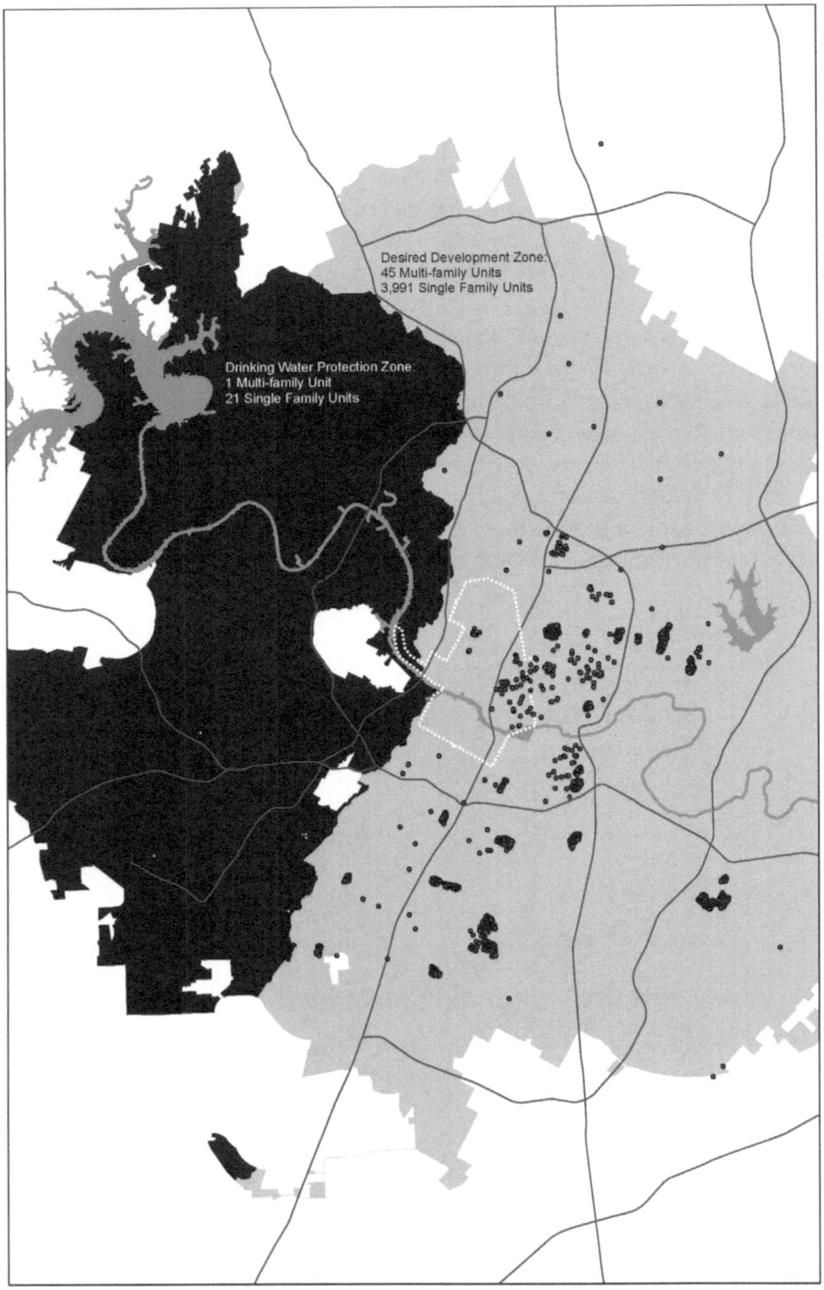

Figure 10.7 S.M.A.R.T. Housing Distribution in Relation to the 1928 Plan. This figure overlays the distribution of S.M.A.R.T. Housing on the 1928 Plan, which demonstrates that S.M.A.R.T. Housing was consciously designed as an anti-gentrification, or sociotechnical, code.

plants or electrical water-pumping stations). The city administrators and planners who wrote and politically supported the S.M.A.R.T. Housing code clearly understood housing as a necessary component of urban infrastructure. There is, then, considerable irony that the city used precisely the same tools—infrastructure codes—to help Latino and African-American families to stay in their east Austin neighborhoods in 2000 as it did to forcibly move them there in 1928.

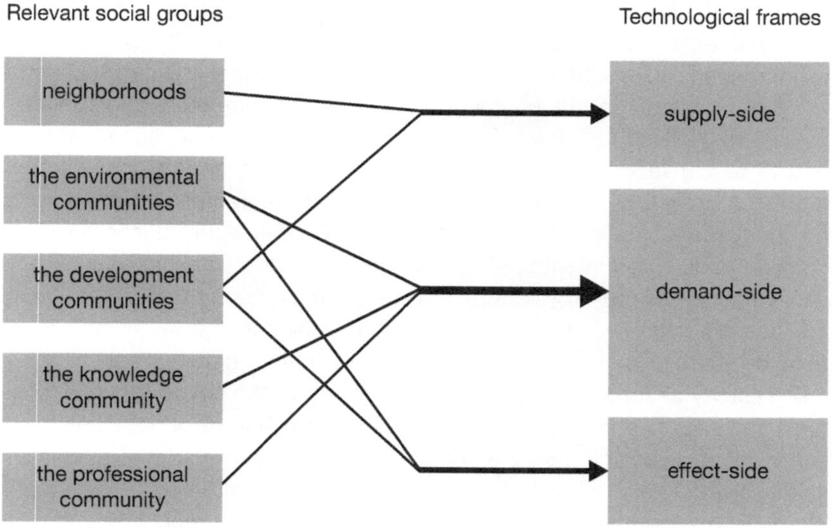

Figure 10.8 Relationship of Relevant Social Groups to Technological Frames, 2012.

After 2008, the initial excitement about S.M.A.R.T. Housing faded, as the economy and other variables changed. By mid 2010, one S.M.A.R.T. Housing progenitor said that, "the program is now effectively dead." Although the global housing and financial crises of this period certainly contributed to the program's demise, external factors were not the only cause. The as yet incomplete third phase of this story, the AFI, provides some insight into the constant realignment of frames and groups that influence the city and its form.

Figure 10.8 illustrates the vectors of attraction between relevant social groups and subgroups involved in S.M.A.R.T. Housing and the technological frames inhabited by actors in 2007. It was into this field of play that the advocates for the AFI wandered.

THE ALLEY FLAT INITIATIVE, 2005–

S.M.A.R.T. Housing became less attractive to for-profit housing developers after 2008, because incentives to developers and homeowners alike were no longer adequate to offset growing economic risks in a downturned economy. Non-profit developers, however, continued to employ it. One of these was the AFI, a partnership between the University of Texas Center for Sustainable Development (UTCSD; an academic research center founded in 2001),[33] the GNDC (a not-for-profit housing developer that has been active since the late 1970s),[34] and the ACDDC (a not-for-profit community design center founded in 2005).[35] The GNDC board of directors is comprised entirely of individuals who live in east-side neighborhoods and thus directly represent community interests.

What the partners recognized was that the particular conditions of Austin's development pattern provided an opportunity to focus the goals of the S.M.A.R.T. Housing code on one type of property—property owned by long-time residents that could accommodate what came to be called an "alley flat." Although the pressures of gentrification are strongest in the near-east-side neighborhoods, inhabited by mostly Latino families, those same neighborhoods have four characteristics that appeared ideal for redevelopment of a kind that would benefit threatened homeowners rather than for-profit developers, using traditional techniques. First, by contemporary standards, the density of these neighborhoods is less than urban. Another way to interpret this condition is to say that modestly sized bungalows located on generous lots provided increasingly difficult to find land suitable for infill units. Second, Latino families tend to be conservative borrowers. In fact, in 2000, long-term homeowners with income levels below 80 percent of the median family income owned more than 60 percent of single-family houses in the near-east-side neighborhoods.[36] In other words, many threatened families are "land poor," meaning that, if they want to remain in their community, and thus preserve their way of life, there is a positive incentive to make economic use of that otherwise non-liquid resource. Third, the existing infrastructure is central to the city's plan to grow in an easterly direction, and so there is incentive for the city to improve long-neglected east-side infrastructure. And fourth, east-side neighborhoods have a network of alleys that makes parking and access to back yards economically inexpensive.

As "designers" in the broad sense, the AFI partners were able to put these four conditions together and conceive an initiative to provide energy-efficient and free-standing secondary houses, of 850 square feet or less, that might serve an extended family.[37] Such an infill strategy would allow grandparents, adult children, or other relatives to consolidate social and economic capital. An alternative scenario would be to rent units to students or others in the community, thus producing enough income to pay escalating taxes. A geographic information system analysis supervised by the authors and completed by graduate students indicated that contemporary building codes would permit the construction of 3,300 alley flats (Figure 10.9).[38] If, however, lots without alley access were also included, that number would increase to more than 40,000—an amount that would have measurable impact in meeting Austin's 2020 climate protection goals.[39]

Understanding housing as infrastructure in a more aggressive and integrated manner would, the partners reasoned, produce multiple benefits for multiple social groups. We found that municipal and utility engineers tend to think of any new house as a *unit of consumption*, because, no matter how efficient, most new homes still require some water, power, and other municipal services, and, even relatively efficient houses built in the suburbs disrupt valuable ecological services, such as storm-water absorption by soils and carbon sequestration by trees, that are provided by undisturbed land.

However, what if small, new houses meant to serve extended or intergenerational families of modest means were tucked into existing neighborhoods, without disrupting neighborhood scale or requiring the extension of existing sewers, water lines, or the electrical grid? And what if these small houses produced energy from solar sources, as well as captured and used rainwater on site, so that both potable and storm water did not have to be pumped around the city? Most people are unaware that, in Austin, as in most cities, pumping water up and down hills is the single largest municipal expenditure of electrical energy and thus the single largest contributor to climate change. Such small houses could, then, be understood as *units of production* rather than of *consumption*. In this reframed context, a distributed approach to affordable housing would provide valuable services to the city that would

Figure 10.9 Austin's Alley Network. Ordinances in effect in 2008 would permit the construction of 3,300 homes in the inner city. Without restrictive ordinances, that number could increase to 9,600, and, if properties without alleys were included, to 43,000.

benefit all taxpayers by improving water quality, reducing energy costs, and reducing the public cost to care for the elderly, the poor, and the disabled. The extended families that live in such houses could also benefit by consolidating family resources. Integrating social and technical problem-solving into a single, yet flexible code would be more effective in realizing city goals, and it would also require that many individuals, organizations, departments, and utilities collaborate in the making of even smarter housing. A team of interdisciplinary graduate students calculated that building 40,000 alley flats could take more than 1,800 cars off the road, reduce annual carbon dioxide emissions by more than 8,000 tons, and provide comparable ecological services to 25,930 acres of forest—an area about the same as central Austin (Figure 10.10).[40]

As of August 2012, a modest two alley flats had been constructed, and 11 others were at various stages of development (Figures 10.11 and 10.12). Each of these exceeds the minimum 1-star energy-efficient requirement to receive S.M.A.R.T. Housing incentives—they have received the maximum rating of five. Although construction costs are on the low side of city norms, annual utility costs are less than 70 percent of city norms, which are themselves 10 percent below the regional norm. From these limited criteria, alley flats are a small demonstration that the S.M.A.R.T. code might be expanded, or transformed, to also be a sociotechnical code that links housing for people of modest means, who have been historically and systematically discriminated against, to climate protection strategies that are in the interest of the city, state, nation, and biosphere.

Although existing city codes allow alley flats to be built in neighborhoods that have explicitly accepted them, to say that the process of gaining city permits has been smooth or efficient would be a gross overstatement. The labyrinth of often-conflicting codes that must be negotiated in the process of day-to-day development is enough to make even the most hard-nosed developer seek another line of work. As one of the staff progenitors of the code observed, "S.M.A.R.T. Housing needs fixin'." In other words, the complexity and dysfunctional nature of prescriptions, incentives, and performance standards have themselves become a disincentive to achieve articulated goals.

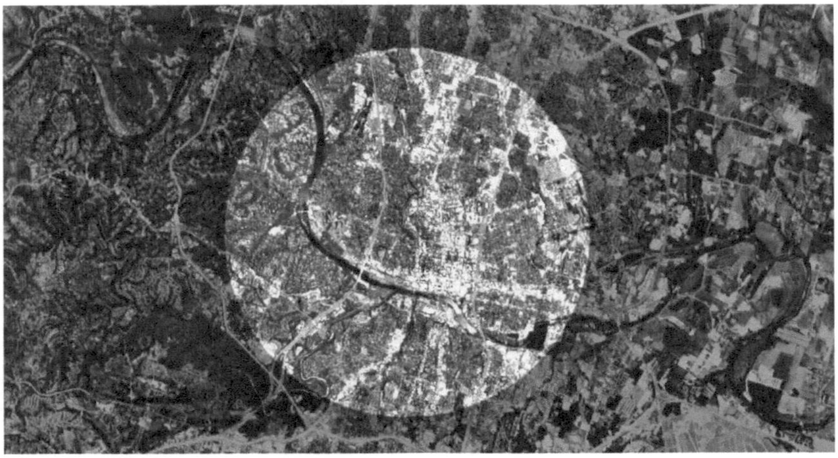

Figure 10.10 Ecosystem Service Equivalent. The production of 3,300 alley flats would provide the same amount of ecosystem services (primarily in carbon sequestration and oxygen production) as 25,390 acres of native forest at the center of the city.

Figure 10.11 Alley Flat 1. Designed by University of Texas architecture students and supervised by the Austin Community Design and Development Center.

Figure 10.12 Alley Flat 2. Designed by University of Texas architecture students, pictured, and supervised by the Austin Community Design and Development Center.

Social Groups Relevant to the AFI

The process of designing, permitting, and building a few small alley flats has taught the partnership a great deal with regard to the social groups that are relevant to putting houses on the ground. A brief look at the still evolving field of action will demonstrate the dynamic nature of groups and the need to continually reconstruct relationships between and to them.

Neighborhoods are alternately supportive or antagonistic toward alley flats, depending on how they interpret focal issues over time. In the case of the Guadalupe neighborhood, not only is this housing type a historical norm, but one of the partners has previously added five new alley flats to the housing stock. Adding two more was, then, not a significant issue. However, in the César Chavez neighborhood next door, for-profit developers have bought properties, added alley flats, subdivided the property as condominiums, and then sold each unit separately at a substantial profit. This practice has not only raised taxes in the neighborhood, but has also displaced significant numbers of families. The lesson learned is that all alley flats are not equal. A building type, separated from not-for-profit economic motives, financial strategies, and sustainable building technologies, can do both social and environmental harm. In other words, agency does not lie in the physical form or "type" itself—as we defined the term in Chapter 3, but in the coupling of physical, social, technical, and environmental elements of the system.

In the west-side environmental community, some find public good even in the construction of expensive alley flats, because they contribute to greater urban density, thus reducing suburban greenfield development and its attendant consequences. Their frame does not yet include the gentrification effects of this kind of environmental action. The same can generally be said with regard to the knowledge and professional communities with regard to the AFI. In both cases, individuals tend to see achieving the goals of the city's 2020 Climate Protection Plan in terms of efficiency—as a simple measure of input over output. In concrete terms, this means that placing large solar arrays or rainwater collection systems on the large flat roofs of institutional, industrial, and commercial buildings is a better investment than placing these systems on the small roofs of alley flats. Such reasoning is perfectly rational, because the systems of production and management established by large utilities rely on a structure of relationships between people and things that is more like those employed by large corporate entities than those of small households in which English may not be spoken. The frame inhabited by utility executives sees the benefit that would accrue to corporate partners as neutral and natural, but the benefit that might accrue to small homeowners as fraught with technical and managerial difficulty, because they are not organized in a way that would allow the utility to manage a distributed system in the manner to which it is accustomed. Its frame *is* sociotechnical, but it fails to recognize how the system it favors benefits corporate partners and hurts small households of modest means. There is, however, an equally rational way to reframe a system of public good that couples the environmental, technical, *and* social factors of the system.

Reframing Alley Flats

Above, we documented that S.M.A.R.T. Housing succeeded, to a significant degree, because advocates were able to make affordable housing a focal issue and then align the frames of relevant social groups at critical times. As one kind of S.M.A.R.T. Housing, alley flats have benefitted from that work. At the time of writing, however, the AFI had not yet succeeded in gathering the resources and aligning the frames necessary to get significant numbers of homes built. What this research has taught us is that a two-level approach is likely to be successful—one that works at the scale of municipal policy and one that works from the scale of grassroots engagement. Such a two-level approach is designed to rearrange the vectors of attraction between relevant social groups and technological frames, as illustrated in Figure 10.13. By attracting some members of neighborhood organizations, the knowledge community, and the professional community to the effect-side frame, it just might be possible to forge a regenerated coalition with enough influence to write a new alley flat code for the city. This work is ongoing.

At the municipal scale, advocates have, over a period of 6 or 7 years, introduced the concept to key individuals in the various departments of city government and to key city council members. As a result, the relationship of relevant social groups to technological frames has shifted, as illustrated in Figure 10.13. In August 2011, the city's chief sustainability officer approached the partnership with a proposal to develop a Green Alley Demonstration Project that would demonstrate "what sustainability might look like." City funds would be used to reconstruct the alley itself as a storm water filtration system, and the AFI partnership would work with homeowners to design, build, finance, and monitor as many as 10 alley flats on a single alley that would also sequester storm water and produce energy. Academics in the partnership would study pre- and post-construction conditions of the coupled systems, including the biophysical characteristics of alleys, the socioeconomic characteristics of households, and the sociotechnical characteristics of the utilities that manage the infrastructures affected. It is far too early to predict the outcomes of this 5–6-year urban experiment in sustainable development, but the experiment itself provides, as we argued in Chapter 4, the field required for frame transformation of relevant social groups through collaborative action.

At the grassroots scale, advocates were engaged in drafting a comprehensive "Alley Flat Code," at the time of writing, that would pull together, and revise, the far-flung city regulations that now permit "secondary dwelling units." The code-writing team includes not only the original AFI partners, but also key individuals engaged in the Community Action Network, members of the city staff, and citizens engaged in redrafting the City Development Code. Together, this hybrid group will introduce the proposed code to the city manager's office and mid-level "champions" in each relevant utility and city department—particularly Public Works, Watershed Protection, Austin Energy, and the Water Utility—before introducing it to appropriate citizen boards and city council members for action. As in the municipal scale of action, we expect that the activity of writing and vetting the code will alter our frames of interpretation and the code itself, as it moves from hand to hand.

In sum, our investigation of S.M.A.R.T. Housing and the AFI demonstrates two related propositions: First, relevant social groups interpret focal

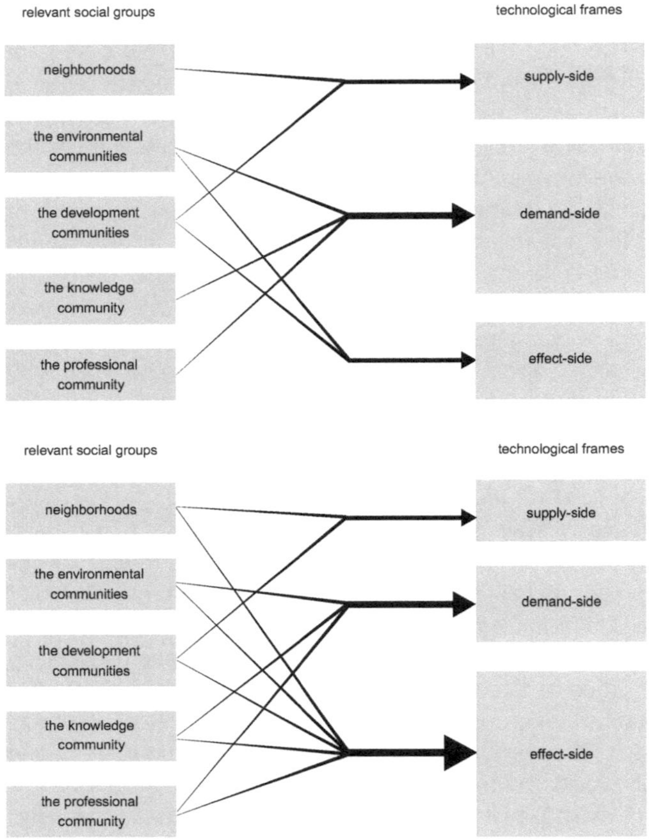

Figure 10.13 Relationship of Relevant Social Groups to Technological Frames, 2008 and 2012. By comparing the direction and weight of the relationships in these two figures, the reader can visualize how relationships were reframed through action.

issues through technological frames and act to reconstruct the technological codes that influence the form of the city. It is collaborative action that serves to align, realign, and ultimately transform frames through direct action. In turn, the form of the city enhances or reduces the capacity of the urban ecology, including the relevant social groups that influence its operation.

Second, this hypothesis can be used as a tool to design action in other places. We can recommend such action, however, only so long as designers take care to ground their action in local focal issues and engage local social groups relevant to those issues. Our claim that this tool can be generalized is based on our study of the DRM, which took place in thousands of locales in the United States, as well as S.M.A.R.T. Housing, which is a case unique to Austin.

The historical satisfaction found in this case is that our reasoning began by analyzing the sociotechnical framing of infrastructure used by segregationists in Austin's 1928 City Plan. That reasoning was turned on its head by the progenitors of S.M.A.R.T. Housing who have, in turn, inspired the activists engaged in the AFI. This unexpected storyline brings us to the final chapter, in which we speculate what our findings mean for the exercise of judgment in all the contemporary design disciplines, but architecture in particular.

Chapter 11

Sociotechnical Coding as Design

> A practitioner exercises disciplined judgment by providing a solution that not only responds to the task at hand in a manner that can be recognized as responsive, but expresses its own status in a way that refers to other such judgments, and to the practice of making judgments of a particular sort.[1]
>
> (David Brain, 1991)

At the outset of this book, we argued that there is a problem with, perhaps even a crisis of, architectural judgment in the United States. In a period such as our own—one with radically changing social, economic, and environmental conditions—what criteria should practitioners use to judge their actions and works? Above, sociologist David Brain suggests that the professionals, presumably in any age, should exercise judgment that is disciplined by years of study and on-the-job training. He also holds that professional judgment refers to the history of "other such judgments . . . of a particular sort." For the design disciplines, that history of judgment is, of course, the *canon*, as we defined it in Chapter 1—the collection of exemplary works used by experts in the field as the "basis for judgment" in determining the significance of any particular architectural work.

The problem we recognized in the literature reviewed in Chapter 1 is, however, that the canon itself is now a scene of struggle between constituencies that favor only some of the 20 modes of judgment that constitute contemporary architectural discourse. At best, these modes can be distilled to five or perhaps three—*art studies* (the investigation of intention and meaning), *technology studies* (the investigation of environmental, social, and purely technical issues), or *professional culture* (the practice of management, pedagogy, methods, competitions, and ethics). We are tempted to say that this 20-way, 5-way or 3-way conflict is a false one. Why not, after all, serve all modes of reasoning equally well—and in synthesis? To simply answer "yes" to this rhetorical question because it sounds reasonable would be purely hypothetical, or ungrounded—it would be to ignore the evidence constructed in the nine chapters sandwiched between the introduction and this conclusion that document the various methods by which architectural judgment is codified in favor of one social group or another. Our project has been, then, to question architectural judgment and so make it more transparent and accountable to those it should serve.

In this concluding chapter, our goal is to, first, consider if designers have already become irrelevant in the struggle to code architectural production. Assuming that it is never too late to make a difference, the following sections consider two contemporary social movements in which designers might take relevant action: the *certification movement* and the *sustainable consumption movement*. Taken together, these social movements provide the background to finally state 10 propositions that might guide relevant action by designers of all kinds. These propositions are designed to provide direction in the difficult problem of judging, coding, or certifying architecture in the future.

ARE ARCHITECTS AN *IRRELEVANT* SOCIAL GROUP?

> The challenge . . . is for architects to look beyond their traditional role and reinvent themselves as interpretive intermediaries, thereby escaping their perceived inability to act within existing constraints. Certainly, this suggests a very different view of the architect as a visionary who designs buildings almost single-handedly.[2]

This challenge, issued by Fischer and Guy, derives from an empirical study of contemporary conditions in practice. Through interviews and a broad review of the relevant literature, they examine how the dramatic proliferations of new codes related to climate change are affecting all of the design professions. On the basis of their research, and that by Imrie and Street,[3] there is little doubt that those practitioners who interpret conditions only through art studies perceive a sudden and undesirable shift toward the authority of technology studies and professional culture as dominant modes of architectural judgment. To prop up this observation, advocates of technology studies quote statistics that support an atmosphere of crisis. In this new atmosphere, advocates of professional culture see, in turn, new market opportunities. On the basis of our study of frame analysis in Chapter 4, it is hardly surprising, then, that conflict has arisen in the discipline regarding the question of judgment. Fischer and Guy offer several observations that might move these three frames of interpretation toward alignment, or transformation, rather than further alienation:

First, they argue new regulations are an opportunity for architects to gain support for "'good design,' as opposed to simply 'safe design'." As have other observers, they document how the new codes have become a "maze" to practitioners and building managers alike, not because the goals of regulation are inherently too complicated to grasp, but because of the ad hoc way in which they have been cobbled together under the pressure of constantly changing conditions—as we found in our case studies of the ADA and S.M.A.R.T. Housing. Given such volatile and chaotic conditions, Fischer and Guy hold that, "The enforcement regime is at risk of crumbling under the weight of increasing responsibilities and systemic failures."[4] Rather than complain about the increasing burden of regulation, the authors recommend that architects become more relevant in the regulatory crisis by repositioning themselves in the market as "interpretive intermediaries." By this term, they do not mean a "bridge" or a low-level "go-between, but as primary actors in the field of construction who lead the process of interpreting codes in action."[5] We concur—designers might exert more leadership in the creative project of code-making. In addition to designing singular material compositions, architects might become interpretive intermediaries in the public talk required to imagine how we might live differently than we do. This is to suggest that architects should reframe design activity as being, not the articulation of objects, but the coevolution of design practices, technology, and culture.

As we argued in Chapter 3, coding (at least in the United States) is typically a process of voluntary yet prescriptive regulation by second-party industrial groups, based on empirical analysis by experts, followed by state and municipal government adoption, interpretation, and localization. Regulation is, then, a call-and-response minuet. As we argued in Chapters 7 and 10, implementation of any code is also its reinterpretation. The opportunity is for architects to expand their definition of "design" beyond material composition and embrace code-making as a collective, politically significant, and creative act. The *certification revolution* and those who promote *sustainable consumption* provide the immediate opportunity for designers to act collectively, politically, and creatively in the redefinition of architectural judgment as relevant to contemporary problems defined outside of the discipline.

The Certification Revolution

The core of the certification revolution, its neoliberal promoters argue, relies on an inherent two-part contradiction within late capitalism: First, the process of international "branding" or eco-labeling expands a company's opportunity to sell its products in global rather than local markets. This is an observation we made throughout the book in the context of technological standardization. However, certification advocates further observe that, if a brand name becomes tarnished by negative social or environmental consequences, which are subsequently made public through the media, the marketability of the brand can be seriously compromised. The case of Nike (exposed in 1997 as operating unsafe sweatshops in Indonesia) and the case of Apple (exposed in 2012 for similar labor practices in Schenzen, China) come to mind. In both cases, manufacturers were forced by the power of public opinion to alter production methods or working conditions. Contemporary retailers selling iPods, to continue the example, are sensitive to an increasingly aware and critical customer base. Activist customers routinely put pressure on producers (including service providers such as architects) and suppliers (including building material suppliers such as Home Depot) to conform to more progressive standards, such specifying or selling Forest Stewardship Council (FSC)-certified lumber. The direct and indirect vulnerability of producers to skeptical, and potentially disloyal, consumers thus opens the door to third-party certification companies to negotiate standards with stakeholders—not only those in industry and consumer advocates, but environmentally and socially motivated NGOs as well.[6] New kinds of judgment related to goods and services are taking place, not only in the building industry, but in literally every arena of production, from electronics (Energy Star) to furnishings (Green Seal). The contemporary certification movement is clearly a sumptuary code, as defined in Chapter 6, because certification is an attempt to limit consumption by all or some members of society to that which is more "sustainable." However, product certification also employs methods derived from the "economic codes" documented in Chapter 7—prescription, incentive, and performance. Certification in the real world is, then, a hybrid method of coding—it is only the most recent attempt to modify architectural production.

The implications of these observations, at least for some, are that we have already entered a new era of global governance, one legislated not only by nation-states and international corporations, but also by civil society—groups of volunteers who find common cause for, and in, action.[7] To make civil society more potent and corporations (or design firms) more compliant, Conroy holds that three related actions are required: First, activists must create a "market campaign" by a third-party NGO that can put pressure on producers and service providers to reform their practices. Second, the third-party NGO must create a "stakeholder-based set of standards" that includes all relevant social groups—industry, environmental groups, insurance companies, social equity advocates, and, eventually, government. Third, the diverse stakeholder group must create a "credible independent mechanism for certifying companies" over time and space.

The point of these observations is that, in architectural certification programs, as in successful material and food certification programs, third-party certifiers must *align* or *transform* the frames of relevant social groups, as we defined this term in Chapter 4, if the certification criteria are to be successful.[8] We argue that getting people to alter their habits requires that activists bring tacit codes to consciousness and then work toward aligning, transforming, and codifying common interests with all relevant social groups.[9]

The potential power of "third-party certification" is found in our analysis of standard-making in the United States. Unlike most other countries, standards, codes, and regulations of most kinds are made, not by government, but by first-party industries or second-party industry organizations operating under the umbrella of organizations such as NSI, UL, or the International Standards Organization (ISO). Although these second-party standard-makers operate under professional codes of ethics, we established in Chapter 3 that second-party certifiers exist and operate to benefit the interests of members and their stockholders, not the general health, safety, and welfare of all citizens. Consumers are, or should be, justifiably skeptical of second-party standards. What the advocates of third-party certification hope to accomplish is what federalists have failed to do over nearly 250 years—to include the previously excluded sectors of society in the making of more credible standards that will benefit, not only industry, government, and retailers, but also the general population, by establishing a field of contract certainty rather than one of distrust.[10]

Certification advocates point to the FSC as a particularly successful example of third-party certification. This is because FSC actually audits the production of lumber products throughout the production chain and, thereby, is able to certify measurable impacts to consumers with considerable credibility. In contrast, ISO 14000 Environmental Certification (a second-party certifier) is only a specification for a management system—it does not certify that companies "have actually put these systems into practice or achieved improved environmental results."[11] In other words, there is no system in place for companies using ISO 14000 standards to certify compliance, only intent, which may be more "green-wash" than substance.

Industry and its representatives in government have, of course, been resistant to what they consider to be outside interference by third-party NGOs. Like other "green" or "fair" certifiers, FSC has been challenged by second-party industry groups, in this case by the American Forest and Paper Association, which invented its own certification system—the Sustainable Forestry Initiative—in order to subvert the more rigorous forestry practices promoted by FSC and adopted by LEED. Conroy, overoptimistically in our view, argues that none of the industry-sponsored "copy-cat systems" has achieved "effective legitimacy in the eyes of civil society and the marketplace."[12]

It is, then, too early to accept the "certification revolution" as a singular pathway to urban sustainability, or to suggest that the participation of the design community will suddenly make design relevant to ordinary citizens. However, rather than reject the code-making efforts of energetic civil society groups such as the USGBC, it will be more helpful to put that movement in the broader context of our consumer society and the new sumptuary codes that just might transform the very concept of consumption.

Sustainable Consumption

Although the certification movement has indeed come a long way, others who study the concept of "sustainable consumption" are far less enthusiastic about the inevitable ability of the third-party certification movement to discipline the "invisible hand" of the market. For example, Lawrence Busch is skeptical that the market has the capacity to expand its influence, not through monopoly, but by creating "differentiated standards," such as ISO 14000, LEED, SEED, Green Globes, etc., that compete with each other for market share. He further argues,

> The widespread use of market standards, certifications, and accreditations to differentiate has led to another, seemingly oxymoronic pair of extremes not envisioned by neoliberals: a world in which everyone is constantly confronted by a vast—indeed, overwhelming—range of decisions, many of which are life-changing, *and* where everyone is subject to incessant checking and audit, certification and accreditation.[13]

In this darker view of the move toward certification, we may be entering something like the *judgment age*, an updated version of the *information age*, in which the availability of thousands of minute judgments makes them unmanageable and unwanted—just like the 83 email and text messages that have piled up in your inboxes as you have read this chapter. The problem is that one of those unwanted messages might indeed change your life, requiring that you at least scan them all, or accept unreasonable risk. In such a world, those who seek authoritative and trustworthy judgments by experts either become enslaved by making "what looks like choices"[14] in the market, or lack the capacity to make informed judgments at all, because they don't have a smartphone. This condition is but one reflection of the general shift in the first half of the 20th century from the federalist desire to regulate production for the benefit of all to the anti-federalist desire in the second half of the century to deregulate production, and thus optimize private choices, for the benefit of only the most capable.[15] One result of that shift is increasing inequality in the general population—those who have the tools and time to judge, and those who don't.[16]

A second result of the move toward architectural certification is the delusion that "political consumerism" can sustain a fundamentally unsustainable system.[17] Andrew Szasz refers to this delusion as an "inverted quarantine," or the idea that, by buying only products certified as sustainable—office buildings, houses, cars, clothing, food, pet food, etc.—we will isolate ourselves from a toxic environment.[18] Such a false sense of private security, Szasz argues, tends only to "anesthetize" us from engaging in genuine public political action that might alter the system as a whole. By thinking of ourselves as *educated* or even *political consumers*, rather than as citizens-at-risk, these skeptics argue that we imprison judgment within an ill-fated neoliberal paradigm that privatizes well-being.[19]

In our view, such skepticism is well warranted. That doesn't require, however, that we should ignore the certification movement as another seemingly attractive, yet inherently flawed, strategy of neoliberalism. Rather, it suggests that we might understand the certification movement as we did the early DRM or the S.M.A.R.T. Housing initiative—not as silver bullets, but as one opportunity for civil society groups to align the many interpretations of "sustainability" through action—action that might not only improve public as well as private conditions, but also hatch new ideas. What that means in concrete terms will vary from place to place, but it is those local initiatives that could add up, through mediated public talk, to become a social movement as robust as the DRM.[20]

Certifying Architecture

LEED—the building certification system developed by the USGBC—is but one of the many NGOs that are attempting to create measures that will credibly inform architectural production. The LEED measures developed thus far have had significant influence. At the time of writing, almost 2 billion square feet of commercial space have been certified, 15,000 companies are affiliated at the national level, and 79 regional chapters in the United States (not including 21 chapters in other countries) have mobilized over 20,000 civil society volunteers.[21] These are impressive numbers that suggest "green building" has become a bona fide social movement.[22] However, LEED standards, and those of competing NGOs, remain contested in many corners of the building industry and in academia. In the terms we discussed in Chapter 2, the system has not yet come to "closure"—meaning that the definition of a "sustainable" technology, building, space, or place has not been agreed upon by relevant social groups. The good news is that, unlike most technology innovators, USGBC has remained open to criticism and demonstrates willingness to continually revise its criteria for judgment, opening up more space for collaborators.[23]

Will LEED, or some other future coalition of assessment systems, replace the canon of architecture? That is unlikely. Will a new generation of leaders in the field alter the criteria for admission into the canon to also include performance criteria? Almost certainly! Our view is that accounting for many different kinds of performance will democratize and politicize the canon in healthy ways. However, it is as yet unclear to what degree sociotechnical performance, in addition to environmental performance, will be measured, and by whom.

Three emergent tools may point us in a productive direction: the *REGEN Tool*, *ICLEI*, and *SEED*. First is the proposal for "regenerative design,"[24] and a companion "Regen Tool," by Svec, Berkebile, and Todd. Their proposal is not for a building assessment tool in the orthodox sense, but for "a forum, a repository of information and a framework that are capable of stimulating dialogue among a diversity of practitioners and decision-makers with interdisciplinary backgrounds and viewpoints." The tool is intended to be "tailored specifically to each place and each project" as a decision-making, or judgment-making process backed by empirical data—what Faulconbridge describes as the "mobilization" and localization of "green knowledges" through the process of "bricolage."[25] In short, the "regen tool [is] a tool for thinking"[26] or judgment by locally oriented but Internet-connected civil society groups. The tool challenges professional conventions that encourage the hoarding of proprietary information and a legal system that is risk-averse and thus inhibits transformation of the general building culture. As conceived, however, the REGEN Tool falls short of catalyzing agency for the general population, let alone underrepresented groups, because it limits participation to design professionals and the usual cast of decision-makers. In contrast, Nye and Hargreaves hold that, without the participation of non-experts—building owners, managers, and at least some users—it will be impossible to "create a shared commitment, encouraging creativity and innovation, building confidence, fostering a sense of shared responsibility, and providing a forum where participants can challenge received ways of doing things."[27] Heiskanen and Lovio come to a similar conclusion in their study of sustainable and "experimental" building techniques in Finland. They found, "that the communication gap between producers and users can, by and large, be filled by the introduction of new communication skills and methods," and that, "improved communication may be the best way to produce novel innovations in the housing sector."[28] Given such empirical findings, there is no reason—save software design—that the REGEN Tool could not also be made more accessible to the communities being affected by expert decision-making.

The second emerging tool works at the scale of the community, rather than the building, as Berkebile and his colleagues encourage. ICLEI—Local Governments for Sustainability USA (formerly the International Council for Local Environmental Initiatives)—is now developing a "national, consensus-based framework for gauging the sustainability and livability of U.S. communities," called the STAR Community Index (SCI).[29] This tool, like LEED (which is an SCI partner), is a member-based effort to allow definitions and standards of sustainability to emerge from civil society groups, rather than being handed down by experts.The SCI is, however, in its infancy and has yet to demonstrate how collected data will represent those interests that generally remain invisible.

The third tool is the SEED Network—an acronym for *social, economic*, and *environmental design*.[30] At the time of writing, SEED has successfully brought the issue of social equity as a dimension of sustainability into the mainstream professional literature, and to the attention of dominant institutions such as the American Institute of Architects (AIA), by creating a social equity certification system that can be added to LEED or ICLEI. What SEED has not yet accomplished is to make this frame of interpretation matter to the other relevant social groups that dominate the construction industry—banks, mortgage lenders, insurance companies, general contractors, and governments. Unlike the REGEN Tool and ICLEI, SEED will, no doubt, remain outside normative practice and draw a critical line in the sand that distinguishes what its progenitors consider to be genuinely equitable and what is, in their view, mere green-wash.[31] By adopting such an outsider, more radical, and uncompromising position, SEED will perform the useful task of disciplining those who work to reform neoliberal institutions from within—at least so long as SEED's position is not overtly "moralizing or appealing to individual altruism."[32] However, to be clear, working from the inside is not necessarily a compromising task. As we argued in Chapter 6, the transformation of traditional sumptuary codes, or codes of taste, into life-enhancing codes of public distinction is a radical and difficult project.[33]

In sum, the contemporary conversations concerning certification, regenerative design, and community design are forms of public talk about how the social and environmental performance of places influences what we think of as beautiful, or excellent.[34] This hybrid conversation, which includes not only architects, but engineers, artists, public policymakers, municipal managers, and a host of others, is extremely encouraging, because it contributes to the potency of civil society governance of the built world.[35] For architects, there could not be a better moment to assume an appropriate level of leadership and responsibility for social change, and thereby become a social group more relevant to the development of a sustainable building culture. To do so will require repositioning the discipline in both the market and within civil society.[36]

Toward that end, our conclusion consists of 10 propositions derived from the historical and empirical research in the preceding chapters. We hope these will be helpful in the project of producing sociotechnical codes for a future we hope to construct, inhabit, and continually reconstruct.

TEN PROPOSITIONS FOR SOCIOTECHNICAL CODE-MAKING

The following propositions can be considered sub-hypotheses of the general hypothesis stated above. They are offered in no particular order and are occasionally overlapping. Although they derive from our case studies, which are highly particular, we have argued above that they will be helpful to others engaged in action research. It is, however, the readers' responsibility to adapt them to the conditions where they are applied.

1. All codes, whether we recognize it or not, influence not only technology (in the broad sense of the term), but also related biophysical and social systems. If we accept this proposition, it requires that code-making institutions include citizens trained or equipped by experience to make judgments in each of those dimensions—technical, biophysical, and social.

Some will argue that we should also include aesthetic decision-making in this recipe. We agree, provisionally. But, if those with primary interest in aesthetic standards wish to participate in coding the future, they should be prepared to employ empirical evidence and sound reasoning in the reconstruction of the canon.

2. Tacit codes, or those that we carry around in the back of our heads without being able to articulate them, can be effective in preserving life-enhancing traditions. However, they are also powerful inhibitors of coordinated technological, biophysical, and social change. The project of a democratic society is to bring tacit codes to consciousness and publicly codify them to be more efficient, more environmentally friendly, and more just.

This is a radical proposition for action and one inherently incompatible with the concept of multiculturalism. Rather than seek the preservation of traditional cultures that depend on tacit codes, this proposition seeks the self-conscious production of new hybrid cultures. It is, then, inherently an aspiration appropriate to citizens of the United States. In making such a proposal, however, we do not embrace the doctrines of American exceptionalism. Rather, we look forward to constructing solidarity with democrats everywhere.

3. Sumptuary codes are a potentially powerful tool in the project to reduce resource consumption without restoring authoritarian, class-based bans. Contemporary sumptuary codes might, instead, positively reward behavior by citizens that is demonstrated to be environmentally and socially distinctive.

Sumptuary codes are social rules, or behavioral codes, that attempt to influence what citizens should and shouldn't consume, distinguish, or discourage. For example, architect Raphael Sperry has argued that it is irrational to grant the design for a new prison a distinction for environmental performance (as USGBC's LEED certification system would allow), because that criterion of distinction simply ignores the social costs of producing prisoners and the prisons in which to house them. We now understand that producing goods with ever-increasing efficiency will not be enough to satisfy ever-increasing rates of consumption by ever-increasing numbers of people. In other words, supply-side economics will necessarily be tempered, not only by demand-side theory, but also by what we characterize as effect-side theory—the ability to see and account for the unintended consequences of action on underrepresented groups.

4. Economic codes—prescription, incentive- and performance-based regulations—will not disappear anytime soon in our neoliberal economy. As we argued in Chapter 7, each has some benefit. They can, however, be made far more democratic and effective through third-party certification and transparent administration—the latter being an idea that both federalists and anti-federalists might embrace.

Only the most enlightened producers of goods and services welcome third-party activists to the table. But it is precisely in this arena of judgment that professional designers of all kinds might make significant contributions and thus exercise leadership, rather than remaining outside of civil society discourse in the interest of maintaining a "critical" stance.

5. Design networks are technical, environmental, and social—it is not possible to achieve technological change without social and environmental consequences, or to achieve social change without technological and environmental consequences. To realize technological, environmental and social change deemed desirable by citizens, those who conceptualize action and those who implement it must work together.

We argued in Chapter 2 that this proposition holds that *successful* technological or environmental networks cannot be conceptualized by one group of politicians (who may have little knowledge of the technical side of the system) and implemented by another group of technocrats (who may have little investment in the social side of the system, but who run the machines of road-making, planning, or water supply).

6. The incremental change of technological codes may reduce short-term conflict, but incrementalism also reduces the transparency of technological storylines and suppresses long-term social learning.

This proposition reflects the desire of entrepreneurs of all kinds for *contract certainty*—the need to have clear rules that reduce risk and render deals and designs to have predictable outcomes. Slicing up technological change into increments small enough for contractors, investors, or voters to be able to calculate the economic effect of code changes is, as President Jefferson argued in 1789, prudent in the short term. Incremental change consciously avoids confrontation with tacit codes, as we discussed them in Chapter 4. However, incremental steps by themselves tend to complicate codes and obscure the consideration of long-term alternatives—the technological storylines that inspire a society to make large and difficult changes. There is, then, a dialectic of conflict and clarity: Too much conflict curbs technological change, and too little curbs the social learning required to take bold steps toward an alternative future. Conflict can be productive.

7. Code-making can shift, or externalize, the cost and responsibility for designing and building infrastructure from communities to developers and investors. Doing so, however, obfuscates the social and ecological effects of public technological choices.

Architect Randy Croxton has argued, with some humorous intent, that "building-to-code" is but one step above criminal activity. In Chapter 3, we argued that codes are generally minimum standards for developers to follow, not an expression of community aspirations. By abdicating responsibility for the design and construction of infrastructure (understood broadly), municipalities may indeed save taxpayers a few short-term dollars. However, externalizing that responsibility also excludes public and professional input into imagining preferred futures.

8. The design of sustainable cities must integrate both production and consumption as reciprocal sides of a single system.

Systems of production and consumption are made up, not only of technologies, resources, and artifacts, but also of people. For example, gentrification cannot occur without the production of "gentrifiers." This is to say that the social displacement of relatively poor people by relatively richer ones is not an abstract process involving automatons governed only by global economic structures. Rather, society has produced a class of people who see it not only in their interest, but also in the interest of the city, to act in this way. Yes, gentrifiers may be influenced by global economic structures, but they also make choices of their own in the places in which they choose to live. We are arguing, then, that, just as society has unconsciously created a system of rewards that encourage unsustainable consumption, we should consciously work toward producing a system of rewards that encourage sustainable consumption. We might do so by granting individuals distinction in society for living and acting in a sustainable fashion.

9. As a prerequisite for action, working to fix goals and creating a common language to discuss them is an admirable but misguided assumption. Action reframes both goals and the language used to define them.

Waiting for competing social groups to agree, a priori, on language that will fix the meaning of "sustainable," "affordable," or "distributed" will be counter-productive for two related reasons: First, scientific analysis and design are social practices that seek different, but related, products. Scientific analysis hopes to accurately describe, through language, causal relations between variables so that, all things remaining equal, those relations may prove helpful to problem-solvers in the future. Designs, however, are proposals for action in the present, because the actors involved understand that all other things *never* remain equal—conditions of economy, ecology, and politics are in a constant state of evolution. Waiting for meaning to become fixed would only mean that the conditions receptive to action would pass us by. In this evolutionary context, buildings are not "eternal truths," but a timely mobilization of material artifacts and social agreements requiring and enjoying constant renovation.

The second reason why waiting for language to find consensus is counterproductive is that the meaning of our words emerges through action. As we argued above, this is not necessarily an epistemological position—it is to say that design, science, and democracy are not separate and distinct practices, but one and the same way of life. It is to hold that *action is inquiry*, or, turned inside out, it is to hold that both *design and science are politics by another name*.

We also found that the process of finding common norms, codes, and values requires the integration of technological frames through cycles of action, experimentation, and reflection. By this, we mean that it is only *action* toward a goal, even one vaguely shared by competing social groups, that allows us to recognize the value of our neighbor's perspective—a realization we are not likely to reach through the parsing of words alone. This proposition suggests, then, that, if the technological codes that guide city-making are the by-products of experimental inquiry, code-making is but one form of democratic experimentation. Code-making is not, then, a final declaration of "the truth," or the Law; be it about gentrification or any other focal issue, it is a way to test what works best in the making of cities. This is why cities need to create for themselves spaces of experimentation—spaces where designers and other collaborators can test possibilities.

10. Codes must constantly evolve in response to changing conditions and goals.

This proposition follows from the previous one. As economic, technological, or ecological conditions change, old agreements come into conflict, because new kinds of action are required. The implications of this proposition for municipalities, or any institution, is that investment in staff and public talk is required to keep agreements alive, flexible, and in a position to lead technological choices, rather than respond to them defensively.

Finally, these ten propositions are not rules or codes in themselves. Rather, they are suggestions for experimentation, intended to expand the arena in which creative designers act.

Glossary

The specialized terms developed in the book are necessary to describe the dynamic conditions we found through historical and empirical investigation. Brief definitions of these specialized terms provide the reader with a distilled theoretical framework of the book as a whole.

code This term is both a noun and a verb. As a noun it has two dominant meanings: (1.) It refers to a system of signals for transforming information from one form into another, as in semaphore signaling, a computer "access code," or a "genetic code." Or (2.), we use the term *code* to mean an extra-technological law that governs behavior as well as the design and construction of artifacts and spaces. Codes can be placed within a hierarchy that begins with metaethics, and includes ethics, laws, codes, ordinances, standards, and operating practices. Codes stipulate not only a standard for behavior, as in a professional code of conduct, but also a standard for material production, as in a technological or building code.

building code A typical building code provision is, for example, the prescription that the exterior doors of public buildings must open outward (International Conference of Building Officials (ICBO)), or that the vertical rise of steps and stairs shall not be less than 4 inches nor more than 7 inches (ICBO). These particular requirements are, however, social rather than purely technological in origin, because they are intended to mediate human behavior in the case of emergencies such as fires in buildings. In general, one can say that building codes both reflect and enforce social values. They are, then, a historical index of how social values regarding the safety, health, and welfare of individuals and communities are materialized as the built world. We further categorize technological and building codes into four subcategories: *tacit*, *sumptuary*, *economic*, and *socio-technical* codes.

tacit code Tacit knowledge is generally understood to be that which is embedded in cultural practices—it is knowledge that is difficult for individuals to articulate because they carry it around in the back of their heads—it is not formally codified in the modern sense. Tacit codes are similar, but should be understood as a subset of tacit knowledge. Tacit building codes are, then, a third-order subset—they are the rules, procedures, and habits that discipline how we build, or what Davis refers to as our "building culture." Although tacit codes of all kinds may be unspoken, they still "frame" acceptable behavior and thus regulate what we can and can't do in predictable ways.

sumptuary codes The word "sumptuary" is an archaic one and derives from the Latin pertaining to "regulating or limiting expense."

In the medieval societies of Europe, Japan, and China, sumptuary codes regulated, not only the dress of all classes of people, so as to make their social rank legible in public spaces, but also architectural representation and material construction systems. Sumptuary codes are, then, those that regulate, not only the appearance of individuals, but also expenditures related to consumption made by those individuals—how lavish or large their houses might be, for example. Although most people assume that sumptuary codes have long since disappeared, we find that they are still very much with us and, surprisingly, provide a contemporary method to distinguish individuals who consume community resources sustainably.

economic codes Economic codes regulate artifacts and spaces primarily to enhance what private and public code-makers determine to be economically beneficial for society as a whole. Economic codes are of three types: prescriptive, incentive-, and performance-based:

> **prescriptive codes** By prescribing universal characteristics of a class of artifacts or spaces in detail, code-makers enhance the exchange value of, for example, a pound of 16 penny nails or a parking space across their spatial jurisdiction. Standardization also reduces the possibility of conflict between persons using different standards. Although prescriptive codes appear essential in some contexts, they are universally unpopular, because they require a centralized and technocratic form of governance to make them effective.
>
> **incentive-based codes** In lieu of prescribing standards for artifacts and spaces, code-makers have more and more frequently turned to incentives, such as granting a height variance to a developer in exchange for building publicly desired amenities such as parks, for which code-makers lack the political backing to prescribe or finance through taxation. Incentives are designed to reward risk-takers in both the private and public realms and can, therefore, devolve into simple capitalistic deal-making that gives up some public goods in favor of others.
>
> **performance-based codes** Rather than prescribe the exact size, shape, and technical qualities of artifacts or spaces that can be made, or introduce economic incentives designed to attract those qualities, performance-based codes specify only the outcomes to be achieved—if they meet or exceed basic prescriptions. The apparent benefit of performance-based criteria is that public and private interests are rewarded for creativity and context-dependent problem-solving. The apparent detriment is that the cost of demonstrating compliance is borne by the applicant and so excludes people of modest means from exercising this option.

sociotechnical codes This category of code emerges from acknowledgment that, whether or not we recognize it, all technological codes have, not only environmental consequences, but also social ones.

We demonstrate this claim empirically, through study of the Americans with Disabilities Act and the case of S.M.A.R.T. Housing in Austin, Texas. On these grounds, we propose that sociotechnical codes differ from tacit, sumptuary, and economic codes primarily in the conscious intention of code-makers to change social and environmental conditions for specific social groups through technological change. If all codes are implicit sociotechnical codes, then the process through which they are socially constructed and continually evaluated should change to become explicit. The act of coding should include individuals with the training or experience to anticipate both environmental and social consequences, as well as purely technological ones.

As a verb, to code (or encode) something is to assign it an identity or to classify it as belonging to a group of things perceived to be of similar kind, as in "multistory buildings" or "mud huts." And, as in these two examples, our codes derive from social values as much as technological characteristics. To decode something is to reconstruct the social values and reasoning from which the code was initially constructed as a technological standard by code-makers.

hypothesis Our primary empirical finding is that there is a consistent and predictable relationship between three primary variables that drive code-making in the United States: *relevant social groups*, *technological frames*, and the *focal issues*. These terms are defined as follows:

relevant social groups This term is defined best by Cowan as social groups that "influence the creation, the demand for, the production, the diffusion, the acceptance, or the opposition to new technologies."[1]

technological frames This term derives from the works of Erving Goffman and Wiebe Bijker. By it we mean that adult members of all social groups inhabit common frames of interpretation that organize our perceptions of the events that take place around us, as well as how we expect people to behave as events unfold. More specifically, our technological frames condition our expectations of the knowledge, practices, and things required to solve our problems. We found technological frames to be of three kinds: *supply*-side, *demand*-side, and *affect*-side.

supply-side Seen through a supply-side technological frame, any system can be made more productive by the removal of obstacles to efficiency, if the system is narrowly defined. Seen through a supply-side frame, technological change is generally viewed with skepticism, because it tends to upset established relationships within the system.

demand-side Seen through a demand-side technological frame, no system can be assessed in isolation of its external affects, or affects absorbed by other systems. Technological change is generally viewed optimistically, because it is likely to expand relationships across systems.

effect-side For those who inhabit the supply- or demand-side frame, technological change is viewed through a priori values. For those who inhabit the effect-side frame, however, technologies are neither good nor bad in essence. Rather, their value depends on who is affected by change, how they are affected, and when.

focal issues In the cases studied, we found public conflicts, or what we call focal issues, tend to dominate public consciousness and obscure other issues that compete for attention. Focal issues dominate public discourse because they embody core tensions or identities that have developed in the community over time.

Although these three variables, and their sub-variables, are modified by global economies and the cultural politics of particular places, we find the relationship between them to be consistent. Stated as four sequential sub-hypotheses, we find that:

H1. *Relevant social groups (RSGs) interpret focal issues from within shared technological frames.* RSGs have an a priori disposition to interpret events, conditions, and possibilities in a particular way.

H2. *Technological frames are said to be generative if they catalyze action intended to improve (or degrade) conditions for a particular social group.* Technological frames are not fixed. Rather, they can move RSGs to act in uncertain conditions that challenge a priori dispositions.

H3. *Generative frames are said to be regenerative if they transform, realign, and/or expand RSGs through action.* Through leadership-in-action, the frames of singular RSGs can be transformed and thus aligned with other RSGs and life-enhancing environmental conditions.

H4. *Regenerative technological frames are said to be successful if they produce codes that materialize life-enhancing built environments that, in turn, develop the agency of relevant groups.* New hybrid frames of interpretation, which emerge through collective action, can improve the capacity of specific social groups to act on their own behalf by producing codes that, in turn, make the built environment easier to navigate or more receptive to specific kinds of action valued by the RSG.

Notes

General Introduction

1 Mumford, Lewis. 1963[1934]. *Technics and Civilization* (pp. 427, 417). New York: Harvest/HBJ.

2 Hard, Mikael, and Andrew Jamison. 2005. *Hubris and Hybrids: A Cultural History of Technology and Science*. New York and London: Routledge. See also, Scott, James C. 1998. *Seeing Like a State: How Certain Schemes to Improve the Human Condition Have Failed*. New Haven, CN: Yale University Press.

3 We have adopted Howard Davis' use of this term, by which he means, "the coordinated system of knowledge, rules, procedures, and habits that surround the building process in any given place and time." See: Davis, Howard. 2006. *The Culture of Building* (p. 5). New York and Oxford, UK: Oxford University Press.

4 For a counter-argument, see: Guggenheim, Michael, and Ola Soderstrom, eds. 2010. *Re-shaping Cities: How Global Mobility Transforms Architectural and Urban Form*. Abingdon, UK and New York: Routledge. These authors hold that, "Cities are generally considered as expressions of the region in which they are situated. This book tells another story. It shows that cities are on the move, that they are produced by globally circulating architects, ideas, and materials" (p. 3).

5 Carmona, Matthew. 2009. "Design Coding and the Creative, Market and Regulatory Tyrannies of Practice." In, *Urban Studies* 46 (12):2643–2667. Here and elsewhere, Carmona examines design coding in the UK.

6 Duany, Andrés. 2004. "Notes Towards a Reason to Code." In, *Perspecta; The MIT Press on behalf of Perspecta* 35 (Building Codes). See also, Duany, Andrés. 1993. "Coding America." In, *ANY* 1 (1):14–19.

7 Duany, Andrés. 2012. "Foreword," in Talen, Emily. 2012. *City Rules: How Regulations Affect Urban Form*. Washington, DC: Island Press.

8 Parolek, Daniel G., Karen Parolek, and Paul C. Crawford. 2008. *Form-based Codes: A Guide for Planners, Urban Designers, Municipalities, and Developers*. New York: Wiley.

9 The dualisms of modern, or Cartesian, philosophy have been the subject of critique by all post-modern philosophers, from Nietzsche onward. One of the most influential has been Heidegger: See: Heidegger, Martin. 1977. "The Age of the World Picture." In, *The Question Concerning Technology and Other Essays*. Edited by W. Lovitt. New York: Harper and Rowe. More recently, and directly related to architecture, pragmatist and STS scholars have challenged the dualism of the humanities and technology. See: Yaneva, Albena. 2012. *Mapping Controversies in Architecture*. Farnham, UK: Ashgate.

10 It will come as a surprise to some that there is an organized discipline known by this name. Don Ihde has argued that the field formally emerged in the works of an obscure German–American philosopher in the late 19th century. See: Ihde, Don. 1979. *Technics and Praxis*. Rotterdam, The Netherlands: Dordrecht. Others have assumed that the discourse began with Martin Heidegger only after World War II; see: Heidegger. 1977[1935]. *The Question Concerning Technology and Other Essays*. No matter the origin, the contemporary field is made rich with major contributions by Albert Borgman, Andrew Feenberg, Larry Hickman, Andrew Light, Carl Mitcham, Paul Thompson, Langdon Winner, and many others.

11 Sismondo, Sergio. 2009. *An Introduction to Science and Technology Studies*. 2nd ed. Chichester, UK: John Wiley & Sons.

12 MacKenzie, Donald, and Wajcman, Judy, eds. 1999. *The Social Shaping of Technology*. 2nd ed. Philadelphia, PA: Open University Press.

13 Interdisciplinary scholars are fond of saying that the world did not come in disciplines, and so studying it through our own limited categories tells us more about ourselves than the world itself.
14 Kayden, Jerold S. 2004. "Understanding the 'Code' of Codes." In, *Perspecta: The Yale Architectural Journal* (35).
15 Conroy, Michael E. 2007. *Branded! How the "Certification Revolution" Is Transforming Global Corporations.* Gabriola Island, BC: New Society Publishers.
16 See, for example: Frampton, Kenneth. 1991. "Reflection on the Autonomy of Architecture: A Critique of Contemporary Production." In, *Out of Site: A Social Criticism of Architecture.* Edited by Diane Ghirardo (pp. 17–26). Seattle, WA: Bay Press. See also, Larson, Magali Sarfatti. 1993. *Behind the Postmodern Façade.* University of California Press; Habracken, Joseph W. 2005. *Palladio's Children: Essays on the Everyday Environment and the Architect.* Edited by Jonathan Teicher. London: Taylor & Francis; Imrie, Rob, and Emma Street. 2011. *Architectural Design and Regulations.* London: Wiley–Backwell; Ingersoll, Richard. 1991. "Context and Modernity. Delft, June 12–15, 1990." In, *Journal of Architectural Education (1984–)* 44 (2):124–125; and Thorpe, Ann. 2012. *Architecture and Design Versus Consumerism: How Design Activism Confronts Growth.* London and New York: Earthscan; Taylor & Francis. Kindle Edition.

Chapter 1

1 Vitruvius.1960[15 BCE]. *Ten Books on Architecture.* Translated by Morris Hicky Morgan. New York: Dover Publications.
2 Frampton, Kenneth. 1983. "Toward a Critical Regionalism: Six Points for an Architecture of Resistance." In, *The Anti-Aesthetic: Essays on Postmodern Culture.* Edited by Hal Foster. Seattle, WA: Bay Press. Beginning in the 1980s, shortly after philosopher Martin Heidegger's powerful critique of modern technology first appeared in English, contemporary architects adopted the idea of *techne* as their own because it seemed to provide a conceptual bridge between art and technology. Heidegger argued that our modern manner of engaging the world through technology is not simply one that is faster or more efficient than that of Vitruvius, but one that is ontologically distinct from any previous age. Heidegger holds that,

> The word *techne* denotes . . . a way of knowing. . . . *Techne*, as knowledge experienced in the Greek manner, is a bringing forth of beings in that it *brings forth* what is present in such *out of* concealedness and specifically *into* the unconcealedness of their appearance; *techne* never signifies the action of making.
>
> (1977[1935], p. 180)

3 On the Greek term *metis*, see Scott. *Seeing Like a State.*
4 Davis. *The Culture of Building.*
5 According to the *American Heritage Dictionary of the English Language* (1981; edited by William Morris. Boston, MA: Houghton Mifflin Company), the Semetic root word of "canon" is "kana," which links the concept to the Greek word for "reed," "canyon," and "canal" and, thus, the controlled flow of water. Another interpretation is offered in: Tzonis, A., and L. Lefaivre. 1992. *Classical Architecture: The Poetics of Order.* MIT Press. Tzonis and Lefaivre hold, "Rather than a free-wheeling style, the Canon of Classical Architecture is a tool for design-thinking about space, through space, and organizing activities and objects within space."
6 Bourdieu, P. 1984[1979]. *Distinction: A Social Critique of the Judgment of Taste* (p. 2). Harvard University Press. Bourdieu more specifically argues that, "A work of art has meaning and interest only for someone who possesses the cultural competence, that is, the code, into which it is encoded."
7 Habracken. *Palladio's Children.*
8 Larson. *Behind the Postmodern Façade.* Larson holds that, "Of Vitruvian definition—architecture is the combination of 'firmness, commodity, and delight'—only delight was not claimed by credentialed or otherwise expert rivals" (p. 72). Although her claim is related to the end of the century, the process of transforming architectural production from that of a people, to that of an individual architect–artist, begins with Palladio and other architects of the period.
9 Habracken, *Palladio's Children.*

10 Latour has referred to such systems as "immutable mobiles." He means, by this term, that, once phenomena can be reduced to abstractions such as maps or money, they can be transported elsewhere and manipulated at a distance. Codification of the classical orders operates in a similar way. See: Latour, Bruno. 1986. "Visualization and Cognition: Thinking with eyes and hands." *Knowledge and Society* 6:1–40.

11 Schön, Donald A. 1987. *Educating the Reflective Practitioner* (p. 30). San Francisco, CA: Jossey-Bass.

12 See also, Bozdoğan, Sibel. 1999. "Architectural History in Professional Education: Reflections on Postcolonial Challenges to the Modern Survey." In, *Journal of Architectural Education (1984–)* 52 (4):207–215.

13 Crouch, D.P., and J.G. Johnson. 2001. *Traditions in Architecture: Africa, America, Asia, and Oceania* (p. 3). New York: Oxford University Press.

14. Of the many who have moved beyond these limits, Dave Hickey may be the closest to our view. See, for example: Hickey, Dave. 1997. *Air Guitar: Essays on Art & Democracy*. New York: Art Issues Press; distributed by D.A.P., Distributed Art Publishers.

15 Boyer, Ernest L., and Lee D. Mitgang. A Special Report. 1996. *Building Community: A New Future for Architecture Education and Practice*. Ewing, NJ: California Princeton Fulfillment Services.

16 Boyer and Mitgang. 1996. *Building Community*. See also, Larson. *Behind the Postmodern Façade*.

17 John Dewey's proposal for direct engagement and transformation of the everyday was in direct contrast to the Critical Theory admonition for withdrawal from everyday life. See: Dewey, John. 1980[1934]. *Art as Experience*. New York: Perigree, Penguin.

18 Adorno, Theodor W. 1983. *Aesthetic Theory*. Translated by Gretel Adorno and Rolf Tiedemann; translated by Christian Lenhardt. Boston: Routledge and Kegan Paul.

19 Hays, K. Michael. 1998. *Architecture Theory Since 1968*. Cambridge, MA: The MIT Press.

20 Thorpe. *Architecture and Design Versus Consumerism*. See also, Bell, Jeffrey A. 2011. "Undoing the Subject: Deleuze and the Makings of a Sustainable Life." In, *New Directions in Sustainable Design*. Edited by A. Parr and M. Zaretsky. New York: Routledge. See also: Doucet, Isabelle, and Kenny Cupers. 2009. "Agency in Architecture: Reframing Criticality in Theory and Practice."In, *Footprint: Delft School of Design Journal*:1–6.

21 For an example of pragmatic theory building, see: Yaneva. *Mapping Controversies in Architecture*. For an example of anti-theoretical, action-oriented architecture, see: Bell, Bryan, ed. 2004. *Good Deeds, Good Design: Community Service Through Architecture*. New York: Princeton Architectural Press.

22 Eisenman, Peter. 2000. "Autonomy and the Will to be Critical." In, *Dialogue: Architecture + Design + Culture* (pp. 61–62).

23 Bergdoll, Barry, and Reinhold Martin, eds. 2011. *Foreclosed: Rehousing the American Dream*. New York: Museum of Modern Art. Accessed July 29, 2012 at: www.moma.org/interactives/exhibitions/2012/foreclosed/.

24 For one example of serious reconsideration of the suburb, see: Dunham-Jones, Ellen, and June Williamson. 2009. *Retrofitting Suburbia: Urban Design Solutions for Redesigning Suburbs*. New York: John Wiley and Sons.

25 Bell, Bryan. Thursday, February 16, 2012. "MoMA Misses by 99%." In, *Metropolis: Point of View*. New York: Metropolis Magazine. Accessed July 29, 2012 at: www.metropolismag.com/pov/20120216/moma-misses-by-99.

26 The term, "*l'art pour l'art*," or "art for art's sake," is generally credited to Théophile Gautier (1811–1872) and was adopted by those romantics who objected to the premodern idea that art should serve a moral or didactic purpose, particularly one controlled by religious authority. In contemporary life, architect Frank Gehry makes a similar romantic claim, but one that discounts the authority of science with regard to climate change rather than that of the church. He argues:

> We've just been through a very expressionist period where people have had a lot of money and it's coming to a screeching halt because of the culture around architecture. It's a kind of backlash. They're saying to focus on sustainability, on social problems, that the architecture should come second. It just seems so thoughtless to throw out the baby with the bathwater. It becomes a mantra for less talented people to get their way I guess.

In the context of this interview, Gehry dismisses motivations other than "*l'art pour l'art*" as being outside the boundaries of the canon and a tool employed by the "less talented" to attract legitimation. See: Zakaria, Fareed. 2011. A Conversation with Frank Gehry: *How to Innovate: Inside the Mind of Master Architect Frank Gehry.* Available at: www.yousendit.com/dl?phi_action=app/orchestrateDownload&rurl=https%253A%252F%252Fwww.yousendit.com%252Ftransfer.php%253Faction%253Dbatch_download%2526batch_id%253DT2dmTkF1dzhlcEpBSXRVag, aired September 4, 2011.

27 In their collaborative and empirical study of public participation in architectural process, Jenkins, Forsythe, et al. come to very similar conclusions. In their view, architects have historically felt their profession to be privileged and isolated from normative concerns. In their study of contemporary practice, they found three linked conceptual and analytic issues to lie beneath the disengagement of architects from social concerns, "knowledge, value and power" (p. 148). Because, they argue, architects are trained to consider architectural knowledge to be unique and, thus, superior to other forms of knowledge, the self-imposed isolation of architects promotes the "vicious circle of limited social participation and appreciation of architecture throughout society" (p. 149). They found that architectural knowledge has become increasingly opaque to other citizens and, thus, seemingly irrelevant. "This context leads to a situation where architects create a value system for architecture which is not necessarily that widely accepted socially—this closed value system being used in many situations as a defense mechanism" (p. 150) to prop up the waning authority of the profession within the building industry. They conclude that, "widening social participation in the architectural process comes down to how value is created and who creates this value, and how it is affected by power relations and played out in terms of knowledge" (p. 150). See: Jenkins, Paul, and Leslie Forsyth, eds. 2010. *Architecture, Participation and Society.* London, Routledge.

28 For Gehry's version of architectural autonomy, see: Zakaria. A Conversation with Frank Gehry.

29 Imrie and Street. *Architectural Design and Regulations*; Ingersoll. "Context and Modernity. Delft, June 12–15, 1990.". See also, Boyer and Mitgang. *Building Community.*

30 Owen, Ceridwen, and Kim Dovey. 2008. "Fields of Sustainable Architecture." In, *The Journal of Architecture* 13 (1):9–21.

31 Bourdieu, Pierre. 1993. *The Field of Cultural Production.* New York: Columbia University Press.

32 Wang, David. 2003. "Categories of ACSA Conference Papers: A Critical Evaluation of Architectural Research in Light of Social Science Methodological Frameworks." In, *Journal of Architectural Education* 56 (4):50–56. Wang conducted a content analysis of papers given at conferences sponsored bythe Associated Collegiate Schools of Architecture. But, where Wang sought to determine the "ways of knowing" employed by architects in research, our emphasis was more topical: we asked "what do they want to know about." Although the two studies differ in the categories constructed, they arrive at very sympathetic conclusions about the nature of architectural research.

33 In addition to the authors, the team includes graduate students Meghan Kleon and Cayce Bean.

34 Zaknic, Ivan. 1989. "Le Corbusier San Fin Review: [*Voyage d'Orient: Carnets; La Chaux-de Fonds et Jeanneret avant Le Corbusier; Le Corbusier, le passé a réaction poétique; Le Corbusier Secret; Les mains de Le Corbusier; Le Corbusier à Cap-Martin; Le Corbusier*]." In, *Journal of Architectural Education (1984–)* 42 (3):49–59. Rowley, Ellen. 2009. "Review [Le Corbusier: The Art of Architecture]." In, *Journal of Architectural Education* 63 (1):147–149. Hartoonian, Gevork. 1989. "Mies van der Rohe: The Genealogy of Column and Wall." In, *Journal of Architectural Education (1984–)* 42 (2):43–50. Hartoonian, Gevork. 1994. "Review: The Artless Word: Mies van der Rohe on the Building Art by Fritz Neumeyer." In, *Journal of Architectural Education (1984–)* 47 (3):180–181. Stankard, Mark. 2002. "Re-covering Mies van der Rohe's Weissenhof: The Ultimate Surface." In, *Journal of Architectural Education* 55 (4):247–256. Ott, Randall. 2003. "Review [Mies in Berlin and Mies in America]." In, *Journal of Architectural Education* 56 (4):69–75. James, Kathleen. 1995. "Louis Kahn's Indian Institute of Management's Courtyard: Form versus Function." In, *Journal of Architectural Education (1984–)* 49 (1):38–49. Goode, Terrence. 2002. "Review [Louis Kahn's Situated Modernism]." In, *Journal of Architectural Education* 56 (2):56–56. Morshed, Adnan. 2005. "Review [Architecture as a Means of Filial Discovery: Nathaniel Kahn's

My Architect The Louis Kahn Project]." In, *Journal of Architectural Education* 58 (3):54–60. Ashraf, Kazi K. 2009. "Review [Louis I. Kahn: The Making of a Room]." In, *Journal of Architectural Education* 63 (1):141–142. Sargeant, John. 1982. "Review [Frank Lloyd Wright's Hanna House: The Client's Report]." *JAE* 36 (1):54–55. Mostoller, Michael. 1985. "The Towers of Frank Lloyd Wright." In, *Journal of Architectural Education (1984–)* 38 (2):13–17. Donoian, John, Dennis Doordan, and Sarah Smith. 1986. "'A Magnificent Adventure': An Interview with Mrs. Sarah (Melvyn) Maxwell Smith about the Smith House by Frank Lloyd Wright." In, *Journal of Architectural Education (1984–)* 39 (4):7–10. Long, David G. De. 1993. "Review: The Wright Space: Pattern and Meaning in Frank Lloyd Wright's Houses by Grant Hildebrand." In, *Journal of Architectural Education (1984–)* 47 (2):116–117.

35 Streatfield, David C. 1983. "Review [Common Landscape of America, 1580–1845]." In, *Journal of Architectural Education* 37 (1):27–28. MacDonald, William L. 1988. "Roman Urbanism." In, *Journal of Architectural Education (1984–)* 41 (3):29–32. Fazio, Michael. 1991. "Review: Interpreting Southern Antebellum Architecture in the 1990s—Reviewed work(s): *Architecture of the Old South: Virginia* by Mills Lane; *Architecture of the Old South: South Carolina* by Mills Lane; *Architecture of the Old South: North Carolina* by Mills Lane; *Architecture of the Old South: Georgia* by Mills Lane; *Architecture of the Old South: Mississippi/Alabama* by Mills Lane." In, *Journal of Architectural Education (1984–)* 44 (4):225–234. Vidler, Anthony. 1991. "Researching Revolutionary Architecture." In, *Journal of Architectural Education (1984–)* 44 (4):206–210. Marcuse, Harold. 1995. "Review: Architecture and Auschwitz." In, *Journal of Architectural Education (1984–)* 49 (2):123–128. Long, Christopher. 2001. "An Alternative Path to Modernism: Carl König and Architectural Education at the Vienna Technische Hochschule, 1890–1913." *Journal of Architectural Education* 55 (1):21–30.

36 Chase, John. 1991. "The Role of Consumerism in American Architecture." In, *Journal of Architectural Education (1984–)* 44 (4):211–224. Sutton, Sharon Egretta. 2003. "Review [Children in the City, Home, Neighborhood, and Community and Growing Up in an Urbanizing World and Creating Better Cities with Children and Youth: A Manual for Participation and the Growing Up in Cities Project]." In, *Journal of Architectural Education* 57 (2):55–61. Hee, Limin. 2006. "Review [Architourism: Authentic, Escapist, Exotic, Spectacular—Edited by Joan Ockman and Salomon Frausto]." In, *Journal of Architectural Education* 60 (1):71–72. Borden, Gail Peter. 2007. "Propositions for Suburban Living." In, *Journal of Architectural Education* 61 (1):76–83. Atkin, Tony, and Carol Herselle Krinsky. 1996. "Cultural Identity in Modern Native American Architecture: A Case Study." In, *Journal of Architectural Education (1984–)* 49 (4):237–245.

37 Pressman, Norman. 1983. "Review: [The Aesthetic Townscape and The Visual and Spatial Structure of Landscapes]." In, *Journal of Architectural Education* 37 (2):27–30. Anderton, Frances. 1989. "Learning from Jaipur." In, *Journal of Architectural Education (1984–)* 42 (4):15–24. Rujivacharakul, Vimalin. 2010." Ghosts of Asia: Fergusson's Haunted Mansion and the Architectural History of Asia in a Post-Said World." In, *Journal of Architectural Education* 63 (2):161–165.

38 Bluestone, Daniel. 1994. "Preservation and Renewal in Post-World War II Chicago." *Journal of Architectural Education (1984–)* 47 (4):210–223. Shapiro, Kelli. 2007. "From Modernism to McDonald's." In, *Journal of Architectural Education* 61 (2):6–14. Dodds, George. 2007." Editorial." In, *Journal of Architectural Education* 61 (2):3. Yan, X. Winston. 1996. "Carrying Forward Heritage: A Review of Contextualism in New Construction in Beijing." In, *Journal of Architectural Education (1984–)* 50 (2):115–126. Poon, Ben Ho-Sing. 2001. "Buildings Recycled—City Refurbished." In, *Journal of Architectural Education* 54 (3):191–194. Mayo, James M. 1990. "Review: Icons and Aliens: Law, Aesthetics, and Environmental Change by John J. Costonis." In, *Journal of Architectural Education (1984–)* 43 (3):47–49. Loh, Laurence. 2010. "Conserving for Change." In, *Journal of Architectural Education* 63 (2):71–73.

39 Wang, David. 2003. "Categories of ACSA Conference Papers." Groat, Linda N. 1992. "Rescuing Architecture from the Cul-de-Sac." In, *Journal of Architectural Education (1984–)* 45 (3):138–146. Scherr, Richard. 1991. "Architecture as Index: Toward a Theory of Contingency." In, *Journal of Architectural Education (1984–)* 44 (3):172–181. Dutton, Thomas. 2000. "Review [The Anaesthetics of Architecture]." *Journal of Architectural Education* 53 (4):239–249.

40 Stiny, George Nicholas. 1985. "Computing with Form and Meaning in Architecture." In, *Journal of Architectural Education (1984–)* 39 (1):7–19. Hewitt, Mark. 1985. "Representational Forms and

Modes of Conception: An Approach to the History of Architectural Drawing." In, *Journal of Architectural Education (1984–)* 39 (2):2–9. Weingarden, Lauren S. 1985. "Aesthetics Politicized: William Morris to the Bauhaus." In, *Journal of Architectural Education (1984–)* 38 (3):8–13. Gusevich, Miriam. 1986. "Meaning and Means in Urban Design: A Case Study in American Urbanism, South La Salle Street, Chicago." In, *Journal of Architectural Education (1984–)* 39 (3):24–30. Walker, Gerald. 1987. "Architecture, Method and the Poetic Image." In, *Journal of Architectural Education (1984–)* 40 (2):85–86. Lewis, Diane. 1987. "Program: The Literary Counterpart of the Architectural Work." In, *Journal of Architectural Education (1984–)* 40 (2):45–45. McClung, William Alexander. 1988. "Dialectics of Literary Cities." In, *Journal of Architectural Education (1984–)*41 (3):33–37. Legault, Réjean. 1991. "Architecture and Historical Representation." In, *Journal of Architectural Education (1984–)*44 (4):200–205. Schwarzer, Mitchell. 1991. "Gathered This Unruly Folk: The Textural Colligation of Historical Knowledge on Architecture." In, *Journal of Architectural Education (1984–)*44(3):144–149. Wang, David. 2002. "Review [Words and Buildings: A Vocabulary of Modern Architecture]." In, *Journal of Architectural Education* 55 (4):272–275. Hewitt, Mark A. 1984. "Books of Drawings, Books on Drawing, Books about Drawings Review: [Masterpieces of Architectural Drawing and Great Drawings from the Collection of the Royal Institute of British Architects and The Plan of St. Gall in Brief and Architecture of the Twentieth Century in Drawings and Architectural Drawing: The Art and the Process]." In, *Journal of Architectural Education (1984–)*38 (1):29–30. Crowe, Norman A., and Steven W. Hurtt. 1986. "Visual Notes and the Acquisition of Architectural Knowledge." In, *Journal of Architectural Education (1984–)*39 (3):6–16. Yates, Penny W. 1999. "Review: Architectural Representation and the Perspective Hinge by Alberto Pérez-Gómez; Louise Pelletier." In, *Journal of Architectural Education (1984–)*53 (1):51. Anderson, Alex T. 2002. "On the Human Figure in Architectural Representation." In, *Journal of Architectural Education* 55 (4):238–246. Gino, Alex. 2003. "Changing Rooms." In, *Journal of Architectural Education* 56 (4):32–36. Wilcox, Glenn. 2004. "The Medium and the Thing Itself." In, *Journal of Architectural Education* 58 (2):25–27.

41 Zuk, Radoslav. 1983. "A Music Lesson." In, *Journal of Architectural Education* 36 (3):2–6. Bell, David H. 1987. "Reflection." In, *Journal of Architectural Education (1984–)* 41 (1):2–3. Bernstein, Gerald S. 1985. "The Architecture of Repression: The Built Environment of George Orwell's 1984." In, *Journal of Architectural Education (1984–)* 38 (2):26–28. Sauda, Eric. 1987. "Three Small Architectural Dramas in the Form of a Pair." In, *Journal of Architectural Education (1984–)* 40 (2):69–71. Ghirardo, Diane. 1989. "Editorial." In, *Journal of Architectural Education (1984–)* 43 (1):2. Pecora, Vincent P. 1995. "Review: Architecture and theText: The (S)crypts of Joyce and Piranesi by Jennifer Bloomer." In, *Journal of Architectural Education (1984–)* 48 (4):275–277. Pearlman, Jill. 1998. "Review: Bauhaus in America by Judith Pearlman." In, *Journal of Architectural Education (1984–)* 51 (3):204. Prakash, Vikramaditya. 2001. "Between Objectivity and Illusion: Architectural Photography in the Colonial Frame." In, *Journal of Architectural Education* 55 (1):13–20. Sung, Doris Kim. 2001. "Incorporations: Exploring the Space between Body, Mechanism, and Imagination." In, *Journal of Architectural Education* 54 (4):260. Henderson, Susan R. 2003. "Review [The Gray Cloth]." In, *Journal of Architectural Education* 56 (4):69–75. Borys, Ann Marie. 2004. "Lume di Lume: A Theory of Light and Its Effects." *Journal of Architectural Education* 57 (4):3–9. Dimendberg, Edward. 2005. "Review [Zoomscape: Architecture in Motion and Media]." In, *Journal of Architectural Education* 58 (4):63–71. Beaudoin, Thierry, Sinsha Brdar, Nicolas Marier, Patrick Morand, and Marc Pape. 2006. "Playtime." In, *Journal of Architectural Education* 59 (4):26–30. Bonnemaison, Sarah, Ronit, Eisenbach, and Robert Gon. 2006. "Introduction." In, *Journal of Architectural Education* 59 (4):3–11. Brownell, Blaine. 2008. "Assembling Light." In, *Journal of Architectural Education* 62 (2):30–36. Weinstein, Beth. 2008. "Flamand and His Architectural Entourage." In, *Journal of Architectural Education* 61 (4):25–33. Balmer, Jeffrey. 2008. "Review [Cinematic Urbanism: A History of the Modern from Reelto Real—Edited by NezarAlsayyad]." In, *Journal of Architectural Education* 61 (4):136–137.

42 Hayden, Dolores. 1988. "Placemaking, Preservation and Urban History." In, *Journal of Architectural Education (1984–)* 41 (3):45–51. Joines-Novotny, Laura. 1996. "Czech Town Squares: Ten Spatial Patterns." In, *Journal of Architectural Education (1984–)* 50 (1):22–31. Friedman, D. S. 1995. "Public Things in the Modern City: Belated Notes on 'Tilted Arc' and the Vietnam

Veterans Memorial." In, *Journal of Architectural Education (1984–)* 49 (2):62–78. Allen, Barbara. 2006. "Interview with Gene Cizek." Journal of Architectural Education 60 (1):26–29. Song, Linn. 2007. "The Muenster City Library." In, *Journal of Architectural Education* 60 (3):12–20. Yoon, J. Meejin. 2008. "Public Works." In, *Journal of Architectural Education* 61 (4):59–68. Morozov, Petia. 2009. "Review [Did Someone Say Participate? An Atlas of Spatial Practice—Markus Miessen and Shumon Basar]." In, *Journal of Architectural Education* 62 (4):134–135. Willis, Daniel. 1994. "Review: On Weathering: The Life of Buildings in Time by Mohsen Mostafavi; David Leatherbarrow." In, *Journal of Architectural Education (1984–)* 48 (2):126–129. Deamer, Peggy. 1999. "Introduction." In, *Journal of Architectural Education (1984–)* 53 (1):35. Chi, Lily. 1999. "Wind Gate." In, *Journal of Architectural Education (1984–)* 53 (1):42–43. Schumacher, Thomas L. 2002. "'The Outside is the Result of an Inside' Some Sources of One of Modernism's Most Persistent Doctrines." In, *Journal of Architectural Education* 56 (1):22. Scarpo, Bob. 2002. "Review [The Room in Context: Design Beyond Boundaries]." In, *Journal of Architectural Education* 55 (3):197–201. Rickenbacker, Shawn L. 2003. "Performative Surfaces." In, *Journal of Architectural Education* 57 (2):18–21. Veikos, Cathrine. 2006. "To Enter the Work." In, *Journal of Architectural Education* 59 (4):71–80. Rufford, Juliet. 2008. "Out of Site." In, *Journal of Architectural Education* 61 (4):34–42. Snyder, Alison B. 2008. "Review [AD Interior Atmospheres—Edited by Julieanna Preston]." In, *Journal of Architectural Education* 62 (2):70–71.

43 Trabalzi, Ferruccio. 1989. "Primavalle: Urban Reservation in Rome." In, *Journal of Architectural Education (1984–)* 42 (3):38–46. Shin, Chunghoon. 2010. "Review [Globalization, the City and Civil Society in Pacific Asia: The Social Production of Civic Spaces]." In, *Journal of Architectural Education* 63 (2):175–176. Satler, Gail. 2003. "New York City Restaurants: Vernaculars of Global Designing." In, *Journal of Architectural Education* 56 (3):27–39. Gillem, Mark. 2005. "America Town: Planning the Outposts of Empire." *Journal of Architectural Education* 58 (3):5–12. Bloch, Robin, and Melinda Silverman. 1989. "Response to Owen, 'Architecture and Apartheid'." In, *Journal of Architectural Education (1984–)* 42 (3):24–25. Bell, Matthew J., and Cheryl A. O'Neill. 1994. "A Public Library for Evanston, Illinois." In, *Journal of Architectural Education (1984–)* 47 (3):129–134. Crawford, Margaret. 1995. "Contesting the Public Realm: Struggles over Public Space in Los Angeles." In, *Journal of Architectural Education (1984–)* 49 (1):4–9.

44 Kingsley, Karen. 1988. "Gender Issues in Teaching Architectural History." *Journal of Architectural Education (1984–)* 41 (2):21–25. Travis, Jack. 1993. "African American Architecture: From Idea to Published Product." In, *Journal of Architectural Education (1984–)* 47 (1):60–62. Stratigakos, Despina. 2001. "Architects in Skirts: The Public Image of Women Architects in Wilhelmine Germany." In, *Journal of Architectural Education* 55 (2):90–100. Rüedi Ray, Katerina. 2001. "Bauhaus Hausfraus: Gender Formation In Design Education." In, *Journal of Architectural Education* 55 (2):73–80. Murphy, Amy. 2002. "Review [Gender and Architecture]." In, *Journal of Architectural Education* 55 (3):197–201. Merwood Salisbury, Joanna. 2008. "Review [Women in Modernism: Making Places in Architecture—Edited by Beverly Willis, Gwendolyn Wright, Sarah Herda, Toshiko Mori, and Karen Stein]." In, *Journal of Architectural Education* 61 (4):144–145. Wright, Gwendolyn. 1982. "Review: [The Grand Domestic Revolution: A History of Feminist Designs for American Homes, Neighborhoods, and Cities]." In, *Journal of Architectural Education* 36 (2):31–32. Wilkins, Craig L. 2000. "(W)rapped Space: The Architecture of Hip Hop." In, *Journal of Architectural Education* 54 (1):7–19. Weddle, Robert. 2001. "Housing and Technological Reform in Interwar France: The Case of the Cité de la Muette." In, *Journal of Architectural Education* 54 (3):167–175. Jordan, Coleman A. 2007. "Rhizomorphics of Race and Space." In, *Journal of Architectural Education* 60 (4):48–59. Moore, Sandy. 1987. "Review: [Learning through the Built Environment]." *Journal of Architectural Education (1984–)* 40 (4):31. Tanzer, Kim, and Caroline Constant. 2001. "Center for Women's Studies and Gender Research, University of Florida, 1994–2000." In, *Journal of Architectural Education* 55 (2):81–89. Anthony, Kathryn H. 2002. "Designing for Diversity: Implications for Architectural Education in the Twenty-first Century." In, *Journal of Architectural Education* 55 (4):257–267. Smith, Glenn L. 2004. "Review [Metaphors and Questions in Harlem harlemworld: Metropolis as Metaphor]." In, *Journal of Architectural Education* 58 (2):57–61. Widodo, Johannes. 2010. "Current State of Modern Asian Architecture Discourse and Networking." In, *Journal of Architectural Education* 63 (2):79–81. Merwood

Salisbury. "Review [Women in Modernism: Making Places in Architecture—Edited by Beverly Willis, Gwendolyn Wright, Sarah Herda, Toshiko Mori, and Karen Stein]." Bloch and Silverman. "Response to Owen, 'Architecture and Apartheid'." Fouche, Rayvon. 2002. "Review [Sites of Memory]." *Journal of Architectural Education* 56 (1):57. Erdman, Jori. 2006. "Studio South." In, *Journal of Architectural Education* 59 (4):19–25. Jordan. "Rhizomorphics of Race and Space."

45 Polledri, Paolo. 1988. "Urbanism and Economics: Industrial Activities in Eighteenth-Century Venice." In, *Journal of Architectural Education (1984–)* 41 (3):15–19. Tonton, Jacqueline. 2004. "Review [Building Suburbia. Green Fields and Urban Growth, 1820–2000 and A Field Guide to Sprawl]." In, *Journal of Architectural Education* 58 (2):57–61. Payton, Neal I. 1985. "Review: [Campus: An American Planning Tradition]." In, *Journal of Architectural Education (1984–)* 39 (1):32. Celik, Zeynep, and Diane Favro. 1988. "Methods of Urban History." In, *Journal of Architectural Education (1984–)* 41 (3):4–9. Jones, Kay Bea. 1990. "Genus and Genius: An Architectural Morphology of Urban Genoa." In, *Journal of Architectural Education (1984–)* 43 (4):16–26. Kaplan, Archie. 1991. "Review: City: Rediscovering the Center by William H. Whyte." In, *Journal of Architectural Education (1984–)* 44 (4):241–242. Hakim, Besim S. 1995. "Review: Redesigning the American Dream." In, *Journal of Architectural Education (1984–)* 49 (2):129–131.

46 Baird, David. 1999. "The Mobile Studio Project." In, *Journal of Architectural Education (1984–)* 5 (1):44–45. Brandes, Uwe Steven. 2004. "Review [Good Deeds, Good Design: Community Service through Architecture and Consensus Design: Socially Inclusive Process]." In, *Journal of Architectural Education* 58 (2):57–61. Samuels, Linda C. 2005. "Review [Samuel Mockbee and the Rural Studio: Community Architecture]." In, *Journal of Architectural Education* 58 (3):54–60. Real, Patricio Del. 2009. "Ye Shall Receive": The Rural Studio and the Gift of Architecture." In, *Journal of Architectural Education* 62 (4):123–126. Bell Jr., Robert R. 2006. "Citizen Architect: An Educator's Response to Crisis." In, *Journal of Architectural Education* 60 (1):22–23. Blakely, Edward J. 2006. "A Cry for a City: What Is Happening to New Orleans?" In, *Journal of Architectural Education* 60 (1):9–12. Read, Gray. 2008. "Review [Architects Without Frontiers: War, Reconstruction and Design Responsibility—Edited by Esther Charlesworth]." In, *Journal of Architectural Education* 61 (3):65–66. Corser, Robert, and Nils Gore. 2009. "Insurgent Architecture: An Alternative Approach to Design-Build." In, *Journal of Architectural Education* 62 (4):32–39. Perkes, David. 2009. "A Useful Practice." In, *Journal of Architectural Education* 62 (4):64–71. Jann, Marga, and Stephen Platt. 2009. "Philanthropic Architecture: Nongovernmental Development Projects in Latin America." In, *Journal of Architectural Education* 62 (4):82–91. Shall, Scott. 2009. "Review [Design Like You Give a Damn: Architectural Responses to Humanitarian Crises—Architecture for Humanity and Expanding Architecture: Design as Activism—Edited by Bryan Bell and Katie Wakeford]." In, *Journal of Architectural Education* 62 (4):132–134. Francis, Mark. 1983. "Community Design." *Journal of Architectural Education* 37 (1):14–19. Mann, Dennis Alan. 1985. "Between Traditionalism and Modernism: Approaches to a Vernacular Architecture." In, *Journal of Architectural Education (1984–)* 39 (2):10–16. Jones, Kay Bea. 1995. "Review: House Rules by Mark Robbins 'Assemblage' 24." In, *Journal of Architectural Education (1984–)* 49 (1):53–56. Allen, Barbara L., and Roberta M. Feldman. 2000. "Editorial: Beyond Expert Culture." In, *Journal of Architectural Education* 53 (3):128–129. Ellin, Nan. 2000. "Participatory Architecture on the Parisian Periphery: Lucien Kroll's Vignes Blanches." In, *Journal of Architectural Education* 53 (3):178–183. Schneekloth, Lynda H., and Robert G. Shibley. 2000. "Implacing Architecture into the Practice of Placemaking." In, *Journal of Architectural Education* 53 (3):130–140. Hou, Jeffrey, and Michael Rios. 2003. "Community-Driven Place Making: The Social Practice of Participatory Design in the Making of Union Point Park." In, *Journal of Architectural Education* 57 (1):19–27. Sabatino, Michelangelo. 2008. "Review [Third Ward TX—A Documentary About Art, Life, and Real Estate—Edited by Andrew Garrison, director and Nancy Bless, Andrew Garrison, Noland Walker, producers]." In, *Journal of Architectural Education* 62 (1):78–79. Crosbie, Michael J. 2010. "Review [The Judicious Eye: Architecture Against the Other Arts]." In, *Journal of Architectural Education* 63 (2):177–178.

47 Dean, Edward. 1984. "The New Foreign Import: Manufactured Housing Systems." In, *Journal of Architectural Education (1984–)* 37 (3/4):12–19. Weddle. 2001. Park, Jin-Ho. 2004. "An Integral Approach to Design Strategies and Construction Systems. R. M. Schindler's 'Schindler Shelters'."

In, *Journal of Architectural Education* 58 (2):29–38. Weinthal, Lois. 2006. "House Lab." In, *Journal of Architectural Education* 60 (2):25–28. Shane, Graham. 1990. "Review: Street Performance; The Homeless Vehicle Project." In, *Journal of Architectural Education (1984–)* 43 (4):37–42. AlSayyad, Nezar. 1992. "Housing, Culture, and Environment: A Review of Two Conferences. 'Housing Environments: A Cross-Cultural Perspective'. University of California, San Diego, May 1991. 'Design for Desert Living'. University of Arizona, Tucson, July 1991." In, *Journal of Architectural Education (1984–)* 46 (1):63–64. Sturges, William Gould. 1992. "An Exploration of the Relationships Between Houses and Forests in American History." In, *Journal of Architectural Education (1984–)* 46 (2):66–75. Bernard, Catherine E. 1993. "Housing InternationalConference. Cairo, Egypt, February 23–27, 1992." In, *Journal of Architectural Education (1984–)* 46 (3):189–190. Winston, E. Perry. 1998. "Review: Good Neighbors: Affordable Family Housing by Tom Jones, William Pettus, Mike Pyatok. The Architecture of Affordable Housing by Sam Davis. Democratic Architecture: Practical Solutions to Today's Housing Crisis by Donald MacDonald." In, *Journal of Architectural Education (1984–)* 52 (2):124–126. Allen. "Interview with Gene Cizek."

48 MacKenzie, Donald, and Wajcman, Judy. 1999. *The Social Shaping of Technology*. 2nd ed. Philadelphia, PA: Open University Press.

49 Dunay, Robert, Joseph Wheeler, and Robert Schubert. 2006. "No Compromise." In, *Journal of Architectural Education* 60 (2):8–17. Stuart, John A. 2003. "Review [The Glass State: The Technology of the Spectacle, Paris, 1981–1998]." In, *Journal of Architectural Education* 56 (4):69–75. Zell, Maureen, and Marc Roehrle. 2003. "Reconsideration of the Shed: Garage + Workshop." In, *Journal of Architectural Education* 56 (4):30–31. Hartoonian. "Mies van der Rohe: The Genealogy of Column and Wall." Tenhaaf, Nell. 1987. "Pandora Revisited: Art and New Technologies." In, *Journal of Architectural Education (1984–)* 40 (4):18–23. McCleary, Peter. 1988. "Some Characteristics of a New Concept of Technology." In, *Journal of Architectural Education (1984–)* 42 (1):4–9. Allen, Barbara L. 1997. "Introduction." In, *Journal of Architectural Education (1984–)* 51 (1):3–4. Cavanagh, Ted. 1997. "Balloon Houses: The Original Aspects of Conventional Wood-Frame Construction Re Examined." In, *Journal of Architectural Education (1984–)* 51 (1):5–15. Al-Kodmany, Kheir. 2000. "Public Participation: Technology and Democracy." In, *Journal of Architectural Education* 53 (4):220–228. Burns, Carol J. 2001. "A Manufactured Housing Studio: Home/On the Highway." In, *Journal of Architectural Education* 55 (1):51–57. Frampton, Kenneth, and Steven A. Moore. 2001. "Technology and Place." *Journal of Architectural Education* 54 (3):121–122. Cuff, Dana. 2003. "Immanent Domain: Pervasive Computing and the Public Realm." In, *Journal of Architectural Education* 57 (1):43–49. Snyder, Vincent. 2005. "Review [Refabricating ARCHITECTURE: How Manufacturing Methodologies Are Poised to Transform Building Construction]." In, *Journal of Architectural Education* 59 (1):51–52.

50 Mostoller. "The Towers of Frank Lloyd Wright." Matthias, Stephen. 1988. "Courting the House." In, *Journal of Architectural Education (1984–)* 42 (1):48–53. Senft, Carolyn. 1994. "Review: The Staircase: History and Theories by John Templer. The Staircase: Studies of Hazards, Falls, and Safer Design by John Templer." In, *Journal of Architectural Education (1984–)*48 (2):129–131. Clarke, David W. 1996. "Review: The Gas Station in America by John A. Jakle; Keith A. Sculle. Grain Elevators by Lisa Mahar-Keplinger." In, *Journal of Architectural Education (1984–)* 50 (1):74–75. Franck, Karen A., and Lynda H. Schneekloth. 1996. "Review: Ordering Space: Types in Architecture and Design." In, *Journal of Architectural Education (1984–)* 50 (2):128–130. Solomon, Jonathan D. 2010. "Learning from Louis Vuitton." In, *Journal of Architectural Education* 63 (2):67–70.

51 Wasley, James. 2000. "Safe Houses and Green Architecture: Reflections on the Lessons of the Chemically Sensitive." In, *Journal of Architectural Education* 53 (4):207–215. Allen, Barbara. 2007. "Cities, Poverty, and the Environment Review [Planet of Slums and 10th Venice Architecture Biennale: Cities, Architecture and Society and Power, Justice, and the Environment: A Critical Appraisal of the Environmental Movement and Sustainable Communities and the Challenge of Environmental Justice]." In, *Journal of Architectural Education* 60 (4):67–71. Meyboom, A. 2009. "Infrastructure as Practice." In, *Journal of Architectural Education* 62:72–81. Sowell, Jason, and Nichole Wiedemann. 2009. "Sponge Urbanism: The Cellular Redevelopment of New Orleans." In, *Journal of Architectural Education* 62 (4):24–31. Guy, Simon, and Graham Farmer. 2001.

"Reinterpreting Sustainable Architecture: The Place of Technology." In, *Journal of Architectural Education* 54 (3):140–148. Canizaro, Vincent B. 2001. "Review [The Land That Could Be: Environmentalism and Democracy in the Twenty-First Century]." In, *Journal of Architectural Education* 54 (3):198–201. Fuglem, Terri, and Bruce Webb. 2005. "Introduction." In, *Journal of Architectural Education* 58 (4):3. Guy, Simon, and Steven A. Moore. 2007. "Sustainable Architecture and the Pluralist Imagination." In, *Journal of Architectural Education* 60 (4):15–23. Canizaro, Vince, and Kim Tanzer. 2008. "The JAE Sustainability Issue." In, *Journal of Architectural Education* 62 (1): 67.

52 Frampton. "Toward a Critical Regionalism." See also, Moore, Steven A. 2001b. "Technology, Place, and the Nonmodern Thesis." In, *Journal of Architectural Education* 54 (3):130–139. Testa, Peter. 1987. "Tradition and Actuality in the Antonio Carlos Siza House." In, *Journal of Architectural Education (1984–)* 40 (4):24–30. Dovey, Kim. 2000. "Myth and Media: Constructing Aboriginal Architecture." *Journal of Architectural Education* 54 (1):2–6. Eggener, Keith L. 2002. "Placing Resistance: A Critique of Critical Regionalism." In, *Journal of Architectural Education* 55 (4): 228–237. Barton, Greg. 2006. "The Trailerization of New Orleans." In, *Journal of Architectural Education* 60 (1):17. Owen, Graham. 2006. "In Dark Waters: Opportunity and Opportunism in the Reconstruction of New Orleans." In, *Journal of Architectural Education* 60 (1):7–9. Lara, Fernando Luiz. 2009. "Modernism Made Vernacular: The Brazilian Case." In, *Journal of Architectural Education* 63 (1):41–50.

53 Wolf, Harry. 1987. "Observations on Education." In, *Journal of Architectural Education (1984–)* 40 (2):91–93. Hinson, David. 2007. "Design as Research." In, *Journal of Architectural Education* 61 (1):23–26. Tisi, Rodrigo. 2008. "B + S + P + T + PL + M." In, *Journal of Architectural Education* 61 (4):69–75. McBride, Jacquelin Spangler. 1984. "The Case Method in Architecture Education." In, *Journal of Architectural Education (1984–)* 37 (3/4):10–11. Smith, Kendra Schank. 1990. "Architectural Sketches and the Power of Caricature." In, *Journal of Architectural Education (1984–)* 44 (1):49–58.

54 Thomas, Helen. 2004. "Invention in the Shadow of History: Joseph Rykwert at the University of Essex." In, *Journal of Architectural Education* 58 (2):39–45. Burgess, Peter G. 1984. "Review: [The Image of the Architect]." In, *Journal of Architectural Education (1984–)* 38 (1):30. Koester, Robert J. 1988. "Review: [Architecture as Environmental Communication]." In, *Journal of Architectural Education (1984–)* 42 (1):54–55.

55 Bell, David H. 1987. "Reflection." In, *Journal of Architectural Education (1984–)* 41 (1):2–3. Barrie, Thomas. 2007. "Book Review [Built upon Love: Architectural Longing after Ethics and Aesthetics —Edited by Alberto Pérez-Gómez]." In, *Journal of Architectural Education* 60 (3):51–52. Britton, Karla. 2009. "Review [God, Creativity, and Evolution: The Argument from Design(ers)—Michael Benedikt and God Is the Good We Do: Theology of Theopraxy—Edited by Michael Benedikt]." In, *Journal of Architectural Education* 62 (4):135–137.

Chapter 2

1 Marx, L. 2010. "Technology: The Emergence of a Hazardous Concept." In, *Technology and Culture* 51 (3):568.

2 MacKenzie and Wajcman. *The Social Shaping of Technology.*

3 Marx. "Technology," p. 575.

4 See: Hess, D.J. 1997. *Science Studies: An Advanced Introduction.* New York: New York University Press; and Sismondo. *An Introduction to Science and Technology Studies.*

5 Leatherbarrow, David. 2005[2010]. "Architecture's Unscripted Performance." In, *Performative Architecture: Beyond Instrumentality.* Edited by Branko Kolarevic and Ali Malkawi (p. 7). New York and London: Spon Press.

6 Mayntz, Renate, and Thomas P. Hughes, eds. 1988. *The Development of Large Technical Systems* (p. 68). Frankfurt am Main and Boulder, CO: Campus Verlag and Westview Press.

7 Giddens, Anthony. 1994. In, *Explorations in Planning Theory.* Edited by Seymour J. Mandelbaum, Luigi Mazza, and Robert W. Burchell (pp. 189–190). New Brunswick, NJ: Center for Urban Policy Research. For an updated version of "agency" related specifically to architecture, see: Awan, Nishat, Tatjana Schneider, and Jeremy Till. 2011. *Spatial Agency: Other Ways of Doing Architecture.* London: Routledge.

8 Marx, "Technology."

9 Peet, for example, holds that the study of geography in the late 19th century was dominated by the doctrines of Social Darwinism and environmental determinism in order to legitimate imperial conquest. In this context, environmental determinists held that African or Native American cultures were inherently inferior, owing to the natural environments in which they developed—a thinly veiled form of racism. See: Peet, Richard. 1985. "The Social Origins of Environmental Determinism." In, *Annals of the Association of American Geographers* 75 (3):309–333.

10 In contrast to environmental determinism, economic determinists hold that economic structures determine the course of human history. The doctrines of Marxism are the primary exemplar of this position. See: Marx, Karl. 1908. *Kapital.* 4th ed. London: W. Reeves.

11 The idea that technologies drive the evolution of social history is best investigated in: Smith, Merritt Rowe, and Leo Marx. 1994. *Does Technology Drive History?: The Dilemma of Technological Determinism*. Cambridge, MA: MIT Press.

12 Contemporary social constructivists have been characterized as "social determinists," meaning that genetic predisposition, the physical environment, economic structures, or the appearance of new technologies all take the back seat to social choices in determining the course of human history. For example, see: Latour, Bruno. 2004. *Politics of Nature: How to Bring Science into Democracy.* Translated by C. Porter. Cambridge, MA: Harvard University Press. Original edition, *Politiques de la Nature,* Editions de la Couverte.

13 Diamandis, Peter H., and Steven Kotler. 2012. *Abundance: The Future is Better Than You Think.* New York: Free Press.

14 Urban Design Associates, Ray Gindroz, Rob Robinson, et al. 2004. *The Architectural Pattern Book: A Tool for Building Great Neighborhoods.* New York: W.W. Norton & Company.

15 Elliott, Cecil D. 1992.*Technics in Architecture: The Development of Materials and Systems for Buildings* (p. vi). Cambridge, MA: MIT Press.

16 Meyer, Hannes. 1990[1928]. "Building." In, *Programs and Manifestoes on 20th-Century Architecture.* Edited by Ulrich Conrads (p. 117). Cambridge, MA: MIT Press.

17 Guggenheim, Michael. 2010. "(Un-)Building Social Systems: The Concrete Foundations of Society." In, *Observando Systemas.* Edited by Ignacio Farias. Mexico: Universidad Iberoamericana.

18 Kolarevic, Branko, and Ali M. Malkawi, eds. 2005[2010]. *Performative Architecture: Beyond Instrumentality.* New York and London: Spon Press.

19 See: Leatherbarrow. "Architecture's Unscripted Performance." In his essay, Leatherbarrow argues that:

> Events do not result from technique or technical knowledge. This is because foresight is essential to technological thought. Technique is always participatory, it is a form of knowledge that leads to preconceived results. Because events arise out of a past that we do not know, they cannot be produced technically. Putting the matter more forcefully, performative architecture is not the outcome of building or design technology, even up-to-the-minute digital technology. All technique can give architecture is enhanced functionality.
>
> (p. 11)

In this passage and others, Leatherbarrow seems to grant building limited agency in the manner that ANT theorists do—in a frame of interaction that is relational, uncertain, and unmeasurable. He succinctly holds that: "When the building is freed from technological and aesthetic intentionalities, we discover its lateral connections to an environment and social milieu that is not of anyone's making, still less of design and planning" (p. 16).

20 For example, see: Latour. *Politics of Nature.*

21 Lefebvre, Henri. 1991. *The Production of Space.* Translated by Donald Nicholson-Smith. Cambridge, MA: Blackwell Press; Oxford, UK: Basil Blackwell Publishers.

22 Awan, Schneider, and Till. *Spatial Agency.*

23 Lang, Jon. 1980. "The Built Environment and Social Behavior: Architectural Determinism Reexamined." In, *Via* IV (1980): 146–153. Lang observes the architect's ability to determine social outcomes is "deeply embedded" in architectural discourse, and he goes on to document substantial claims to architectural determinism in the writings of Ebenezer Howard, Le Corbusier, Richard Neutra, Frank Lloyd Wright, and Alison and Peter Smithson.

24 For example, see: Gonchar, Joann. 2007. "Schools Make the Grade." In, *Architectural Record* 195 (7):129.
25 Sailer, Kersten, Andrew Budgen, Nathan Lonsdale, Alasdare Turner, and Alan Penn. 2009. "Evidence-Based Design: Theoretical and Practical Reflections of an Emerging Approach in Office Design." In, *Undisciplined! Design Research and Society Conference*, 2008, 119:1–19. Sheffield, UK: Sheffield Hallam University.
26 Gidieon, Sigfried. 1963[1941]. *Space, Time, and Architecture: The Growth of a New Tradition.* 4th ed. Cambridge, MA: Harvard University Press.
27 Cavanagh. "Balloon Houses."
28 Davis. *The Culture of Building.*
29 Sailer, et al. "Evidence-Based Design."
30 In particular, see the works of Max Horkheimer (1895–1973), Theodor Adorno (1903–1969), Herbert Marcuse (1898–1979), and Jürgen Habermas (1929–).
31 Rorty, Richard. 1998. *Achieving Our Country* (p. 94). Cambridge, MA: Harvard University Press.
32 Lang. "The Built Environment and Social Behavior," p. 149. For another investigation of design agency, see also, Woodhouse, Edward, and Jason W. Patton. 2004. "Design by Society: Science and Technology Studies and the Social Shaping of Design." In, *Design Issues* 20 (3):1–12.
33 See: Pevsner, N. 1976. *A History of Building Types* (p. 6). Princeton, NJ: Princeton University Press. Although the book was not completed until 1976, Pevsner developed the idea of such a history at Gottenheim in 1930. He does recognize many earlier authors in developing the idea of the "architectural type," including: Blondel, J.-F. 1771. *Cours d'architecture civile.* Vol.2; Durand, L.-N.-L. 1802–1809. *Précis des leçons d'architecture données à l'Ecole Polytechnique*; Gourlier, Charles. 1825–1850. *Choix d'édifices publique projetés et construits en France depuis le commencement du XIX siècle*; Reynaud, Leonce. 1850–1858. *Traité d'architecture*; Planat, P. 1888–1895. *Encyclopédie de l'architecture et de la construction*; and Guadet, Julien. 1902–1904. *Eléments et théorie de l'architecture.* He also claims, however, that no historian had previously compiled an organized history in this fashion.
34 Pevsner. *A History of Building Types*, p. 9.
35 Leatherbarrow. "Architecture's Unscripted Performance."
36 Rossi, Aldo. 1982. *The Architecture of the City, with an Introduction by Peter Eisenman.* Translated by Diane Ghirardo and Joan Ockman. Cambridge, MA: MIT Press.
37 Hans Robert Jauss is the principal progenitor of reception theory; see: Jauss, Hans Robert. 1989. *Question and Answer: Forms of Dialogic Understanding: Edited, Translated, and With a Foreword by Michael Hays.* Minneapolis, MN: University of Minnesota Press.
38 Holub, Robert. 1984. *Reception Theory: A Critical Introduction* (p. 2). London: Methuen.
39 Moore, Steven A. 2001a.*Technology and Place: Sustainable Architecture and the Blueprint Farm.* Austin, TX: University of Texas Press.
40 Freire, Paulo. 1970. *Cultural Action for Freedom.* Cambridge, MA: Harvard Educational Review.
41 McLaughlin, Thomas. 1996. *Street Smarts and Critical Theory: Listening to the Vernacular.* Madison, WI: The University of Wisconsin Press.
42 Bell. *Good Deeds, Good Design*; Architecture for Humanity. 2006. *Design Like you Give a Damn: Architectural Response to Humanitarian Crisis.* New York: Metropolis Books.
43 Palleroni, Sergio. 2004. *Studio at Large: Architecture in Service of Global Communities.* Seattle, WA: University of Washington Press.
44 Perkes. "A Useful Practice," p. 64.
45 Ibid., p. 68.
46 Thorpe, while remaining within the Critical Theory paradigm, has developed a participatory and engaged theory of social change and design. See: Thorpe. *Architecture and Design versus Consumerism.*
47 For example, in a lecture at the University of Texas at Austin, September 19, 2011, architect Stanley Saitowitz used the common strategy of comparing architectural to medical knowledge in holding that, "You wouldn't want anyone but a doctor operating on you, so why would you encourage untrained people to think they can design for you?" Personal observation.
48 *The Oxford English Dictionary.* "scientific method." Retrieved October 12, 2011, from: www.oed.com/view/Entry/172685?redirectedFrom=scientific%20method#eid23962743

49 For a critique of the scientist's objectivity, see: Latour. *Politics of Nature.*

50 Sailer, et al. "Evidence-Based Design."

51 Achterhuis, Hans. 2001[1999]. *American Philosophy of Technology.* Edited by Don Ihde, The Indiana Series in the Philosophy of Technology. Bloomington and Indianapolis, IN: Indiana University Press. See also, Higgs, Eric, et al. 2000. *Technology and the Good Life.* University of Chicago Press.

52 Richard Ingersoll has paralleled Achterhuis' argument in the field of architecture; see: Richard Ingersoll. 1996. "Second Nature: On the Social Bond of Ecology and Architecture." In, *Reconstructing Architecture: Critical Discourses and Social Practices.* Edited by Tom Dutton and Lian Hurst Mann (pp. 119–157). Minneapolis. MN: University of Minnesota Press.

53 Among others with a firm stake in the intuitive nature of design, Michael Benedikt has proposed that an in-depth case study basis is required for architectural criticism to salvage that practice from irrelevance. See: Benedikt, Michael. 2009. "On the Role of Architectural Criticism Today." In, *Journal of Architectural Education* 62 (3):6–7. Even more relevant is the proposal for *regenerative design* accompanied by a public archive of post-occupancy data by Svec, Berkebile, and Todd. See: Svec, Phaedra, Robert Berkebile, and Joel Ann Todd. 2012. "REGEN: Toward a Tool for Regenerative Thinking." In, *Building Research & Information* 40 (1):81–94.

54 BRE Global, BREEAM. 2012. Available at: www.breeam.org (accessed April 20, 2012).

55 U.S. Green Building Council. 2012a. *Leadership in Energy and Environmental Design* (LEED). USGBC 2012. Available at: www.usgbc.org (accessed April 20, 2012).

56 Japan Sustainable Building Consortium. 2012. CASBEE. Available at: www.ibec.or.jp/CASBEE/english/ (accessed July 15, 2012).

57 Council for Scientific and Industrial Research, SBAT Tool. 2012. Available at: www.csir.co.za/Built_environment/Architectural_sciences/sbat.html (accessed April 20, 2012).

58 Cascadia Region Building Council. 2008, 2009. *Code and Regulatory Barriers to the Living Building Challenge for Sustainable, Affordable, Residential Development (SARD).* Vancouver, WA: International Living Future Institute.

59 German Sustainable Building Council. 2012. DGNB Certificate. Available at: www.dgnb.de/en/ (accessed April 20, 2012).

60 For Green Globes standards, see: Green Globes. 2012. *The Practical Building Rating System: The Green Globes system.* Available at: www.greenglobes.com/ (accessed December 12, 2012).

61 Cole, Raymond. 2005. "Building Environmental Assessment Methods: Redefining Intentions and Roles." In, *Building Research & Information* 35 (5): 462. For a summary of the contested efficacy of LEED as a building assessment system, see: Roberts, Tristan. 2010. "USGBC, LEED Targeted by Class-Action Suit." *GreenSource.* Retrieved 15 November 2011 from: http://greensource.construction.com/news/2010/100719GBCI.asp. This article originally appeared on Building Green.com.

62 Wilson, Barbara B. 2010. *Social Movement Toward Spatial Justice.* Dissertation. University of Texas at Austin.

63 See: Barber, Jeffrey. 2007. "Mapping the Movement to Achieve Sustainable Production and Consumption in North America." In, *Journal of Cleaner Production* 15 (6):499–512; Bentivegna, V., S. Curwell, M. Deakin, P. Lombardi, G. Mitchell, and P. Nijkamp. 2002. "A Vision and Methodology for Integrated Sustainable Urban Development." In, *Building Research & Information* 30 (2):83–94; Cole, Raymond. 2006. "Shared Markets: Coexisting Building Environmental Assessment Methods." In, *Building Research & Information* 34 (4):357–371; Hersh, Stuart. 2009. "Duh: Designing Affordable Housing." Austin, TX; Imrie, Rob, and Emma Street. 2009b. "Risk, Regulation and the Practices of Architects." In, *Urban Studies* 46 (12):2555–2576; Jackson, Tim, and Nic Marks. 1999. "Consumption, Sustainable Welfare and Human Needs—with Reference to UK Expenditure Patterns between 1954 and 1994." In, *Ecological Economics* 28 (3):421–441.

64 For a discussion how competing storylines influence the trajectory of history, see: Moore, Steven A. 2007. *Alternative Routes to the Sustainable City: Austin, Curitiba and Frankfurt.* Lanham, MD: Lexington Books, Rowman & Littlefield.

65 For a discussion of the "hybrid imagination" through which some ideas appropriate others, see: Hard and Jamison. *Hubris and Hybrids.*

66 Winner, Langdon. 1977. *Autonomous Technology: Technics out-of-Control as a Theme in Political Thought.* Cambridge, MA: MIT Press.

67 For a more in-depth discussion of STS literature with regard to architecture, see: Moore. *Technology and Place.*

68 MacKenzie and Wajcman. *The Social Shaping of Technology.*

69 For a general introduction to the field, see: Hess. *Science Studies*; and Sismondo. *An Introduction to Science and Technology Studies.*

70 Bijker, Wiebe E. 1995. *Of Bicycles, Bakelites, and Bulbs: Toward a Theory of Sociotechnical Change.* Cambridge, MA: MIT Press.

71 Bijker, Wiebe E. 1987. "The Social Construction of Bakelite: Toward a Theory of Invention." In, *The Social Construction of Technological Systems: New Directions in the Sociology and History of Technology.* Edited by Wiebe Bijker, Thomas Hughes, and Trevor Pinch. Cambridge, MA: MIT Press.

72 Cowan, Ruth. 1985. "How the Refrigerator Got its Hum." In, *The Social Shaping of Technology.* Edited by D. MacKenzie and Judy Wajcman. Philadelphia, PA: Open University Press.

73 That said, buildings are "obdurate," meaning that the materialization of agreements is costly to renovate. See: Hommels, Anique. 2005. *Unbuilding Cities: Obduracy in Urban Sociotechnical Change.* Edited by W. E. Bijker, W. Bernard Carlson, and Trevor Pinch, *Inside Technology.* Cambridge, MA: MIT Press. See also, Hughes, Thomas. 1995. "Technological Momentum." In, *Does Technology Drive History?* Edited by M.R. Smith and L. Marx. Cambridge, MA: MIT Press.

74 Hughes, Thomas P. 1985. "Edison and Electric Light." In, *The Social Shaping of Technology.* Edited by D. MacKenzie and Judy Wajcman. Philadelphia, PA: Open University Press.

75 Latour, Bruno. 1987. *Science in Action.* Cambridge, MA: Harvard University Press.

76 See: Leatherbarrow. "Architecture's Unscripted Performance"; and Rahim, Ali. 2010 [2005]. "Performativity: Beyond Efficiency and optimization in Architecture." In, *Performative Architecture: Beyond Instrumentality.* Edited by Branko Kolarevic and Ali Malkawi. New York and London: Spon Press.

77 Yaneva, Albena. 2009. *The Making of a Building: A Pragmatist Approach to Architecture.* Oxford, UK: Peter Lang.

78 Collins, H.M., and Steven Yearley. 1992. "Epistemological Chicken." In, *Science as Practice and Culture.* Edited by Andrew Pickering (pp. 301–326, p. 322). Chicago, IL: University of Chicago Press.

79 Callon, Michel, and Bruno Latour. 1992. "Don't Throw the Baby out with the Bath School! A Reply to Collins and Yearley." In, *Science as Practice and Culture.* Edited by Andrew Pickering (pp. 343–366, p. 359). Chicago, IL: University of Chicago.

80 Bruun, Henrik, and Janne Hukkinen. 2003. "Crossing Boundaries: An Integrative Framework for Studying Technology Change." In, *Social Studies of Science* 33 (1): 95–116.

81 William James has argued that,

> The truth of an idea is not a stagnant property inherent in it. Truth *happens* to an idea. It *becomes* true, is *made* true by events. Its verity *is* in fact an event, a process: the process namely of its verifying itself, its veri-*fication.* Its validity is the process of its valid-*ation.*
>
> (emphasis original)

This is not to suggest that facts become true just because people think they are so, but because they act in a way that makes them so. See: James, William. 1907. *Pragmatism, a New Name for Some Old Ways of Thinking; Popular Lectures on Philosophy* (p. 547). New York: Longmans, Green, and Co.

Chapter 3

1 Busch, Lawrence. 2011. *Standards: Recipes for Reality.* Edited by Goeffrey Bowker and Paul N. Edwards (p. 73). Cambridge, MA: MIT Press.

2 Timmermans, S., and S. Epstein. "A World of Standards but not a Standard World: Toward a Sociology of Standards and Standardization." In, *Annual Review of Sociology* 36 (2010):70.

3 Timmermans and Epstein." A World of Standards but not a Standard World," p. 70.

4 See: Rider, Traci Jones. 2009. *Understanding Green Building Guidelines for Students and Young Professionals*. New York: W.W. Norton. In her useful "how to" book, Rider observes that, "If the design and construction industries tried to look at all issues comprehensively for each project, the effort would be so overwhelming that nothing would get done," p. 12.

5 Brownsword, Roger, and Karen Yeung, eds. 2008. *Regulating Technologies: Legal Futures, Regulatory Frames, and Technological Fixes* (p. 4). Oxford, UK and Portland, OR: Hart Publishing.

6 Mitchell, Don. 2003. *The Right to the City: Social Justice and the Fight for Public Space*. New York: The Guilford Press.

7 Soja, E. 2009. "The City and Spatial Justice." In, *Justice Spatiale / Spatial Justice* September (1):31.

8 Lefebvre. *The Production of Space*.

9 Dikeç, M. 2001. "Justice and the Spatial Imagination." In, *Environment and Planning A* (33):1790.

10 Castells, Manuel. 1977. *The Urban Question: A Marxist Approach*. Translated by Alan Sheridan. London: Edward Arnold.

11 Pickvance, C. 2003. "From Urban Social Movements to Urban Movements." In, *International Journal of Urban and Regional Research* 21 (1):103.

12 Castells, Manuel. 1983. *The City and the Grassroots: A Cross-cultural Theory of Urban Social Movements* (p. 336). Berkeley, CA: University of California Press.

13 Fainstein, S., and C.H. 1995. "Urban Social Movements." In, *Theories of Urban Politics*. Edited by G.S. David Judge and Harold Wolman (pp. 181–204). London: Sage.

14 Talen. *City Rules*.

15 Fischler, Raphael. 1998. "Health, Safety, and the General Welfare: Markets, Politics, and Social Science in Early Land-Use Regulation and Community Design." In, *Journal of Urban History* 24 (6):676.

16 Ibid., p. 675. Fischler holds that, "Class- and race-based exclusion was a conscious rationale of building and land-use regulation from its very first days."

17 Silver, Christopher. 1997. "The Racial Origins of Zoning in American Cities." In, *Urban Planning and the African American Community: In the Shadows*. Edited by June Manning Thomas and Marsha Ritzdorf. Thousand Oaks, CA: Sage Publications.

18 Talen. *City Rules*, p. 90.

19 Fischler, Raphael. "Health, Safety, and the General Welfare," p. 687.

20 Ibid., p. 690.

21 Knack, Ruth, Stuart Meck, and Israel Stollman. 1996. "The Real Story Behind the Standard Planning and Zoning Acts of the 1920s." In, *Land Use Law* (February).

22 Talen.*City Rules*, p. 29.

23 Revell, Keith D. 2005. *Building Gotham: Civic Culture and Public Policy in New York City, 1898–1938*. Baltimore, MD: The Johns Hopkins Press.

24 Cited in: Knack et al. "The Real Story Behind the Standard Planning and Zoning Acts of the 1920s."

25 *Village of Euclid, Ohio v. Ambler Realty Co.*, 272 US 365 (1926).

26 Ibid., p. 3.

27 Cited in: Weber, Gustavus A. 1925. *The Bureau of Standards: Its History, Activities, and Organization*. Baltimore, MD: The Johns Hopkins Press.

28 Cited in: Fischer, Louis Albert. 1925. *History of the Standard Weights and Measures of the United States* (p. 2). United States Bureau of Standards Miscellaneous Publications. Washington, DC: Government Printing Office, citing *Messages and Papers of the Presidents*, 1, p. 66.

29 Weber. *The Bureau of Standards*, p. 3, citing *American State Papers*, Misc. Vol. I, p. 19.

30 Cochrane, Rexmond Canning. 1976. *Measures for Progress: A History of the National Bureau of Standards, America in Two Centuries, an Inventory* (p. 23). New York: Arno Press.

31 Cochrane. *Measures for Progress*, p. 15.

32 Weber. *The Bureau of Standards*.

33 In 1799, the Fifth Congress, second session "passed an act ordering that the surveyor shall . . . examine and try the weights, measures, and other instruments used in ascertaining the duties on imports with standards to be provided by each collector at the public expense for that purpose." "This was the first act passed by Congress in regard to weights and measures." Fischer. *History of the Standard Weights and Measures of the United States*, p. 3, citing *Statutes at Large*, 1, p. 643.

34 Weber. *The Bureau of Standards*, pp. 7–9.

35 "Joint resolution providing for the [construction and] distribution of weights and measures." Cochrane. *Measures for Progress*, p. 537.

36 The NBS was subsequently renamed the National Institute for Standards and Technology (NIST). See: NIST. 2009. "National Institute of Standards and Technology." Available at: www.nist.gov/index.html (accessed May 3, 2012).

37 "The standards which the Bureau is authorized to deal with have been designated as standards of measurement, standard values of constants, standards of quality, standards of mechanical performance, and standards of practice." Weber. *The Bureau of Standards*, p. 78.

38 Cochrane. *Measures for Progress*, p. 16.

39 It is fair to say that Jefferson may have been the first anti-federalist, at least in his attitude toward states' rights, a small federal government, and debt reduction.

40 Turbin, J. 2011. "Return to Gold Standard Gaining Traction with Presidential Candidates." In, *International Business Times* (October 10).

41 Olshan, M.A. 1993. "Standards Making Organizations and the Rationalization of American Life." In, *Sociological Quarterly* 34 2:319–335.

42 Weber. *The Bureau of Standards*, pp. 74, 206, 210.

43 Russell, A.L. 2009. "Industrial Legislatures: Consensus Standardization in the Second and Third Industrial Revolutions." In, *Enterprise and Society* 10 (4):661.

44 Olshan. "Standards Making Organizations and the Rationalization of American Life," p. 322.

45 Mallard, A. 1998. "Compare, Standardize and Settle Agreement." In, *Social Studies of Science* 28 (4):571.

46 Olshan. "Standards Making Organizations and the Rationalization of American Life." See also, Busch. *Standards: Recipes for Reality*.

47 Olshan. "Standards Making Organizations and the Rationalization of American Life," p. 325.

48

> ANSI is often asked about the total number of standards (and standards setting bodies) in the United States. It is estimated that in the U.S. today there are hundreds of "traditional" standards developing organizations—with the 20 largest SDOs producing 90% of the standards—and hundreds more "non-traditional" standards development bodies, such as consortia. This means that the level of U.S. participation is quite expansive as the groups themselves are comprised of individual committees made up of experts addressing the technical requirements of standards within their specific area of expertise. At year-end 2006, about 200 of these standards developers were accredited by ANSI; there were more than 10,000 American National Standards (ANS).

See: American National Standards Institute. ANSI. Available at: www.ansi.org/membership/overview/overview.aspx?menuid=2 (accessed August 13, 2011).

49 A rare public critique of this process was aired on the radio program, *On the Media*, wherein host Alex Goldman interviewed Carl Malamud.

> Malamud's interested in what are called "incorporation by reference." The phrase describes laws that have references to safety standards embedded in them. For instance, a law that says your car has to have turning signals will also include standards about how bright or how large the turn signals have to be. Malamud's gripe is that frequently, those standards are written by private companies, and those companies hold the copyright to the standards. That means that even though the standards are part of a law everyone has to follow, citizens have to pay—sometimes several hundreds of dollars—for the privilege of looking at them.

See: Goldman, Alex. 2012. "Carl Malamud's Box of Goodies." *On the Media*. Available at: www.onthemedia.org/blogs/on-the-media/2012/apr/13/carl-malamuds-box-goodies/ (accessed April 16, 2012).

50 Busch. *Standards*, p. 23.

51 American National Standards Institute. ANSI. The organization's website states that, membership offers "the opportunity to build relationships that empower members with a voice and influence over the standardization and conformity assessment decisions that *directly affect their business*"

(our emphasis). The point is that ANSI exists to promote the business interests of its member organizations, rather than the interests of citizens as a whole.

52 Oligarchy is generally defined as "rule by the few." That definition is demonstrated by a brief article written in 2010 by Mark Ames, then the chief lobbyist for the American Society of Heating and Refrigeration Engineers (ASHRAE), a major ANSI constituent group. Ames was concerned with what the American Clean Energy and Security Act (H.R. 2454), the American Clean Energy Leadership Act (S. 1462), the American Power Act (not yet introduced), and the Practical Energy and Climate Plan Act (S. 3464) would "mean for *us*? The short answer: a lot" (our emphasis). What is significant about the author's perspective is that he sees the pending federal legislation promoted by the Obama administration, in response to climate change data, as a threat to ASHRAE's recognized authority. He holds that "the potential of the federal government to write standards in place of ASHRAE represents a new ingredient to our standards-making process." It is tacit recognition that, until these pieces of legislation were introduced, government, and citizens, did not have effective authority to regulate energy consumption and its attendant consequences. See: Ames, Mark. 2010. "Energy Bills & 90.1 Targets." In, *ASHRAE Journal* August:71. See also, Busch. *Standards*, p. 236. Busch argues that: "Because individuals and small firms lack the capital and expertise to participate effectively in TSRs, they become subject to governance by dominant firms in the supply chain."

53 Noble, David F. 1977. *America by Design: Science, Technology and the Rise of Corporate Capitalism*. New York: Alfred A. Knopf. Although Noble's critique of corporate capitalism in the United States has been criticized as overstated, or missing some essential issues, it has also been accepted as having contributed significantly to the field. There is little doubt that his *essentialization* of managerial character is overstated. See also, Chandler, Alfred E. Jr. 1978. Book review. In, *Technology and Culture* 19 (3):569–572.

54 Hess, David J. 2007. *Alternative Pathways in Science and Industry: Activism, Innovation, and the Environment in an Era of Globalization*. Cambridge, MA: MIT Press.

55 Henderson provides an excellent comparative case study that demonstrates how two municipalities, in different states, have interpreted and codified "straw bale" technology in very different ways. See: Henderson, Kathryn. 2006. "Ethics, Culture, and Structure in the Negotiation of Straw Bale Building Codes." In, *Science, Technology and Human Values* 31 (3):261–288.

56 Another source of mandate for action by code-makers can be citizen complaints. Since 2007, when the City of Austin began its 311 call service to divert less urgent calls from the emergency 911 service, the most calls (30,416) of 10 categories for 2009 concerned code compliance issues. See: Gandara, Ricardo. 2010. "311 Calls Up Over Past Years." In, *Austin American Statesman*, November 26.

57 Cochrane. *Measures for Progress*, p. 15.

58 Krislov, S. 1997. *How Nations Choose Product Standards and Standards Change Nations*. Pittsburgh, PA: University of Pittsburgh Press.

59 Shove, E., and M. Moezzi. 2002. "What do Standards Standardize?" Paper read at, *Human and Social Dimensions of Energy Use: Understanding Markets and Demand*. EECE, Panel 8. *Human and Social Dimensions of Energy Use: Understanding Markets and Demand*. Available at: www.eceee.org/conference_proceedings/ACEEE_buildings/2002/Panel_8 (accessed January 9, 2013).

60 For a comparison of the organic food labeling controversy and that of sustainable, or "green," architecture, see: Moore, Steven A., and Nathan Engstrom. 2005. "The Social Construction of 'Green' Building Codes: Competing Models by Industry, Government and NGOs." In, *Sustainable Architectures: Natures and Cultures in Europe and North America*. Edited by Simon Guy and Steven A. Moore (pp. 51–70). London: Routhedge/Spon.

61 Hess, David J. 2001. "Selecting Technology, Science, and Medicine." In, *Alternative Pathways in Globalization*. Vol. V. 1. Edited by D.J. Hess. Niskayuna, NY: David J. Hess.

62 Conroy. *Branded!*

63 Bartky, I.R. 1989. "The Adoption of Standard Time." *Technology and Culture* 30 (1):25–56.

64 Adshead, Julie, ed. 2011. *Green Buildings and the Law*. Cib, the International Council for Research and Innovation in Buildings and Construction. London: Spon Press.

65 Cochrane. *Measures for progress*, p. 151.

66 WCED. 1987. *Our Common Future*. New York: United Nations World Council on Economic Development.

67 This general claim is supported by an editorial plea for regulatory simplicity in: *The Economist*. 2012. "Over-regulated America: The home of laissez-faire is being suffocated by excessive and badly written regulation." *The Economist*, February 19, 2012. Editors argued that: "Unlike Europeans, whose lives have long been circumscribed by meddling governments and diktats from Brussels, Americans are supposed to be free to choose, for better or for worse. Yet for some time America has been straying from this ideal" (p. 1). "Two forces make American laws too complex. One is hubris. Many lawmakers seem to believe that they can lay down rules to govern every eventuality. . . . The other force that makes American laws complex is lobbying" (p. 2).

> More important, rules need to be much simpler. When regulators try to write an all-purpose instruction manual, the truly important dos and don'ts are lost in an ocean of verbiage. Far better to lay down broad goals and prescribe only what is strictly necessary to achieve them. Legislators should pass simple rules, and leave regulators to enforce them.
>
> (p. 3)

68 Imrie and Street. *Architectural Design and Regulations*.

69 Talen. *City Rules*.

70 Latour. *Science in Action*. See also, Hommels. *Unbuilding Cities*.

71 Imrie, Rob, and Emma Street. 2009a. "Regulating Design: The Practices of Architecture, Governance and Control." In, *Urban Studies* 46 (12):2507–2518.

72 Talen. *City Rules*.

73 One salient example of an experimental space dedicated to affordable housing is that created by architect Mike Reynolds near Taos, New Mexico. Although the political or technological "style" of Reynolds' experiment may not be transferable, the process of creating it may be. See: Hodge, Oliver. 2007. *Garbage Warrior*—a film about eco architecture by Oliver Hodge, available at: www.garbagewarrior.com/. A second example is a case of technological innovation and regulation resistance in Lagunitas, California. David Lee Hoffman, who has quietly avoided building permits for some 40 years, constructed a nearly hidden live/work space of several structures, ponds, and fields and has perfected a method of aging rare tealeaves. By recycling gray water, composting, and building earthen environments particularly well suited to rare worms, he has innovated where others have not. This is a classic case of innovation unfettered by regulation. Unfortunately, Marin County sued Hoffman in 2012 and threatens to demolish the structures, because they violate building and public health laws. See: Brown, Patricia Leigh. 2012. "Hippie Holdout, a Fight over Worms and Moats." In, *New York Times*, Monday, April 23, A9–A11.

74 Dewey, John. 1954. *The Public and Its Problems*. Chicago: Swallow Press. See also, Fischer, Frank. 2000. *Citizens, Experts, and the Environment: The Politics of Local Knowledge*. Durham, NC and London: Duke University Press.

Chapter 4

1 Brain, David. 1991. "Practical Knowledge and Occupational Control: The Professionalization of Architecture in the United States." In, *Sociological Forum* 6 (2):260.

2 Foucault, Michel. 1977[1975]. *Discipline and Punish: The Birth of the Prison* (p. 218). New York: Pantheon.

3 Brain, "Practical Knowledge," p. 260.

4 Ben-Joseph, Eran. 2005. *The Code of the City: Standards and the Hidden Language of Place Making*. Edited by Robert Gottlieb, Urban and Industrial Environments. Cambridge, MA and London: MIT Press.

5 Shah, Rajiv C., and Jay P. Kesan. 2007. "How Architecture Regulates." In, *Journal of Architectural and Planning Research* 24 (4):350–359.

6 See: Winner. *Autonomous Technology*; and Feenberg, Andrew. 1991. *Critical Theory of Technology*. New York: Oxford University Press.

7 Bourdieu. *The Field of Cultural Production.*

8 Owen and Dovey. "Fields of Sustainable Architecture."

9 Moore, Steven A., and Andrew Karvonen. 2007. "Sustainable Architecture in Context: STS and Design Thinking." In, *Science Studies* 21 (1):29–46.

10 Goffman, Erving. 1974. *Frame Analysis: An Essay on the Organization of Experience with a New Foreword by Bennet Berger* (p. 2). Boston, MA: Northeastern University Press.

11 Ibid., p. 8.

12 A former student of ours reported that she quit architecture school after she was strenuously criticized by a studio instructor for introducing criteria borrowed from social psychology into the design of an elementary school.

13 Goffman. *Frame Analysis,* p. 83.

14 Ibid., p. 303.

15 Ibid., p. 338.

16 This is a position also argued by Larry Hickman. See: Hickman, Larry. 2007. *Pragmatism as Post-Postmodernism.* New York: Fordham University Press.

17 Hacking, Ian. 2004. "Between Michel Foucault and Erving Goffman: Between Discourse in the Abstract and Face-to-Face Interaction." In, *Economy and Society* 33 (3):279.

18 Kuypers, Jim A. 2009. *Rhetorical Criticism: Perspectives in Action.* Lanham, MD: Lexington Press.

19 Moore. *Technology and Place.*

20 Marx, Karl. 1978. "Division of Labour and Manufacture." In, *Capital* Vol. 1. *The Marx–Engels Reader.* Edited by Robert C. Tucker. New York: Norton.

21 Cochrane, Willard. 1978. *The Development of American Agriculture: A Historical Analysis.* Minneapolis, MN: University of Minnesota Press.

22 Bijker. *Of Bicycles, Bakelites, and Bulbs.*

23 Aibar, E., and Bijker, W. 1997. "Constructing a City: The Cerda Plan for the extension of Barcelona." In, *Science, Technology, & Human Values* 22 (1):3–30.

24 Soris y Puig, Arturo, ed. 1999. *Cerda: The Five Bases of the General Theory of Urbanization.* Barcelona, Spain: Electa.

25 Bijker, Wiebe E., and Karin Bijsterveld. 2000. "Women Walking through Plans: Technology, Democracy, and Gender Identity." In, *Technology and Culture* 41 (3):485–515.

26 Ibid., p. 489.

27 Ibid., p. 487.

28 Ibid., p. 490.

29 Cowan, Ruth Schwartz. 1989. "The Consumption Junction: A Proposal for Research Strategies in the Sociology of Technology." In, *The Social Construction of Technological Systems* (p. 262). Cambridge, MA: MIT Press.

30 Bijker and Bijsterveld. "Women Walking through Plans," p. 504.

31 Ibid., p. 506.

32 Ibid., p. 506, n. 61. See also, Bijker. *Of Bicycles, Bakelites, and Bulbs.*

33 Brain. "Practical Knowledge," pp. 260–261. Brain, in his study of the professionalization of architecture, makes almost exactly the same observation as Bijker, using different language. Citing Abbott (p. 823), Brain argues that,

> status within the profession . . . is granted on the basis of purity: "the ability to exclude non-professional issues or irrelevant issues from practice." Purity is attributed to an exemplification of the categories and classifications of a cultural system. Professional practitioners develop a system of judgments and purity and impurity that are used in the attribution of relative status within the profession and are associated with positions in a professional division of labor.

See: Abbott, Andrew. 1981. "Status and Status Strain in the Professions." In, *American Journal of Sociology* 86:819–835.

34 Bijker and Bijsterveld. "Women Walking through Plans," p. 507.

35 Davidson, Elizabeth J. 2002. "Technology Frames and Framing: A Socio-Cognitive Investigation of requirements Determination." In, *MIS Quarterly* 26 (4):329–358.

36 Mehalik, Matthew M., and Michael E. Gorman. 2006. "A Framework for Strategic Network Design Assessment, Decision Making, and Moral Imagination." In, *Science, Technology & Human Values* 31 (3):289–308.

37 Moore. *Technology and Place*; Guy and Farmer. "Reinterpreting Sustainable Architecture."

38 Guy, Simon, and Steven A. Moore. 2005. *Sustainable Architectures: Natures and Cultures in Europe and North America*. London: Routledge/Spon.

Chapter 5

1 Davis. *The Culture of Building*, p. 5.

2 Hubka, T. 1984. *Big House, Little House, Back House, Barn: The Connected Farm Buildings of New England*. Lebanon, NH: The University Press of New England.

3 In Critical Theory, the term "vernacular" has been used in a far more sophisticated manner than in everyday conversation. McLaughlin, for example, argues that,

> Vernacular theories could be thought of in terms of what Michael Foucault has called "subjugated knowledges." A "subjugated knowledge" is an "autonomous, non-centralized kind of theoretical production, one that is to say whose validity is not dependent on the approval of the established regimes of thought." Foucault contrasts these knowledges with "the tyranny of globalizing discourses."
>
> (McLaughlin. *Street Smarts and Critical Theory*, p. 7)

4 AlSayyad, Nezarr. 2006. "Foreword." In, *Vernacular Architecture in the Twenty-First Century*. Edited by Lindsay and Marcel Vellinga Asquith (p. xvii). London: Taylor & Francis.

5 Asquith, Lindsay, and Marcel Vellinga. 2006. *Vernacular Architecture in the Twenty-First Century* (p. 5). London: Taylor & Francis.

6 Rudofsky, Bernard. 1965[1987]. *Architecture Without Architects: A Short Introduction to Non-Pedigreed Architecture* (p. 3). Albuquerque, NM: University of New Mexico Press. Original edition, Museum of Modern Art, New York.

7 Norberg-Schulz, Christian. 1979. *Genius Loci: Towards a Phenomenology of Architecture*. New York: Rizzoli.

8 Oliver, Paul. 1987. *Dwellings: The Houses across the World*. Austin, TX: University of Texas Press.

9 Rapoport, Amos. 1969. *House Form and Culture*. Edited by Richard E. Dahlberg, Foundations of Cultural Geography. Englewood Cliffs, NJ: Prentice-Hall.

10 Davis. *The Culture of Building*.

11 Meyer. "Building," p. 116.

12 Shepheard, P. (2003). *Artificial Love: A Story of Machines and Architecture*. Cambridge, MA: MIT Press.

13 Walter Gropius is a central figure in the development of modern architecture and, perhaps for that reason, escapes easy categorization at one end or the other of core art-versus-science debates. Although he clearly embraced modern science, he was no less supportive of the architect as "artist." In his *Architecture and Design in the Age of Science*, Gropius articulated a vision of architectural practice as democratic, collaborative, and artistic. See: Gropius, Walter. 1952. *Architecture and Design in the Age of Science*. New York: Spiral Press.

14 Conrads, U. 1990. *Programs and Manifestoes on 20th-Century Architecture* (p. 29). Cambridge, MA: MIT Press.

15 Berlin, Isaiah. 2006. *Political Ideas in the Romantic Age: Their Rise and Influence on Modern Thought, with an Introduction by Joshua L. Cherniss*. Edited by Henry Hardy. Princeton, NJ: Princeton University Press.

16 Vattimo, Gianni. 1991. *The End of Modernity* (p. 166). Baltimore, MD: Johns Hopkins University Press.

17 Wolin, Richard. 2004. *The Seduction of Unreason: The Intellectual Romance with Fascism: From Nietzsche to Postmodernism*. Princeton, NJ: Princeton University Press.

18 Latour, Bruno. 1993. *We Have Never Been Modern*. Translated by Catherine Porter. Cambridge, MA: Harvard University Press.

19 Davis. *The Culture of Building*, p. 149.

20 Umbach, Maiken, and Bernd Huppauf. 2005. *Vernacular Modernism: Heimat, Globalization and the Built Environment* (pp. 5–11). Stanford, CA: Stanford University Press.
21 Glassie, Henry. 1975. *Folk Housing in Middle Virginia: A Structural Analysis of Historic Artifacts* (p. 114). Knoxville, TN: University of Tennessee Press.
22 Ibid., p. 115.
23 Glassie, Henry. 2000. *Vernacular Architecture.* Edited by George Jevremovic, William T. Sumner, and Henry Glassie (p. 20). Philadelphia, PA: Material Culture; Bloomington, IN: Indiana University Press.
24 Lara. "Modernism made vernacular," p. 45.
25 Lara. "Modernism made vernacular," p. 49.
26 Holub. *Reception Theory.*
27 Jamison, Andrew. 2010. "Climate Change Knowledge and Social Movement Theory." In, *Wiley Interdisciplinary Reviews: Climate change.* Aalborg, Denmark: Aalborg University.
28 Horkheimer, Max, and Theodor Adorno. 1947[1944]. *Dialectic of Enlightenment.* Amsterdam, The Netherlands: Querido. Original edition, *Dialektik der Aufklärung: Philosophische Fragmente.*
29 Lefebvre. *The Production of Space.*
30 Morse, Richard M. 1974. *From Community to Metropolis: A Biography of São Paulo, Brazil.* New York: Octagon Books.
31 Lima, Zeuler R.M.A. 2006. "The Faces of Janus: Modernism and Hybridization in the Architecture of Lina Bo Bardi." In, *Journal of Architecture* 11 (2):257–264.
32 da Costa Meyer, Esther. 2002. "After the Flood: Lino Bo Bardi's Glass House." In, *Harvard Design Magazine,* Winter/Spring:1–12.
33 Ibid.
34 Lima. "The Faces of Janus," p. 261.
35 Ferraz, Marcello Carvalho. 2010. Interview with Kristine Stiphany, August 10. São Paulo, Brazil.
36 Lima, Zeuler R.M.A. 2005. "Preservation as Confrontation: The Work of Lina Bo Bardi." In, *Journal of Historic Preservation, History, Theory and Criticism* 2 (Jan):24–33.
37 Lima. "The Faces of Janus", p. 263.
38 Ferraz. Interview with Kristine Stiphany.
39 Lima. "The Faces of Janus," p. 265.
40 Davis has argued,

> The more distant loci of control, the increase of the quantity and specificity of abstract documents of control, and the growth of litigious atmosphere in the construction industry and in the building culture as a whole have developed hand in hand. Together they have removed people's ability to carefully apply human discretion to the making of buildings and have contributed to the abstract and fragmented nature of the modern built landscape.
>
> (*The Culture of Building,* p. 200)

41 Lima. "The Faces of Janus," p. 265.
42 This frame is closest to that inhabited by Christopher Alexander and colleagues. See: Alexander, C., S. Ishikawa, and M. Silverstein. 1977. *A Pattern Language: Towns, Buildings, Construction.* New York: Oxford University Press.
43 Feenberg, Andrew. 2010. "Incommensurable Paradigms: Values and the Environment." In, *Pragmatic Sustainability: Theoretical and Practical Tools.* Edited by Steven A. Moore (pp. 276–288). London: Routledge.

Chapter 6

1 Levy, Janet E. 1979. "Evidence of Social Stratification in Bronze Age Denmark." In, *Journal of Field Archaeology* 6 (1):49–56. With regard to Rome, see: Massey, Jonathan 2004. "New Necessities: Modernist Aesthetic Discipline." In, *Perspecta* 35 (Building Codes):112–133.
2 *American Heritage Dictionary of the English Language.*
3 Hollander, S.C. 1984. "Sumptuary Legislation: Demarketing by Edict." In, *Journal of Macromarketing* 4 (1):4.
4 In fact, there are more than three types of sumptuary code, but, in the context of this book, the others are minor. For example, medieval Jews forbade themselves to wear sumptuous clothing

for fear of retribution from Gentiles. See: Community of Carpentras. In, *The Jewish Quarterly Review* 18 (4):357–383.

5 The Sustainable Consumption Research and Action Initiative, or SCORAI, is a major source of this discourse. See: www.scorai.org/

6 Thorpe. *Architecture & Design versus Consumerism.* Kindle location 4413.

7 A third minor tradition of sumptuary coding is prohibition against influence peddling. The Romans, for example, instituted codes against treating senators to lavish meals and other forms of consumption, which remain a part of contemporary government. See Dauster, Molly Ann Rosser. 1996. *Roman Sumptuary Legislation, History.* Lubbock, TX: Texas Tech University. A fourth minor tradition of sumptuary coding is documented by Roth (Roth, Cecil. 1928. "Sumptuary Laws of the Community of Carpentras." In, *The Jewish Quarterly Review* 18 (4):357–383), and is related to the *external* adoption by European Jewish communities of apparel restrictions intended to avoid envy by Christian neighbors, inevitably followed by cycles of persecution. We could find no productive contemporary use for this tradition. Although these two forms of sumptuary coding are worthy of study, they do not contribute significantly to our interests in this chapter, and so we have excluded them.

8 Hooper, Wilfrid. 1915. "The Tudor Sumptuary Laws." In, *The English Historical Review* 30 (119):437.

9 Freudenberger, Herman. 1963. "Fashion, Sumptuary Laws, and Business." In, *The Business History Review* 37 (1/2):37–48.

10 Hess. *Alternative Pathways in Science and Industry.*

11 Schumacher, E.F. 1973. *Small is Beautiful: Economics as if People Mattered.* London: Bond & Briggs.

12 Canizaro, Vincent. 2007. *Architectural Regionalism: Collected Writings on Place, Identity, Modernity, and Tradition.* New York: Princeton Architectural Press.

13 Berry, Wendell. 1978. *The Unsettling of America.* New York: Avon.

14 Diamond, Jared. 2005. *Collapse: How Societies Choose to Fail or Succeed.* New York: Penguin, citing: Totman, Conrad. 2007. *Japan's Imperial Forest, Goryōrin, 1889–1945: With a Supporting Study of the Kan/Min Division of Woodland in Early Meiji Japan, 1871–1876.* Folkestone, UK: Global Oriental. pp. 299–301). See also, Coaldrake, William H. 1981. "Edo Architecture and Tokugawa Law." In, *Monumenta Nipponica* (Sophia University) 36 (3):235–284.

15 Ishikawa, Eisuke. 2000. *Japan in the Edo Period—An Ecologically Conscious Society (O-edo ecology jijo).* Kodansha Publishing Company.

16 Hunt, Alan. 1996. "The Governance of Consumption: Sumptuary Laws and Shifting Forms of Regulation." In, *Economy and Society* 25 (3):410–427. See also, Hunt, A. 1996b. *Governance of the Consuming Passions: A History of Sumptuary Law.* London: Macmillan Press.

17 Goodrich, Peter. 1998. "Review: Signs Taken for Wonders: Community, Identity," and "A History of Sumptuary Law." In, *Law & Social Inquiry* 23 (3):707–728.

18 Lim, Regina Mapua. 2006. "Cultural Sustainability and Development: Drukpa and Burman Vernacular Architecture," In, *Designing Sustainable Cities in the Developing World.* Edited by Roger Zetter. Farnham, UK: Ashgate; Hunt, Alan. 1998. *Governance of the Consuming Passions: A History of Sumptuary Law.* Chicago, IL: University of Chicago.

19 Beebe, Barton. 2010. "Intellectual Property Law and the Sumptuary Code." In, *Harvard Law Review* 123 (4):886.

20 Levy. "Evidence of Social Stratification in Bronze Age Denmark."

21 Beebe. "Intellectual Property Law and the Sumptuary Code," pp. 809–889.

22 Dauster. *Roman Sumptuary Legislation.*

23 Bourdieu. *Distinction,* p. 466.

24 "A Thirteenth-Century Castilian Sumptuary Law." 1963. In, *Business History Review* 37 (1/2):98–100.

25 Hooper. "The Tudor Sumptuary Laws," p. 433.

26 Baldwin, F.E. 1926. *Sumptuary Legislation and Personal Regulation in England.* Baltimore, MD: Johns Hopkins Press.

27 Grignon, Marc, and Juliana Maxim. 1995. "Convenance, Caractère, and the Public Sphere." In, *Journal of Architectural Education (1984–)* 49 (1):30. The authors cite Norbert Elias as holding

"in this court society—all members of the society are involved in a ceaseless struggle for status and prestige." See: Norbert, Elias. 1983. *The Court Society*. Translated by Edmund Jephcott (p. 63). Oxford, UK: Basil Blackwell.

28 Hooper. "The Tudor Sumptuary Laws," p. 437.

29 Freudenberger. "Fashion, Sumptuary Laws, and Business."

30 Stilgoe, John. 1982. *Common Landscapes of America: 1580–1845* (pp. 34–42). New Haven, CT: Yale University Press.

31 Coaldrake, William H. 1988. "The Gatehouse of the Shogun's Senior Councillor: Building Design and Status Symbolism in Japanese Architecture of the Late Edo Period." In, *The Journal of the Society of Architectural Historians* 47 (4):397–410.

32 Grignon and Maxim. "Convenance, Caractère, and the Public Sphere,"p. 29. The authors rely on a key text by Habermas. See: Habermas, Jürgen. 1991. *The Structural Transformation of the Public Sphere*. Translated by Thomas Burger. Cambridge, MA: MIT Press. See also, Bourdieu. *Distinction*, p. 252. Here, Bourdieu also makes a specific connection between sumptuary and taste codes in saying:

> The symbolic struggles over being and seeming, over the symbolic manifestations which the sense of appropriateness, as strict as the old sumptuary laws, assigns to the different social conditions ("Who does he think he is?"), separating, for example, natural "grace" from usurped "airs and graces," are both based and focused on the degree of freedom from one's "station" that is allowed by the specific logic of symbolic manifestations.

33 The periodization of explicit sumptuary codes and implicit taste codes is very fuzzy, because they are two parts of the same social phenomenon and varied spatially. In Chapter 2, we argued that, as early as Palladio in the 16th century, taste was a powerful determinant.

34 Grignon and Maxim. "Convenance, Caractère, and the Public Sphere," p. 32.

35 Foucault, Michel. 1977. *Discipline and Punish: The Birth of the Prison*. New York: Pantheon.

36 Massey, Jonathan 2004. "New Necessities: Modernist Aesthetic Discipline." In, *Perspecta* 35 (Building Codes):112–133.

37 We are indebted to historian Richard Cleary for these insights; personal email 28 July 2011.

38 Picon, Antoine. 2004. "The Ghost of Architecture: The Project and Its Codification." In, *Perspecta: The Yale Architectural Journal*. Edited by Elijah and Stephanie Tuerk Huge (p. 11). Cambridge, MA: MIT Press.

39 Grignon and Maxim. "Convenance, Caractère, and the Public Sphere," p. 32.

40 Sumptuary architectural codes can, of course, work in the opposite direction, by propping up or reinforcing a coming social order, such as that proposed by Albert Speer and the Nazis.

41 Bourdieu. *Distinction*, p. 466.

42 Ibid., p. 471.

43 Ibid., p. 374.

44 Scott. *Seeing Like a State*. Scott has argued, for example, that such reductive assumptions would be laughable if not occasionally so tragic. Yet, he observes that some utopian projects of modern architecture have continued to operate with this same goal in mind, yet no more successfully.

45 Shively, Donald H. 1964. "Sumptuary Regulation and Status in Early Tokugawa Japan." In, *Harvard Journal of Asiatic Studies* 25:123–164; See also, Cox, Noel. 2006. "Tudor Sumptuary Laws and Academical Dress: An Act Against Wearing of Costly Apparel 1509 and an Act for Reformation of Excess in Apparel 1533." In, *Transactions of the Burgon Society* 6:15–43.

46 Beebe. "Intellectual Property Law and the Sumptuary Code," p. 811, cites several archaic examples of early Japanese and European sumptuary codes that "were almost invariably ignored, circumvented, or openly defied," even when penalties were extreme.

47 Ibid., p. 812.

48 Bourdieu. *Distinction*, p. 477.

49 See also Ponte, Lucille M. 2009. "Echoes of the Sumptuary Impulse: Considering the Threads of Social Identity, Public Morality, and Economic Protectionism under the Proposed Design Piracy Prohibition Act." Florida Coastal School of Law.

50 Thorpe. *Architecture and Design versus Consumerism*. Kindle locations 1676–1678.

51 Beebe. "Intellectual Property Law and the Sumptuary Code," p. 812.
52 Lynes, Russell. 1954[1949]. *The Tastemakers* (p. 4). The Universal Library. New York: Grosset and Dunlap.
53 Beebe. "Intellectual Property Law and the Sumptuary Code," p. 825.
54 There is disagreement among historians concerning terminology. Where Upton distinguishes between "pattern books" and "style books," Jandl distinguishes between "builders' guides" and "pattern books"; see: Jandl, H. Ward. 1991. *Yesterday's Houses of Tomorrow*. Washington, DC: The Preservation Press; National Trust for Historic Preservation. We have adopted Upton's terms.
55 Upton, Dell 1984. "Pattern Books and Professionalism: Aspects of the Transformation of Domestic Architecture in America, 1800–1860." *Winterthur Portfolio* 19 (2/3):107–150.
56 Ibid., p. 116.
57 Ibid., p. 124.
58 Downing, Andrew Jackson (1815–1852). 1968[1850]. *The Architecture of Country Houses* (p. 18). Reprinted. New York: Da Capo Press. Original edition, New York; D. Appleton, 1861.
59 Ibid.
60 Upton. "Pattern Books and Professionalism," p. 154.
61 Lynes. *The Tastemakers*.
62 Davidson, Chandler. 1990. *Race and Class in Texas Politics*. Princeton, NJ: Princeton University Press.
63 Although both Republicans and Democrats tend to see populists as crude in their politics, it is of interest to note that pragmatists, who emerged at about the same time, had more sympathy. Not because pragmatists shared the anti-intellectual posture of populists, but because they shared a skeptical position regarding any claim toward inherent superiority, intelligence, or tastes of the dominant class. See: Menand, Louis. 2001. *The Metaphysical Club*. New York: Farrar, Straus, Giroux.
64 Jandl. *Yesterday's Houses of Tomorrow*.
65 Stevenson, Katherine Cole, and H. Ward Jandl. 1986. *Houses by Mail: A Guide to Houses From Sears, Roebuck and Company*. Washington, DC: Preservation Press.
66 Ibid., p. 32.
67 Davis. *The Culture of Building*.
68 Urban Design Associates, Ray Gindroz, Rob Robinson, et al. 2004. *The Architectural Pattern Book: A Tool for Building Great Neighborhoods*. New York: W.W. Norton & Company.
69 Chase. "The Role of Consumerism in American Architecture."
70 Jackson, J.B. 1985. "Urban Circumstances." In, *Design Quarterly*, pp. 25–29.
71 For example, the on-stage conflict between Frank Gehry and CNU advocate Fred Kent (president of Project for Public Spaces), at the 2009 Aspen Ideas Conference, demonstrates the distaste that FBC advocates have for both crass commercialism and the world of high design. Architect Robert Adam summed the situation up by saying, "being famous is not going to be enough to allow you to drive over local people, and conspire with star-struck bureaucrats to flummox elected committees? One thing that hasn't changed much since the eighties is public taste for architecture. There's good research evidence for this and any cultural historian will tell you that fundamentals like this don't change quickly." See: Adam, Robert. 2009. "Chelsea Changed Everything." In, *Building Magazine* July 10:27. Available at: www.building.co.uk/comment/chelsea-changed-everything/3144511.article (accessed April 9, 2013); and Adam, Robert. 2012. "Good urbanism and the 'starchitects'." In, *Congress for New Urbanism 2009*. Available at: www.cnu.org/cnu-salons/2009/07/good-urbanism-and-starchitects (accessed May 5, 2012).
72 Cited in: Talen, Emily. 2009b. *The Codes Project* (p. 157). National Science Foundation 2009. Available at: http://codesproject.asu.edu/ (accessed March 11, 2009).
73 Parolek et al. *Form-Based Codes*, p. 10.
74 Tilly, Charles. 2004. *Social Movements, 1768–2004*. Boulder, CO: Paradigm Publishers.
75 Parolek et al. *Form-Based Codes*. These authors identify the FBC movement as a whole with the ancient authors cited. The book is a good example of the first or conservative advocacy.
76 Architect Michael Pyatok characterizes the group this way:

> As an architect I can sympathize with the professional tendency of the CNU to try to solve our society's problems within the framework of our architectural and urban design disciplines. However, it is clear that the CNU leadership needs to significantly broaden its membership so it can recognize that the creation of physical interventions is not the end, but rather the means, for building jobs, community self-sufficiency and political empowerment. Until then, we will continue to see from CNU the "sticks and bricks" interventions that merely raise property values and displace the very people we should be trying to help.

See: Pyatok, Michael. "The Narrow Base of the New Urbanists." *Planners Network*. Available at: www.plannersnetwork.org/2002/04/the-narrow-base-of-the-new-urbanists/ (accessed April 6, 2013).

77 Talen's *The Codes Project* is the best example of this second, or progressive, type of FBC advocacy. See also: Talen, Emily. 2009a. "Design by the Rules: The Historical Underpinnings of Form-Based Codes." In, *Journal of the American Planning Association* 75 (2):144–160.

78 Ibid., p. 157.

79 Carmona, Matthew, Stephen Marshall, and Quentin Stevens. 2006. *Design Codes: Their Use and Potential*. Oxford, UK: Elsevier; see also Duany, Andres. 1993. "Coding America." In, *ANY* 1 (1):14–19; and Carmona, Matthew. 2003. "English Design Policies: How Have They Fared?" In, *Environment and Planning B: Planning and Design* 30 (6):911–931.

80 Neyfak, Leon. 2011. "Green Building: Are Cities the Best Place to Live? Are Suburbs OK? A Fight Grows in Urban Planning, With Harvard at the Center." In, *Boston Globe*, January 30, 2011. In the theoretical battle between the advocates of FBCs and Landscape Urbanism, Duany is cited as saying, "What you're seeing is the New Urbanism (FBCs) about to swallow the landscape urbanists." His plan now, Duany held, is to systematically "assimilate" the language and strategies that have made his opponents such a white-hot brand. "We're trying to upgrade ourselves. I'm not gonna say, 'We're gonna flick 'em off the table because they're a bunch of lawn apologists.' I'm gonna say, 'For God's sake, these guys took over Harvard!'" A visit to recent projects of Duany Plater-Zyberk (at: http://dpz.com) will confirm that the firm claims to be employing the most recent technological strategies to achieve "environmental sustainability."

81 In a similar vein, psychologist Tim Kasser argues that, "a strong MVO (Materialistic Value Orientation) is one way in which people attempt to compensate for worries and doubts about their self-worth, their ability to cope effectively with challenges, and their safety in a relatively unpredictable world" (p. 14). Extending that empirical finding, he holds, "that the ideology encouraged by our culture of consumption undermines the personal well-being and need satisfaction of those who accept its values," and "a strong MVO also leads people to engage in behaviors and hold attitudes damaging to our communities and to the world's ecological health" (p. 21). See: Kasser, Tim, and Allen D. Kanner. 2003. "Psychology and Consumer Culture: The Struggle for a Good Life in a Materialistic World." In, *American Psychological Association* (APA), 1st ed. (pp. 10–23).

82 Duany, Andres, and David Brain. 2005. "Regulating as if Humans Matter: The Transect and Post-Suburban Planning." In, *Regulating Place: Standards and the Shaping of Urban America*. Edited by E. and T.S. Szold Ben-Joseph. New York: Routledge.

83 Karvonen, Andrew. 2008. *Botanizing the Asphalt: Politics of Urban Drainage*. Doctoral Dissertation. Austin, TX: The University of Texas.

84 Farr, Douglas. 2008. *Sustainable Urbanism: Urban Design with Nature*. New York: Wiley.

85 Discussed and illustrated in, Farr. *Sustainable Urbanism* (pp. 234–237). This project, developed by the Seattle Housing Authority and designed by Mithun Architects + Designers + Planners includes 50 percent affordable housing units and advanced stormwater management technologies that reduced storm flows into the adjacent creek by 65 percent.

86 Hosey, Lance. 2012. *The Shape of Green: Aesthetics, Ecology and Design*. Washington, DC: Island Press. Hosey makes an almost opposite claim. In his view, we need to scientize design so as to make the biophysical patterns lodged in our subconscious more evident in architecture, and thus irresistible to users. His assumption is that our criteria for making architectural judgments are hard-wired rather than socially constructed. Our position is that it need not be one or the other, but that both innate and socially learned responses are operable.

Chapter 7

1 Misa, T.J., Philip Brey, and Andrew Feenberg (2003). *Modernity and Technology* (p. 10). Cambridge, MA: MIT Press.

2 Feenberg, Andrew. 2003. "Pragmatism and Critical Theory of Technology." *Techne* 7 (1):42–49.

3 Cited in: Melosi, M. (2000). *The Sanitary City: Urban Infrastructure in America from Colonial Times to the Present* (p. 8). Baltimore, MD: Johns Hopkins University Press.

4 We are indebted to Michael Oden for this insight.

5 Goldberger, Paul. 2010. "Review." *The New Yorker*, August 9, p. 79.

6 Frantzen, Jason. 2010. Herzog and De Meuron design team member. Email communication, October 4.

7 Bruno Latour wrote this text under the pseudonym of Jim Johnson, in a special issue of *Social Problems* (1988). In his view, it is not that human agency can be placed in the door closer by code-makers, but that the relationship between humans and door closers is one of "quasi-objects and quasi-subjects" (p. 306). See: Johnson, Jim. 1988. "Mixing Humans and Nonhumans Together: The Sociology of a Door-Closer." In, *Social Problems, University of California Press on Behalf of the Society for the Study of Social Problems* 35 (3):298–310.

8 Cited in: Scott. *Seeing Like a State*, p. 139. Similar objections are made by contemporary complexity theorists. For example, see: McDaniel, Rueben R., and Holly Jordan Lanham. (2010). "Sustainable Development: Complexity and the Problem of Balance." In, *Pragmatic Sustainability:Theoretical and Practical Tools*. Edited by Steven A. Moore (pp. 51–66). London: Routledge.

9 AISC. 2011. *Our Mission: Making Structural Steel the Material of Choice*. American Institute of Steel Construction 1921. Available at: www.aisc.org/contactUs.aspx?ekfrm=248&id=4974 (accessed August 12, 2011).

10 Busch. *Standards*.

11 For one example of how prescriptive code-makers are resistant to change that may be in the public interest, see: Price, Asher. 2012. "New gray water rules on tap." In, *Austin American-Statesman*, Monday, July 2, pp. A1–A4.

12 See: Noble. *America by Design*. By the mid 1970s, Noble argued that a class of "corporate liberal managers," who are the graduates of the best schools of engineering—particularly the Massachusetts Institute of Technology—had become central shapers of modern business and corporate culture in North America. This is to say that North American culture and the economy in general had become technocratic.

13 Imrie and Street. *Architectural Design and Regulations*.

14 Beck, U. 1992. *Risk Society: Towards a New Modernity*. Thousand Oaks, CA: Sage.

15 Lauria, M. 1997. *Reconstructing Urban Regime Theory: Regulating Urban Politics in a Global Economy*. Thousand Oaks, CA: Sage.

16 *Village of Euclid, Ohio v. Ambler Realty Co.*, 272 US 365 (1926).

17 Oden, Michael. 2011. Private email correspondence, July 26.

18 Hadjisophocleous, G.V., N. Benichou, et al. (1998). "Literature Review of Performance-Based Fire Codes and Design Environment." In, *Journal of Fire Protection Engineering* 9 (1):12–40. See also: Hurley, Morgan J. (2006). "The practice of performance-based design." In, *Fire Protection Engineering* (29):2; Lutzkendorf, T., and David Lorenz. (2006). "Using an Integrated Performance Approach in Building Assessment Tools." In, *Building Research & Information* 34 (4):334–356.

19 Hurley. "The Practice of Performance-Based Design." Hurley specifically holds that performance-based codes have two functions: "(1) as a means to determine equivalency to a prescriptive code or standard, or (2) as an approach to achieve broadly defined . . . goals and objectives."

20 Ben-Joseph. *The Code of the City*.

21 We have previously used the case of the Commerzbank tower in Frankfurt, designed by Sir Norman Foster & Partners, to make the same point. The two cases are strikingly similar. See, Moore, Steven A., and Barbara B. Wilson. 2009. "Contested Construction of Green Building Codes in North America: The Case of the Alley Flat Initiative." In, *Urban Studies* 46 (12):2617–2642.

22 Fortmeyer, Russell. 2008. "Architecture, Engineering, and the Germans." In, *Architectural Record* 196 (January):44–49. See also: Tsui, S.C., and W.K. Chow. 2003. "Possibility of applying a

performance-based approach for designing means of escape in a public transport interchange." In, *Architectural Science* 46 (3):279–290.

23 Brown, Bay. 2004. "Enlightened Behavior." In, *Architecture* 93 (February):58–63.

24 International Code Council. 2001. *ICC Performance Code for Buildings and Facilities*. Falls Church, VA: International Code Council, Inc. The ICC Performance Code,

> clearly defines the objectives for achieving the intended levels of occupant safety, property protection and community welfare. It provides a framework to achieve the defined objectives in terms of tolerable levels of damage and magnitude of design events, such as fire and natural hazards. . . . This code is distinctly different from the prescriptive code, which directs the user to a single solution to address a safety concern for a building or facility. The performance code allows the user to systematically achieve various solutions.
>
> (p. iii)

However, it allows exiting prescriptive codes "as an acceptable method," (p. 85).

25 For a general assessment of how performance-based codes reward creativity, see: Qualtrough, S. 2006. "Cracking the Performance Code: Where the Most Successful Firms Squeeze to Gain an Extra Competitive Edge." In, *Office Products International* (158):52–56.

26 Otto, Greg. 2010. Project engineer with BuroHappold, New York. Email communication, October 10 .

27 Dewey, J. 1887. *Psychology*, Vol. 2 (p. 39). Carbondale: Southern Illinois University Press.

28 Dewey also argues that, "the meaning of words is not fully transportable, but relies on the context in which they are used." Dewey questions, then, the application of any universal code. See, Dewey, J. 1991. "General Theory of Propositions." In, *John Dewey: The Later Works*, Vol. 12. Edited by J.A. Boydston (pp. 283–309). Carbondale, IL: Southern Illinois University Press. With regard to "context-rich knowledge," see also, Moore and Karvonen. "Sustainable Architecture in Context."

29 A paraphrase of Dewey by Larry Hickman. In, Hickman, L.A. 2001. *Philosophical Tools for a Technological Culture: Putting Pragmatism to Work*. Bloomington, IN: Indiana University Press.

30 Behnisch, Stefan. 2010. *An Interview With the Architect of Genzyme's Headquarters Building, Genzyme Center, in Cambridge, Massachusetts*. Available at: http://link.brightcove.com/services/player/bcpid23629764001?bctid=23632903001 (accessed July 12, 2011).

31 Hickman. *Philosophical Tools for a Technological Culture*, p. 77.

32 Foliente, Greg C. 2000. "Developments in Performance-Based Building Codes and Standards." In, *Forest Products Journal* 50 (7/8):12–21. Foliente more specifically holds that a

> prescriptive solution would "imply" a certain level of performance, but this is not explicitly or quantitatively stated. Thus it would take a tremendous amount of work to demonstrate that another solution . . . would equal this unspecified performance level. In contrast, a performance-based code would have a clear and quantified description of required performance.

That "tremendous amount of work" by engineers is very expensive.

33 Dewey, John. 1991[1927]. *The Public and its Problems* (p. 207). New York: H. Holt [reprinted: Athens, OH: Swallow Press, Ohio University Press]. The Swallow Press, which was then in Denver, also reprinted the original essay in 1954. See also: Fischer. *Citizens, Experts, and the Environment*, and: Fischer, F. 2009. *Democracy and Expertise: Reorienting Public Inquiry*. New York: Oxford University Press.

34 See: Allen and Feldman. "Editorial." For an extended case study that examines this claim, see also: Allen, B.L. 2003. *Uneasy Alchemy: Citizens and Experts in Louisiana's Chemical Corridor Disputes*. Cambridge, MA: MIT Press.

35 Gross, J. 2008. "Community Benefits Agreements: Definitions, Values, and Legal Enforceability." In, *Journal of Affordable Housing* 17 (1–2):36–51.

Notes

Introduction

1 Flyvbjerg, Bent. 2006. "Five Misunderstandings About Case-Study Research." In, *Qualitative Inquiry* (12):219–245.

2 Strauss, A. and Corbin, J. 1987. *Basics of Qualitative Research*. Newbury Park, CA: Sage.

3 See: Spradley, James P. 1980. *Participant Observation*. New York: Harcourt Brace Javanovich; Schön. *Educating the Reflective Practitioner*, Kemmis, Stephen, and Robin McTaggart. 2005. "Participatory Action Research." In, *The Handbook of Qualitative Research*. Edited by N.K. Denzin and Y.S. Lincoln. London: Sage Publications; and Jamison. "Climate Change Knowledge and Social Movement Theory."

4 Simon, Herbert. 1969. *The Sciences of the Artificial* (pp. 55–56). Cambridge, MA: MIT Press.

Chapter 8

1 Cowan. "The Consumption Junction," p. 262.

2 In general, see the works of John C. Turner and Henri Tajfel.

3 Yin, Robert K. 2003. *Case Study Research: Design and Methods*. 3rd ed. (pp. 150–151). Thousand Oaks, CA: Sage Publications.

4 See: Sismondo. *An Introduction to Science and Technology Studies*; Cowan. "The Consumption Junction," pp. 260–271.

5 Snow, David A., E. Burke Rochford, Steven K. Worden, and Robert D. Benford. 1986. "Frame Alignment Processes, Micromobilization, and Movement Participation." In, *American Sociological Review* 51 (4):464–481.

6 The term "code-switcher" appears to derive from Peter Berger's *Invitation to Sociology* (1963). However, rather than the term "code-switcher," Berger describes the process of "alternation" or "the ability to switch between different frames of reference." Cited in: Collins and Yearley. "Epistemological Chicken," p. 310.

7 Goffman. *Frame Analysis*; Pinch, T.J., and Bijker, W.E. 1985. "The Social Construction of Facts and Artifacts: Or how the Sociology of Science and the Science of Sociology of Technology Might Benefit Each Other." In, *The Social Construction of Technological Systems*. Cambridge, MA: MIT Press.

8 In general, mortgage lenders and real-estate appraisers do not yet include energy efficiency as a value to the homeowner.

9 For a historical review of the *Precautionary Principle* in relation to sustainable development, see: Kibert, Charles J., Martha C. Monroe, Anna L. Peterson, Richard R. Plate, and Leslie Paul Thiele. 2012. *Working Toward Sustainability: Ethical Decision Making in a Technological World*. New York: Wiley.

10 This is what Haraway has referred to as "situated knowledge." See, Haraway, Donna. 1995. "Situated Knowledge: The Science Question in Feminism and the Privilege of Partial Perspective." In, *Technology and the Politics of Knowledge*. Edited by A. Freenberg and A. Hannay. Bloomington, IN: Indiana University Press.

11 Moore and Engstrom. "The Social Construction of 'Green' Building Codes." In this study, we found that catastrophic natural (e.g., hurricanes) and cultural events (e.g., riots) tend to catalyze action related to long suppressed or ignored focal issues.

12 Moore and Karvonen. "Sustainable Architecture in Context."

13 See: Long, Joshua. 2010. *Weird City: Sense of Place and Creative Resistance in Austin, Texas*. Austin, TX: University of Texas Press; Orum, Anthony. 1987. *Power, Money and the People: The Making of Modern Austin*. Austin: Texas Monthly Press; and Swearingen, William Scott. 2010. *Environmental City: People, Place, Politics, and the Meaning of Modern Austin*. Austin, TX: University of Texas Press.

14 Snow et al. "Frame Alignment Processes, Micromobilization, and Movement Participation," p. 464.

15 Moore and Engstrom. "The Social Construction of 'Green' Building Codes," pp. 51–70.

16 Snow et al. "Frame Alignment Processes, Micromobilization, and Movement Participation," p. 473.

17 Jamison, Andrew. 2001. *The Making of Green Knowledge: Environmental Politics and Cultural Transformation*. Cambridge, UK, and New York: Cambridge University Press.

18 Tarrow, S. 1998. *Power in Movement: Social Movements and Contentious Politics*. Cambridge, UK: Cambridge University Press.
19 Simon. *The Sciences of the Artificial*.
20 Klandermans, B. 1997. *The Social Psychology of Protest* (p. 44). Oxford, UK: Basil Blackwell.
21 Tilly. *Social Movements, 1768–2004*.
22 Bijker, Wiebe E. 1993. "Do Not Despair: There Is Life After Constructivism." In, *Science, Technology & Human Values* 18 (1):113–138.

Chapter 9

1 Roberts, E.V. 1983. "When Others Speak for You, You Lose." In, *Disability Rights and Independent Living Archive* January.
2 Baynton, D.C. 2001. "Disability and the Justification of Inequality in American History." In, *The New Disability History*. Edited by P.K. Longmore and L. Umansky (pp. 33–57). New York: New York University.
3 Braddock, D. and S.L. Parish. 2001. "An Institutional History of Disability." In, *The Handbook of Disability Studies*. Edited by Gary L. Albrecht, Katherine D. Seelman, and Michael Bury (p. 11). Thousand Oaks, CA: Sage.
4 Young, I.M. 1990. *Justice and the Politics of Difference*. Princeton, NJ: Princeton University Press.
5 Skull, A. 1984. *Decarceration: Community Treatment and the Deviant—A Radical View*. 2nd ed. (p. 39). Rutgers, NJ: Rutgers University Press.
6 Scott. *Seeing Like a State*, p. 11.
7 Imrie, Rob 1996. *Disability and the City: International Perspectives* (p. 11). New York: St. Martin's Press.
8 Zames Fleischer, D., and Frieda Zames. 2001. *The Disability Rights Movement*. Philadelphia, PA: Temple University Press.
9 Groce, Nora Ellen. 1992. *The U.S. Role in International Disability Activities: A History and a Look Towards the Future: A Study Commissioned by the World Institute on Disability, the World Rehabilitation Fund and Rehabilitation International*. New York: Rehabilitation International.
10 Gallagher, Hugh Gregory. 1985. *FDR's Splendid Deception*. New York: Dodd, Mead, and Co.
11 Zames Fleischer and Zames. *The Disability Rights Movement*, p. 7.
12 Ibid., p. 36.
13 Ibid., p. 33.
14 McAdams, Doug. 1999. *Political Process and the Development of Black Insurgency, 1930–1970* (p. 184). Chicago, IL: University of Chicago Press.
15 Goldman, Peter. 1970. *Report from Black America* (p. 77). Cambridge, MA: Schenkman Publishing.
16 *Introduction to the World Institute on Disability Proposal Summary*. Bancroft Archives.1983.
17 Oda, J. 1995. "Highlights from Speeches by Ed Roberts." Edward V. Roberts Papers, BANC MSS 99/34 cz, carton 11, folder 30 (p. 3). The Bancroft Library, University of California, Berkeley.
18 Ibid., p. 4.
19 Roberts, E.V. 1980. *The Emergence of the Disabled Civil Rights Movement*. Berkeley, CA: Disability Rights and Independent Living Movement Archive. May 19.
20 Ibid.
21 Oda. "Highlights from Speeches by Ed Roberts," p. 6.
22 Zames Fleischer and Zames. *The Disability Rights Movement*, p. 39.
23 Pelka, F. 1997. *The ABC-CLIO Companion to The Disability Rights Movement* (p. 62). Santa Barbara, CA: ABC-CLIO.
24 Ibid., p. 12.
25 Zames Fleischer and Zames. *The Disability Rights Movement*, p. 83.
26 Davis, Lennard. 2002. *Bending over Backwards: Disability, Dismodernism, and Other Difficult Positions* (p. 50). New York: NYU Press.
27 National Institute of Building Sciences. 2010. *Whole Building Design Guide; History of Accessible Building Design*. Available at: www.wbdg.org/design/accessible_history.php (accessed September 5, 2011). For more on the history of the ANSI, see Chapter 4.

28 Longmore, P.K., and L. Umansky. 2001. "Disability History: From the Margins to the Mainstream." In, *The New Disability History*. Edited by P.K. Longmore and L. Umansky (pp. 1–29). New York: New York University.

29 Cannon, D. 1989. "Design for All Persons: The Architectural Barriers Act and Public Transit." In, *Journal of Rehabilitation* 55 (2):10–12.

30 Shapiro, J.P. 1994. *No Pity* (p. 65). New York: Three Rivers Press.

31 Roberts, S.V. 1978. "The Handicapped Are Emerging As a Vocal Political Action Group." In, *New York Times* June 19.

32 Scotch, Richard K. 2001. *From Good Will to Civil Rights: Transforming Federal Disability Policy*. Philadelphia, PA: Temple University Press.

33 Pelka. *The ABC-CLIO Companion to The Disability Rights Movement*, p. 10.

34 Shapiro. *No Pity*, p. 66.

35 Ibid., p. 68.

36 Zames Fleischer and Zames. *The Disability Rights Movement*, p. 78.

37 Scotch. *From Good Will to Civil Rights*.

38 Pelka. *The ABC-CLIO Companion to The Disability Rights Movement*, p. 279.

39 Kaplan, D. 1998. "Attorney, National Policy Advocate, and Spokesperson for Disability Rights Organizations, 1976–1990s." In, *Disability Rights and Independent Living Movement Oral History Series*. Edited by S. Bonney. Berkeley, CA: Regional Oral History Office, The Bancroft Library.

40 Imrie. *Disability and the City*, p. 63.

41 Pelka. *The ABC-CLIO Companion to The Disability Rights Movement*, p. 20.

42 Breslin, M.L. 1996–1998. "Selections From Cofounder and Director of the Disability Rights Education and Defense Fund, Movement Strategist." In, *Disability Rights and Independent Living Movement Oral History Series*. Edited by S. O'Hara. Berkeley, CA: Regional Oral History Office, The Bancroft Library.

43 Eyerman, Ron, and Andrew Jamison. 1991. *Social Movements: A Cognitive Approach*. University Park: Pennsylvania State University. Eyerman and Jamison built on the concept of collective action to develop the term cognitive praxis, which is meant to denote the important role social movements play in the production of new forms of societal knowledge through their collective appropriation of civic space.

44 Hughes, Thomas P. 2004. *Human-Built World: How to Think About Technology and Culture*. Chicago, IL: University of Chicago Press.

45 Chan, S. 2005. "Disabled Criticize Taxi Access." In, *New York Times*; Marshall, C. 2008. "Near the Golden Gate, Seeking Broader Access to Parks." In, *New York Times* March 18; Neuman, W. 2008. "$1 Billion Later, New York's Subway Elevators Still Fail." In, *New York Times* May 19.

46 Ibid.

47 Feenberg, Andrew. 1995. "Subversive Rationalization: Technology, Power, and Democracy." In, *Technology and the Politics of Knowledge*. Edited by Andrew Feenberg and Alistair Hannay, Bloomington, IN: Indiana University Press, pp. 3–22.

48 McDaniel and Lanham. "Sustainable Development."

49 Pear, R. 2008. "Plan Seeks More Access for Disabled." In, *New York Times* June 16.

50 Congress for New Urbanism website, *History*. Available at: www.cnu.org/history (accessed November 27, 2011).

51 *New Urban News*. 2009. "Common ground found for urbanism and the disabled." March 1.

52 Roberts, E.V. 1983. "When Others Speak for You, You Lose."

53 Haraway. "Situated Knowledges," pp. 175–191.

Chapter 10

1 Monsho, Anoa. 2004. "From East Austin to East End: Gentrification in Motion." In, *Good Life Magazine: A Monthly Journal of Austin Stories* November.

2 Allen, Bertram Leon. 1989. *Blacks in Austin* (p. 7). Published by the Author.

3 Connell, Earl Monroe. 1925. *The Mexican Population of Austin, Texas* (p. 2). Thesis. Austin, TX: University of Texas at Austin.

4 Orum. *Power, Money and the People*, p. 175.

5 "CLARKSVILLE, TX." Available at: www.tshaonline.org/handbook/online/articles/hpc01 (accessed April 9, 2013).

6 Monsho. "From East Austin to East End."

7 Ibid.

8 U.S. Environmental Protection Agency. 1992. Available at: http://nepis.epa.gov/Exe/ZyNET.exe/P1002PDG.TXT?ZyActionD=ZyDocument&Client=EPA&Index=2000+Thru+2005&Docs=&Query=&Time=&EndTime=&SearchMethod=1&TocRestrict=n&Toc=&TocEntry=&QField=&QFieldYear=&QFieldMonth=&QFieldDay=&IntQFieldOp=0&ExtQFieldOp=0&XmlQuery=&File=D%3A%5Czyfiles%5CIndex%20Data%5C00thru05%5CTxt%5C00000017%5CP1002PDG.txt&User=ANONYMOUS&Password=anonymous&SortMethod=h%7C&MaximumDocuments=1&FuzzyDegree=0&ImageQuality=r75g8/r75g8/x150y150g16/i425&Display=p%7Cf&DefSeekPage=x&SearchBack=ZyActionL&Back=ZyActionS&BackDesc=Results%20page&MaximumPages=1&ZyEntry=1&SeekPage=x&ZyPURL (accessed November 29, 2011). For a review of environmental racism, see Agyeman, Julian, Robert D. Bullard, and Bob Evans. 2003. *Just Sustainabilities: Development in an Unequal World*. Cambridge, MA: MIT Press.

9 PODER. 2010. People Organized in the Defense of Earth and her Resources 2010. Available at: www.poder-texas.org/ (accessed November 27, 2011).

10 Sierra Club Sprawl Report. 2000. Available at: www.sierraclub.org/sprawl/50statesurvey/ (accessed March 29, 2013).

11 Swearingen. *Environmental City*, p. 91.

12 Ibid. This cultural geography of Austin's "struggle to save its soul" provides a detailed account of the "Keep Austin Weird" campaign.

13 City of Austin, Watershed Protection Department, Barton Creek Watershed. Available at: www.austintexas.gov/page/watershed-protection-ordinance (accessed April 9, 2013).

14 Monsho, "From East Austin to East End."

15 Kennedy, Maureen, and Paul Leonard. 2001. *Dealing with Neighborhood Change: A Primer on Gentrification and Policy Choices* (p. 5). April.

16 Mueller, Elizabeth. 2008. *The Alley Flat Initiative: Financial Model Overview*. Unpublished graduate student report conducted under faculty supervision, the University of Texas School of Architecture, Community and Regional Planning Program. Authors' file.

17 See: Swearingen, *Environmental City*, for a demonstration of how environmentalists in west Austin interpreted the situation.

18 Gentrification Committee. 2001. *Gentrification Committee Report*. Austin, TX: Planning Commission and Community Development Commission. See also: Staff Task Force, Joe Canales Chair. 2003. *Staff Task Force on Gentrification in East Austin*. Austin, TX: City of Austin.

19 Lees, Loretta, Tom Slater, and Elvin Wyly, eds. 2010. *The Gentrification Reader*. London: Routledge.

20 This claim is consistent with Haraway's claim that "situated knowledge" is more objective than abstract, or scientific, knowledge. See, Haraway. "Situated Knowledge."

21 Swearingen. *Environmental City*, pp. 104–116.

22 Moore. *Alternative Routes to the Sustainable City*. In this text, Austin is one of three in-depth case studies of cities that aspire to develop sustainably. That history need not be retold here.

23 In this 1987 history of Austin, Orum documents the political confrontation between the development community and an emergent environmental community that has dominated political life in the city since the 1950s. Orum, *Power, Money and the People*. At the date of Orum's book, however, some of the most defining moments of Austin's environmental movement had not yet unfolded. More recently, Swearingen has written a history of environmentalism in the city in which the "growth machine" of developers is similarly pitted against environmentalists concerned with "quality of life." Strangely, however, Swearingen's detailed history includes a single reference (in a footnote) to the relationship of environmental action and race relations, discussed in Chapter 9.

24 Moore. *Alternative Routes to the Sustainable City*, Chapter 2.

25 For example, in 2010, PODER was strongly advocating for the closure and relocation of the Pure Castings Company, "a polluter of heavy metals" located less than a block from an elementary school, and its replacement with affordable housing. See: PODER. People Organized in the Defense of Earth and her Resources 2010.

26 Livable City. 2010. *Livablecity: Quality of Life for all Austin* 2010. Available at: www.liveablecity.org/; Hill Country Conservancy. 2010. *Hill Country Conservancy: Here Forever.* Available at: www.hillcountryconservancy.org/ (accessed August 15, 2010).

27 Imbroscio, David L. 1997. *Reconstructing City Politics: Alternative Economic Development and Urban Regimes*. Thousand Oaks, CA: Sage Publications; Lauria. *Reconstructing Urban Regime Theory*.

28 Younger, Margalit, Heather R. Morrow-Almeida, Stephen M. Vindigni, and Andrew L. Dannenberg. 2008. "The Built Environment, Climate Change, and Health Opportunities for Co-Benefits." In, *Journal of Preventative Medicine* 35 (5):517–526.

29 Production housing builders such as KB Homes, for example, have planned "water sense" communities and have also introduced a "net-zero energy" home at an affordable cost. Combined with other more predictable examples of "frame expansion" by niche home builders, the trend is significant. Personal communication with Roger Arriaga, V.P. for Governmental Affairs, K Homes, Austin, Texas; September 28, 2011.

30 Pecan Street Project. 2010. *Pecan Street Project Report* (p. 8). PSP is a collaboration of the University of Texas, the Environmental Defense Fund, the Greater Austin Chamber of Commerce, Austin Energy, and the City of Austin. The Environmental Defense Fund subsequently recruited 11 corporate partners that continue to "re-imagine Austin's energy distribution system in a way that can support and accelerate the installation and management of smarter and cleaner electricity services." In short, these visionary academics, public policymakers, industry engineers, and business boosters had the intellectual capacity to imagine a system of distributed infrastructure and "smart controls" that would allow Austinites to take control of how much, and when, they consume energy and water. In the process of reducing their own energy bills, PSP progenitors argued, citizens would reduce GHG emissions, along with unwanted effects such as childhood asthma and degraded water quality. They would also avoid the very costly alternative of building new coal-powered generating capacity. Add to this the imaginative proposal to make Austin the home of the nation's first hybrid plug-in automobile fleet, which would draw electricity at night—when it is very cheap—and thus contribute further to balancing Austin Energy's peak demand cycles, and you have, in their eyes, a blueprint for sustainable urban development. Their vision, together with the public investment opportunity, is a very exciting one indeed.

31 See also Toohey, Marty. 2009. "Will Clean Power Hurt Poor?" In, *Austin American Statesman* B1–B4.

32 AFHC. 2010. *S.M.A.R.T. Housing*™. City of Austin 2010. Available at: www.austintexas.gov//sites/default/files/files/Housing/Application_Center/RHDA/FY_12-13/rhda_fy1213_guidelines_attachments.pdf (accessed June 18, 2010). See also: AHFC. 2004. *S.M.A.R.T. Housing™ as a Tool to Reduce Regulatory Barriers for Housing, as a Component of Smart Growth September 2004*. Austin, TX: Austin Housing Finance Corporation.

33 One of the authors is a founder of the UTCSD, and the other is its current director.

34 As a community-based, not-for-profit affordable housing developer, GNDC had been developing "alley flats" for decades before the academics associated with the UTCSD came along and gave them that name.

35 One of the authors is a co-founder of ACDDC, and the other has served as chair of the Board of Directors since its founding in 2005.

36 City of Austin, Demographics. Available at: www.austintexas.gov/. Accessed 15 July 2011.

37 Alley flats are, of course, hardly a new idea. In other cities, they are called "back houses," "dependencies," "secondary apartments," "mother-in-law apartments," laneway houses," or, more formally, "secondary dwelling units." See: Moore, Steven A., and Sergio Palleroni. 2008. "The Alley Flat Initiative: An Alternative Route to the Sustainable City." In, *Working Paper Series*. Edited by Elizabeth Mueller. Austin: The University of Texas Center for Sustainable Development.

38 This number includes only lots in neighborhoods that have accepted a specific overlay ordinance that allows secondary dwelling units. Were all neighborhoods included, the number of units possible would approximately double.

39 Moore and Palleroni, "Alley Flat Initiative."

40 Ibid., pp. 86–138.

Chapter 11

1 Brain. "Practical Knowledge and Occupational Control," p. 260.

2 Fischer, Jan, and Simon Guy. 2009. "Re-interpreting Regulations: Architects as Intermediaries for Low-carbon Buildings." In, *Urban Studies* 46 (12):2577–2594.

3 Imrie and Street. *Architectural Design and Regulations.*

4 Fischer and Guy. "Re-interpreting Regulations," pp. 2590–2591.

5 Talen. *City Rules.*

6 The literature on third-party certification has become very broad and linked to that on the topic of consumption. For a popular manifesto on the topic, see: Conroy. *Branded!* For an accessible, yet theoretical, source, see: Thorpe. *Architecture and Design versus Consumerism.* For a scholarly example, see: Micheletti, M., and D. Stolle. 2007. "Mobilizing Consumers to Take Responsibility for Global Social Justice." In, *The ANNALS of the American Academy of Political and Social Science* 611 (1):157–175.

7 David Hess has previously proposed a civil society approach to sustainable development. See: Hess. *Alternative Pathways in Science and Industry.*

8 See also: Cashore, Benjamine, Graeme Auld, and Deanna Newsom. 2004. *Governing Through Markets: Forest Certification and the Emergence of Non-state Authority.* New Haven, CT: Yale University Press.

9 Gram-Hanssen, Kirsten. 2010. "Standby Consumption in Households Analyzed With a Practice Theory Approach." *Journal of Industrial Ecology* 14 (1):150–165.

10 An early third-party certification program is "Green Seal." See: GreenSeal. 2012. *The Original Green Seal of Approval Since 1989.* Available at: www.greenseal.org/ (accessed December 12, 2012).

11 Conroy. *Branded!*, p. 15.

12 Ibid., p. 87.

13 Busch. *Standards*, p. 292.

14 Shove, Elizabeth. 2004. *Comfort, Cleanliness and Convenience: The Social Organization of Normality.* Oxford, UK and New York: Berg Publishers.

15 According to Salecl, although "liberal democratic capitalism glorifies the idea of choice . . . what is on offer is primarily a consumerist model of choosing," but that, "the choice of a new form of social organization, of different ways in which society might develop in the future" is not on offer (p. 154). See: Salecl, Renata. 2010. *Choice.* London: Profile Books. Available at: http://UTXA.eblib.com/patron/FullRecord.aspx?p=708923

16 Hilton, Matthew. 2007. "Consumers and the State Since the Second World War." In, *The ANNALS of the American Academy of Political and Social Science* 611 (1):66–81.

17 Micheletti and Stolle. "Mobilizing Consumers to Take Responsibility for Global Social Justice."

18 Szasz, Andrew. 2007. *Shopping Our Way to Safety: How We Changed from Protecting the Environment to Protecting Ourselves.* Minneapolis, MN: University of Minnesota Press.

19 Seyfang, Gill. 2009. "The New Economics of Sustainable Consumption: Seeds of Change." In, *The New Economics of Sustainable Consumption.* Edited by D. Elliott. New York: Palgrave Macmillan.

20 Sociologist Juliet Schor has studied the early 20th-century critique of American consumer culture through the eyes of Thorsten Veblen, the Frankfurt School, and John Kenneth Galbraith. Although she grants that the recent scholarship cited above (Busch, Seyfang, Szasz, Hilton, et al.) has rightly characterized these early critiques of American consumerism as "totalizing," biased against middle-class norms, and lacking empirical backing, she also holds that the recent literature on "sustainable consumption" might build upon that set of earlier observations in productive ways. The certification movement might indeed contribute to making consumption more sustainable by employing some of the insights developed in our analysis of sumptuary codes in

Chapter 6. See: Schor, Juliet B. 2007. In, "Defense of Consumer Critique: Revisiting the Consumption Debates of the Twentieth Century." In, *The ANNALS of the American Academy of Political and Social Science* (611):16–30.

21 U.S. Green Building Council. 2012b. *An Introduction to LEED.* Available at: www.usgbc.org/DisplayPage.aspx?CategoryID=19 (accessed January 10, 2012).

22 The significance of this point is that USGBC has established a social process to catalyze and administer environmental change through construction. The buildings themselves have agency only to the degree that they are coupled to those social systems. See: Harvey, David. 2000. *Spaces of Hope.* Berkeley, CA: University of California Press.

23 For example, see: Moore, Steven A., and Elizabeth Walsh. 2012; in press. "The Problem of Judging Architecture." In, *Beyond LEED: Regenerative Design, A Symposium.* Edited by S.A. Moore. Austin, TX: The University of Texas Center for Sustainable Design. Available at: http://soa.utexas.edu/beyondleed/index.html

24 The term "regenerative design" was originally coined by John Tillman Lyle. See: Lyle, John Tillman. 1994. *Regenerative Design for Sustainable Development.* New York: Wiley. For a discussion of the social side of regenerative design, see also: Moore. *Technology and Place.*

25 Faulconbridge, James. 2012. "Mobile 'Green' Design Knowledge: Institutions, Bricolage and the Rational Production of Embedded Sustainable Building Designs." In, *Transactions of the Institute of British Geographers.* London: Royal Geographic Society (with the Institute of British Geographers).

26 Svec et al. "REGEN," pp. 81, 83, 91.

27 Nye, Michael, and Tom Hargreaves. 2010. "Exploring the Social Dynamics of Proenvironmental Behavior Change." *Journal of Industrial Ecology* 14 (1):146.

28 Heiskanen, Eva, and Raimo Lovio. 2010. "User–Producer Interaction in Housing Energy Innovations." In, *Journal of Industrial Ecology* 14 (1) (January 1):91–102.

29 ICLEIUSA. 2010. *STAR Community Index.* ICLEI Local Governments for Sustainability USA 2010. Available at: www.icleiusa.org/sustainability/star-community-index

30 SEED. 2012. *The SEED Network.* Design Corps. Available at: www.seed-network.org/ (accessed July 1, 2012).

31 This claim is made on the basis of personal conversation with Bryan Bell, the progenitor of SEED; June 10, 2012.

32 Tukker, Arnold, Maurie J. Cohen, Klaus Hubacek, and Oksana Mont. 2010. "The Impacts of Household Consumption and Options for Change." In, *Journal of Industrial Ecology* 14 (1) (January 1):21.

33 From the literature of sustainable consumption, Holt argues similarly that, "the only option, structurally speaking, is to develop a set of tastes in opposition to materialism: consuming that emphasizes the metaphysical over the material—idealism—is prestigious currency in the cultural sphere." See: Holt, Douglas B. 1998. "Does Cultural Capital Structure American Consumption?" In, *Journal of Consumer Research* 25 (1) (June):1–25. For another sympathetic proposal, see also: Sassatelli, Roberta, and Federica Davolio. 2010. "Consumption, Pleasure and Politics. Slow Food and the Politico-aesthetic Problematization of Food." In, *Journal of Consumer Culture* 10 (2):202–232.

34 For example, see: Braham, William, and Daniel Willis. 2012. *Architecture and Energy: Questions about Performance and Style.* Greater Philadelphia Innovation Cluster (GPIC) 2012. Accessed January 10 2012. See also: Hosey, Lance. 2010. "The G-List: Is the Rift Between Design Excellence and Environmental Performance Getting Wider?" *Architect* July 27. In preparation for this article, Hosey conducted an informal survey of 52 well-known figures in the field of "green building." He asked each to nominate the best green building of the past 10 years, so that he might compare the list of nominees to a similar list of "best buildings" published by *Vanity Fair* magazine, using a similar technique of interviewing well-known figures in the field of high design. He concluded that the lists diverged to a significant degree and that, "Someday, maybe standards of 'good design' and 'green design' will match, but we're not there yet. Not by a long shot."

35 The Sustainable Consumption Research and Action Initiative, or SCORAI, is a major source of this discourse. See: www.scorai.org/

36 The AIA, the primary organization that represents professional architects in and to the public realm, has taken many actions and formed subgroups supportive of sustainable design. The organization has, however, been most active in protecting its membership from the threats of designing environments using unorthodox technologies. Such protections are afforded by revisions to standard contracts that shift risks for claims of reduced energy use or increased social equity away from architects to third-party certification groups. As we argued in Chapter 3, technologies cannot change without change to the social agreements that enable their use. For example, see: Blott, Nicole. 2011. *News Release: American Institute of Architects Announces Guide for Sustainability Projects*. Washington, DC: AIA.

Glossary

1 Cowan. "The Consumption Junction."

References

"A Thirteenth-Century Castilian Sumptuary Law." 1963. In, *Business History Review* 37 (1/2):98–100.

Abbott, Andrew. 1981. "Status and Status Strain in the Professions." In, *American Journal of Sociology* 86:819–835.

Achterhuis, Hans. 2001[1999]. *American Philosophy of Technology*. Edited by Don Ihde. The Indiana Series in the Philosophy of Technology. Bloomington and Indianapolis, IN: Indiana University Press.

Adam, Robert. 2009. "Chelsea Changed Everything." In, *Building Magazine* July 10:27. Available at: www.building.co.uk/comment/chelsea-changed-everything/3144511.article (accessed April 9, 2013).

—— 2012. "Good urbanism and the 'starchitects'." In, *Congress for New Urbanism 2009*. Available at: www.cnu.org/cnu-salons/2009/07/good-urbanism-and-starchitects (accessed May 5, 2012).

Adorno, Theodor W. 1983. *Aesthetic Theory*. Edited by Gretel Adorno and Rolf Tiedemann; translated by Christian Lenhardt. Boston, MA: Routledge and Kegan Paul.

Adshead, Julie, ed. 2011. *Green Buildings and the Law*. CIB, the International Council for Research and Innovation in Buildings and Construction. London: Spon Press.

AHFC. 2004. *S.M.A.R.T. Housing™ as a Tool to Reduce Regulatory Barriers for Housing, as a Component of Smart Growth*. September. Austin, TX: Austin Housing Finance Corporation.

AFHC. 2010. *S.M.A.R.T. Housing™*. City of Austin 2010. Available at: www.austintexas.gov// sites/default/files/files/Housing/Application_Center/RHDA/FY_12-13/rhda_fy1213_guidelines_attachments.pdf (accessed April 8, 2013).

Agyeman, Julian, Robert D. Bullard, and Bob Evans. 2003. *Just Sustainabilities: Development in an Unequal World*. Cambridge, MA: MIT Press.

Aibar, E., and Bijker, W. 1997. "Constructing a City: The Cerda Plan for the extension of Barcelona." In, *Science, Technology, & Human Values* 22 (1):3–30.

AISC. 2011. *Our Mission: Making Structural Steel the Material of Choice*. American Institute of Steel Construction 1921. Available at: www.aisc.org/contactUs.aspx?ekfrm=248&id=4974 (accessed August 12, 2011).

Alexander, C., S. Ishikawa, and M. Silverstein. 1977. *A Pattern Language: Towns, Buildings, Construction*. New York: Oxford University Press.

Al-Kodmany, Kheir. 2000. "Public Participation: Technology and Democracy." In, *Journal of Architectural Education* 53 (4):220–228.

Allen, Barbara. 2003. *Uneasy Alchemy: Citizens and Experts in Louisiana's Chemical Corridor Disputes*. Cambridge, MA: MIT Press.

—— 2006. "Interview with Gene Cizek." In, *Journal of Architectural Education* 60 (1):26–29.

—— 2007. "Cities, Poverty, and the Environment Review [Planet of Slums AND 10th Venice Architecture Biennale: Cities, Architecture and Society AND Power, Justice, and the Environment: A Critical Appraisal of the Environmental Movement AND Sustainable Communities and the Challenge of Environmental Justice]." In, *Journal of Architectural Education* 60 (4):67–71.

Allen, Barbara L. 1997. "Introduction." In, *Journal of Architectural Education (1984–)* 51 (1):3–4.

Allen, Barbara L., and Roberta M. Feldman. 2000. "Editorial: Beyond Expert Culture." In, *Journal of Architectural Education* 53 (3):128–129.

Allen, Bertram Leon. 1989. *Blacks in Austin*. Published by the Author.

AlSayyad, Nezar. 1992. "Housing, Culture, and Environment: A Review of Two Conferences. 'Housing Environments: A Cross-Cultural Perspective.' University of California, San Diego, May 1991. 'Design for Desert Living.' University of Arizona, Tucson, July 1991." In, *Journal of Architectural Education (1984–)* 46 (1):63–64.

—— 2006. "Foreword." In, *Vernacular Architecture in the Twenty-First Century*. Edited by Lindsay and Marcel Vellinga Asquith (p. xvii). London: Taylor & Francis.

American Heritage Dictionary of the English Language. 1981. Edited by William Morris. Boston, MA: Houghton Mifflin Company.

Ames, Mark. 2010. "Energy Bills & 90.1 Targets." In, *ASHRAE Journal* August:71.

Anderson, Alex T. 2002. "On the Human Figure in Architectural Representation." In, *Journal of Architectural Education* 55 (4):238–246.

Anderton, Frances. 1989. "Learning From Jaipur." In, *Journal of Architectural Education (1984–)* 42 (4):15–24.

ANSI. *American National Standards Institute*. Available at: www.ansi.org/membership/overview/overview.aspx?menuid=2 (accessed August 13, 2011).

Anthony, Kathryn H. 2002. "Designing for Diversity: Implications for Architectural Education in the Twenty-First Century." In, *Journal of Architectural Education* 55 (4):257–267.

Architecture for Humanity. 2006. *Design Like you Give a Damn: Architectural Response to Humanitarian Crisis*. New York: Metropolis Books.

Ashraf, Kazi K. 2009. "Review [Louis I. Kahn: The Making of a Room]." In, *Journal of Architectural Education* 63 (1):141–142.

Asquith, Lindsay, and Marcel Vellinga. 2006. *Vernacular Architecture in the Twenty-First Century*. London: Taylor & Francis.

Atkin, Tony, and Carol Herselle Krinsky. 1996. "Cultural Identity in Modern Native American Architecture: A Case Study." In, *Journal of Architectural Education (1984–)* 49 (4):237–245.

Awan, Nishat, Tatjana Schneider, and Jeremy Till. 2011. *Spatial Agency: Other Ways of Doing Architecture*. London: Routledge.

Baird, David. 1999. "The Mobile Studio Project." In, *Journal of Architectural Education (1984–)* 5 (1):44–45.

Balmer, Jeffrey. 2008. "Review [Cinematic Urbanism: A History of the Modern from Reel to Real—Edited by Nezar Alsayyad]." In, *Journal of Architectural Education* 61 (4):136–137.

Baldwin, F.E. 1926. *Sumptuary Legislation and Personal Regulation in England*. Baltimore, MD: Johns Hopkins Press.

Barber, Jeffrey. 2007. "Mapping the Movement to Achieve Sustainable Production and Consumption in North America." In, *Journal of Cleaner Production* 15 (6):499–512.

Barrie, Thomas. 2007. "Book Review [Built upon Love: Architectural Longing after Ethics and Aesthetics—Edited by Alberto Pérez-Gómez]." In, *Journal of Architectural Education* 60 (3):51–52.

Bartky, I.R. 1989. "The Adoption of Standard Time." In, *Technology and Culture* 30 (1):25–56.

Barton, Greg. 2006. "The Trailerization of New Orleans." In, *Journal of Architectural Education* 60 (1):17.

Baynton, D.C. 2001. "Disability and the Justification of Inequality in American History." In, *The New Disability History*. Edited by P.K. Longmore and L. Umansky (pp. 33–57). New York: New York University.

Beaudoin, Thierry, Sinsha Brdar, Nicolas Marier, Patrick Morand, and Marc Pape. 2006. "Playtime." In, *Journal of Architectural Education* 59 (4):26–30.

Beck, U. (1992). *Risk Society: Towards a New Modernity*. Thousand Oaks, CA: Sage.

Beebe, Barton. 2010. "Intellectual Property Law and the Sumptuary Code." In, *Harvard Law Review* no. 123 (4):809–889.

Behnisch, Stefan. (2010). "An Interview With the Architect of Genzyme's Headquarters Building, Genzyme Center, in Cambridge, Massachusetts." Available at: http://link.brightcove.com/services/player/bcpid23629764001?bctid=23632903001 (accessed February 12, 2011).

Bell, Bryan, ed. 2004. *Good Deeds, Good Design: Community Service Through Architecture*. New York: Princeton Architectural Press.

—— 2012. "MoMA Misses by 99%." In, *Metropolis Point of View. Metropolis Magazine*. Thursday, February 16. Available at: www.metropolismag.com/pov/20120216/moma-misses-by-99 (accessed July 29, 2012).

Bell, David H. 1987. "Reflection." In, *Journal of Architectural Education (1984–)* 41 (1):2–3.

Bell, Jeffrey A. 2011. "Undoing the Subject: Deleuze and the Makings of a Sustainable Life." In, *New Directions in Sustainable Design*. Edited by A. Parr and M. Zaretsky. New York: Routledge.

Bell, Matthew J., and Cheryl A. O'Neill. 1994. "A Public Library for Evanston, Illinois." In, *Journal of Architectural Education (1984–)* 47 (3):129–134.

Bell Jr., Robert R. 2006. "Citizen Architect: An Educator's Response to Crisis." In, *Journal of Architectural Education* 60 (1):22–23.

Benedikt, Michael. 2009. "On the Role of Architectural Criticism Today." In, *Journal of Architectural Education* 62 (3):6–7.

Ben-Joseph, Eran. 2005. *The Code of the City: Standards and the Hidden Language of Place Making*. Edited by Robert Gottlieb, Urban and Industrial Environments. Cambridge, MA and London: MIT Press.

Bentivegna, V., S. Curwell, M. Deakin, P. Lombardi, G. Mitchell, and P. Nijkamp. 2002. "A Vision and Methodology for Integrated Sustainable Urban Development." In, *Building Research & Information* 30 (2):83–94.

Bergdoll, Barry, and Reinhold Martin, eds. 2011. *Foreclosed: Rehousing the American Dream*. New York: Museum of Modern Art. Available at: www.moma.org/interactives/exhibitions/2012/foreclosed/ (accessed July 28, 2012).

Berlin, Isaiah. 2006. *Political Ideas in the Romantic Age: Their Rise and Influence on Modern Thought, With an Introduction by Joshua L. Cherniss*. Edited by Henry Hardy. Princeton, NJ: Princeton University Press.

Bernard, Catherine E. 1993. "Housing International Conference. Cairo, Egypt, February 23–27, 1992." In, *Journal of Architectural Education (1984–)* 46 (3):189–190.

Bernstein, Gerald S. 1985. "The Architecture of Repression: The Built Environment of George Orwell's 1984." In, *Journal of Architectural Education (1984–)*38 (2):26–28.

Berry, Wendell. 1978. *The Unsettling of America*. New York: Avon.

Bijker, Wiebe E. 1987. "The Social Construction of Bakelite: Toward a Theory of Invention." In, *The Social Construction of Technological Systems: New Directions in the Sociology and History of Technology*. Edited by Wiebe Bijker, Thomas Hughes, and Trevor Pinch. Cambridge, MA: MIT Press.

Bijker, Wiebe E. 1993. "Do Not Despair: There Is Life After Constructivism." In, *Science, Technology & Human Values* 18 (1):113–138.

Bijker, Wiebe E. 1995. *Of Bicycles, Bakelites, and Bulbs: Toward a Theory of Sociotechnical Change*. Cambridge, MA: MIT Press.

Bijker, Wiebe E., and Karin Bijsterveld. 2000. "Women Walking through Plans: Technology, Democracy, and Gender Identity." In, *Technology and Culture* 41 (3):485–515.

Blakely, Edward J. 2006. "A Cry for a City: What Is Happening to New Orleans." In, *Journal of Architectural Education* 60 (1):9–12.

Blondel, J.-F. 1771. *Cours d'architecture civile*. Vol.2. Cited by Pevsner.

Bloch, Robin, and Melinda Silverman. 1989. "Response to Owen, 'Architecture and Apartheid'." In, *Journal of Architectural Education (1984–)* no. 42 (3):24–25.

Blott, Nicole. 2011. "News Release: American Institute of Architects Announces Guide for Sustainability Projects." Washington, DC: AIA.

Bluestone, Daniel. 1994. "Preservation and Renewal in Post-World War II Chicago." In, *Journal of Architectural Education (1984–)* 47 (4):210–223.

Bonnemaison, Sarah, Ronit Eisenbach, and Robert Gon. 2006. "Introduction." In, *Journal of Architectural Education* 59 (4):3–11.

Borden, Gail Peter. 2007. "Propositions for Suburban Living." In, *Journal of Architectural Education* 61(1):76–83.

Borys, Ann Marie. 2004. "Lume di Lume: A Theory of Light and Its Effects." In, *Journal of Architectural Education* 57 (4):3–9.

Bourdieu, Pierre. 1984[1979]. *Distinction: A Social Critique of the Judgment of Taste*. Cambridge, MA: Harvard University Press.

Bourdieu, Pierre. 1993. *The Field of Cultural Production*. New York: Columbia University Press.

Boyer, Ernest L., and Lee D. Mitgang. A Special Report. 1996. *Building Community: A New Future for Architecture Education and Practice.* Ewing, NJ: California Princeton Fulfillment Services.

Bozdoğan, Sibel. 1999. "Architectural History in Professional Education: Reflections on Postcolonial Challenges to the Modern Survey." In, *Journal of Architectural Education (1984–)* 52 (4):207–215.

Braddock, D., and S.L.Parish. 2001. "An Institutional History of Disability." In, *The Handbook of Disability Studies.* Edited by Gary L. Albrecht, Katherine D. Seelman, and Michael Bury (p. 11). Thousand Oaks, CA: Sage.

Braham, William, and Daniel Willis. 2012. *Architecture and Energy: Questions about Performance and Style.* Greater Philadelphia Innovation Cluster (GPIC).

Brain, David. 1991. "Practical Knowledge and Occupational Control: The Professionalization of Architecture in the United States." In, *Sociological Forum* 6(2).

Brandes, Uwe Steven. 2004. "Review: *Good Deeds, Good Design: Community Service through Architecture* and *Consensus Design: Socially Inclusive Process.*" In, *Journal of Architectural Education* no. 58 (2):57–61.

BRE Global, BREEAM. 2012. Available at: www.breeam.org (accessed April 20, 2012).

Breslin, M.L. 1996–1998. "Selections From Cofounder and Director of the Disability Rights Education and Defense Fund, Movement Strategist." In, *Disability Rights and Independent Living Movement Oral History Series.* Edited by S. O'Hara. Berkeley, CA: Regional Oral History Office, The Bancroft Library.

Britton, Karla. 2009. "Review: *God, Creativity, and Evolution: The Argument from Design(ers)*, by Michael Benedikt, and *God Is the Good We Do: Theology of Theopraxy*, Edited by Michael Benedikt." In, *Journal of Architectural Education* no. 62 (4):135–137.

Brown, Bay. 2004. "Enlightened Behavior." In, *Architecture* 93 (February):58–63.

Brown, Patricia Leigh. 2012. "In Hippie Holdout, a Fight over Worms and Moats." In, *New York Times*, Monday, April 23, pp. A9–A11.

Brownell, Blaine. 2008. "Assembling Light." In, *Journal of Architectural Education* 62 (2):30–36.

Brownsword, Roger, and Karen Yeung, eds. 2008. *Regulating Technologies: Legal Futures, Regulatory Frames, and Technological Fixes* (p. 4). Oxford, UK and Portland, OR: Hart Publishing.

Bruun, Henrik, and Janne Hukkinen. 2003. "Crossing Boundaries: An Integrative Framework for Studying Technology Change." In, *Social Studies of Science* 33 (1):95–116.

Burgess, Peter G. 1984. "Review: *The Image of the Architect.*" In, *Journal of Architectural Education (1984–)* no. 38 (1):30–30.

Burns, Carol J. 2001. "A Manufactured Housing Studio: Home/On the Highway." In, *Journal of Architectural Education* 55 (1):51–57.

Busch, Lawrence. 2011. *Standards: Recipes for Reality.* Edited by Geoffrey Bowker and Paul N. Edwards. Cambridge, MA: MIT Press.

Callon, Michel, and Bruno Latour. 1992. "Don't Throw the Baby Out With the Bath School! A Reply to Collins and Yearley." In, *Science as Practice and Culture.* Edited by Andrew Pickering (pp. 343–366). Chicago, IL: University of Chicago,.

Canizaro, Vincent. 2001. "Review: *The Land That Could Be: Environmentalism and Democracy in the Twenty-First Century.*" In, *Journal of Architectural Education* no. 54 (3):198–201.

—— 2007. *Architectural Regionalism: Collected Writings on Place, Identity, Modernity, and Tradition.* New York: Princeton Architectural Press.

—— and Kim Tanzer. 2008. "The JAE Sustainability Issue." In, *Journal of Architectural Education* 62 (1):67.

Cannon, D. 1989. "Design for All Persons: The Architectural Barriers Act and Public Transit." In, *Journal of Rehabilitation* 55 (2):10–12.

Carmona, Matthew. 2003. "English Design Policies: How Have They Fared?" In, *Environment and Planning B: Planning and Design* 30 (6):911–931.

—— 2009. "Design Coding and the Creative, Market and Regulatory Tyrannies of Practice." In, *Urban Studies* 46 (12):2643–2667.

—— Stephen Marshall, and Quentin Stevens. 2006. *Design Codes: Their Use and Potential.* Oxford, UK: Elsevier.

References

Cavanagh, Ted. 1997. "Balloon Houses: The Original Aspects of Conventional Wood-Frame Construction Re-Examined." In, *Journal of Architectural Education (1984–)* 51 (1):5–15.

Cascadia Region Building Council. 2008, 2009. *Code and Regulatory Barriers to the Living Building Challenge for Sustainable, Affordable, Residential Development (SARD).* Vancouver, WA: International Living Future Institute. Available at: https://ilbi.org/education/reports/codestudy3 (accessed October 5, 2010).

Cashore, Benjamine, Graeme Auld, and Deanna Newsom. 2004. *Governing Through Markets: Forest Certification and the Emergence of Non-state Authority.* New Haven, CT: Yale University Press.

Castells, Manuel. 1977. *The Urban Question: A Marxist Approach.* Translated by Alan Sheridan. London: Edward Arnold.

—— 1983. *The City and the Grassroots: A Cross-cultural Theory of Urban Social Movements.* Berkeley, CA: University of California Press.

Celik, Zeynep, and Diane Favro. 1988. "Methods of Urban History." In, *Journal of Architectural Education (1984–)* 41 (3):4–9.

Chan, S. 2005. "Disabled Criticize Taxi Access." In, *New York Times,* April 21. Available at: www.nytimes.com (accessed February 20, 2009)

Chandler, Alfred E. Jr. 1978. "Book Review." In, *Technology and Culture* 19 (3):569–572.

Chase, John. 1991. "The Role of Consumerism in American Architecture." In, *Journal of Architectural Education (1984–)* 44 (4):211–224.

Chi, Lily. 1999. "Wind Gate." In, *Journal of Architectural Education (1984–)* 53 (1):42–43.

City of Austin. Demographics. Available at: www.austintexas.gov/ (accessed July 15, 2011).

City of Austin. Watershed Protection Department, Barton Creek Watershed. Available at: www.austintexas.gov/page/watershed-protection-ordinance (accessed April 9, 2013).

Clarke, David W. 1996. "Review: *The Gas Station in America* by John A. Jakle and Keith A. Sculle and *Grain Elevators* by Lisa Mahar-Keplinger." In, *Journal of Architectural Education (1984–)* 50 (1):74–75.

"Clarksville, TX." Available at: www.tshaonline.org/handbook/online/articles/hpc01 (accessed April 9, 2013).

Coaldrake, William H. 1981. "Edo Architecture and Tokugawa Law." In, *Monumenta Nipponica* (Sophia University) 36 (3):235–284.

—— 1988. "The Gatehouse of the Shogun's Senior Councillor: Building Design and Status Symbolism in Japanese Architecture of the Late Edo Period." In, *The Journal of the Society of Architectural Historians* 47 (4):397–410.

Cochrane, Rexmond Canning. 1976. *Measures for Progress: A History of the National Bureau of Standards, America in Two Centuries, an Inventory.* New York: Arno Press.

Cochrane, Willard. 1978. *The Development of American Agriculture: A Historical Analysis.* Minneapolis, MN: University of Minnesota Press.

Cole, Raymond. 2005. "Building Environmental Assessment Methods: Redefining Intentions and Roles." In, *Building Research & Information* 35 (5): 462.

—— 2006. "Shared Markets: Coexisting Building Environmental Assessment Methods." In, *Building Research & Information* 34 (4):357–371.

Collins, H.M., and Steven Yearley. 1992. "Epistemological Chicken." In, *Science as Practice and Culture.* Edited by Andrew Pickering (pp. 301–326). Chicago, IL: University of Chicago Press.

Community of Carpentras. In, *The Jewish Quarterly Review* 18 (4):357–383.

Congress for New Urbanism Website. *History.* Available at: www.cnu.org/history (accessed November 27, 2011).

Connell, Earl Monroe. 1925. *The Mexican Population of Austin, Texas.* Thesis. University of Texas at Austin.

Conrads, U. 1990. *Programs and Manifestoes on 20th-century Architecture.* Cambridge, MA: MIT Press.

Conroy, Michael E. 2007. *Branded! How the "Certification Revolution" is Transforming Global Corporations.* Gabriola Island, BC: New Society Publishers.

Corser, Robert, and Nils Gore. 2009. "Insurgent Architecture: An Alternative Approach to Design-Build." In, *Journal of Architectural Education* 62 (4):32–39.

Council for Scientific and Industrial Research. 2012. SBAT Tool. Available at: www.csir.co.za/Built_environment/Architectural_sciences/sbat.html (accessed April 20, 2012).

Cowan, Ruth Schwartz. 1985. "How the Refrigerator Got its Hum." In, *The Social Shaping of Technology*. Edited by Donald MacKenzie and Judy Wajcman. Philadelphia, PA: Open University Press.

—— 1989. "The Consumption Junction: A Proposal for Research Strategies in the Sociology of Technology." In, *The Social Construction of Technological Systems*. Cambridge, MA: MIT Press.

Cox, Noel. 2006. "Tudor Sumptuary Laws and Academical Dress: An Act Against Wearing of Costly Apparel 1509 and an Act for Reformation of Excess in Apparel 1533." In, *Transactions of the Burgon Society* 6:15–43.

Crawford, Margaret. 1995. "Contesting the Public Realm: Struggles over Public Space in Los Angeles." In, *Journal of Architectural Education (1984–)* 49 (1):4–9.

Crosbie, Michael J. 2010. "Review: *The Judicious Eye: Architecture Against the Other Arts*." In, *Journal of Architectural Education* no. 63 (2):177–178.

Crouch, D.P., and J.G. Johnson. 2001. *Traditions in Architecture*. New York: Oxford University.

Crowe, Norman A., and Steven W. Hurtt. 1986. "Visual Notes and the Acquisition of Architectural Knowledge." In, *Journal of Architectural Education (1984–)* 39 (3):6–16.

Cuff, Dana. 2003. "Immanent Domain: Pervasive Computing and the Public Realm." In, *Journal of Architectural Education* 57 (1):43–49.

da Costa Meyer, Esther. 2002. "After the Flood: Lino Bo Bardi's Glass House." In, *Harvard Design Magazine* Winter/Spring:1–12.

Dauster, Molly Ann Rosser. 1996[1928]. "Roman Sumptuary Legislation." In, *History*. Lubbock, TX: Texas Tech University.

Davidson, Chandler. 1990. *Race and Class in Texas Politics*. Princeton, NJ: Princeton University Press.

Davidson, Elizabeth J. 2002. "Technology Frames and Framing: A Socio-cognitive Investigation of Requirements Determination." In, *MIS Quarterly* 26 (4):329–358.

Davis, Howard. 2006. *The Culture of Building*. New York: Oxford University Press.

Davis, Lennard. 2002. *Bending Over Backwards: Disability, Dismodernism, and Other Difficult Positions*. New York: NYU Press.

Deamer, Peggy. 1999. "Introduction." In, *Journal of Architectural Education (1984–)* 53 (1):35.

Dean, Edward. 1984. "The New Foreign Import: Manufactured Housing Systems." In, *Journal of Architectural Education (1984–)* 37 (3/4):12–19.

Dewey, J. 1887. *Psychology* . Vol. 2. Carbondale, IL: Southern Illinois University.

—— 1991[1927]. *The Public and its Problems*. New York: H. Holt [reprinted: Athens, OH: Swallow Press, Ohio University Press].

—— 1980[1934]. *Art as Experience*. New York: Perigree, Penguin.

—— 1991. "General Theory of Propositions." In, *John Dewey: The Later Works*. Vol. 12. Edited by J.A. Boydston (pp. 283–309). Carbondale, IL: Southern Illinois University Press.

Diamandis, Peter H., and Steven Kotler. 2012. *Abundance: The Future is Better than You Think*. New York: Free Press.

Diamond, Jared. 2005. *Collapse: How Societies Choose to Fail or Succeed*. New York: Penguin.

Dikeç, M. 2001. "Justice and the Spatial Imagination." In, *Environment and Planning A* 3.

Dimendberg, Edward. 2005. "Review: *Zoomscape: Architecture in Motion and Media*." In, *Journal of Architectural Education* no. 58 (4):63–71.

Dodds, George. 2007. "Editorial." In, *Journal of Architectural Education* 61 (2):3.

Donoian, John, Dennis Doordan, and Sarah Smith. 1986. "'A Magnificent Adventure': An Interview with Mrs. Sarah (Melvyn) Maxwell Smith about the Smith House by Frank Lloyd Wright." In, *Journal of Architectural Education (1984–)* 39 (4):7–10.

Doucet, Isabelle, and Kenny Cupers. 2009. "Agency in Architecture: Reframing Criticality in Theory and Practice." In, *Footprint: Delft School of Design Journal*:1–6.

Dovey, Kim. 2000. "Myth and Media: Constructing Aboriginal Architecture." In, *Journal of Architectural Education* 54 (1):2–6.

Downing, Andrew Jackson. 1968[1850]. *The Architecture of Country Houses*. Reprint ed. New York: Da Capo Press. Original edition. 1861. New York: D. Appleton.

Duany, Andrés. 1993. "Coding America." In, *ANY* 1 (1):14–19.

—— 2004. "Notes Towards a Reason to Code." In, *Perspecta; The MIT Press on behalf of Perspecta* 35 (Building Codes).

—— and David Brain. 2005. "Regulating as if Humans Matter: The Transect and Post-Suburban Planning." In, *Regulating Place: Standards and the Shaping of Urban America*. Edited by E. Ben-Joseph and T.S. Szold. New York: Routledge.

Dunay, Robert, Joseph Wheeler, and Robert Schubert. 2006. "No Compromise." In, *Journal of Architectural Education* (2):8–17.

Dunham-Jones, Ellen, and June Williamson. 2009. *Retrofitting Suburbia: Urban Design Solutions for Redesigning Suburbs*. New York: John Wiley and Sons.

Durand, L.-N.-L. 1802–1809. *Précis des leçons d'architecture données a l'Ecole Polytechnique*. Cited by Pevsner.

Dutton, Thomas. 2000. "Review: *The Anaesthetics of Architecture*." In, *Journal of Architectural Education* no. 53(4):239–249.

The Economist. 2012. "Over-regulated America: The Home of Laissez-Faire is Being Suffocated by Excessive and Badly Written Regulation." In, *The Economist* February 19, 2012.

Eggener, Keith L. 2002. "Placing Resistance: A Critique of Critical Regionalism." In, *Journal of Architectural Education* 55 (4):228–237.

Eisenman, Peter. 2000. "Autonomy and the Will to be Critical." In, *Dialogue: Architecture + Design + Culture* (042).

Ellin, Nan. 2000. "Participatory Architecture on the Parisian Periphery: Lucien Kroll's Vignes Blanches." In, *Journal of Architectural Education* 53 (3):178–183.

Elliott, Cecil D. 1992. *Technics in Architecture: The Development of Materials and Systems for Buildings*. Cambridge, MA: MIT Press.

Erdman, Jori. 2006. "Studio South." In, *Journal of Architectural Education* 59 (4):19–25.

Eyerman, Ron, and Andrew Jamison. 1991. *Social Movements: A Cognitive Approach*. University Park, PA: Pennsylvania State University.

Fainstein, S., and C. Hirst (1995). "Urban Social Movements." In, *Theories of Urban Politics*. Edited by David Judge, Gerry Stoker, and Harold Wolman. London: Sage.

Farr, Douglas. 2008. *Sustainable Urbanism: Urban Design with Nature*. New York: Wiley.

Faulconbridge, James. 2012. "Mobile 'Green' Design Knowledge: Institutions, Bricolage and the Rational Production of Embedded Sustainable Building Designs." In, *Transactions of the Institute of British Geographers*. London: Royal Geographic Society (with the Institute of British Geographers).

Fazio, Michael. 1991. "Review: Interpreting Southern Antebellum Architecture in the 1990s—Reviewed work(s): *Architecture of the Old South: Virginia*, by Mills Lane; *Architecture of the Old South: South Carolina*, by Mills Lane; *Architecture of the Old South: North Carolina*, by Mills Lane; *Architecture of the Old South: Georgia*, by Mills Lane; *Architecture of the Old South: Mississippi/Alabama*, by Mills Lane." In, *Journal of Architectural Education (1984–)* 44 (4):225–234.

Feenberg, Andrew. 1991. *Critical Theory of Technology*. New York: Oxford University Press.

—— 1995. "Subversive Rationalization: Technology, Power, and Democracy." In, *Technology and the Politics of Knowledge*. Edited by Andrew Feenberg and Alistair Hannay. Bloomington, IN: Indiana University Press.

—— 2003. "Pragmatism and Critical Theory of Technology." In, *Techne* 7 (1):42–49.

—— 2010. "Incommensurable Paradigms: Values and the Environment." In *Pragmatic Sustainability: Theoretical and Practical Tools*. Edited by Steven A. Moore (pp. 276–288). London: Routledge.

Ferraz, Marcello Carvalho. 2010. *Interview with Kristine Stiphany*, August 10. São Paulo, Brazil.

Fischer, Frank. 2000. *Citizens, Experts, and the Environment: The Politics of Local Knowledge*. Durham, NC and London: Duke University Press.

—— 2009. *Democracy and Expertise: Reorienting Public Inquiry*. New York: Oxford University Press.

Fischer, Jan, and Simon Guy. 2009. "Re-interpreting Regulations: Architects as Intermediaries for Low-Carbon Buildings." In, *Urban Studies* 46 (12):2577–2594.

Fischer, Louis Albert. 1925. *History of the Standard Weights and Measures of the United States.* Washington, DC: U.S. Bureau of Standards Miscellaneous Publications, Government Printing Office.

Fischler, Raphael. 1998. "Health, Safety, and the General Welfare: Markets, Politics, and Social Science in Early Land-Use Regulation and Community Design." In, *Journal of Urban History* 24 (6):676.

Flyvbjerg, Bent. 2006. "Five Misunderstandings About Case-Study Research." In, *Qualitative Inquiry* (12):219–245.

Foliente, Greg C. 2000. "Developments in Performance-Based Building Codes and Standards." In, *Forest Products Journal* 50 (7/8):12–21.

Fortmeyer, Russell. 2008. "Architecture, Engineering, and the Germans." In, *Architectural Record* 196 (January):44–49.

Foucault, Michel. 1977[1975]. *Discipline and Punish: The Birth of the Prison.* New York: Pantheon.

Fouche, Rayvon. 2002. "Review: *Sites of Memory.*" In, *Journal of Architectural Education* no. 56 (1):57–57.

Frampton, Kenneth. 1983. "Toward a Critical Regionalism: Six Points for an Architecture of Resistance". In, *The Anti-Aesthetic: Essays on Postmodern Culture.* Edited by Hal Foster. Seattle, WA: Bay Press.

—— 1991. "Reflection on the Autonomy of Architecture: A Critique of Contemporary Production." In, *Out of Site: A Social Criticism of Architecture.* Edited by Diane Ghirardo (pp. 17–26). Seattle, WA: Bay Press.

—— and Steven A. Moore. 2001. "Technology and Place." In, *Journal of Architectural Education* 54 (3):121–122.

Francis, Mark. 1983. "Community Design." In, *Journal of Architectural Education* 37 (1):14–19.

Franck, Karen A., and Lynda H. Schneekloth. 1996. "Review: *Ordering Space: Types in Architecture and Design.*" In, *Journal of Architectural Education (1984–)* 50 (2):128–130.

Freire, Paulo. 1970. *Cultural Action for Freedom.* Cambridge, MA: Harvard Educational Review.

Freudenberger, Herman. 1963. "Fashion, Sumptuary Laws, and Business." In, *The Business History Review* 37 (1/2):37–48.

Friedman, D.S. 1995. "Public Things in the Modern City: Belated Notes on 'Tilted Arc' and the Vietnam Veterans Memorial." In, *Journal of Architectural Education (1984–)* 49 (2):62–78.

Fuglem, Terri, and Bruce Webb. 2005. "Introduction." In, *Journal of Architectural Education* 58 (4):3.

Gallagher, Hugh Gregory. 1985. *FDR's Splendid Deception.* New York: Dodd, Mead, and Co.

Gandara, Ricardo. 2010. "311 Calls up over Past Years." In, *American Statesman,* 26 November.

Gentrification Committee. 2001. *Gentrification Committee Report.* Austin, TX: Planning Commission and Community Development Commission.

German Sustainable Building Council. 2012. DGNB Certificate. Available at: www.dgnb.de/en/ (accessed April 20, 2012).

Giddens, Anthony. 1994. In, *Explorations in Planning Theory.* Edited by Seymour J. Mandelbaum, Luigi Mazza, and Robert W. Burchell (pp. 189–190). New Brunswick, NJ: Center for Urban Policy Research.

Gidieon, Sigfried. 1963[1941]. *Space, Time, and Architecture: The Growth of a New Tradition.* 4th ed. Cambridge, MA: Harvard University Press.

Gillem, Mark. 2005. "America Town: Planning the Outposts of Empire." In, *Journal of Architectural Education* 58 (3):5–12.

Ghirardo, Diane. 1989. "Editorial." In, *Journal of Architectural Education (1984–)* 43 (1):2.

Gino, Alex. 2003. "Changing Rooms." In, *Journal of Architectural Education* 56 (4):32–36.

Glassie, Henry. 1975. *Folk Housing in Middle Virginia: A Structural Analysis of Historic Artifacts.* Knoxville, TN: University of Tennessee Press.

—— 2000. *Vernacular Architecture.* Edited by George Jevremovic, William T. Sumner, and Henry Glassie. Philadelphia, PA: Material Culture; Bloomington: Indiana University Press.

Goffman, Erving. 1974. *Frame Analysis: An Essay on the Organization of Experience with a New Foreword by Bennet Berger.* Boston, MA: Northeastern University Press.

Goldberger, Paul. 2010. "Review." In, *The New Yorker* August 9.

Goldman, Alex. 2012. "Carl Malamud's Box of Goodies." In, *On the Media*. Available at: www.onthemedia.org/blogs/on-the-media/2012/apr/13/carl-malamuds-box-goodies/ (accessed April 16, 2012).

Goldman, Peter. 1970. *Report from Black America*. Cambridge, MA: Schenkman Publishing.

Gonchar, Joann. 2007. "Schools Make the Grade." In, *Architectural Record* 195 (7):129.

Goode, Terrence. 2002. "Review: *Louis Kahn's Situated Modernism*." In, *Journal of Architectural Education* no. 56 (2):56–56.

Goodrich, Peter. 1998. "Review: 'Signs Taken for Wonders: Community, Identity,' and 'A History of Sumptuary Law'." In, *Law & Social Inquiry* 23 (3):707–728.

Gourlier, Charles. 1825–1850. Choix d'édifices publique projetés et construits en France depuis le commencement du XIX siècle. Cited by Pevsner.

Gram-Hanssen, Kirsten. 2010. "Standby Consumption in Households Analyzed With a Practice Theory Approach." In, *Journal of Industrial Ecology* 14 (1):150–165.

Green Globes. 2012. *The Practical Building Rating System: The Green Globes System*. Available at: www.greenglobes.com (accessed December 12, 2012).

GreenSeal. 2012.*The Original Green Seal of Approval Since 1989*. Available at: www.greenseal.org/ (accessed December 12, 2012).

Groce, Nora Ellen. 1992. *The U.S. Role in International Disability Activities: A History and a Look Towards the Future: A Study Commissioned by the World Institute on Disability, the World Rehabilitation Fund and Rehabilitation International*. New York: Rehabilitation International.

Grignon, Marc, and Juliana Maxim. 1995. "Convenance, Caractère, and the Public Sphere." In, *Journal of Architectural Education (1984–)* 49 (1):30.

Groat, Linda N. 1992. "Rescuing Architecture from the Cul-de-Sac." In, *Journal of Architectural Education (1984–)* 45 (3):138–146.

Gropius, Walter. 1952. *Architecture and Design in the Age of Science*. New York: Spiral Press.

Gross, J. 2008. "Community Benefits Agreements: Definitions, Values, and Legal Enforceability." In, *Journal of Affordable Housing* 17 (1–2):36–51.

Guadet, Julien. 1902–1904. *Eléments et théorie de l'architecture*. Cited by Pevsner.

Guggenheim, Michael. 2010. "(Un-)Building Social Systems. The Concrete Foundations of Society." In, *Observando Systemas*. Edited by Ignacio Farias. Mexico: Universidad Iberoamericana.

—— and Ola Soderstrom, eds. 2010. *Re-shaping Cities: How Global Mobility Transforms Architectural and Urban Form*. Abingdon, UK, and New York: Routledge.

Gusevich, Miriam. 1986. "Meaning and Means in Urban Design: A Case Study in American Urbanism, South La Salle Street, Chicago." In, *Journal of Architectural Education (1984–)* 39 (3):24–30.

Guy, Simon, and Graham Farmer. 2001. "Reinterpreting Sustainable Architecture: The Place of Technology." *Journal of Architectural Education* 54 (3):140–148.

—— and Steven A. Moore. 2005. *Sustainable Architectures: Natures and Cultures in Europe and North America*. London: Routledge/Spon.

—— and —— 2007. "Sustainable Architecture and the Pluralist Imagination." In, *Journal of Architectural Education* 60 (4):15–23.

Habermas, Jürgen. 1991. *The Structural Transformation of the Public Sphere*. Translated by Thomas Burger. Cambridge, MA: MIT Press. Cited by Grignon and Maxim.

Habracken, Joseph W. 2005. *Palladio's Children: Essays on the Everyday Environment and the Architect*. Edited by Jonathan Teicher. London: Taylor & Francis.

Hacking, Ian. 2004. "Between Michel Foucault and Erving Goffman: Between Discourse in the Abstract and Face-to-Face Interaction." In, *Economy and Society* 33 (3):279.

Hadjisophocleous, G.V., N. Benichou, et al. (1998). "Literature Review of Performance-Based Fire Codes and Design Environment." In, *Journal of Fire Protection Engineering* 9 (1):12–40.

Hakim, Besim S. 1995. "Review: Redesigning the American Dream." In, *Journal of Architectural Education (1984–)* 49 (2):129–131.

Haraway, Donna 1995. "Situated Knowledge: The Science Question in Feminism and the Privilege of Partial Perspective." In, *Technology & the Politics of Knowledge*. Edited by Andrew Feenberg and Alistair Hannay. Bloomington, IN: Indiana University Press.

Hard, Mikael, and Andrew Jamison. 2005. *Hubris and Hybrids: A Cultural History of Technology and Science*. New York and London: Routledge.

Hartoonian, Gevork. 1989. "Mies van der Rohe: The Genealogy of Column and Wall." In, *Journal of Architectural Education (1984–)* 42 (2):43–50.

—— 1994. "Review: The Artless Word: Mies van der Rohe on the Building Art by Fritz Neumeyer." In, *Journal of Architectural Education (1984–)* 47 (3):180–181.

Harvey, David. 2000. *Spaces of Hope*. Berkeley, CA: University of California Press.

Hayden, Dolores. 1988. "Place Making, Preservation and Urban History." In, *Journal of Architectural Education (1984–)* 41 (3):45–51.

Hays, K. Michael. 1998. *Architecture Theory Since 1968*. Cambridge, MA: The MIT Press.

Hee, Limin. 2006. "Review: *Architourism: Authentic, Escapist, Exotic, Spectacular*, Edited by Joan Ockman and Salomon Frausto." In, *Journal of Architectural Education* no. 60 (1):71–72.

Heidegger, Martin. 1977[1935]. *The Question Concerning Technology and Other Essays*. Translated and with an introduction by William Lovitt. New York: Harper & Row.

—— 1977. "The Age of the World Picture." In, *The Question Concerning Technology and Other Essays*. Edited by W. Lovitt. New York: Harper and Rowe.

Heiskanen, Eva, and Raimo Lovio. 2010. "User–Producer Interaction in Housing Energy Innovations." In, *Journal of Industrial Ecology* 14 (1)(January 1):91–102.

Henderson, Kathryn. 2006. "Ethics, Culture, and Structure in the Negotiation of Straw Bale Building Codes." In, *Science, Technology and Human Values* 31 (3):261–288.

Henderson, Susan R. 2003. "Review: *The Gray Cloth*." *Journal of Architectural Education* no. 56 (4):69–75.

Hersh, Stuart. 2009. "Duh: Designing Affordable Housing." Unpublished MS. Austin, TX.

Hess, David J. 1997. *Science Studies: An Advanced Introduction*. New York: New York University Press.

—— 2001. "Selecting Technology, Science, and Medicine." In, *Alternative Pathways in Globalization*. Vol. V. 1. Edited by D.J. Hess. Niskayuna, NY: David J. Hess.

—— 2007. *Alternative Pathways in Science and Industry: Activism, Innovation, and the Environment in an Era of Globalization*. Cambridge, MA: MIT Press.

Hewitt, Mark A. 1984. "Books of Drawings, Books on Drawing, Books about Drawings Review: *Masterpieces of Architectural Drawing* and *Great Drawings from the Collection of the Royal Institute of British Architects* and *The Plan of St. Gall in Brief* and *Architecture of the Twentieth Century in Drawings* and *Architectural Drawing: The Art and the Process*." In, *Journal of Architectural Education (1984–)* no. 38 (1):29–30.

—— 1985. "Representational Forms and Modes of Conception: An Approach to the History of Architectural Drawing." In, *Journal of Architectural Education (1984–)* 39 (2):2–9.

Hickey, Dave. 1997. *Air Guitar: Essays on Art & Democracy*. New York: Art Issues Press; Distributed by Distributed Art Publishers.

Hickman, Larry A. 2001. *Philosophical Tools for a Technological Culture: Putting Pragmatism to Work*. Bloomington, IN: Indiana University Press.

Higgs, Eric, et al. 2000. *Technology and the Good Life*. Chicago, IL: University of Chicago Press.

Hill Country Conservancy. 2010. *Hill Country Conservancy: Here Forever, 2010*. Available at: www.hillcountryconservancy.org/ (accessed August 15, 2010).

Hilton, Matthew. 2007. "Consumers and the State since the Second World War." In, *The ANNALS of the American Academy of Political and Social Science* 611 (1):66–81.

Hinson, David. 2007. "Design as Research." In, *Journal of Architectural Education* 61 (1):23–26.

Hollander, S.C. 1984. "Sumptuary Legislation: Demarketing by Edict." In, *Journal of Macromarketing* 4 (1):4.

Holt, Douglas B. 1998. "Does Cultural Capital Structure American Consumption?" In, *Journal of Consumer Research* 25 (1)(June):1–25.

Holub, Robert C. 1984. *Reception Theory: A Critical Introduction*. London: Methuen.

Hommels, Anique. 2005. *Unbuilding Cities: Obduracy in Urban Sociotechnical Change*. Edited by W.E. Bijker, W. Bernard Carlson, and Trevor Pinch, Inside Technology Series. Cambridge, MA: MIT Press.

Hooper, Wilfrid. 1915. "The Tudor Sumptuary Laws." In, *The English Historical Review* 30 (119):437.

Horkheimer, Max, and Theodor Adorno. 1947[1944]. *Dialectic of Enlightenment*. Amsterdam: Querido. Original edition, *Dialektik der Aufklärung: philosophische Fragmente*.

Hosey, Lance. 2010. "The G-List: Is the Rift Between Design Excellence and Environmental Performance Getting Wider?" *Architect*, 27 July.

—— 2012. *The Shape of Green: Aesthetics, Ecology and Design*. Washington, DC: Island Press.

Hou, Jeffrey, and Michael Rios. 2003. "Community-Driven Place Making: The Social Practice of Participatory Design in the Making of Union Point Park." In, *Journal of Architectural Education* 57 (1):19–27.

Hubka, T. 1984. *Big House, Little House, Back House, Barn: The Connected Farm Buildings of New England*. Lebanon, NH. The University Press of New England.

Hughes, Thomas P. 1985. "Edison and Electric Light." In, *The Social Shaping of Technology*. Edited by Donald MacKenzie and Judy Wajcman. Philadelphia, PA: Open University Press.

—— 1995. "Technological Momentum." In, *Does Technology Drive History?* Edited by M.R. Smith and L. Marx. Cambridge, MA: MIT Press.

—— 2004. *Human-Built World: How to Think About Technology and Culture*. Chicago, IL: University of Chicago Press.

Hunt, Alan 1996. "The Governance of Consumption: Sumptuary Laws and Shifting Forms of Regulation." In, *Economy and Society* 25 (3):410–427.

—— 1998. *Governance of the Consuming Passions: A History of Sumptuary Law*. Chicago, IL: University of Chicago.

ICLEIUSA. STAR Community Index. ICLEI Local Governments for Sustainability USA 2010. Available at: www.icleiusa.org/sustainability/star-community-index (accessed May 25, 2013).

Ihde, Don. 1979. *Technics and Praxis*. Rotterdam, The Netherlands: Dordrecht.

Imbroscio, David L. 1997. *Reconstructing City Politics: Alternative Economic Development and Urban Regimes*. Thousand Oaks, CA: Sage Publications.

Imrie, Rob. 1996. *Disability and the City: International Perspectives*. New York: St. Martin's Press.

—— and Emma Street. 2009a. "Regulating Design: The Practices of Architecture, Governance and Control." In, *Urban Studies* 46 (12):2507–2518.

—— and —— 2009b. "Risk, Regulation and the Practices of Architects." In, *Urban Studies* 46 (12):2555–2576.

—— 2011. *Architectural Design and Regulations*. London: Wiley-Backwell.

Ingersoll, Richard. 1991. "Context and Modernity. Delft, June 12–15, 1990." In, *Journal of Architectural Education (1984–)* 44 (2):124–125.

—— 1996. "Second Nature: On the Social Bond of Ecology and Architecture." In, *Reconstructing Architecture: Critical Discourses and Social Practices*. Edited by Tom Dutton and Lian Hurst Mann. Minneapolis, MN: University of Minnesota Press.

International Code Council. (2001). *ICC Performance Code for Buildings and Facilities*. Falls Church, VA: International Code Council, Inc.

Ishikawa, Eisuke. 2000. *Japan in the Edo Period—An Ecologically-Conscious Society* [*O-edo ecology jijo*]. Kodansha Publishing Company.

Jackson, J.B. 1985. "Urban Circumstances." In, *Design Quarterly*:25–29.

Jackson, Tim, and Nic Marks. 1999. "Consumption, Sustainable Welfare and Human Needs—with Reference to UK Expenditure Patterns between 1954 and 1994." In, *Ecological Economics* 28 (3):421–441.

James, Kathleen. 1995. "Louis Kahn's Indian Institute of Management's Courtyard: Form versus Function." In, *Journal of Architectural Education (1984–)*49 (1):38–49.

James, William. 1907. *Pragmatism, a New Name for Some Old Ways Of Thinking: Popular Lectures on Philosophy*. New York: Longmans, Green, and Co.

Jamison, Andrew. 2001. *The Making of Green Knowledge: Environmental Politics and Cultural Transformation*. Cambridge, UK and New York: Cambridge University Press.

—— 2010. "Climate Change Knowledge and Social Movement Theory." In, *Wiley Interdisciplinary Reviews: Climate Change*. Aalborg University.

Jandl, H. Ward. 1991. *Yesterday's Houses of Tomorrow*. Washington, DC: The Preservation Press; National Trust for Historic Preservation.

Jann, Marga, and Stephen Platt. 2009. "Philanthropic Architecture: Nongovernmental Development Projects in Latin America." In, *Journal of Architectural Education* 62 (4):82–91.

Japan Sustainable Building Consortium. 2012. CASBEE. Available at: www.ibec.or.jp/CASBEE/english/

Jauss, Hans Robert. 1989. *Question and Answer: Forms of Dialogic Understanding*. Edited, translated, and with a foreword by Michael Hays. Minneapolis, MN: University of Minnesota Press.

Jenkins, Paul, and Leslie Forsyth. 2010. *Architecture, Participation and Society*. London: Routledge.

Johnson, Jim. 1988. "Mixing Humans and Nonhumans Together: The Sociology of a Door-Closer." In, *Social Problems, University of California Press on Behalf of the Society for the Study of Social Problems* 35 (3):298–310.

Joines-Novotny, Laura. 1996. "Czech Town Squares: Ten Spatial Patterns." In, *Journal of Architectural Education (1984–)* 50 (1):22–31.

Jones, Kay Bea. 1990. "Genus and Genius: An Architectural Morphology of Urban Genoa." In, *Journal of Architectural Education (1984–)* 43 (4):16–26.

Jones, Kay Bea. 1995. "Review: House Rules by Mark Robbins 'Assemblage' 24." In, *Journal of Architectural Education (1984–)* 49 (1):53–56.

Jordan, Coleman A. 2007. "Rhizomorphics of Race and Space." In, *Journal of Architectural Education* 60 (4):48–59.

Kaplan, Archie. 1991. "Review: *City: Rediscovering the Center*, by William H. Whyte." In, *Journal of Architectural Education (1984–)* 44 (4):241–242.

Kaplan, D. 1998. *Attorney, National Policy Advocate, and Spokesperson for Disability Rights Organizations, 1976–1990s*. Edited by S. Bonney. Disability Rights and Independent Living Movement Oral History Series. Berkeley, CA: Regional Oral History Office, The Bancroft Library.

Kasser, Tim, and Allen D. Kanner. 2003. "Psychology and Consumer Culture: The Struggle for a Good Life in a Materialistic World." In, *American Psychological Association (APA)*, 1st ed. (pp. 13–22).

Karvonen, Andrew. 2008. *Botanizing the Asphalt: Politics of Urban Drainage*. Doctoral dissertation. The University of Texas.

Kayden, Jerold S. 2004. "Understanding the 'Code' of Codes." In, *Perspecta: The Yale Architectural Journal* (35).

Kemmis, Stephen, and Robin McTaggart. 2005. "Participatory Action Research." In, *The Handbook of Qualitative Research*. Edited by N.K. Denzin and Y.S. Lincoln. London: Sage Publications.

Kennedy, Maureen, and Paul Leonard. 2001. "Dealing with Neighborhood Change: A Primer on Gentrification and Policy Choices." April. Brookings Institution Center on Urban and Metropolitan Policy.

Kibert, Charles J., Martha C. Monroe, Anna L. Peterson, Richard R. Plate, and Leslie Paul Thiele. 2012. *Working Toward Sustainability: Ethical Decision Making in a Technological World*. New York: Wiley.

Kingsley, Karen. 1988. "Gender Issues in Teaching Architectural History." In, *Journal of Architectural Education (1984–)* 41 (2):21–25.

Klandermans, B. 1997. *The Social Psychology of Protest*. Oxford, UK: Basil Blackwell.

Knack, Ruth, Stuart Meck, and Israel Stollman. 1996. "The Real Story Behind the Standard Planning and Zoning Acts of the 1920s." In, *Land Use Law* (February).

Koester, Robert J. 1988. "Review: *Architecture as Environmental Communication*." In, *Journal of Architectural Education (1984–)* no. 42 (1):54–55.

Kolarevic, Branko, and Ali M. Malkawi, eds. 2010[2005]. *Performative Architecture: Beyond Instrumentality*. New York and London: Spon Press.

Krislov, S. 1997. *How Nations Choose Product Standards and Standards Change Nations*. Pittsburgh, PA: University of Pittsburgh Press.

Kuypers, Jim A. 2009. *Rhetorical Criticism: Perspectives in Action*. Lanham, MD: Lexington Press.

Lang, Jon. 1980. "The Built Environment and Social Behavior: Architectural Determinism Reexamined." In, *Via* IV:146–153.

Lara, Fernando Luiz. 2009. "Modernism Made Vernacular: The Brazilian Case." In, *Journal of Architectural Education* 63 (1):41–50.

Larson, Megali Sarfatti. 1993. *Behind the Postmodern Facade: Architectural Change in the Late Twentieth-century*. Berkeley, CA: University of California Press.

Latour, Bruno. 1986. "Visualization and Cognition: Thinking With Eyes and Hands." In, *Knowledge and Society* 6:1–40.

—— 1987. *Science in Action*. Cambridge, MA: Harvard University Press.

—— 1993. *We Have Never Been Modern*. Translated by Catherine Porter. Cambridge, MA: Harvard University Press.

—— 2004. *Politics of Nature: How to Bring Science Into Democracy*. Translated by C. Porter. Cambridge, MA: Harvard University Press. Original edition, Politiques de la Nature, Editions de la Couverte.

Lauria, M. (1997). *Reconstructing Urban Regime Theory: Regulating Urban Politics in a Global Economy*. Thousand Oaks, CA: Sage.

Leatherbarrow, David. 2005[2010]. "Architecture's Unscripted Performance." In, *Performative Architecture: Beyond Instrumentality*. Edited by Branko Kolarevic and Ali M. Malkawi. New York and London: Spon Press.

Lees, Loretta, Tom Slater, and Elvin Wyly, eds. 2010. *The Gentrification Reader*. London: Routledge.

Lefebvre, Henri. 1991. *The Production of Space*. Translated by Donald Nicholson-Smith. Cambridge, MA: Blackwell Press; Oxford, UK: Basil Blackwell Publishers.

Legault, Réjean. 1991. "Architecture and Historical Representation." In, *Journal of Architectural Education (1984–)* 44 (4):200–205.

Levy, Janet E. 1979. "Evidence of Social Stratification in Bronze Age Denmark." In, *Journal of Field Archaeology* 6 (1):49–56.

Lewis, Diane. 1987. "Program: The Literary Counterpart of the Architectural Work." In, *Journal of Architectural Education (1984–)* 40 (2):45.

Lim, Regina Mapua. 2006. "Cultural Sustainability and Development: Drukpa and Burman Vernacular Architecture." In, *Designing Sustainable Cities in the Developing World*. Edited by Roger Zetter. Farnham, UK: Ashgate.

Lima, Zeuler R.M.A. 2005. "Preservation as Confrontation: The Work of Lina Bo Bardi." In, *Journal of Historic Preservation, History, Theory and Criticism* 2 (Jan.):24–33.

—— 2006. "The faces of Janus: Modernism and Hybridization in the Architecture of Lina Bo Bardi." In, *Journal of Architecture* 11 (2):257–264.

Livable City. 2010. *Livablecity: Quality of Life for all Austin*. Available at: www.liveablecity.org/ (accessed August 15, 2010).

Loh, Laurence. 2010. "Conserving for Change." In, *Journal of Architectural Education* 63 (2):71–73.

Long, Christopher. 2001. "An Alternative Path to Modernism: Carl König and Architectural Education at the Vienna Technische Hochschule, 1890–1913." In, *Journal of Architectural Education* 55 (1):21–30.

Long, David G. De. 1993. "Review: *The Wright Space: Pattern and Meaning in Frank Lloyd Wright's Houses*, by Grant Hildebrand." In, *Journal of Architectural Education (1984–)* 47 (2):116–117.

Long, Joshua. 2010. *Weird City: Sense of Place and Creative Resistance in Austin, Texas*. Austin, TX: University of Texas Press.

Longmore, P. K. and L. Umansky. 2001. "Disability History: From the Margins to the Mainstream." In, *The New Disability History*. Edited by P.K. Longmore and L. Umansky (pp. 1–29). New York: New York University.

Lutzkendorf, T., and D. Lorenz. (2006). "Using an Integrated Performance Approach in Building Assessment Tools." In, *Building Research & Information* 34(4):334–356.

Lyle, John Tillman. 1994. *Regenerative Design for Sustainable Development*. New York: Wiley.

Lynes, Russell. 1954[1949]. *The Tastemakers*. The Universal Library. New York: Grosset and Dunlap.

MacDonald, William L. 1988. "Roman Urbanism." In, *Journal of Architectural Education (1984–)* 41 (3):29–32.

MacKenzie, Donald, and Wajcman, Judy. 1999. *The Social Shaping of Technology*. 2nd ed. Philadelphia, PA: Open University Press.

Mallard, A. 1998. "Compare, Standardize and Settle Agreement." In, *Social Studies of Science* 28 (4):571.

Mann, Dennis Alan. 1985. "Between Traditionalism and Modernism: Approaches to a Vernacular Architecture." In, *Journal of Architectural Education (1984–)* 39 (2):10–16.

Marcuse, Harold. 1995. "Review: *Architecture and Auschwitz*." In, *Journal of Architectural Education (1984–)*49 (2):123–128.

Marshall, C. (2008). "Near the Golden Gate, Seeking Broader Access to Parks." In, *New York Times* March 18.

Marx, Karl. 1908. *Kapital.* 4th ed. London: W. Reeves.

—— 1978. "Division of Labour and Manufacture." in, *Capital.* Vol. 1. *The Marx–Engels Reader.* Edited by Robert C. Tucker. New York: Norton.

Marx, Leo. 2010. "Technology: The Emergence of a Hazardous Concept." In, *Technology and Culture* 51 (3):568.

Massey, Jonathan. 2004. "New Necessities: Modernist Aesthetic Discipline." In, *Perspecta* 35 (Building Codes):112–133.

Matthias, Stephen. 1988. "Courting the House." In, *Journal of Architectural Education (1984–)* 42 (1):48–53.

Mayntz, Renate, and Thomas P. Hughes, eds. 1988. *The Development of Large Technical Systems.* Frankfurt am Main and Boulder, CO: Campus Verlag and Westview Press.

Mayo, James M. 1990. "Review: *Icons and Aliens: Law, Aesthetics, and Environmental Change,* by John J. Costonis." In, *Journal of Architectural Education (1984–)* 43 (3):47–49.

McAdams, Doug. 1999. *Political Process and the Development of Black Insurgency, 1930–1970.* Chicago, IL: University of Chicago Press.

McBride, Jacquelin Spangler. 1984. "The Case Method in Architecture Education." In, *Journal of Architectural Education (1984–)* 37 (3/4):10–11.

McCleary, Peter. 1988. "Some Characteristics of a New Concept of Technology." In, *Journal of Architectural Education (1984–)* 42 (1):4–9.

McClung, William Alexander. 1988. "Dialectics of Literary Cities." In, *Journal of Architectural Education (1984–)* 41 (3):33–37.

McDaniel, Rueben R., and Holly Jordan Lanham. 2010. "Sustainable Development: Complexity and the Problem of Balance." In, *Pragmatic Sustainability: Theoretical and Practical Tools.* Edited by Steven A. Moore. London: Routledge.

McLaughlin, Thomas. 1996. *Street Smarts and Critical Theory: Listening to the Vernacular.* Madison, WI: The University of Wisconsin Press.

Mehalik, Matthew M., and Michael E. Gorman. 2006. "A Framework for Strategic Network Design Assessment, Decision Making, and Moral Imagination." In, *Science, Technology & Human Values* 31 (3):289–308.

Melosi, M. (2000). *The Sanitary City: Urban Infrastructure In America from Colonial Times to the Present.* Baltimore, MD: Johns Hopkins University Press.

Menand, Louis. 2001. *The Metaphysical Club.* New York: Farrar, Straus, Giroux.

Merwood Salisbury, Joanna. 2008. "Review: *Women in Modernism: Making Places in Architecture,* Edited by Beverly Willis, Gwendolyn Wright, Sarah Herda, Toshiko Mori, and Karen Stein." In, *Journal of Architectural Education* no. 61 (4):144–145.

Meyboom, A. 2009. "Infrastructure as Practice." In, *Journal of Architectural Education* 62:72–81.

Meyer, Hannes. 1990. "Building." In, *Programs and Manifestoes on 20th-Century Architecture.* Edited by Ulrich Conrads. Cambridge, MA: MIT Press.

Micheletti, M., and D. Stolle. 2007. "Mobilizing Consumers to Take Responsibility for Global Social Justice." In, *The ANNALS of the American Academy of Political and Social Science* 611 (1):157–175.

Misa, T.J., Philip Brey, and Andrew Feenberg. (2003). *Modernity and Technology.* Cambridge, MA: MIT Press.

Mitchell, Don. 2003. *The Right to the City: Social Justice and the Fight for Public Space.* New York: The Guilford Press.

Monsho, Anoa. 2004. "From East Austin to East End: Gentrification in Motion." In, *Good Life Magazine: A Monthly Journal of Austin Stories* November.

Moore, Sandy. 1987. "Review: *Learning through the Built Environment.*" In, *Journal of Architectural Education (1984–)* no. 40 (4):31–31.

Moore, Steven A. 2001a. *Technology and Place. Sustainable Architecture and the Blueprint Farm.* Austin, TX: University of Texas Press.

—— 2001b. "Technology, Place, and the Nonmodern Thesis." In, *Journal of Architectural Education* 54 (3):130–139.

—— 2007. *Alternative Routes to the Sustainable City: Austin, Curitiba and Frankfurt*. Lanham, MD: Lexington Books, Rowman & Littlefield.

—— and Andrew Karvonen. 2007. "Sustainable Architecture in Context: STS and Design Thinking." *Science Studies*:29–46.

—— and Barbara B. Wilson. 2009. "Contested Construction of Green Building Codes in North America: The Case of the Alley Flat Initiative." In, *Urban Studies* 46 (12):2617–2642.

—— and Nathan Engstrom. 2005. "The Social Construction of 'Green' Building Codes: Competing Models by Industry, Government and Ngos." In, *Sustainable Architectures: Natures and Cultures in Europe and North America*. Edited by Simon Guy and Steven A. Moore (pp. 51–70). London: Routhedge/Spon.

—— and Sergio Palleroni. 2008. "The Alley Flat Initiative: An Alternative Route to the Sustainable City." In, *Working Paper Series*. Edited by Elizabeth Mueller. Austin, TX: The University of Texas Center for Sustainable Development.

—— and Elizabeth Walsh. 2012. "The Problem of Judging Architecture." In, *Beyond LEED: Regenerative Design, A Symposium*. Edited by S. A. Moore. Austin: The University of Texas Center for Sustainable Design. Available at: http://soa.utexas.edu/beyondleed/index.html (accessed May 25, 2013).

Morozov, Petia. 2009. "Review: *Did Someone Say Participate? An Atlas of Spatial Practice*, by Markus Miessen and Shumon Basar." In, *Journal of Architectural Education* no. 62 (4):134–135.

Morse, Richard M. 1974. *From Community to Metropolis: A Biography of São Paulo, Brazil*. New York: Octagon Books.

Morshed, Adnan. 2005. "Review: *Architecture as a Means of Filial Discovery: Nathaniel Kahn's My Architect The Louis Kahn Project*." In, *Journal of Architectural Education* no. 58 (3):54–60.

Mostoller, Michael. 1985. "The Towers of Frank Lloyd Wright." In, *Journal of Architectural Education (1984–)* 38 (2):13–17.

Mueller, Elizabeth. 2008. *The Alley Flat Initiative: Financial Model Overview*. Unpublished graduate student report conducted under faculty supervision. The University of Texas School of Architecture, Community and Regional Planning Program. Authors' file.

Mumford, Lewis. 1963[1934]. *Technics and Civilization*. New York: Harvest/HBJ.

Murphy, Amy. 2002. "Review: *Gender and Architecture*." In, *Journal of Architectural Education* no. 55 (3):197–201.

National Institute of Building Sciences. 2010. *Whole Building Design Guide*; *History of Accessible Building Design*. Available at: www.wbdg.org/design/accessible_history.php (accessed September 5, 2011).

Neuman, W. 2008. "$1 Billion Later, New York's Subway Elevators Still Fail." In, *New York Times* May 19.

New Urban News. 2009. "Common ground found for urbanism and the disabled." March 1.

Neyfak, Leon. 2011. "Green Building: Are Cities the Best Place to Live? Are Suburbs OK? A Fight Grows in Urban Planning, with Harvard at the Center." In, *Boston Globe*, January 30.

NIST. 2009. "National Institute of Standards and Technology." Available at: www.nist.gov/index.html (accessed May 3 2012).

Noble, David F. 1977. *America by Design: Science, Technology and the Rise of Corporate Capitalism*. New York: Alfred A. Knopf.

Norberg-Schulz, Christian. 1979. *Genius Loci: Towards a Phenomenology of Architecture*. New York: Rizzoli.

Norbert, Elias. 1983. *The Court Society*. Translated by Edmund Jephcott. Oxford: Basil Blackwell.

Nye, Michael, and Tom Hargreaves. 2010. "Exploring the Social Dynamics of Proenvironmental Behavior Change." In, *Journal of Industrial Ecology* 14 (1):137–149.

Oda, J. 1995. "Highlights from Speeches by Ed Roberts." Edward V. Roberts Papers, BANC MSS 99/34 cz, carton 11, folder 30. The Bancroft Library, University of California, Berkeley.

Oden, Michael. 2011. Private email correspondence, July 26.

Oliver, Paul. 1987. *Dwellings: The Houses Across the World*. Austin, TX: University of Texas Press.

Olshan, M.A. 1993. "Standards Making Organizations and the Rationalization of American Life." In, *Sociological quarterly* 34 (2):319–335.

Orum, Anthony. 1987. *Power, Money and the People: The Making of Modern Austin*. Austin, TX: Texas Monthly Press.

Otto, Greg. 2010. Project engineer with Buro Happold, New York. Email communication, October 10.

Ott, Randall. 2003. "Review: *Mies in Berlin* and *Mies in America*." In, *Journal of Architectural Education* no. 56 (4):69–75.

Owen, Ceridwen, and Kim Dovey. 2008. "Fields of Sustainable Architecture." In, *Journal of Architecture* 13 (1):9–21.

Owen, Graham. 2006. "In Dark Waters: Opportunity and Opportunism in the Reconstruction of New Orleans." In, *Journal of Architectural Education* 60 (1):7–9.

Oxford English Dictionary. 2011. "scientific method." Available at: www.oed.com/view/Entry/172685?redirectedFrom=scientific%20method#eid23962743 (accessed October 12).

Palleroni, Sergio. 2004. *Studio at Large: Architecture in Service of Global Communities*. Seattle, WA: University of Washington Press.

Park, Jin-Ho. 2004. "An Integral Approach to Design Strategies and Construction Systems: R. M. Schindler's 'Schindler Shelters'." In, *Journal of Architectural Education* 58 (2):29–38.

Parolek, Daniel G., Karen Parolek, and Paul C. Crawford. 2008. *Form-Based Codes: A Guide for Planners, Urban Designers, Municipalities, and Developers*. New York: Wiley.

Payton, Neal I. 1985. "Review: *Campus: An American Planning Tradition*." *Journal of Architectural Education (1984–)* no. 39 (1):32–32.

Pear, R. 2008. "Plan Seeks More Access for Disabled." In, *New York Times* June 16.

Pearlman, Jill. 1998. "Review: *Bauhaus in America*, by Judith Pearlman." In, *Journal of Architectural Education (1984–)* 51 (3):204.

Pecan Street Project. 2010. *Pecan Street Project Report*. Available at: www.pecanstreet.org/ (accessed January 9, 2013).

Pecora, Vincent P. 1995. "Review: *Architecture and the Text: The (S)crypts of Joyce and Piranesi*, by Jennifer Bloomer." In, *Journal of Architectural Education (1984–)* 48 (4):275–277.

Peet, Richard. 1985. "The Social Origins of Environmental Determinism." In, *Annals of the Association of American Geographers* 75 (3):309–333.

Pelka, F. 1997. *The ABC–CLIO Companion to the Disability Rights Movement*. Santa Barbara, CA: ABC–CLIO.

Perkes, David. 2009. "A Useful Practice." In, *Journal of Architectural Education* 62 (4):64–71.

Pevsner, N. 1976. *A History of Building Types*. Princeton, NJ: Princeton University Press.

Pickvance, C. 2003. "From Urban Social Movements to Urban Movements." In, *International Journal of Urban and Regional Research* 21 (1).

Picon, Antoine. 2004. "The Ghost of Architecture: The Project and Its Codification." In, *Perspecta: The Yale Architectural Journal*. Edited by Elijah and Stephanie Tuerk Huge (pp. 8–19). Cambridge, MA: MIT Press.

Pinch, T.J., and W.E. Bijker. 1985. "The Social Construction of Facts and Artifacts: Or How the Sociology of Science and the Science of Sociology of Technology Might Benefit Each Other." In, *The Social Construction of Technological Systems*. Cambridge, MA: MIT Press.

Planat, P. (1888–1895). *Encyclopédie de l'architecture et de la construction*. Cited by Pevsner.

Plater-Zyberk, Elizabeth. 2008. "Foreword." In, *Form-Based Codes: A Guide for Planners, Urban Designers, Municipalities, and Developers*. Edited by Daniel G. Parolek, Karen Parolek, and Paul C. Crawford (pp. ix–xii). New York: Wiley.

PODER. 2010. People Organized in the Defense of Earth and her Resources. Available at: www.poder-texas.org/ (accessed November 27, 2011).

Polledri, Paolo. 1988. "Urbanism and Economics: Industrial Activities in Eighteenth-Century Venice." In, *Journal of Architectural Education (1984–)*41 (3):15–19.

Ponte, Lucille M. 2009. "Echoes of the Sumptuary Impulse: Considering the Threads of Social Identity, Public Morality, and Economic Protectionism under the Proposed Design Piracy Prohibition Act." Florida Coastal School of Law.

Poon, Ben Ho-Sing. 2001. "Buildings Recycled—City Refurbished." In, *Journal of Architectural Education* 54 (3):191–194.

Prakash, Vikramaditya. 2001. "Between Objectivity and Illusion: Architectural Photography in the Colonial Frame." In, *Journal of Architectural Education* 55 (1):13–20.

Pressman, Norman. 1983. "Review: *The Aesthetic Townscape* and *The Visual and Spatial Structure of Landscapes*." In, *Journal of Architectural Education* no. 37 (2):27–30.

Price, Asher. 2012. "New Gray Water Rules On Tap." In, *Austin American-Statesman* Monday, July 2:A1–A4.

Pyatok, Michael. 2008. "The Narrow Base of the New Urbanists." *Planners Network*. Available at: www.plannersnetwork.org/2002/04/the-narrow-base-of-the-new-urbanists/ (accessed April 6, 2013).

Qualtrough, S. (2006). "Cracking the Performance Code: Where the Most Successful Firms Squeeze to Gain an Extra Competitive Edge." In, *Office Products International* (158):52–56.

Rahim, Ali. 2010[2005]. "Performativity: Beyond Efficiency and Optimization in Architecture." In, *Performative Architecture: Beyond Instrumentality*. Edited by Branko Kolarevic and Ali M. Malkawi. New York and London: Spon Press.

Rapoport, Amos. 1969. *House Form and Culture*. Edited by Richard E. Dahlberg. Foundations of Cultural Geography. Englewood Cliffs, NJ: Prentice-Hall.

Read, Gray. 2008. "Review: *Architects without Frontiers: War, Reconstruction and Design Responsibility*, Edited by Esther Charlesworth." In, *Journal of Architectural Education* no. 61 (3):65–66.

Real, Patricio Del. 2009. "'Ye Shall Receive': The Rural Studio and the Gift of Architecture." In, *Journal of Architectural Education* 62 (4):123–126.

Revell, Keith D. 2005. *Building Gotham: Civic Culture and Public Policy in New York City, 1898–1938*. Baltimore, MD: The Johns Hopkins Press.

Reynaud, Leonce. (1850–1858). *Traité d'architecture*. Cited by Pevsner.

Rickenbacker, Shawn L. 2003. "Performative Surfaces." *Journal of Architectural Education* 57 (2):18–21.

Rider, Traci Jones. 2009. *Understanding Green Building Guidelines for Students and Young Professionals*. New York: W.W. Norton.

Roberts, E.V. 1980. *The Emergence of the Disabled Civil Rights Movement*. Berkeley, CA: Disability Rights and Independent Living Movement Archive.

—— 1983. "When Others Speak for You, You Lose." Disability Rights and Independent Living Archive. Berkeley, CA.

Roberts, S.V. 1978. "The Handicapped Are Emerging As a Vocal Political Action Group." In, *New York Times* June 19.

Roberts, Tristan. 2010. "USGBC, LEED Targeted by Class-Action Suit." *GreenSource*. Available at: http://greensource.construction.com/news/2010/100719GBCI.asp (accessed November 15, 2011). This article originally appeared on BuildingGreen.com.

Rorty, Richard. 1998. *Achieving Our Country*. Cambridge, MA: Harvard University Press.

Rossi, Aldo. 1982. *The Architecture of the City, with an Introduction by Peter Eisenman*. Translated by Diane Ghirardo and Joan Ockman. Cambridge, MA: MIT Press.

Roth, Cecil. 1928. "Sumptuary Laws of the Community of Carpentras." In, *The Jewish Quarterly Review* 18 (4):357–383.

Rowley, Ellen. 2009. "Review: *Le Corbusier: The Art of Architecture*." In, *Journal of Architectural Education* 63 (1):147–149.

Rudofsky, Bernard. 1987[1965]. *Architecture Without Architects; A Short Introduction to Non-Pedigreed Architecture*. Albuquerque, MN: University of New Mexico Press. Original edition, Museum of Modern Art, New York.

Rüedi Ray, Katerina. 2001. "Bauhaus Hausfraus: Gender Formation In Design Education." In, *Journal of Architectural Education* 55 (2):73–80.

Rufford, Juliet. 2008. "Out of Site." In, *Journal of Architectural Education* 61 (4):34–42.

Russell, A.L. 2009. "'Industrial Legislatures': Consensus Standardization in the Second and Third Industrial Revolutions." In, *Enterprise and Society* 10 (4):661.

Rujivacharakul, Vimalin. 2010. "Ghosts of Asia: Fergusson's Haunted Mansion and the Architectural History of Asia in a Post-Said World." In, *Journal of Architectural Education* 63 (2):161–165.

Sabatino, Michelangelo. 2008. "Review: *Third Ward TX—A Documentary About Art, Life, and Real Estate*, edited by Andrew Garrison, director, and Nancy Bless, Andrew Garrison, Noland Walker, producers." In, *Journal of Architectural Education* no. 62 (1):78–79.

Sailer, Kersten, Andrew Budgen, Nathan Lonsdale, Alasdare Turner, and Alan Penn. 2009. "Evidence-Based Design: Theoretical and Practical Reflections of an Emerging Approach in Office Design." In, *Undisciplined! Design Research and Society Conference*, 2008, 119/1–19. Sheffield, UK: Sheffield Hallam University.

Salecl, Renata. 2011. *Choice*. London: Profile Books. Available at: http://UTXA.eblib.com/patron/FullRecord.aspx?p=708923

Samuels, Linda C. 2005. "Review: *Samuel Mockbee and the Rural Studio: Community Architecture*." In, *Journal of Architectural Education* no. 58 (3):54–60.

Sargeant, John. 1982. "Review: *Frank Lloyd Wright's Hanna House: The Client's Report*." In, *Journal of Architectural Education* no. 36 (1):54–55.

Sassatelli, Roberta, and Federica Davolio. 2010. "Consumption, Pleasure and Politics. Slow Food and the Politico-Aesthetic Problematization of Food." In, *Journal of Consumer Culture* 10 (2):202–232.

Satler, Gail. 2003. "New York City Restaurants: Vernaculars of Global Designing." In, *Journal of Architectural Education* 56 (3):27–39.

Sauda, Eric. 1987. "Three Small Architectural Dramas in the Form of a Pair." In, *Journal of Architectural Education (1984–)* 40 (2):69–71.

Scarpo, Bob. 2002. "Review: *The Room in Context: Design Beyond Boundaries*." In, *Journal of Architectural Education* no. 55 (3):197–201.

Scherr, Richard. 1991. "Architecture as Index: Toward a Theory of Contingency." In, *Journal of Architectural Education (1984–)* 44 (3):172–181.

Schneekloth, Lynda H., and Robert G. Shibley. 2000. "Implacing Architecture into the Practice of Placemaking." In, *Journal of Architectural Education* 53 (3):130–140.

Schön, Donald A. 1987. *Educating the Reflective Practitioner*. San Francisco, CA: Jossey-Bass.

Schor, Juliet B. 2007. "In Defense of Consumer Critique: Revisiting the Consumption Debates of the Twentieth Century." In, *The ANNALS of the American Academy of Political and Social Science* (611):16–30.

Schumacher, E.F. 1973. *Small is Beautiful: Economics as if People Mattered*. London: Bond & Briggs.

Schumacher, Thomas L. 2002. "'The Outside is the Result of an Inside': Some Sources of One of Modernism's Most Persistent Doctrines." In, *Journal of Architectural Education* 56 (1):22.

Schwarzer, Mitchell. 1991. "Gathered This Unruly Folk: The Textural Colligation of Historical Knowledge of Architecture." In, *Journal of Architectural Education (1984–)* 44 (3):144–149.

Scotch, Richard K. 2001. *From Good Will to Civil Rights: Transforming Federal Disability Policy*. Philadelphia, PA: Temple University Press.

Scott, James C. 1998. *Seeing Like a State: How Certain Schemes to Improve the Human Condition Have Failed*. New Haven, CN: Yale University Press.

SEED. 2012. *The SEED Network*. Design Corps. Available at: www.seed-network.org/ (accessed July 1, 2012).

Seyfang, Gill. 2009. "The New Economics of Sustainable Consumption: Seeds of Change." In, *The New Economics of Sustainable Consumption*. Edited by D. Elliott. New York: Palgrave Macmillan.

Senft, Carolyn. 1994. "Review: *The Staircase: History and Theories*, by John Templer; *The Staircase: Studies of Hazards, Falls, and Safer Design*, by John Templer." In, *Journal of Architectural Education (1984–)* 48 (2):129–131.

Shah, Rajiv C., and Jay P. Kesan. 2007. "How Architecture Regulates." In, *Journal of Architectural and Planning Research* 24 (4).

Shall, Scott. 2009. "Review: *Design Like You Give a Damn: Architectural Responses to Humanitarian Crises—Architecture for Humanity* and *Expanding Architecture: Design as Activism*, Edited by Bryan Bell and Katie Wakeford." In, *Journal of Architectural Education* no. 62 (4):132–134.

Shane, Graham. 1990. "Review: Street Performance; The Homeless Vehicle Project." In, *Journal of Architectural Education (1984–)* 43 (4):37–42.

Shapiro, J.P. 1994. *No Pity*. New York: Three Rivers Press.

Shapiro, Kelli. 2007. "From Modernism to McDonald's." In, *Journal of Architectural Education* 61 (2):6–14.

Shepheard, P. (2003). *Artificial Love: A Story of Machines and Architecture*. Cambridge, MA: MIT Press.

Shin, Chunghoon. 2010. "Review: *Globalization, the City and Civil Society in Pacific Asia: The Social Production of Civic Spaces.*" In, *Journal of Architectural Education* no. 63 (2):175–176.

Shively, Donald H. 1964. "Sumptuary Regulation and Status in Early Tokugawa Japan." In, *Harvard Journal of Asiatic Studies* 25:123–164.

Shove, E., and M. Moezzi. 2002. "What do Standards Standardize." Paper read at, *Human and Social Dimensions of Energy Use: Understanding Markets and Demand.* EECE, Panel 8. *Human and Social Dimensions of Energy Use: Understanding Markets and Demand.* Available at: www.eceee.org/conference_proceedings/ACEEE_buildings/2002/Panel_8 (accessed January 9, 2013).

Shove, Elizabeth. 2004. *Comfort, Cleanliness and Convenience: The Social Organization of Normality.* Oxford, UK and New York: Berg Publishers.

Sierra Club Sprawl Report. 2000. Available at: www.sierraclub.org/sprawl/50statesurvey/ (accessed March 29, 2013).

Silver, Christopher. 1997. "The Racial Origins of Zoning in American Cities." In, *Urban Planning and the African American Community: In the Shadows.* Edited by June Manning Thomas and Marsha Ritzdorf. Thousand Oaks, CA: Sage Publications.

Simon, Herbert. 1969. *The Sciences of the Artificial.* Cambridge, MA: MIT Press.

Sismondo, Sergio. 2009. *An Introduction to Science and Technology Studies.* 2nd ed. Chichester, UK: John Wiley & Sons.

Skull, A. 1984. *Decarceration: Community treatment and the deviant—A Radical View.* 2nd ed. Rutgers, NJ: Rutgers University Press.

Smith, Glenn L. 2004. "Review: *Metaphors and Questions in Harlem* and *Harlemworld: Metropolis as Metaphor.*" In, *Journal of Architectural Education* no. 58 (2):57–61.

Smith, Kendra Schank. 1990. "Architectural Sketches and the Power of Caricature." In, *Journal of Architectural Education (1984–)* 44 (1):49–58.

Smith, Merritt Rowe, and Leo Marx. 1994. *Does Technology Drive History? The Dilemma of Technological Determinism.* Cambridge, MA: MIT Press.

Snow, David A., E. Burke Rochford, Steven K. Worden, and Robert D. Benford. 1986. "Frame Alignment Processes, Micromobilization, and Movement Participation." In, *American Sociological Review* 51 (4):464–481.

Snyder, Alison B. 2008. "Review: *AD Interior Atmospheres*, Edited by Julieanna Preston." In, *Journal of Architectural Education* no. 62 (2):70–71.

Snyder, Vincent. 2005. "Review: *refabricating ARCHITECTURE: How Manufacturing Methodologies Are Poised to Transform Building Construction.*" In, *Journal of Architectural Education* no. 59 (1):51–52.

Soja, E. 2009. "The City and Spatial Justice." In, *Justice Spatiale | Spatial Justice* 1 (September).

Solomon, Jonathan D. 2010. "Learning from Louis Vuitton." In, *Journal of Architectural Education* 63 (2):67–70.

Song, Linn. 2007. "The Muenster City Library." In, *Journal of Architectural Education* 60 (3):12–20.

Soris y Puig, Arturo, ed. 1999. *Cerda: The Five Bases of the General Theory of Urbanization.* Barcelona, Spain: Electa.

Sowell, Jason, and Nichole Wiedemann. 2009. "Sponge Urbanism: The Cellular Redevelopment of New Orleans." In, *Journal of Architectural Education* 62 (4):24–31.

Spradley, James P. 1980. *Participant Observation.* New York: Harcourt Brace Javanovich.

Staff Task Force, Joe Canales Chair. 2003. *Staff Task Force on Gentrification in East Austin.* Austin, TX: City of Austin.

Stankard, Mark. 2002. "Re-covering Mies van der Rohe's Weissenhof: The Ultimate Surface." In, *Journal of Architectural Education* 55 (4):247–256.

Stevenson, Katherine Cole, and H. Ward Jandl. 1986. *Houses by Mail: A Guide to Houses From Sears, Roebuck and Company.* Washington, DC: Preservation Press.

Stilgoe, John. 1982. *Common Landscapes of America: 1580–1845.* New Haven, CT: Yale University Press.

Stiny, George Nicholas. 1985. "Computing with Form and Meaning in Architecture." In, *Journal of Architectural Education (1984–)* 39 (1):7–19.

Stratigakos, Despina. 2001. "Architects in Skirts: The Public Image of Women Architects in Wilhelmine Germany." In, *Journal of Architectural Education* 55 (2):90–100.

Streatfield, David C. 1983. "Review: *Common Landscape of America, 1580–1845.*" In, *Journal of Architectural Education* no. 37 (1):27–28.

Strauss, A., and Corbin, J. 1987. *Basics of Qualitative Research.* Newbury Park, CA: Sage.

Stuart, John A. 2003. "Review: *The Glass State: The Technology of the Spectacle, Paris, 1981–1998.*" In, *Journal of Architectural Education* no. 56 (4):69–75.

Sturges, William Gould. 1992. "An Exploration of the Relationships Between Houses and Forests in American History." *Journal of Architectural Education (1984–)* 46 (2):66–75.

Sung, Doris Kim. 2001. "Incorporations: Exploring the Space between Body, Mechanism, and Imagination." In, *Journal of Architectural Education* 54 (4):260.

The Sustainable Consumption Research and Action Initiative (SCORAI). Available at: www.scorai.org/ (accessed April 6, 2013).

Sutton, Sharon Egretta. 2003. "Review: *Children in the City, Home, Neighborhood, and Community* and *Growing Up in an Urbanizing World* and *Creating Better Cities with Children and Youth: A Manual for Participation* and *The Growing Up in Cities Project.*" In, *Journal of Architectural Education* no. 57 (2):55–61.

Svec, Phaedra, Robert Berkebile, and Joel Ann Todd. 2012. "REGEN: Toward a Tool for Regenerative Thinking." In, *Building Research & Information* 40 (1):81–94.

Swearingen, William Scott. 2010. *Environmental City: People, Place, Politics, and the Meaning of Modern Austin.* Austin, TX: University of Texas Press.

Szasz, Andrew. 2007. *Shopping Our Way to Safety: How We Changed from Protecting the Environment to Protecting Ourselves.* Minneapolis, MN: University of Minnesota Press.

Talen, Emily. 2009a. "Design by the Rules: The Historical Underpinnings of Form-Based Codes." In, *Journal of the American Planning Association* 75 (2):144–160.

—— 2009b. *The Codes Project.* National Science Foundation. Available at: http://codesproject.asu.edu/ (accessed March 11, 2009).

—— 2012. *City Rules: How Regulations Affect Urban Form.* Wasington, DC: Island Press.

Tanzer, Kim, and Caroline Constant. 2001. "Center for Women's Studies and Gender Research, University of Florida, 1994–2000." In, *Journal of Architectural Education* 55 (2):81–89.

Tarrow, S. 1998. *Power in Movement: Social Movements and Contentious Politics.* Cambridge, UK: Cambridge University Press.

Tenhaaf, Nell. 1987. "Pandora Revisited: Art and New Technologies." In, *Journal of Architectural Education(1984–)* 40 (4):18–23.

Testa, Peter. 1987. "Tradition and Actuality in the Antonio Carlos Siza House." In, *Journal of Architectural Education (1984–)* 40 (4):24–30.

Thomas, Helen. 2004. "Invention in the Shadow of History: Joseph Rykwert at the University of Essex." In, *Journal of Architectural Education* 58 (2):39–45.

Thorpe, Ann. 2012. *Architecture and Design Versus Consumerism: How Design Activism Confronts Growth.* London and New York: Earth Scan; Taylor & Francis. Kindle Edition.

Tilly, Charles. 2004. *Social Movements, 1768–2004.* Boulder, CO: Paradigm Publishers.

Timmermans, S., and S. Epstein. 2010. "A World of Standards but Not a Standard World: Toward a Sociology of Standards and Standardization." In, *Annual Review of Sociology* 36.

Tisi, Rodrigo. 2008. "B + S + P + T + PL + M." In, *Journal of Architectural Education* 61 (4):69–75.

Tonton, Jacqueline. 2004. "Review: *Building Suburbia. Green Fields and Urban Growth, 1820–2000* and *A Field Guide to Sprawl.*" *Journal of Architectural Education* no. 58 (2):57–61.

Toohey, Marty. 2009. "Will Clean Power Hurt Poor?" In, *Austin American Statesman* B1–B4.

Totman, Conrad. 2007. *Japan's Imperial Forest, Goryōrin, 1889–1945: With a Supporting Study of the Kan/Min Division of Woodland in Early Meiji Japan, 1871–1876.* Folkestone, UK: Global Oriental.

Trabalzi, Ferruccio. 1989. "Primavalle: Urban Reservation in Rome." In, *Journal of Architectural Education (1984–)* no. 42 (3):38–46.

Travis, Jack. 1993. "African American Architecture: From Idea to Published Product." In, *Journal of Architectural Education (1984–)* 47 (1):60–62.

Tsui, S.C., and W.K. Chow. (2003). "Possibility of Applying a Performance-Based Approach for Designing Means of Escape in a Public Transport Interchange." In, *Architectural Science* 46(3):279–290.

Tukker, Arnold, Maurie J. Cohen, Klaus Hubacek, and Oksana Mont. 2010. "The Impacts of Household Consumption and Options for Change." In, *Journal of Industrial Ecology* 14 (1):13–30.

Turbin, J. "Return to Gold Standard Gaining Traction with Presidential Candidates." In, *International Business Times* October 10, 2011.

Tzonis, A., and L. Lefaivre. 1992. *Classical Architecture: The Poetics of Order*. Cambridge, MA: MIT Press.

Umbach, Maiken, and Bernd Huppauf. 2005. *Vernacular Modernism: Heimat, Globalization and the Built Environment*. Stanford, CA: Stanford University Press.

Upton, Dell. 1984. "Pattern Books and Professionalism: Aspects of the Transformation of Domestic Architecture in America, 1800–1860." In, *Winterthur Portfolio* 19 (2/3):107–150.

Urban Design Associates, Ray Gindroz, Rob Robinson, et al. 2004. *The Architectural Pattern Book: A Tool for Building Great Neighborhoods*. New York: W.W. Norton & Company.

U.S. Environmental Protection Agency. 1992. Available at: http://nepis.epa.gov/Exe/ZyNET.exe/P1002PDG.TXT?ZyActionD=ZyDocument&Client=EPA&Index=2000+Thru+2005&Docs=&Query=&Time=&EndTime=&SearchMethod=1&TocRestrict=n&Toc=&TocEntry=&QField=&QFieldYear=&QFieldMonth=&QFieldDay=&IntQFieldOp=0&ExtQFieldOp=0&XmlQuery=&File=D%3A%5Czyfiles%5CIndex%20Data%5C00thru05%5CTxt%5C00000017%5CP1002PDG.txt&User=ANONYMOUS&Password=anonymous&SortMethod=h%7C&MaximumDocuments=1&FuzzyDegree=0&ImageQuality=r75g8/r75g8/x150y150g16/i425&Display=p%7Cf&DefSeekPage=x&SearchBack=ZyActionL&Back=ZyActionS&BackDesc=Results%20page&MaximumPages=1&ZyEntry=1&SeekPage=x&ZyPURL (accessed November 29, 2011).

U.S. Green Building Council. 2012a. *Leadership in Energy and Environmental Design* (LEED) Available at: www.usgbc.org (accessed April 20, 2012).

—— 2012b. *An Introduction to LEED*. Available at: www.usgbc.org/DisplayPage.aspx?CategoryID=19 (accessed January 10, 2012).

Vattimo, Gianni. 1991. *The End of Modernity*. Baltimore, MD: Johns Hopkins University Press.

Veikos, Cathrine. 2006. "To Enter the Work." In, *Journal of Architectural Education* 59 (4):71–80.

Vidler, Anthony. 1991. "Researching Revolutionary Architecture." In, *Journal of Architectural Education (1984–)* 44 (4):206–210.

Village of Euclid, Ohio v. Ambler Realty Co., 272 US 365. 1926.

Vitruvius. 1960[15 BCE]. *Ten Books on Architecture*. Translated by Morris Hicky Morgan. New York: Dover Publications.

Walker, Gerald. 1987. "Architecture, Method and the Poetic Image." In, *Journal of Architectural Education (1984–)* 40 (2):85–86.

Wang, David. 2002. "Review: *Words and Buildings: A Vocabulary of Modern Architecture*." In, *Journal of Architectural Education* no. 55 (4):272–275.

—— 2003. "Categories of ACSA Conference Papers: A Critical Evaluation of Architectural Research in Light of Social Science Methodological Frameworks." In, *Journal of Architectural Education* 56 (4):50–56.

Wasley, James. 2000. "Safe Houses and Green Architecture: Reflections on the Lessons of the Chemically Sensitive." In, *Journal of Architectural Education* 53 (4):207–215.

WCED. 1987. *Our Common Future*. New York: United Nations World Council on Economic Development.

Weber, Gustavus A. 1925. *The Bureau of Standards: Its History, Activities, and Organization*. Baltimore, MD: The Johns Hopkins Press.

Weddle, Robert. 2001. "Housing and Technological Reform in Interwar France: The Case of the Cité de la Muette." In, *Journal of Architectural Education* 54 (3):167–175.

Weingarden, Lauren S. 1985. "Aesthetics Politicized: William Morris to the Bauhaus." In, *Journal of Architectural Education (1984–)* 38 (3):8–13.

Weinstein, Beth. 2008. "Flamand and His Architectural Entourage." In, *Journal of Architectural Education* 61 (4):25–33.

Weinthal, Lois. 2006. "House Lab." In, *Journal of Architectural Education* 60 (2):25–28.

Widodo, Johannes. 2010. "Current State of Modern Asian Architecture Discourse and Networking." In, *Journal of Architectural Education* 63 (2):79–81.

Wilcox, Glenn. 2004. "The Medium and the Thing Itself." In, *Journal of Architectural Education* 58 (2):25–27.

Wilkins, Craig L. 2000. "(W)rapped Space: The Architecture of Hip Hop." In, *Journal of Architectural Education* 54 (1):7–19.

Willis, Daniel. 1994. "Review: *On Weathering: The Life of Buildings in Time by Mohsen Mostafavi,* by David Leatherbarrow." In, *Journal of Architectural Education (1984–)* 48 (2):126–129.

Wilson, Barbara B. 2010. *Social Movement Toward Spatial Justice*. Dissertation. University of Texas at Austin.

Winner, Langdon. 1977. *Autonomous Technology: Technics Out-of-Control as a Theme in Political Thought*. Cambridge, MA: MIT Press.

Winston, E. Perry. 1998. "Review: *Good Neighbors: Affordable Family Housing,* by Tom Jones, William Pettus, Mike Pyatok; *The Architecture of Affordable Housing,* by Sam Davis; *Democratic Architecture: Practical Solutions to Today's Housing Crisis,* by Donald MacDonald." In, *Journal of Architectural Education (1984–)* 52 (2):124–126.

Wolf, Harry. 1987. "Observations on Education." In, *Journal of Architectural Education (1984–)* 40 (2):91–93.

Wolin, Richard. 2004.*The Seduction of Unreason: The Intellectual Romance with Fascism: From Nietzsche to Postmodernism*. Princeton, NJ: Princeton University Press.

Woodhouse, Edward, and Patton, Jason W. 2004. "Design by Society: Science and Technology Studies and the Social Shaping of Design." In, *Design Issues* 20 (3):1–12.

World Institute on Disability. 1983. *Introduction to the World Institute on Disability Proposal Summary*. Bancroft Archives.

Wright, Gwendolyn. 1982. "Review: *The Grand Domestic Revolution: A History of Feminist Designs for American Homes, Neighborhoods, and Cities*." In, *Journal of Architectural Education* no. 36 (2):31–32.

Yan, X. Winston. 1996. "Carrying Forward Heritage: A Review of Contextualism in New Construction in Beijing." In, *Journal of Architectural Education (1984–)* 50 (2):115–126.

Yaneva, Albena. 2009. *The Making of a Building: A Pragmatist Approach to Architecture*. Oxford, UK: Peter Lang.

—— 2012. *Mapping Controversies in Architecture*. Farnham, UK: Ashgate.

Yates, Penny W. 1999. "Review: *Architectural Representation and the Perspective Hinge,* by Alberto Pérez-Gómez, Louise Pelletier." In, *Journal of Architectural Education (1984–)* 53 (1):51.

Yin, Robert K. 2003. *Case Study Research: Design and Methods*. 3rd ed. Thousand Oaks, CA: Sage Publications.

Yoon, J. Meejin. 2008. "Public Works." In, *Journal of Architectural Education* 61 (4):59–68.

Young, I.M. 1990. *Justice and the Politics of Difference*. Princeton, NJ: Princeton University Press.

Younger, Margalit, Heather R. Morrow-Almeida, Stephen M. Vindigni, and Andrew L. Dannenberg. 2008. "The Built Environment, Climate Change, and Health Opportunities for Co-Benefits." In, *Journal of Preventative Medicine* 35 (5):517–526.

Zakaria, Fareed. 2011. A Conversation with Frank Gehry: *How to Innovate: Inside the Mind of Master Architect Frank Gehry*. Available at: www.yousendit.com/dl?phi_action=app/orchestrate Download&rurl=https%253A%252F%252Fwww.yousendit.com%252Ftransfer.php%253Faction %253Dbatch_download%2526batch_id%253DT2dmTkF1dzhlcEpBSXRVag (aired September 4, 2011).

Zaknic, Ivan. 1989. "Le Corbusier San Fin Review: *Voyage d'Orient: Carnets*; *La Chaux-de-Fonds et Jeanneret avant Le Corbusier*; *Le Corbusier, le passé a réaction poétique*; *Le Corbusier Secret*; *Les mains de Le Corbusier*; *Le Corbusier à Cap-Martin*; *Le Corbusier*." In, *Journal of Architectural Education (1984–)* no.42 (3):49–59.

Zames Fleischer, D., and Frida Zames. 2001. *The Disability Rights Movement*. Philadelphia, PA: Temple University Press.

Zell, Maureen, and Marc Roehrle. 2003. "Reconsideration of the Shed: Garage + Workshop." In, *Journal of Architectural Education* 56 (4):30–31.

Zuk, Radoslav. 1983. "A Music Lesson." *Journal of Architectural Education* 36 (3):2–6.

Index

Note: Page numbers in *italics* denote figures, those in **bold** denote tables.